Selected Material from

Exploring Writing
Sentences and Paragraphs

Second Edition

John Langan
Atlantic Cape Community College

Department of Language Skills & Student Development
Lansing Community College

Homework
Ch 27 " " mark
Do all but the
yellow, and do journal)

Learning Solutions

Boston   Burr Ridge, IL   Dubuque, IA   New York   San Francisco   St. Louis
Bangkok   Bogotá   Caracas   Lisbon   London   Madrid
Mexico City   Milan   New Delhi   Seoul   Singapore   Sydney   Taipei   Toronto

Selected Material from Exploring Writing: Sentences and Paragraphs
Second Edition
Department of Language Skills & Student Development
Lansing Community College

This book is a McGraw-Hill Learning Solutions textbook and contains select material from the following sources:
Exploring Writing: Sentences and Paragraphs, Second Edition by John Langan. Copyright © 2010, 2008 by The McGraw-Hill Companies, Inc.
Exploring Writing: Sentences and Paragraphs by John Langan. Copyright © 2008 by The McGraw-Hill Companies, Inc.
Both reprinted with permission of the publisher. Many custom published texts are modified versions or adaptations of our best-selling textbooks. Some adaptations are printed in black and white to keep prices at a minimum, while others are in color.

1 2 3 4 5 6 7 8 9 0 WDD WDD 12 11 10

ISBN-13: 978-0-07-745187-5
ISBN-10: 0-07-745187-2

Learning Solutions Specialist: Jenny Harrington
Production Editor: Tina Hermsen
Printer/Binder: Worldcolor
Cover Image: Jaime J. Grant, Photographer
Ra'Mone Gissendanner, Former WRIT 110 Student

ABOUT THE AUTHOR

John Langan has taught reading and writing at Atlantic Cape Community College near Atlantic City, New Jersey, for more than twenty-five years. The author of a popular series of college textbooks on both writing and reading, John enjoys the challenge of developing materials that teach skills in an especially clear and lively way. Before teaching, he earned advanced degrees in writing at Rutgers University and in reading at Rowan University. He also spent a year writing fiction that, he says, "is now at the back of a drawer waiting to be discovered and acclaimed posthumously." While in school, he supported himself by working as a truck driver, a machinist, a battery assembler, a hospital attendant, and apple packer. John now lives with his wife, Judith Nadell, near Philadelphia. In addition to his wife and Philly sports teams, his passions include reading and turning on nonreaders to the pleasure and power of books. Through Townsend Press, his educational publishing company, he has developed the nonprofit "Townsend Library"—a collection of more than fifty new and classic stories that appeal to readers of any age.

BRIEF CONTENTS

PART 4 Readings for Writers

APPENDIXES   585

CONTENTS

PART 4 Readings for Writers

APPENDIXES   585

Exploring Writing

Writing: Skills and Process

PART ONE WILL

- introduce you to the basic principles of effective writing

- present writing as both a skill and a process of discovery

- explain and illustrate the sequence of steps in writing an effective paragraph, including

  - prewriting

  - revising

  - editing

- ask you to write a paragraph

EXPLORING WRITING PROMPT:

Think about the kinds of things people write every day—grocery lists, e-mails to friends and coworkers, notes to family members, and text messages, for example. Keep track of the things you write for seven days. Each time you write something—even if it's only a few words—make a record of it in your journal or notebook. At the end of the week, make a list of all these items.

An Introduction to Writing

RESPONDING TO IMAGES

Do you think that Tiger Woods' prowess on the golf course is more a result of natural talent or hard-earned skill? What about Aretha Franklin's ability to write and perform multiple Grammy-winning hits? Take a few minutes to respond to these questions. In this chapter, you will find the answer as it pertains to one's ability to perform a skill.

Exploring Writing grows out of experiences I had when learning how to write. My early memories of writing in school are not pleasant. In the middle grades I remember getting back paper after paper on which the only comment was "Handwriting very poor." In high school, the night before a book report was due, I would work anxiously at a card table in my bedroom. I was nervous and sweaty because I felt out of my element, like a person who knows only how to open a can of soup being asked to cook a five-course meal. The act of writing was hard enough, and my feeling that I wasn't any good at it made me hate the process all the more.

Luckily, in college I had an instructor who changed my negative attitude about writing. During my first semester in composition, I realized that my instructor repeatedly asked two questions about any paper I wrote: "What is your point?" and "What is your support for that point?" I learned that sound writing consists basically of making a point and then providing evidence to support or develop that point. As I understood, practiced, and mastered these and other principles, I began to write effective papers. By the end of the semester, much of my uneasiness about writing had disappeared. I realized that competent writing is a skill that I or anyone can learn with practice. It is a nuts-and-bolts process consisting of a number of principles and techniques that can be studied and mastered. Furthermore, I learned that although there is no alternative to the work required for competent writing, there is satisfaction to be gained through such work. I no longer feared or hated writing because I knew I could work at it and be good at it.

Exploring Writing: Sentences and Paragraphs explains in a clear and direct way the four basic principles you must learn to write effectively:

1. Start with a clearly stated point that unifies your paragraph or essay.

2. Provide logical, detailed support for your point.

3. Organize and connect your supporting material, always aiming for coherence.

4. Revise and edit so that your sentences are effective and error-free.

This book explains each of these steps in detail and provides many practice materials to help you master them.

Understanding Point and Support

An Important Difference between Writing and Talking

In everyday conversation, you make all kinds of points, or assertions. You say, for example, "I hate my job"; "Sue's a really generous person"; or "That exam was unfair." The points that you make concern such personal matters as well as, at times, larger issues: "A lot of doctors are arrogant"; "The death penalty should exist for certain crimes"; and "Tobacco and marijuana are equally dangerous."

The people you are talking with do not always challenge you to give reasons for your statements. They may know why you feel as you do, they may already agree with you, or they simply may not want to put you on the spot, and so they do not always ask "Why?" But the people who *read* what you write may not know you, agree with you, or feel in any way obliged to you. If you want to communicate effectively with readers, you must provide solid evidence for any point you make. An important difference, then, between writing and talking is this: *In writing, any idea that you advance must be supported with specific reasons or details.*

Think of your readers as reasonable people. They will not take your views on faith, but they *are* willing to consider what you say as long as you support it. Therefore, remember to support any statement that you make with specific evidence.

Point and Support in Two Cartoons

The following two *Peanuts* cartoons will show you quickly and clearly what you need to write effectively. You need to know how to (1) make a point and (2) support the point.

Look for a moment at the following cartoon:

PEANUTS © United Feature Syndicate, Inc.

See if you can answer the following questions:

- What is Snoopy's point in his paper?

Your answer: His point is that _____

- What is his support for his point?

Your answer: _____

Snoopy's point, of course, is that dogs are superior to cats. But he offers no support whatsoever to back up his point. There are two jokes here. First, he is a dog, so he is naturally going to believe that dogs are superior.

The other joke is that his evidence ("They just are, and that's all there is to it!") is no more than empty words. His somewhat guilty look in the last panel suggests that he knows he has not proved his point. To write effectively, you must provide *real* support for your points and opinions.

Now look at this other cartoon about Snoopy as a writer.

PEANUTS © United Feature Syndicate, Inc.

See if you can answer the following questions:

- What is Snoopy's point about the hero in his writing?

Your answer: His point is that _____

- What is his support for his point?

Your answer: _____

Snoopy's point is that the hero's life has been a disaster. This time, Snoopy has an abundance of support for his point: The hapless hero never had any luck, money, friends, love, laughter, applause, fame, or answers. The remaining flaw in Snoopy's composition is that he does not use enough supporting *details* to really prove his point. Instead, he plays the opposites game with his support ("He wanted to be loved. He died unloved."). As readers, we wonder who the hero wanted to be loved by: his mother? a heroine? a beagle? To sympathize with the hero and understand the nature of his disastrous life, we need more specifics. In the final panel of the cartoon, Snoopy has that guilty expression again. Why might he have a hard time ending this paragraph?

Point and Support in a Paragraph

Suppose you and a friend are talking about jobs you have had. You might say about a particular job, "That was the worst one I ever had—a lot of hard work and not much money." For your friend, that might be enough to make your point, and you would not really have to explain your statement. But in writing, your point would have to be backed up with specific reasons and details.

The following is a paragraph written by a student named Mike Cornell about his worst job. A *paragraph* is a short paper of 150 to 200 words. It usually consists of an opening point called a *topic sentence* followed by a series of sentences supporting that point.

My Job at the Crescent Falls Diner and Truck Stop

Working at the Crescent Falls Diner and Truck Stop was the worst job I ever had. First, the work was physically very hard. During my ten-hour days, I had to carry heavy trays of food to the customers, and I had to clean the tables. I washed dishes and then unloaded the delivery truck, lifting sixty-pound cartons of food supplies. The second bad feature was the pay. I had to work at least sixty hours a week to afford next semester's tuition because I got only minimum wage, and I had to share my tips with the kitchen workers too. Finally, the working conditions were horrible. I had to wash dishes in a hot and steamy kitchen. Once, when unloading a truck, I hurt my back so badly I was out of work for a week, without pay! And the boss was a tyrant who hated me because I was a college student. He gave me terrible hours, ridiculed my clothes, and even made racist slurs to my face.

Notice what the specific details in this paragraph do. They provide you, the reader, with a basis for understanding *why* the writer makes this particular point. Through this specific evidence, the writer has explained and successfully communicated the idea that this job was his worst one.

The evidence that supports the point in a paragraph often consists of a series of reasons followed by examples and details that support the reasons. That is true of the previous paragraph: Three reasons are provided, with examples and details that back up those reasons. Supporting evidence in a paper can also consist of anecdotes, personal experiences, facts, studies, statistics, and the opinions of experts.

ACTIVITY 1	Point and Support

The paragraph about the Crescent Falls Diner and Truck Stop, like almost any piece of effective writing, has two essential parts: (1) A point is advanced, and (2) that point is then supported. Taking a minute to outline the paragraph will help you understand these basic parts clearly. Add the words needed to complete the outline that follows.

Point: Working at the Crescent Falls Diner and Truck Stop was the worst job I ever had.

Reason 1: *Work Was Physically hard*

    a. Carried heavy trays while waiting on customers and busing tables

    b. *I had to clean tables*

Reason 2: *The bad feature was the pay*

    a. Got only minimum wage; had to share my tips with others

    b. *had to work sixty hour a week to afford tuition*

Reason 3: *The work conditions were horrible*

    a. Kitchen was hot and steamy

    b. *Unloading truck*

    c. Manager was unfair and insulting

        1. Disliked college students; favored other workers over me

        2. Made insulting remarks about my appearance, race

Fill in the Blanks

ACTIVITY 2

See if you can complete the following statements.

1. An important difference between writing and talking is that in writing we absolutely must *Supported* any statement we make.

2. A *Paragraph* is made up of a point and a collection of specifics that support the point.

An excellent way to get a feel for the paragraph is to write one. Your instructor may ask you to do that now. The only guidelines you need to follow are the ones described here. There is an advantage to writing a paragraph right away, at a point where you have had almost no instruction. This first paragraph will give a quick sense of your needs as a writer and will provide a baseline—a standard of comparison that you and your instructor can use to measure your writing progress during the semester.

WRITING ASSIGNMENT 1

Here, then, is your topic: Write a paragraph on the best or worst job you have ever had. Provide three reasons why your job was the best or the worst, and give plenty of details to develop each of your three reasons.

Notice that the sample paragraph, "My Job at the Crescent Falls Diner and Truck Stop," has the same format your paragraph should have. You should do what this author has done:

- State a point in the first sentence.

- Give three reasons to support the point.

- Introduce each reason clearly with signal words (such as *First of all*, *Second*, and *Finally*).

- Provide details that develop each of the three reasons.

Write or type your paragraph on a separate sheet of paper. After completing the paragraph, hand it in to your instructor.

Writing as a Skill

A realistic attitude about writing must build on the idea that *writing is a skill.* It is a skill like driving, typing, or cooking, and like any skill, it can be learned. If you have the determination to learn, this book will give you the extensive practice needed to develop your writing skills.

People who believe that writing is a "natural gift" rather than a learned skill may think that they are the only ones for whom writing is unbearably difficult. They might feel that everyone else finds writing easy or at least tolerable. Such people typically say, "I'm not any good at writing" or "English was not one of my good subjects." The result of this attitude is that people try to avoid writing, and when they do write, they don't try their best. Their attitude becomes a self-fulfilling prophecy: Their writing fails chiefly because they have convinced themselves that they don't have the "natural talent" needed to write. Unless their attitude changes, they probably will not learn how to write effectively.

Many people find it difficult to do the intense, active thinking that clear writing demands. It is frightening to sit down before a blank sheet of paper or a computer screen and know that an hour later, little on it may be worth keeping. It is frustrating to discover how much of a challenge it is to transfer thoughts and feelings from one's head into words. It is upsetting to find that an apparently simple writing subject often turns out to be complicated. But writing is not an automatic process; for almost everyone, competent writing comes from plain hard work—from determination, sweat, and head-on battle. The good news is that the skill of writing can be mastered, and if you are ready to work, you will learn what you need to know.

Why Does Your Attitude toward Writing Matter?

ACTIVITY 3	How Do You Feel about Writing?

Your attitude toward writing is an important part of learning to write well. To get a sense of just how you feel about writing, read the following statements. Put a check beside those statements with which you agree. (This activity is not a test, so try to be as honest as possible.)

_____✓_____ 1. A good writer should be able to sit down and write a paper straight through without stopping.

_____ 2. Writing is a skill that anyone can learn with practice.

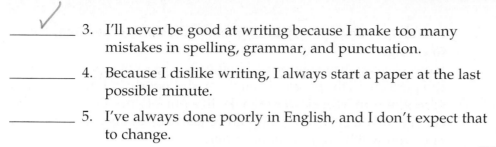

_____ 3. I'll never be good at writing because I make too many mistakes in spelling, grammar, and punctuation.

_____ 4. Because I dislike writing, I always start a paper at the last possible minute.

_____ 5. I've always done poorly in English, and I don't expect that to change.

Now read the following comments about the five statements. The comments will help you see if your attitude is hurting or helping your efforts to become a better writer.

1. **A good writer should be able to sit down and write a paper straight through without stopping.**

   The statement is _false_. Writing is, in fact, a process. It is done not in one easy step but in a series of steps, and seldom at one sitting. If you cannot do a paper all at once, that simply means you are like most of the other people on the planet. It is harmful to carry around the false idea that writing should be an easy matter.

2. **Writing is a skill that anyone can learn with practice.**

   This statement is absolutely true. Writing is a skill, like driving or typing, that you can master with hard work. If you want to learn to write, you can. It is as simple as that. If you believe this, you are ready to learn how to become a competent writer.

   Some people hold the false belief that writing is a natural gift that some have and others do not. Because of this belief, they never make a truly honest effort to learn to write—and so they never learn.

3. **I'll never be good at writing because I make too many mistakes in spelling, grammar, and punctuation.**

   The first concern in good writing should be _content_—what you have to say. Your ideas and feelings are what matter most. You should not worry about spelling, grammar, or punctuation while working on content.

   Unfortunately, some people are so self-conscious about making mistakes that they do not focus on what they want to say. They need to realize that a paper is best done in stages, and that applying the rules can and should wait until a later stage in the writing process. Through review and practice, you will eventually learn how to follow the rules with confidence.

4. **Because I dislike writing, I always start a paper at the last possible minute.**

   This is all too common. You feel you are _going to_ do poorly, and then your behavior ensures that you _will_ do poorly! Your attitude is so negative that you defeat yourself—not even allowing enough time to really try.

   Again, what you need to realize is that writing is a process. Because it is done in steps, you don't have to get it right all at once. Just get started well in advance. If you allow yourself enough time, you'll find a way to make a paper come together.

5. **I've always done poorly in English, and I don't expect that to change.**

    How you may have performed in the *past* does not control how you can perform in the *present*. Even if you did poorly in English in high school, it is in your power to make this one of your best subjects in college. If you believe writing can be learned, and if you work hard at it, you will become a better writer.

In brief, your attitude is crucial. If you believe you are a poor writer and always will be, chances are you will not improve. If you realize you can become a better writer, chances are you *will* improve. Depending on how you allow yourself to think, you can be your own best friend or your own worst enemy.

Writing as a Process of Discovery

In addition to believing that writing is a natural gift, many people believe, mistakenly, that writing should flow in a simple, straight line from the writer's head onto the page. But writing is seldom an easy, one-step journey in which a finished paper comes out in a first draft. The truth is that *writing is a process of discovery* that involves a series of steps, and those steps are very often a zigzag journey. Look at the following illustrations of the writing process:

Seldom the Case

Starting point ————————————————▶ Finished paper

Usually the Case

Starting point ——⋁⫽⋀⋁——▶ Finished paper

Very often, writers do not discover just what they want to write about until they explore their thoughts in writing. For example, Mike Cornell had been asked to write about a best or worst job. Only after he did some freewriting on jobs he liked and disliked did he realize that the most interesting details centered on his job at a diner and truck stop. He discovered his subject in the course of writing.

Another student, Rhonda, talking afterward about a paper she wrote, explained that at first her topic was how she relaxed with her children. But as she accumulated details, she realized after a page of writing that the words *relax* and *children* simply did not go together. Her details were really examples of how she *enjoyed* her children, not how she *relaxed* with them. She sensed that the real focus of her writing should be what she did by herself to relax, and then she thought suddenly that the best time of her week was Thursday after school. "A light clicked on in my head," she explained. "I knew I had my paper." Then it was a matter of detailing exactly what she did to relax on Thursday evenings.

The point is that writing is often a process of exploration and continuing discovery. As you write, you may suddenly switch direction or double back. You may be working on a topic sentence and realize that it could be your concluding thought. Or you may be developing a supporting idea and then decide that it should be the main point of your paper. Chapter 2 will treat the writing process directly. It is important to remember that writers frequently do not know their exact destination as they begin to write. Very often they discover the direction and shape of a paper *during* the process of writing.

Keeping a Journal

Because writing is a skill, it makes sense that the more you practice writing, the better you will write. One excellent way to get practice in writing, even before you begin composing formal paragraphs, is to keep a daily or almost daily journal. Keeping a journal will help you develop the habit of thinking on paper and will show you how ideas can be discovered in the process of writing. A journal can make writing a familiar part of your life and can serve as a continuing source of ideas for papers.

At some point during the day—perhaps during a study period after your last class of the day, right before dinner, or right before going to bed—spend fifteen minutes or so writing in your journal. Keep in mind that you do not have to plan what to write about, be in the mood to write, or worry about making mistakes as you write; just write down whatever words come out. You should write at least one page in each session.

You may want to use a notebook that you can easily carry with you for on-the-spot writing. Or you may decide to type your journal entries on a computer or write on loose-leaf paper that can be transferred later to a journal folder. No matter how you proceed, be sure to date all entries.

Your instructor may ask you to make journal entries a specific number of times a week for a specific number of weeks. He or she may have you turn in your journal every so often for review and feedback. If you are keeping the journal on your own, try to make entries three to five times a week every week of the semester. Your journal can serve as a sourcebook of ideas for possible papers. More important, keeping a journal will help you develop the habit of thinking on paper, and it can help you make writing a familiar part of your life.

Using a Journal to Generate Ideas	ACTIVITY 4

Following is an excerpt from one student's journal. (Sentence-skills mistakes have been corrected to improve readability.) As you read, look for a general point and supporting material that could be the basis for an interesting paper.

October 6

Today a woman came into our department at the store and wanted to know if we had any scrap lumber ten feet long. Ten feet! "Lady," I said, "anything we have that's ten feet long sure as heck isn't scrap." When the boss heard me say that, he

continued

almost canned me. My boss is a company man, down to his toe tips. He wants to make a big impression on his bosses, and he'll run us around like mad all night to make himself look good. He's the most ambitious man I've ever met. If I don't transfer out of Hardware soon, I'm going to go crazy on this job. I'm not ready to quit, though. The time is not right. I want to be here for a year and have another job lined up and have other things right before I quit. It's good the boss wasn't around tonight when another customer wanted me to carry a bookcase he had bought out to his car. He didn't ask me to help him—he <u>expected</u> me to help him. I hate that kind of "You're my servant" attitude, and I told him that carrying stuff out to cars wasn't my job. Ordinarily I go out of my way to give people a hand, but not guys like him. . . .

If the writer of this journal is looking for an idea for a paper, he can probably find several in this single entry. For example, he might write a narrative supporting the point that "In my sales job I have to deal with some irritating customers." See if you can find another idea in this entry that might be the basis for an interesting paragraph. Write your point in the space below.

_____

WRITING ASSIGNMENT 2

Take fifteen minutes to write a journal entry on your own recent experiences at work or in school. What happened to you yesterday or even earlier this morning? On a separate sheet of paper, just start writing about anything that you have said, heard, thought, or felt, and let your thoughts take you where they may.

EXPLORING WRITING ONLINE

Visit each of the following Web sites. Then, for each site, write a sentence that states what its purpose, or main point, is.

eBay: www.ebay.com

Google: www.google.com

YouTube: www.youtube.com

MySpace: www.myspace.com

Wikipedia: www.wikipedia.org

USA.gov: www.usa.gov

RESPONDING TO IMAGES

A lot is happening in this photograph, but we are immediately drawn to one particular interaction. What is the focus (or central point), and how does the photographer guide our eyes and attention to it?

For additional materials on Chapter 1, visit www.mhhe.com/langan.

2

The Writing Process

RESPONDING TO IMAGES

Students often feel uncomfortable sharing their writing with others. How do you feel about letting classmates read your work? Do you feel differently when you post a message to a social blog or forum? Take a few minutes to jot down your responses to these questions. In this chapter, you'll learn about the benefits of having others read and respond to your written work.

How Do You Reach the Goals of Effective Writing?

Even professional writers do not sit down and write a paper automatically, in one draft. Instead, they have to work on it a step at a time. Writing a paper is a process that can be divided into the following steps:

- Prewriting
- Writing the first draft
- Revising
- Editing and proofreading

These steps are described on the following pages.

Prewriting

If you are like many people, you may have trouble getting started writing. A mental block may develop when you sit down before a blank sheet of paper or a blank screen. You may not be able to think of an interesting topic or a point to make about your topic. Or you may have trouble coming up with specific details to support your point. And even after starting a composition, you may hit snags—moments when you wonder "What else can I say?" or "Where do I go next?"

The following pages describe five techniques that will help you think about and develop a topic and get words on paper: (1) freewriting, (2) questioning, (3) making a list, (4) clustering, and (5) preparing a scratch outline. These prewriting techniques help you think about and create material, and they are a central part of the writing process.

Technique 1: Freewriting

When you do not know what to write about a subject or when you are blocked in writing, freewriting sometimes helps. In *freewriting*, you write on your topic for ten minutes. You do not worry about spelling or punctuating correctly, about erasing mistakes, about organizing material, or about finding exact words. You just write without stopping. If you get stuck for words, you write "I am looking for something to say" or repeat words until something comes. There is no need to feel inhibited since mistakes *do not count* and you do not have to hand in your paper.

Freewriting will limber up your writing muscles and make you familiar with the act of writing. It is a way to break through mental blocks about writing. Since you do not have to worry about mistakes, you can focus on discovering what you want to say about a subject. Your initial ideas and impressions will often become clearer after you have gotten them down on paper, and they may lead to other impressions and ideas. Through continued practice in freewriting, you will develop the habit of thinking as you write. And you will learn a technique that is a helpful way to get started on almost any piece of writing.

Freewriting: A Student Model

Mike Cornell's paragraph "My Job at the Crescent Falls Diner and Truck Stop" on page 8 in Chapter 1 was written in response to an assignment to write a composition on the best or worst job he ever had. Mike began by doing some general freewriting and thinking about his jobs. Here is his freewriting:

> I have had good and bad jobs, that's for sure. It was great earning money for the first time. I shoveled snow for my neighbor, a friend of mine and me did the work and had snowball fights along the way. I remember my neighbor reaching into his pocket and pulling out several dollars and handing us the money, it was like magic. Then there was the lawnmowing, which was also a good job. I mowed my aunt's lawn while she was away at work. Then I'd go sit by myself in her cool living room and have a coke she left in the refrigerator for me. And look through all her magazines. Then there was the job at the Crescent Falls diner and truck stop that I had after high school. That was the worst job that left me wiped out after my shift. I had to wait on customers and bus tables while listening to my boss complain. I only got minimum wage. I had to unload delivery trucks. The manager was a real creep, he enjoyed treating all the other guys much better than me. He wouldn't even give me a few days off to go to a wedding, and he made nasty comments about the way I look, my clothes and everything. Even my race. I thought I would make a lot in tips. Then, I find out I have to share them with the other workers. I will never work in a diner again!

At this point, Mike read over his notes, and as he later commented, "I realized that I had several topics. I said to myself, 'What point can I make that I can cover in a paragraph? What do I have the most information about?' I decided to narrow my topic down to my awful job at the diner and truck stop. I figured I would have lots of interesting details for that topic." Mike then did a more focused freewriting to accumulate details for a paragraph on this job:

The job I remember most is the worst job I ever had. I worked at the Crescent Falls diner and truck stop. I put in very long hours and would be totally beat after ten hours of work, six days a week. Most of time waiting on customers and cleaning tables, but also washing dishes in a kitchen that was unbearably hot and steamy, I even had to unload heavy cartons of food from delivery trucks. And I had to keep track of all the cartons I took off. I worked so much that I never had a social life. My boss was always complaining about my work—I didn't get my orders out fast enough, I didn't clean the tables as good as he wanted. I only got minimum wage. The manager was a real creep, he seemed to enjoy irritating me, treating all the other guys much better than me. After a while, I realized he just didn't like college kids. He envied them. He wouldn't even give me a few days off to go to a wedding, and he made nasty comments about the way I look, my clothes and everything. Even my race. I thought I would make a lot in tips. Then, I find out I have to share them with the other workers. Besides the tips, I only got minimum wage. So, I had to work sixty hours a week in that hell whole just to make enough for my first semester's tuition. I will never work in a diner again!

TIP   Notice that there are problems with spelling, grammar, and punctuation in Mike's freewriting. Mike was not worried about such matters, nor should he have been. At this stage, he just wanted to do some thinking on paper and get some material down on the page. He knew that this was a good first step, a good way of getting started, and that he would then be able to go on and shape that material.

You should take the same approach when freewriting: Explore your topic without worrying at all about being "correct." Figuring out what you want to say and getting raw material down on the page should have all of your attention at this early stage of the writing process.

ACTIVITY 1	Freewriting

To get a sense of the freewriting process, take a sheet of paper and freewrite about different jobs you have had and what you liked or did not like about them. See how much material you can accumulate in ten minutes. And remember not to worry about "mistakes"; you're just thinking on paper.

Technique 2: Questioning

In *questioning,* you generate ideas and details by asking as many questions as you can think of about your subject. Such questions include *Why? When? Where? Who? How? In what ways?*

Here are questions that Mike Cornell asked while further developing his paragraph:

Questioning: A Student Model

Questions	Answers
What did I hate about the job?	Very hard work
	Poor pay
	Unfair, nasty manager
	Bad working conditions
How was the work hard?	Carried heavy trays
	Unloaded heavy cartons from trucks, keeping track of what I took off washed dishes
Why was pay poor?	Earned minimum wage
	Had to share tips with coworkers
How was the manager unfair?	Favored coworkers over me when giving days off
	Didn't like college students
	Made insulting remarks about my appearance/race
In what ways were working conditions bad?	Kitchen hot, boss was overly critical of my work

> **TIP**   Asking questions can be an effective way of getting yourself to think about a topic from different angles. The questions can help you generate details about a topic and get ideas on how to organize those details. Notice how asking questions gives Mike a better sense of the different reasons why he hated the job.

Questioning

To get a feel for the questioning process, use a sheet of paper to ask yourself a series of questions about your best and worst jobs. See how many details you can accumulate in ten minutes. And remember again not to be concerned about "mistakes" because you are just thinking on paper.

Technique 3: Making a List

In *making a list,* also known as *brainstorming,* you create a list of ideas and details that relate to your subject. Pile these items up, one after another, without trying to sort out major details from minor ones, or trying to put the details in any special order, or even trying to spell words correctly. Your goal is to accumulate raw material by making up a list of everything about your subject that occurs to you.

After freewriting and questioning, Mike made up the following list of details.

Making a List: A Student Model

Diner and truck stop job—worst one I ever had

Manager was unfair and nasty

Worked ten hours a day, sixty hours a week

Waited on customers, bused tables, cleaned bathrooms

Washed dishes in hot, steamy kitchen, unloaded heavy cartons
     off delivery trucks

Got paid minimum wage

Had no social life

Sometimes had to work overtime—no extra pay

Boss always critical of my work

Manager hated college kids, treated them worse than other workers

Couldn't get a day off to rest or be with friends

---

continued

> No real friends at this job—no social life
>
> Asked for two days off to go to a wedding—no way!
>
> Hurt my back
>
> Had to work at least sixty hours a week to make tuition for first semester in college
>
> Boss was insulting, even made racial remarks
>
> Ridiculed my hair, clothing
>
> Had to share my tips with other workers in the kitchen and cashiers—not just with other servers

TIP One detail led to another as Mike expanded his list. Slowly but surely, more details emerged, some of which he could use in developing his paragraph. By the time you finish making a list, you should be ready to plan an outline of your paragraph and then to write your first draft.

ACTIVITY 3   **Listing**

To get a sense of making a list, use a sheet of paper to list a series of details about one of the best or worst jobs you ever had. Don't worry about deciding whether the details are major or minor; instead, just get down as many details as you can think of in five or ten minutes.

Technique 4: Clustering

Clustering, also known as *diagramming* or *mapping,* is another strategy that can be used to generate material for a paper of any length. This method is helpful for people who like to think in a visual way. In clustering, you use lines, boxes, arrows, and circles to show relationships among the ideas and details that occur to you.

Begin by stating your subject in a few words in the center of a blank sheet of paper. Then, as ideas and details occur to you, put them in boxes or circles around the subject and draw lines to connect them to each other and to the subject. Put minor ideas or details in smaller boxes or circles, and use connecting lines to show how they relate as well.

Keep in mind that there is no right or wrong way of clustering. It is a way to think on paper about how various ideas and details relate to one another. The following is an example of what Mike might have done to develop his ideas:

Clustering: A Student Model

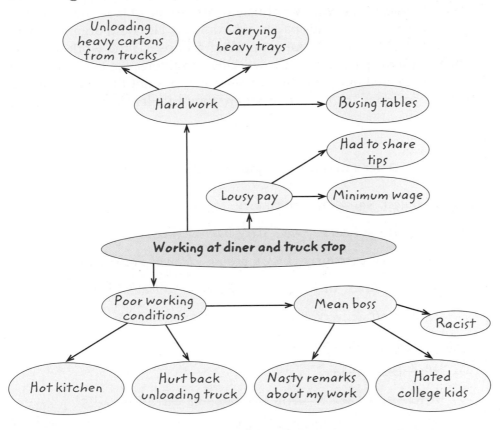

TIP In addition to helping generate material, clustering often suggests ways to organize ideas and details.

Clustering/Diagramming ACTIVITY 4

Use clustering or diagramming to organize the details that you created for the previous activity about a best or worst job (page 22).

Technique 5: Preparing a Scratch Outline

A scratch outline can be the *single most helpful technique* for writing a good paper. A scratch outline often follows freewriting, questioning, making a list, or clustering, but it may also gradually emerge in the midst of these strategies. In fact, trying to make a scratch outline is a good way to see if you need to do more prewriting. If you cannot come up with a solid outline, then you know you need to do more prewriting to clarify your main point and its several kinds of support.

In a scratch outline, you think carefully about the point you are making, the supporting items for that point, and the order in which you will arrange those items. The scratch outline is a plan or blueprint to help you achieve a unified, supported, and well-organized composition.

Scratch Outline: A Student Model

In Mike's case, as he was working on his list of details, he suddenly realized what the plan of his paragraph could be. He could organize many of his details into one of three supporting groups: (1) the work involved in the job, (2) the pay, and (3) the working conditions. He then went back to the list, crossed out items that he now saw did not fit, and numbered the items according to the group where they fit. Here is what Mike did with his list:

Diner and truck stop job—worst one I ever had

3   Manager was unfair and nasty

2   Worked ten hours a day, sixty hours a week

1   Waited on customers, bused tables, cleaned bathrooms

1   Washed dishes in hot, steamy kitchen, unloaded heavy cartons off delivery trucks

2   Got paid minimum wage

~~Had no social life~~

~~A few times had to work overtime—no extra pay~~

3   Boss always critical of my work

3   Manager hated college kids, treated them worse than other workers

~~Couldn't get a day off to rest or be with friends~~

~~No real friends at this job~~

3   Asked for two days off to go to a wedding—no way!

3   Hurt my back

2   Had to work at least sixty hours a week to make tuition for first semester in college

3   Boss was insulting, even made racial remarks

3   Ridiculed my hair, clothing

1   I had to mop floors

2   Had to share my tips with other workers in the kitchen and cashiers—not just with other servers

1   When I interviewed, I didn't know I would also be unloading trucks, cleaning bathrooms

---

Under the list, Mike was now able to prepare his scratch outline:

The diner and truck stop was my worst job.

1. Hard work

2. Lousy pay

3. Poor working conditions

TIP   After all his prewriting, Mike was pleased. He knew that he had a promising composition—one with a clear point and solid support. He saw that he could organize the material into a paragraph with a topic sentence, supporting points, and vivid details. He was now ready to write the first draft of his paragraph, using his outline as a guide. Chances are that if you do enough prewriting and thinking on paper, you will eventually discover the point and support of your paragraph.

Making a Scratch Outline

ACTIVITY 5

Create a scratch outline that could serve as a guide if you were to write a paragraph on your best or worst job experience.

Writing the First Draft

When you write a first draft, be prepared to put in additional thoughts and details that did not emerge during prewriting. And don't worry if you hit a snag. Just leave a blank space or add a comment such as "Do later" and press on to finish the paper. Also, don't worry yet about grammar, punctuation, or spelling. You don't want to take time correcting words or sentences that you may decide to remove later. Instead, make it your goal to state your main idea clearly and develop the content of your paragraph with plenty of specific details.

Writing a First Draft: A Student Model

Here is Mike's first draft, done in longhand:

~~The crescent diner and truck stop job was the pit.~~ Working at the cresent falls diner and Truck Stop was the worst job I ever had. The work was physically very hard. During my ~~long~~ ten hour days I had to carry heavy trays of food to the

continued

custamers, and the tables had to be cleaned.. ~~Then~~, You would wash dishes and then go unload the delivery truck of food supplies. At the same time I had to keep track in my head of all the cartons I had unloaded. The second bad feature that made the job a worst one was the pay. The pay was lousey. I had to work at least sixty hours a week to afford next semester's tuition. I got only minimun wage, and I had to share my tips with the kitchen workers too. And the boss was a creep who hated me cause I was a college student, he gave me lousey hours. Even called me horrible names to my face. DETAILS!

> **TIP**   After Mike finished the first draft, he was able to put it aside until the next day. You will benefit as well if you can allow some time between finishing a draft and starting to revise.

ACTIVITY 6   Drafting

Working with a fellow classmate, see if you can fill in the missing words in the following explanation of Mike's first draft.

1. Mike presents his _____ in the first sentence and then crosses it out and revises it right away to make it read smoothly and clearly.

2. Notice that he continues to accumulate specic supporting details as he writes the draft. For example, he crosses out and replaces "long" with the more specific _____. When talking about his pay, he adds _____.

3. There are various misspellings—for example, _____. Mike doesn't worry about spelling at this point. He just wants to get down as much of the substance of his paragraph as possible.

4. There are various punctuation errors, especially the run-on and the fragment near the (*beginning, middle, end*) _____ of the paragraph.

5. Near the close of his paragraph, Mike can't think of more details to insert, so he simply prints _____ as a reminder to himself for the next draft.

Revising

Revising is as much a stage in the writing process as prewriting, outlining, and doing the first draft. *Revising* means that you rewrite a paragraph or paper, building upon what has already been done in order to make it stronger. One writer has said about revision, "It's like cleaning house—getting rid of all the junk and putting things in the right order." It is not just "straightening up"; instead, you must be ready to roll up your sleeves and do whatever is needed to create an effective paper. Too many students think that a first draft *is* the final one. They start to become writers when they realize that revising a rough draft three or four times is often at the heart of the writing process.

Here are some quick hints that can help make revision easier. First, set your first draft aside for a while. You can then come back to it with a fresher, more objective point of view. Second, work from typed or printed text, preferably double-spaced so you'll have room to handwrite changes later. You'll be able to see the paragraph or paper more impartially if it is typed than if you were just looking at your own familiar handwriting. Next, read your draft aloud. Hearing how your writing sounds will help you pick up problems with meaning as well as with style. Finally, as you do all these things, write additional thoughts and changes above the lines or in the margins of your paper. Your written comments can serve as a guide when you work on the next draft.

There are two stages to the revision process:

- Revising content
- Revising sentences

Revising Content

To revise the content of your paragraph, ask the following questions:

1. Is my paragraph **unified?**

   - Do I have a clear, single point in the first sentence of the paragraph?
   - Does all my evidence support my opening point?

2. Is my paragraph **supported?**

   - Are there separate supporting points for the opening point?
   - Do I have *specific* evidence for each supporting point?
   - Is there *plenty of* specific evidence for the supporting points?

3. Is my paragraph **organized?**

   - Do I have a clear method of organizing my thoughts?
   - Do I use transitions and other connecting words?

Revising Sentences

To revise individual sentences in your paragraph, ask the following questions:

1. Do I use *parallelism* to balance my words and ideas?

2. Do I have a *consistent point of view?*

3. Do I use *specific* words?

4. Do I use *active* verbs?

5. Do I use words effectively by *avoiding slang, clichés, pretentious language,* and *wordiness?*

6. Do I *vary my sentences* in length and structure?

Part 3 of this text will give you practice in revising sentences.

Revising: A Student Model

For his second draft, Mike used a word-processing program on a computer. He then printed out a double-spaced version of his paragraph, leaving himself plenty of room for handwritten revisions. Here is Mike's second draft plus the handwritten changes and additions that became his third draft:

Working at the cresent falls diner and Truck Stop was the worst job I ever had. *First of all* The work was physically very hard. During my ten hour days I had to carry heavy trays of food to the custamers, and ~~the tables had to be cleaned.~~ *I had to clean the tables* ~~You~~ *I* would wash dishes and then go unload the delivery truck, lifting ~~heavy~~ *sixty-pound* cartons of food supplies. ~~At the same time I had to keep track in my head of all the cartons I had unloaded.~~ The second bad feature ~~that made the job a worst one~~ was the pay. ~~The pay was lousey.~~ I had to work at least sixty hours a week to afford next semester's tuition *because* I got only minimun wage, and I had to share my tips with the kitchen workers too. *Finally* The working conditions were horrible. I had to wash dishes *in a hot and steamy kitchen*. Once, when unloading a truck, I hurt my back so badly I was out of work for a week without pay! And the boss was a ~~creep~~ *tyrant* who hated me cause I was a college student, he gave me ~~lousey~~ *terrible* hours. Even ~~called me horrible names~~ *made racist slurs* to my face.

> **T I P**   Mike made his changes in longhand as he worked on the second draft. As you will see when you complete the following activity, a revision should serve to make a paragraph more unified, supported, and organized.

Revising a Draft

Fill in the missing words.

1. To clarify the organization, Mike adds at the beginning of the first supporting point the transitional phrase "_____" and he sets off the third supporting point with the word "_____."

2. In the interest of (*unity, support, organization*) _____, he crosses out the sentence "_____." He realizes that this sentence is not a relevant detail to support the idea that the work was physically hard.

3. To add more (*unity, support, organization*) _____, he changes "heavy cartons" to "_____"; he adds "_____" to his sentence about washing dishes.

4. In the interest of eliminating wordiness, he removes the words "_____" and "_____."

5. To achieve parallelism, he changes "the tables had to be cleaned" to "_____."

6. For greater sentence variety, Mike combines two short sentences beginning the second part of the sentence with "_____."

7. To create a consistent point of view, Mike changes "You would wash dishes" to "_____."

8. Mike becomes more specific by changing "called me horrible names to my face" to "_____."

9. Finally, he replaces the somewhat vague word "creep" with the more precise word "_____."

Editing and Proofreading

The next-to-last major stage in the writing process is editing—checking a paper for mistakes in grammar, punctuation, usage, and spelling. Students often find it hard to edit a paper carefully. They have put so much work into their writing, or so little, that it's almost painful for them to look at the paper one more time. You may simply have to *will* yourself to carry out this important closing step in the writing process. Remember that eliminating sentence-skills mistakes will improve an average paper and help ensure a strong grade on a good paper. Furthermore, as you get into the habit of checking your papers, you will also get into the habit of using sentence skills consistently. They are an integral part of clear, effective writing.

The checklist of sentence skills on the inside back cover of the book will serve as a guide while you are editing your paper.

Here are tips that can help you edit the next-to-final draft of a paper for sentence-skills mistakes:

Editing Tips

1. Have at hand two essential tools: a good dictionary (see Chapter 30) and a grammar handbook (you can use Part 3 of this book).

2. Use a sheet of paper to cover your writing so that you can expose only one sentence at a time. Look for errors in grammar, spelling, and typing. It may help to read each sentence out loud. If the sentence does not read clearly and smoothly, chances are something is wrong.

3. Pay special attention to the kinds of errors you tend to make. For example, if you tend to write run-ons or fragments, be especially on the lookout for these errors.

4. Try to work on a typed and printed draft, where you'll be able to see your writing more objectively than you could on a hand-written page; use a pen with colored ink so that your corrections will stand out.

Proofreading, the final stage in the writing process, means checking a paper carefully for spelling, grammar, punctuation, and other errors. You are ready for this stage when you are satisfied with your choice of supporting details, the order in which they are presented, and the way they and your topic sentence are worded.

At this point in your work, use your dictionary to do final checks on your spelling. Use a grammar handbook (such as the one in Part 3 of this text) to be sure about grammar, punctuation, and usage. Also read through your paper carefully, looking for typing errors, omitted words, and any other errors you may have missed before. Proofreading is often hard to do—again, students have spent so much time with their work, or so little, that they want to avoid it. But if it is done carefully, this important final step will ensure that your paper looks as good as possible.

Proofreading Tips

1. One helpful trick at this stage is to read your paper out loud. You will probably hear awkward wordings and become aware of spots where the punctuation needs to be changed. Make the improvements needed for your sentences to read smoothly and clearly.

2. Another strategy is to read your paper backward, from the last sentence to the first. This helps keep you from getting caught up in the flow of the paper and missing small mistakes—which is easy to do since you're so familiar with what you meant to say.

Editing and Proofreading: A Student Model

After typing into his word-processing file all the revisions in his paragraph, Mike printed out another clean draft. He then turned his attention to editing changes, as shown here:

My Job at the Crescent Falls Diner and Truck Stop

Working at the *C*rescent *F*alls *D*iner and Truck Stop was the worst job I ever had. First of all, the work was physically very hard. During my ten-hour days, I had to carry heavy trays of food to the ~~custamers~~ *customers*, and I had to clean the tables. I ~~would wash~~ *washed* dishes and then ~~go unload~~ *unloaded* the delivery truck, lifting sixty-pound cartons of food supplies. The second bad feature was the pay. I had to work at least sixty hours a week to afford next semester's tuition because I got only ~~minimun~~ *minimum* wage, and I had to share my tips with the kitchen workers too. Finally, the working conditions were horrible. I had to wash dishes in a hot and steamy kitchen. Once, when unloading a truck, I hurt my back so badly I was out of work for a week without pay! And the boss was a tyrant who hated me ~~cause~~ *because* I was a college student; *H*e gave me terrible hours*, ridiculed my clothes, and* Even made racist slurs to my face.

TIP   You can make your changes (as Mike did) in longhand right on the printout of your paper. To note Mike's changes, complete the activity that follows.

Editing and Proofreading a Draft   ACTIVITY 8

Fill in the missing words.

1. As part of his editing, Mike checked and corrected the _____ of two words, *customers* and *minimum*. He also added a _____ between the compound adjective "ten-hour."

2. He added _____ to set off an introductory phrase ("During my ten-hour days") and an introductory word ("Finally").

3. He corrected a run on ("_____
    _____") by replacing the comma with
    a period between the two sentences and by capitalizing the first word of
    the second sentence.

4. He corrected word use by changing "cause" to "_____." He
    eliminated wordiness by changing "I would wash dishes and then go

    unload . . ." to "_____."

5. He corrected _____ by changing "crescent falls diner" to
    "Crescent Falls Diner."

6. Since revision can occur at any stage of the writing process, includ-
    ing editing, Mike makes one of his details more vivid by adding the

    descriptive words "_____."

At this point, all Mike had to do was to enter his corrections, print out
the final draft of the paper, and proofread it for any typos or other careless
errors. He was then ready to hand it in to his instructor.

Tips on Using a Computer

- If you are using your school's computer center, allow enough
  time. You may have to wait for a computer or printer to be free.
  In addition, you may need several sessions at the computer and
  printer to complete your paper.

- Every word-processing program allows you to save your writing
  by pressing one or more keys. Save your work file frequently as
  you write your draft. A saved file is stored safely on the computer
  or network. A file that is not saved will be lost if the computer
  crashes or if the power is turned off.

- Keep your work in two places—the hard drive or network you
  are working on and, if you have one, a backup USB drive. At the
  end of each session with the computer, copy your work onto the
  USB drive or e-mail a copy to yourself. Then if the hard drive or
  network becomes damaged, you'll have the backup copy.

- Print out your work at least at the end of every session. Then
  not only will you have your most recent draft to work on away
  from the computer, but also you'll have a copy in case something
  should happen to your electronic copy.

- Work in single spacing so that you can see as much of your writing
  on the screen at one time as possible. Just before you print out your
  work, change to double spacing.

- Before making major changes in a paper, create a copy of your file.
  For example, if your file is titled "Worst Job," create a file called
  "Worst Job 2." Then make all your changes in that new file. If the
  changes don't work out, you can always go back to the original file.

Using a Computer at Each Stage of the Writing Process

Following are some ways to make word processing a part of your writing.

Prewriting

If you're a fast typist, many kinds of prewriting will work well on the computer. With freewriting in particular, you can get ideas onto the screen almost as quickly as they occur to you. A passing thought that could be productive is not likely to get lost. You may even find it helpful, when freewriting, to dim the screen of your monitor so that you can't see what you're typing. If you temporarily can't see the screen, you won't have to worry about grammar or spelling or typing errors (all of which do not matter in prewriting); instead, you can concentrate on getting down as many ideas and details as possible about your subject.

After any initial freewriting, questioning, and list-making on a computer, it's often very helpful to print out a hard copy of what you've done. With a clean printout in front of you, you'll be able to see everything at once and revise and expand your work with handwritten comments in the margins of the paper.

Word processing also makes it easy for you to experiment with the wording of the point of your paper. You can try a number of versions in a short time. After you have decided on the version that works best, you can easily delete the other versions—or simply move them to a temporary "leftover" section at the end of the paper.

If you have prepared a list of items during prewriting, you may be able to turn that list into an outline right on the screen. Delete the ideas you feel should not be in your paper (saving them at the end of the file in case you change your mind), and add any new ideas that occur to you. Then use the cut and paste functions to shuffle the supporting ideas around until you find the best order for your paper.

Writing Your First Draft

Like many writers, you may want to write out your first draft by hand and then type it into the computer for revision. Even as you type your handwritten draft, you may find yourself making some changes and improvements. And once you have a draft on the screen, or printed out, you will find it much easier to revise than a handwritten one.

If you feel comfortable composing directly on the screen, you can benefit from the computer's special features. For example, if you have written an anecdote in your freewriting that you plan to use in your paper, simply copy the story from your freewriting file and insert it where it fits in your paper. You can refine it then or later. Or if you discover while typing that a sentence is out of place, cut it out from where it is and paste it wherever you wish. And if while writing you realize that an earlier sentence can be expanded, just move your cursor back to that point and type in the added material.

Revising

It is during revision that the virtues of word processing really shine. All substituting, adding, deleting, and rearranging can be done easily within an existing file. All changes instantly take their proper places within the paper, not scribbled above the line or squeezed into the margin. You can concentrate on each change you want to make because you never have to type from scratch or work on a messy draft. You can carefully go through your paper to check that all your supporting evidence is relevant and to add new support as needed here and there. Anything you decide to eliminate can be deleted in a keystroke. Anything you add can be inserted precisely where you choose. If you change your mind, all you have to do is delete or cut and paste. Then you can sweep through the paper, focusing on other changes, such as improving word choice, increasing sentence variety, eliminating wordiness, and so on.

> **TIP**   If you are like many students, you will find it convenient to print out a hard copy of your file at various points throughout the revision. You can then revise in longhand—adding, crossing out, and indicating changes—and later quickly make these changes in the document.

Editing and Proofreading

Editing and proofreading also benefit richly from word processing. Instead of crossing or whiting out mistakes, or rewriting an entire paper to correct numerous errors, you can make all necessary changes within the most recent draft. If you find editing or proofreading on the screen hard on your eyes, print out a copy. Mark any corrections on that copy, and then transfer them to the final draft.

If the word-processing program you're using includes spelling and grammar checks, by all means use them. The spell-check function tells you when a word is not in the computer's dictionary. Keep in mind, however, that the spell-check cannot tell you how to spell a name correctly or when you have mistakenly used, for example, *their* instead of *there*. To a spell-checker, *Thank ewe four the complement* is as correct as *Thank you for the compliment*. Also, use the grammar check with caution. Any errors it doesn't uncover are still your responsibility, and it sometimes points out mistakes when there are none.

A word-processed paper, with its clean look and handsome formatting, looks so good that you may feel it is in better shape than it really is. Do not be fooled by your paper's appearance. Take sufficient time to review your grammar, punctuation, and spelling carefully.

> **TIP**   Even after you hand in your paper, save the computer file. Your instructor may ask you to do some revising, and then the file will save you from having to type the paper from scratch.

Using Peer Review

Often, it is a good idea to have another student respond to your writing before you hand it in to the instructor. On the day a paper is due, or on a day when you are writing papers in class, your instructor may ask you to pair up with another student. That student will read your paper, and you will read his or her paper.

Ideally, read the other paper aloud while your partner listens. If that is not practical, read it in a whisper while he or she looks on. As you read, both you and your partner should look and listen for spots where your reading snags.

Your partner should then read your paper, marking possible trouble spots while doing so. Then each of you should do three things:

1. Identification

On a separate sheet of paper, write at the top the title and author of the composition you have read. Under it, put your name as the reader of the paper.

2. Scratch Outline

"X-ray" the paper for its inner logic by making up a scratch outline. The scratch outline need be no more than twenty words or so, but it should show clearly the logical foundation on which the essay is built. It should identify and summarize the overall point of the paper and the three areas of support for the point.

Your scratch outline should be organized like this:

Point: _____

Support: _____

    1. _____

    2. _____

    3. _____

For example, here is a scratch outline of the paper on page 105 about a new puppy in the house:

Point: *A new puppy can have dramatic effects on a house.*

Support:

    1. *Keeps family awake at night*

    2. *Destroys possessions*

    3. *Causes arguments*

3. Comments

Under the outline, write the heading "Comments." Here is what you should comment on:

- Look at the spots where your reading of the paragraph snagged: Are words missing or misspelled? Is there a lack of parallel structure? Are there mistakes with punctuation? Is the meaning of a sentence confusing? Try to figure out what the problems are and suggest ways of fixing them.

- Are there spots in the composition where you see problem with *unity, support,* or *organization?* (You'll find it helpful to refer to the checklist on the inside back cover of this book.) If so, offer comments. For example, you might say, "More details are needed to back up your main point" or "Some of the supporting details here don't really back up your point."

- Finally, make note of something you really liked about the paragraph, such as good use of transitions or an especially realistic or vivid specific detail.

After you have completed your evaluation of the composition, give it to your partner. Your instructor may provide you with the option of rewriting a piece of work in light of this feedback. Whether or not you rewrite, be sure to hand in the peer evaluation form with your composition.

REFLECTIVE ACTIVITY

1. Has your understanding of the writing process changed since reading Chapter 2? In what ways?

2. Of the four prewriting techniques (freewriting, questioning, making a list, and clustering), which one seems best for the way you might approach a writing assignment?

Review Activities

You now have a good overview of the writing process, from prewriting to drafting to revising to editing. The chapters in Part 2 will deepen your sense of the four goals of effective writing: unity, support, organization or coherence, and sentence skills.

To reinforce much of the information about the writing process that you have learned in this chapter, you can now work through the following review activities:

- Prewriting

- Outlining, drafting, and revising

- Taking a writing inventory

- Chapter review

Prewriting

These activities will give you practice in some of the prewriting strategies you can use to generate material for a paragraph. Although the focus here is on writing a paragraph, the strategies apply to writing an essay as well. See if you can do two or more of these prewriting activities.

Freewriting

REVIEW ACTIVITY 1

On a sheet of paper, freewrite for several minutes about a success or failure in your life. Don't worry about grammar, punctuation, or spelling. Try to write, without stopping, about whatever comes into your head concerning your success or failure.

Questioning

REVIEW ACTIVITY 2

On another sheet of paper, answer the following questions about the success or failure you've started to write about.

1. When did this success or failure occur?

2. Where did it take place?

3. What is one reason you consider this experience a success or failure? Give specific details to illustrate this reason.

4. What is another reason for this success or failure? What are some details that support the second reason?

5. Can you think of a third reason for this success or failure? What are some details that support the third reason?

Clustering

REVIEW ACTIVITY 3

In the center of a blank sheet of paper, write and circle the word *success* or *failure*. Then, around the circle, add reasons and details about this experience. Use a series of boxes, circles, or other shapes, along with connecting lines, to set off the reasons and details. In other words, try to think about and explore your topic in a very visual way.

Making a List

REVIEW ACTIVITY 4

On a separate piece of paper, make a list of details about the success or failure. Don't worry about putting them in a certain order. Just get down as many details about the experience as you can. The list can include specific reasons why the experience was a success or failure and specific details supporting those reasons.

Outlining, Drafting, and Revising

Here you will get practice in the writing steps that follow prewriting: outlining, drafting, revising, editing, and proofreading.

REVIEW ACTIVITY 5	Scratch Outline

On the basis of your prewriting, see if you can prepare a scratch outline made up of your main idea and the three main reasons for your success or failure. Use the form below:

I experienced success or failure when I _____.

Reason 1: _____

Reason 2: _____

Reason 3: _____

REVIEW ACTIVITY 6	First Draft

Now write a first draft of your paragraph. Begin with your topic sentence, stating the success or failure you experienced. Then state the first reason to support your main idea, followed by specific details supporting that reason. Next, state the second reason, followed by specific details supporting that reason. Finally, state the third reason, followed by support.

Don't worry about grammar, punctuation, or spelling. Just concentrate on getting down on paper the details about your experience.

REVIEW ACTIVITY 7	Revising the Draft

Ideally, you will have a chance to put your paragraph aside for a while before writing the second draft. In your second draft, try to do all of the following:

1. Add transition words such as *first of all*, *another*, and *finally* to introduce each of the three reasons why your success or failure occurred.

2. Omit any details that do not truly support your topic sentence.

3. Add more details as needed, making sure you have plenty of support for each of your three reasons.

4. Check to see that your details are vivid and specific. Can you make a supporting detail more concrete? Are there any persuasive, colorful specifics you can add?

5. Try to eliminate wordiness (see pages 428–429) and clichés (see pages 425–426).

6. In general, improve the flow of your writing.

7. Be sure to include a final sentence that rounds off the paragraph, bringing it to a close.

Editing and Proofreading

When you have your almost-final draft of the paragraph, proofread it as follows:

1. Using your dictionary, check any words that you think might be misspelled. Or use a spell-check program on your computer.

2. Using Part 3 of this book, check your paragraph for mistakes in grammar, punctuation, and usage.

3. Read the paragraph aloud, listening for awkward or unclear spots. Make the changes needed for the paragraph to read smoothly and clearly. Even better, see if you can get another person to read the draft aloud to you. The spots that this person has trouble reading are spots where you may have to do some rewriting.

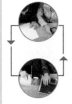

4. Take a sheet of paper and cover your writing so that you can expose and carefully check one line at a time. Or read your writing backward, from the end of the paragraph to the beginning. Look for typing errors, omitted words, and other remaining errors.

Don't fail to edit and proofread carefully. You may be tired of working on your paragraph at this point, but you want to give the extra effort needed to make it as good as possible. A final push can mean the difference between a higher and a lower grade.

Taking a Writing Inventory

Your Approach to Writing

This activity is not a test, so try to be as honest as possible when answering the following questions. Becoming aware of your writing habits can help you make helpful changes in your writing.

1. When you start work on a paper, do you typically do any prewriting?

_____ Yes   _____ Sometimes   _____ No

2. If so, which of the prewriting techniques do you use?

_____ Freewriting   _____ Clustering

_____ Questioning   _____ Scratch outline

_____ List making   _____ Other (please describe)

3. Which prewriting technique or techniques work best for you or do you think will work best for you?

_____

4. Many students have said they find it helpful to handwrite a first draft and then type that draft on a computer. They then print out the draft

and revise it by hand. Describe your own way of drafting and revising a composition.

_____

5. After you write the first draft of a composition, do you have time to set it aside for a while so you can come back to it with a fresh eye?

6. How many drafts do you typically write when doing a paper?

_____

7. When you revise, are you aware that you should be working toward a composition that is unified, solidly supported, and clearly organized? Has this chapter given you a better sense that unity, support, and organization are goals to aim for?

_____

8. Do you revise a paragraph for the effectiveness of its sentences as well as for its content?

_____

9. What (if any) information has this chapter given you about prewriting that you will try to apply in your writing?

_____

10. What (if any) information has this chapter given you about revising that you will try to apply in your writing?

_____

Chapter Review

REVIEW ACTIVITY 10   The Writing Process

Answer each of the following questions by filling in the blank or circling the answer you think is correct.

1. _True or false?_ _____ Writing is a skill that anyone can learn with practice.

2. An effective paragraph or essay is one that
   a. makes a point.
   b. provides specific support.
   c. makes a point and provides specific support.
   d. none of the above.

3. The sentence that states the main idea of a paragraph is known as the

   _____ sentence.

4. Prewriting can help a writer find
   a. a good topic to write about.
   b. a good main point to make about the topic.
   c. enough details to support the main point.
   d. all of the above.

5. One step that everyone should use at some stage of the writing process is to prepare a plan for the paragraph or essay known as a(n) _____.

6. When you start writing, your first concern should be
   a. spelling.
   b. content.
   c. grammar.
   d. punctuation.

7. The words *first, next, then, also, another,* and *finally* are examples of signal words, commonly known as _____.

8. A computer can help a writer
   a. turn a list into an outline.
   b. find just the right words to express a point.
   c. add and delete supporting evidence.
   d. all of the above.

WRITING ASSIGNMENT

All of us have come to various crossroads in our lives—times when we must make an important decision about which course of action to follow. Think about a major decision you had to make (or one you are planning to make). Then write a paragraph on the three reasons for your decision. Start out by describing the decision you have reached. Each of the supporting details that follow should fully explain the reasons for your decision. Here are some examples of major decisions that often confront people:

Enrolling in or dropping out of college

Accepting or quitting a job

Getting married or divorced

Breaking up with a boyfriend or girlfriend

Having a baby

Moving away from home

EXPLORING WRITING ONLINE

In this chapter, you learned that writing is a multistep process. Using your favorite search engine, such as Google, type the words "writing process." Find at least three Web sites that provide helpful information about how to approach writing in this way.

RESPONDING TO IMAGES

1. What process is being illustrated in this image? Translate the steps into written, rather than visual, instructions.

2. How would you illustrate the steps of the writing process visually?

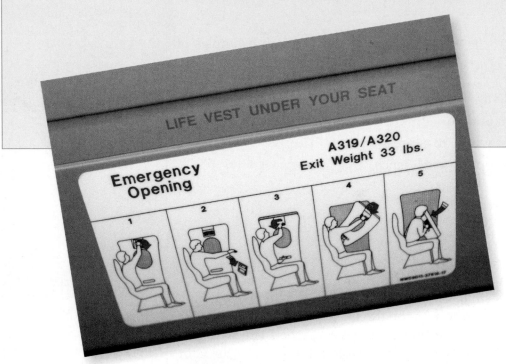

For additional materials on Chapter 2, visit www.mhhe.com/langan.

A WRITER'S TEMPLATE: Across Disciplines

As a college student, you will do a lot of writing. The writing that you do will often involve making a point and supporting that point with reasons and details. Keep this in mind when you read the first draft of the following paragraph written by Desmond for a psychology course, and then answer the questions that follow.

What Do Psychologists Do?

Psychologists study human behavior and the way the mind works. When psychologists conduct experiments, they look for patterns to understand and predict behavior. When psychologists work with people, they ask questions about thoughts, feelings, and actions. Lastly, when psychologists work with people, they also help them change unproductive habits.

Desmond, the writer of the previous paragraph, provided three reasons to support his opening point but not much else. Together with a classmate, complete the following outline by providing two specific supporting details for each of Desmond's three reasons.

Title: What Do Psychologists Do?

Topic sentence: Psychologists study human behavior and the way the mind works.

1. When psychologists conduct experiments, they look for patterns to understand and predict behavior.

    a. _____

    b. _____

2. When psychologists work with people, they ask questions about thoughts, feelings, and actions.

    a. _____

    b. _____

3. Lastly, when psychologists work with people, they also help them change unproductive habits.

    a. _____

    b. _____

Using your outline, revise Desmond's paragraph.

COLLABORATIVE ACTIVITY

EXPLORE WRITING FURTHER

Writing Effective Paragraphs

PART 2 SHOWS YOU HOW TO

- begin a paper by making a point of some kind

- provide specific evidence to support that point

- organize and connect specific evidence

- revise so that your sentences flow smoothly and clearly

- edit so that your sentences are error-free

PART 2 WILL ALSO

- introduce you to nine patterns of paragraph development

- explain and illustrate the differences between a paragraph and an essay

- show you how to evaluate paragraphs and essays for unity, support, coherence, and sentence skills

EXPLORING WRITING PROMPT:

In Part 2, you will learn to make a point and to back it up in paragraphs and essays by using various patterns of development. Among these are (1) exemplification and (2) comparison or contrast.

Consider the following topics:

1. The students I have met since coming to college are, for the most part, _____.

2. The expectations of high school teachers and college professors differ in that _____.

In each blank, write a main point that turns the topic into a central idea. Then write a paragraph that develops each point fully. For topic 1, use examples to support your point, and you will be writing an exemplification paragraph; for topic 2, illustrate how the teachers and professors differ, and you will be writing a comparison or contrast paragraph.

3 CHAPTER

Four Steps for Writing, Four Bases for Revising

RESPONDING TO IMAGES

Has anyone misunderstood something you wrote? What happened? What did you write to make that person get the wrong idea? Take a few minutes to recount your experience. In this chapter, you'll learn how to write clearly so that others don't misinterpret your point.

What Are the Steps to Writing Effective Paragraphs?

To write an effective paragraph, you should begin by making a point, and then go on to support that point with specific evidence. Finally, end your paper with a sentence that rounds off the paragraph and provides a sense of completion.

Step 1: Make a Point

It is often best to state your point in the first sentence of your paragraph, as Mike does in his paragraph about working at a diner and truck stop. The sentence that expresses the main idea, or point, of a paragraph is called the *topic sentence.* Your paragraph will be unified if you make sure that all the details support the point in your topic sentence.

It is helpful to remember that a topic sentence is a *general* statement. The sentences that follow it provide specific support for the general statement.

Understanding the Paragraph	ACTIVITY 1

Each group of sentences in the following activity could be written as a short paragraph. Circle the letter of the topic sentence in each case. To find the topic sentence, ask yourself, "Which is a general statement supported by the specific details in the other three statements?"

Begin by trying the following example item. First circle the letter of the sentence you think expresses the main idea. Then read the explanation.

EXAMPLE

    a. CNN.com provides market trading information.

    b. CNN.com is a good source of national and world news.

    (c.) CNN.com has a lot to offer its readers.

    d. There are many video clips and podcasts available on CNN.com.

> **EXPLANATION:** Sentence *a* explains one important benefit of CNN.com. Sentences *b* and *d* provide other specific advantages of CNN.com. In sentence *c*, however, no one specific benefit is explained. Instead, the words "a lot to offer" refer only generally to such benefits. Therefore, sentence *c* is the topic sentence; it expresses the main idea. The other sentences support that idea by providing examples.

1. a. Food and toiletries can be purchased at bulk prices.

      b. The price of gasoline is cheaper at a warehouse club.

      c. My family and I enjoy shopping at warehouse clubs.

      d. My children love the food samples.

2. a. Instead of talking on the telephone, we send text messages.

    b. People rarely talk to one another these days.

    c. Rather than talking with family members, we sit silently in front of the TV or computer all evening.

    d. In cars, we ignore our traveling companions to listen to the radio.

3. a. Once I completely forgot to study for a history final.

    b. During finals week, something awful always happens.

    c. The city bus was twenty minutes late on the day of my English final.

    d. Another time, the battery in my calculator died during my math final.

4. a. Today's retail environment relies on a variety of technologies.

    b. Cash registers operate on point-of-sale software.

    c. Merchandise is tracked through hand-held barcode scanners.

    d. Anti-shoplifting devices help reduce retail theft.

5. a. The submission techniques in MMA were developed from jujitsu and judo.

    b. Mixed martial arts (MMA) is an evolution of different fighting techniques.

    c. Kickboxing and karate provided MMA with striking techniques.

    d. The clinching techniques in MMA were taken from wrestling and sumo.

Understanding the Topic Sentence

An effective topic sentence does two things. First, it presents the topic of the paragraph. Second, it expresses the writer's attitude or opinion or idea about the topic. For example, look at the following topic sentence:

Professional athletes are overpaid.

In the topic sentence, the topic is *professional athletes*; the writer's idea about the topic is that professional athletes *are overpaid*.

ACTIVITY 2	Topic Sentences

For each topic sentence that follows, underline the topic and double-underline the point of view that the writer takes toward the topic.

EXAMPLES

Living in a small town has many advantages.

Cell phones should be banned in schools.

1. The apartments on Walnut Avenue are a fire hazard.

2. Losing my job turned out to have benefits.

3. Blues is the most interesting form of American music.

4. Our neighbor's backyard is a dangerous place.

5. Paula and Jeff are a stingy couple.

6. Snakes do not deserve their bad reputation.

7. Pollution causes many problems in American cities.

8. New fathers should receive at least two weeks of "paternity leave."

9. People with low self-esteem often need to criticize others.

10. Learning to write effectively is largely a matter of practice.

Identifying Topics, Topic Sentences, and Support

The following activity will sharpen your sense of the differences between topics, topic sentences, and supporting sentences.

Breaking Down the Parts of a Paragraph	ACTIVITY 3

Each group of items below includes one topic, one main idea (expressed in a topic sentence), and two supporting details for that idea. In the space provided, label each item with one of the following:

> T   topic
> MI   main idea
> SD   supporting details

1. _____   a.   The weather in the summer is often hot and sticky.

_____   b.   Summer can be an unpleasant time of year.

_____   c.   Summer.

_____   d.   Bug bites, poison ivy, and allergies are a big part of summertime.

2. _____   a.   The new Ultimate sports car is bound to be very popular.

_____   b.   The company has promised to provide any repairs needed during the first three years at no charge.

_____   c.   Because it gets thirty miles per gallon of gas, it offers real savings on fuel costs.

_____   d.   The new Ultimate sports car.

3. _____   a.   Decorating an apartment doesn't need to be expensive.

_____   b.   A few plants add a touch of color without costing a lot of money.

_____   c.   Inexpensive braided rugs can be bought to match nearly any furniture.

_____   d.   Decorating an apartment.

4. _____   a.   Long practice sessions and busy game schedules take too much time away from schoolwork.

   _____   b.   High school sports.

   _____   c.   The competition between schools may become so intense that, depending on the outcome of one game, athletes are either adored or scorned.

   _____   d.   High school sports put too much pressure on young athletes.

5. _____   a.   After mapping out the best route to your destination, phone ahead for motel reservations.

   _____   b.   A long car trip.

   _____   c.   Following a few guidelines before a long car trip can help you avoid potential problems.

   _____   d.   Have your car's engine tuned as well, and have the tires, brakes, and exhaust system inspected.

Step 2: Back Up Your Point

To support your point, you need to provide specific reasons, examples, and other details that explain and develop it. The more precise and particular your supporting details are, the better your readers can "see," "hear," and "feel" them.

Understanding General versus Specific Ideas

A paragraph is made up of a main idea, which is general, and the specific ideas that support it. So to write well, you must understand the difference between general and specific ideas.

It is helpful to realize that you use general and specific ideas all the time in your everyday life. For example, in choosing a film to rent, you may think, "Which should I rent, an action movie, a comedy, or a romance?" In such a case, *film* is the general idea, and *action movie, comedy,* and *romance* are the specific ideas.

Or you may decide to begin an exercise program. In that case, you might consider walking, pilates, or lifting weights. In this case, *exercise* is the general idea, and *walking, pilates,* and *lifting weights* are the specific ideas.

Or if you are talking to a friend about a date that didn't work out well, you may say, "The dinner was terrible, the car broke down, and we had little to say to each other." In this case, the general idea is *the date didn't work out well,* and the specific ideas are the three reasons you named.

The following activities will give you experience in recognizing the relationship between general and specific. They will also provide a helpful background for the information and additional activities that follow.

Identifying General Ideas

Each group of words consists of one general idea and four specific ideas. The general idea includes all the specific ideas. Underline the general idea in each group.

EXAMPLE

subway   bus   train   <u>public transportation</u>   railway

1. raspy   high-pitched   voice   deep   screechy

2. breakfast food   scrambled eggs   Belgian waffles   smoked bacon   orange juice

3. Mars   Venus   planet   Saturn   Earth

4. pill   syrup   caplet   tablet   pain reliever

5. zoology   botany   chemistry   science   biology

6. surfing   kayaking   water sports   rafting   waterskiing

7. peony   flower   rose   daisy   tulip

8. Indian   Pacific   Atlantic   ocean   Mediterranean

9. ceremony   wedding   funeral   graduation   baptism

10. yup   yeah   yes   yep   yesh

Developing Specific Ideas

In each item below, one idea is general and the others are specific. The general idea includes the specific ones. In the spaces provided, write in two more specific ideas that are covered by the general idea.

EXAMPLE

General: exercises

Specific: chin-ups, jumping jacks, _____sit-ups_____, _____push-ups_____

  HINT   Refer to the images in the margins when answering item 5.

1. *General:* pizza toppings

   Specific: sausage, mushrooms, _____, _____

2. *General:* furniture

   Specific: rocking chair, coffee table, _____, _____

3. *General:* magazines

   Specific: Reader's Digest, Newsweek, _____, _____

4. *General:* birds

   Specific: eagle, pigeon, _____ , _____

5. *General:* music

   Specific: jazz, classical, _____ , _____

6. *General:* cold symptoms

   Specific: aching muscles, watery eyes, _____ , _____

7. *General:* children's games

   Specific: hopscotch, dodgeball, _____ , _____

8. *General:* transportation

   Specific: plane, motorcycle, _____ , _____

9. *General:* city problems

   Specific: overcrowding, pollution, _____ , _____

10. *General:* types of TV shows

    Specific: cartoons, reality shows, _____ , _____

ACTIVITY 6	What Ideas Have in Common

Read each group of specific ideas below. Then circle the letter of the general idea that tells what the specific ideas have in common. Note that the general idea should not be too broad or too narrow. Begin by trying the example item, and then read the explanation that follows.

EXAMPLE

Specific ideas: peeling potatoes, washing dishes, cracking eggs, cleaning out refrigerator

The general idea is

a. household jobs.

b. kitchen tasks.

c. steps in making dinner.

> **EXPLANATION:** It is true that the specific ideas are all household jobs, but they have in common something even more specific—they are all tasks done in the kitchen. Therefore, answer *a* is too broad, and the correct answer is *b*. Answer *c* is too narrow because it doesn't cover all the specific ideas. Although two of them could be steps in making a dinner ("peeling potatoes" and "cracking eggs"), two have nothing to do with making dinner.

1. *Specific ideas:* crowded office, rude coworkers, demanding boss, unreasonable deadlines

   The general idea is

   a.   problems.

   b.   work problems.

   c.   problems with work schedules.

2. *Specific ideas:* cactus, rosebush, fern, daisy

   The general idea is

   a.   plants.

   b.   plants that have thorns.

   c.   plants that grow in the desert.

3. *Specific ideas:* Band-Aids, gauze, antiseptic, aspirin

   The general idea is

   a.   supplies.

   b.   first-aid supplies.

   c.   supplies for treating a headache.

4. *Specific ideas:* trout, whales, salmon, frogs

   The general idea is

   a.   animals.

   b.   fish.

   c.   animals living in water.

5. *Specific ideas:* Hershey bar, lollipop, mints, fudge

   The general idea is

   a.   food.

   b.   candy.

   c.   chocolate.

6. *Specific ideas:* "Go to bed," "Pick up that trash," "Run twenty laps," "Type this letter."

   The general idea is

   a.   remarks.

   b.   orders.

   c.   the boss's orders.

7. *Specific ideas:* "I had no time to study," "The questions were unfair," "I had a headache," "The instructor didn't give us enough time."

   The general idea is

   a.   statements.

   b.   excuses for being late.

   c.   excuses for not doing well on a test.

8. *Specific ideas:* candle, sun, headlight, flashlight

The general idea is

a. things that are very hot.

b. light sources for a home.

c. sources of light.

9. *Specific ideas:* driving with expired license plates, driving over the speed limit, parking without putting money in the meter, driving without a license

The general idea is:

a. ways to cause a traffic accident.

b. traffic problems.

c. ways to get a ticket.

10. *Specific ideas:* "Are we there yet?" "Where do people come from?" "Can I have that toy?" "Do I have to go to bed now?"

The general idea is

a. Things adults say to one another.

b. Things children ask adults.

c. Things children ask at school.

ACTIVITY 7   What Is the General Idea?

In the following items, the specific ideas are given but the general ideas are unstated. Fill in the blanks with the general ideas.

EXAMPLE

General idea: _____ car problems _____

Specific ideas: flat tire   dented bumper
cracked windshield   dirty oil filter

1. *General idea:* _____

Specific ideas: nephew   grandmother
aunt   cousin

2. *General idea:* _____

Specific ideas: boots   sneakers
sandals   slippers

3. *General idea:* _____

Specific ideas: camping   hiking
fishing   hunting

4. *General idea:* _____

Specific ideas: broom   sponge
mop   glass cleaner

5. *General idea:* _____

   Specific ideas: cloudy   sunny
                      snowy   rainy

6. *General idea:* _____

   Specific ideas: Spread mustard on slice of bread
                      Add turkey and cheese
                      Put lettuce on top of cheese
                      Cover with another slice of bread

7. *General idea:* _____

   Specific ideas: thermos of lemonade   insect repellent
                      basket of food   blanket

8. *General idea:* _____

   Specific ideas: fleas in carpeting   loud barking
                      tangled fur   veterinary bills

9. *General idea:* _____

   Specific ideas: diabetes   cancer
                      appendicitis   broken leg

10. *General idea:* _____

    Specific ideas: flooded basements   wet streets
                       rainbow   overflowing rivers

Recognizing Specific Details

Specific details are examples, reasons, particulars, and facts. Such details are needed to support and explain a topic sentence effectively. They provide the evidence needed for us to understand, as well as to feel and experience, a writer's point.

Below is a topic sentence followed by two sets of supporting sentences. Write a check mark next to the set that provides sharp, specific details.

Topic sentence: **Ticket sales for a recent Rolling Stones concert proved that the classic rock band is still very popular.**

_____ a. Fans came from everywhere to buy tickets to the concert. People wanted good seats and were willing to endure a great deal of various kinds of discomfort as they waited in line for many hours. Some people actually waited for days, sleeping at night in uncomfortable circumstances. Good tickets were sold out extremely quickly.

_____ b. The first person in the long ticket line spent three days standing in the hot sun and three nights sleeping on the concrete without even a pillow. The man behind her waited equally long in his wheelchair. The ticket window opened at 10:00 A.M., and the tickets for the good seats—those in front of the stage—were sold out an hour later.

> EXPLANATION: The second set (*b*) provides specific details. Instead of a vague statement about fans who were "willing to endure a great deal of various kinds of discomfort," we get vivid details we can see and picture clearly: "three days standing in the hot sun," "three nights sleeping on the concrete without even a pillow," and "The man behind her waited equally long in his wheelchair."
>
> Instead of a vague statement that tickets were "sold out extremely quickly," we get exact and vivid details: "The ticket window opened at 10:00 A.M., and the tickets for the good seats—those in front of the stage—were sold out an hour later."

Specific details are often like a movie script. They provide us with such clear pictures that we could make a film of them if we wanted to. You would know just how to film the information given in the second set of sentences. You would show the fans in line under a hot sun and, later, sleeping on the concrete. The first person in line would be shown sleeping without a pillow under her head. You would show tickets finally going on sale, and after an hour you could show the ticket seller explaining that all of the seats in front of the stage were sold out.

In contrast, the writer of the first set of sentences (*a*) fails to provide the specific information needed. If you were asked to make a film based on set *a,* you would have to figure out on your own just what particulars to show.

When you are working to provide specific supporting information in a paper, it might help to ask yourself, "Could someone easily film this information?" If the answer is yes, your supporting details are specific enough for your readers to visualize.

ACTIVITY 8	**Specific vs. General Support**

Each topic sentence in this activity is followed by two sets of supporting details. Write *S* (for *specific*) in the space next to the set that provides specific support for the point. Write *G* (for *general*) next to the set that offers only vague general support.

1. *Topic sentence:* Alonzo was relieved when he received the results from his physical exam.

   _____ a. Alonzo's blood pressure was 120/80, which is within the normal range for men. His cholesterol ratio was below 4, which is good for men of his age.

   _____ b. Alonzo's doctor told him that his blood pressure was normal. He also learned that his cholesterol levels were normal.

2. *Topic sentence:* When preparing meals on a budget, canned meats and beans provide cost-effective alternatives.

    _____ a.   Canned meat can be used rather than fresh meat to prepare meals. Canned fish can also be used. Canned beans are another alternative when preparing economical meals.

    _____ b.   Spam can be used instead of sirloin beef to prepare stews and stir-fry dishes. Canned tuna can be used to make baked casseroles and pasta meals. Canned kidney, pinto, and black beans can be used instead of ground beef to make chili and grilled burgers.

3. *Topic sentence:* My college campus provides students with valuable resources.

    _____ a.   The writing tutors at the Learning Center help students find topics and assist them with revision and editing. The reference librarians at the library help students locate appropriate books and online journals for their research papers. The academic advisers at the Counseling Office notify students about required and elective courses during registration.

    _____ b.   Tutors on campus help students with the different stages of their writing. Librarians help students with their research by locating different sources in the library and online. Counselors on campus provide students with useful information on course registration.

4. *Topic sentence:* RateMyProfessor.com provides students with a reliable source of information for finding out information about their professors.

    _____ a.   On RateMyProfessor.com, students evaluate their professors. Professors are scored on their quality of teaching. They are also rated in other areas. The most helpful section of a rating is the user comments.

    _____ b.   On RateMyProfessor.com, students give their professors a "scorecard." Professors are scored on their quality of teaching under the categories "good," "average," and "poor." They are also rated in terms of "easiness," "clarity," and "helpfulness." Some teachers are even awarded a "hot" chili pepper rating. The user comments—the most helpful section of the Web site—allows students to write honestly about what they liked and disliked about their professors.

5. *Topic sentence:* Employers are providing different work options to help employees reduce the cost of commuting to and from work.

    _____ a.   Some employers are allowing their employees to work from home one day a week. Some employers are providing a condensed work week. Some employers are encouraging transportation alternatives and providing public transit incentives.

_____ b. Some employers are allowing employees to telecommute one day a week by using their home computer, the Internet, and phone and video conferencing. Some employers are condensing the work week from five eight-hour days to four ten-hour days. Some employers are encouraging employees to car pool, and they are paying for monthly bus and rail passes.

| ACTIVITY 9 | Specific vs. General Support in a Paragraph |

At several points in each of the following paragraphs, you are given a choice of two sets of supporting details. Write S (for *specific*) in the space next to the set that provides specific support for the point. Write G (for *general*) next to the set that offers only vague, general support.

Paragraph 1

My daughter is as shy as I am, and it breaks my heart to see her dealing with the same problems I had to deal with in my childhood because of my shyness. I feel very sad for her when I see the problems she has making friends.

_____ a. It takes her a long time to begin to do the things other children do to make friends, and her feelings get hurt very easily over one thing or another. She is not at all comfortable about making connections with her classmates at school.

_____ b. She usually spends Christmas vacation alone because by that time of year she doesn't have friends yet. Only when her birthday comes in the summer is she confident enough to invite school friends to her party. Once she sends out the invitations, she almost sleeps by the telephone, waiting for the children to respond. If they say they can't come, her eyes fill with tears.

I recognize very well her signs of shyness, which make her look smaller and more fragile than she really is.

_____ c. When she has to talk to someone she doesn't know well, she speaks in a whisper and stares sideways. Pressing her hands together, she lifts her shoulders as though she wished she could hide her head between them.

_____ d. When she is forced to talk to anyone other than her family and her closest friends, the sound of her voice and the position of her head change. Even her posture changes in a way that makes it look as if she's trying to make her body disappear.

It is hard for me to watch her passing unnoticed at school.

_____ e. She never gets chosen for a special job or privilege, even though she tries her best, practicing in privacy at home. She just doesn't measure up. Worst of all, even her teacher seems to forget her existence much of the time.

_____ f. Although she rehearses in our basement, she never gets chosen for a good part in a play. Her voice is never loud or clear enough. Worst of all, her teacher doesn't call on her in class for days at a time.

Paragraph 2

It is said that the dog is man's best friend, but I strongly believe that the honor belongs to my computer. A computer won't fetch a stick for me, but it can help me entertain myself in many ways.

_____ a. If I am bored, tired, or out of ideas, the computer allows me to explore things that interest me, such as anything relating to the world of professional sports.

_____ b. The other day, I used my computer to visit the National Football League's Web site. I was then able to get injury updates for players on my favorite team, the Philadelphia Eagles.

While the dog is a faithful friend, it does not allow me to be a more responsible person the way my computer does.

_____ c. I use my computer to pay all my bills online. I also use it to balance my checkbook and keep track of my expenses. Now I always know how much money is in my account at the end of the month.

_____ d. The computer helps me be responsible with financial matters because it records my transactions. With the computer, I have access to more information, which allows me to make good decisions with my money.

A dog might help me meet strangers I see in the park, but the computer helps me meet people who share my interests.

_____ e. With my computer, I can go online and find people with every type of hobby or interest. Thousands of blogs and discussion groups are available featuring people from all over the country—and the world. The computer can even allow me to develop meaningful personal relationships with others.

_____ f. Two months ago, I discovered a Web site for people in my community who enjoy hiking. I'm planning to meet a group next Saturday for a day hike. And earlier this year, I met my wonderful fiancée, Shelly, through an online dating service.

Providing Specific Details

| ACTIVITY 10 | **Getting Specific** |

Each of the following sentences contains a general word or words, set off in *italic* type. Substitute sharp, specific words in each case.

EXAMPLE

After the parade, the city street was littered with *garbage.*

After the parade, the city street was littered with multicolored confetti, dirty popcorn, and lifeless balloons.

1. If I had enough money, I'd visit *several places.*

   _____

   _____

2. It took her *a long time* to get home.

   _____

   _____

3. Ron is often stared at because of his *unusual hair color and hairstyle.*

   _____

   _____

4. After you pass *two buildings,* you'll see my house on the left.

   _____

   _____

5. Nia's purse is crammed with *lots of stuff.*

   _____

   _____

6. I bought *some junk food* for the long car trip.

   _____

   _____

7. The floor in the front of my car is covered with *things.*

   _____

   _____

8. When his mother said no to his request for a toy, the child *reacted strongly.*

   _____

   _____

9. Devan gave his girlfriend a *surprise present* for Valentine's Day.

_____

_____

10. My cat can *do a wonderful trick.*

_____

_____

Selecting Details That Fit

The details in your paper must all clearly relate to and support your opening point. If a detail does not support your point, leave it out. Otherwise, your paper will lack unity. For example, see if you can circle the letter of the two sentences that do *not* support the following topic sentence.

Topic sentence: **Tom is a very talented person.**

    a. Tom is always courteous to his professors.

    b. He has created beautiful paintings in his art course.

    c. Tom is the lead singer in a local band.

    d. He won an award in a photography contest.

    e. He is hoping to become a professional photographer.

EXPLANATION: Being courteous may be a virtue, but it is not a talent, so sentence *a* does not support the topic sentence. Also, Tom's desire to become a professional photographer tells us nothing about his talent; thus, sentence *e* does not support the topic sentence either. The other three statements all clearly back up the topic sentence. Each in some way supports the idea that Tom is talented—in art, as a singer, or as a photographer.

Details That Don't Fit   ACTIVITY 11

In each group below, circle the two items that do *not* support the topic sentence.

1. *Topic sentence:* Carla seems attracted only to men who are unavailable.

    a. She once fell in love with a man serving a life sentence in prison.

    b. Her parents worry about her inability to connect with a nice single man.

    c. She wants to get married and have kids before she is thirty.

    d. Her current boyfriend is married.

    e. Recently she had a huge crush on a Catholic priest.

2. *Topic sentence:* Some dog owners have little consideration for other people.

   a. Obedience lessons can be a good experience for both the dog and the owner.

   b. Some dog owners let their dogs leave droppings on the sidewalk or in other people's yards.

   c. They leave the dog home alone for hours, and it barks and howls and wakes the neighbors.

   d. Some people keep very large dogs in small apartments.

   e. Even when small children are playing nearby, owners let their bad-tempered dogs run loose.

3. *Topic sentence:* Dr. Eliot is a very poor teacher.

   a. He cancels class frequently with no explanation.

   b. When a student asks a question that he can't answer, he becomes irritated with the student.

   c. He got his PhD at a university in another country.

   d. He's taught at the college for many years and is on a number of faculty committees.

   e. He puts off grading papers until the end of the semester, and then returns them all at once.

4. *Topic sentence:* Some doctors seem to think it is all right to keep patients waiting.

   a. Pharmaceutical sales representatives sometimes must wait hours to see a doctor.

   b. The doctors stand in the hallway chatting with nurses and secretaries even when they have a waiting room full of patients.

   c. Patients sometimes travel long distances to consult with a particular doctor.

   d. When a patient calls before an appointment to see if the doctor is on time, the answer is often yes even when the doctor is two hours behind schedule.

   e. Some doctors schedule appointments in a way that ensures long lines, to make it appear that they are especially skillful.

5. *Topic sentence:* Several factors were responsible for the staggering loss of lives when the *Titanic* sank.

   a. More than 1,500 people died in the *Titanic* disaster; only 711 survived.

   b. Despite warnings about the presence of icebergs, the captain allowed the *Titanic* to continue at high speed.

   c. If the ship had hit the iceberg head-on, its watertight compartments might have kept it from sinking; however, it hit on the side, resulting in a long, jagged gash through which water poured in.

   d. The *Titanic,* equipped with the very best communication systems available in 1912, sent out SOS messages.

   e. When the captain gave orders to abandon the *Titanic,* many passengers refused because they believed the ship was unsinkable, so many lifeboats were only partly filled.

Providing Details That Fit

Writing Specific Details | ACTIVITY 12

Each topic sentence in this activity is followed by one supporting detail. See if you can add a second detail in each case. Make sure your detail supports the topic sentence.

1. *Topic sentence:* There are valid reasons why students miss deadlines.

    a. Students may have more than one paper to write on any given day.

    b. _____

2. *Topic sentence:* Those who serve in the military make many sacrifices.

    a. They leave their families to serve on tours of duty.

    b. _____

3. *Topic sentence:* Sabrina has such a positive outlook on life.

    a. When she lost her job, she contacted an employment agency right away.

    b. _____

4. *Topic sentence:* There are many advantages to group work.

    a. Everyone has talents to contribute.

    b. _____

5. *Topic sentence:* Everyone should take measures to prevent identity theft.

    a. Passwords should be changed regularly.

    b. _____

Providing Support | ACTIVITY 13

Working in pairs, see if you can add *two* supporting details for each of the following topic sentences.

1. *Topic sentence:* The managers of this apartment building don't care about their renters.

    a. Mrs. Harris has been asking them to fix her leaky faucet for two months.

    b. _____

    c. _____

2. *Topic sentence:* None of the shirts for sale were satisfactory.

    a. Some were attractive but too expensive.

    b. _____

    c. _____

3. *Topic sentence:* After being married for forty years, Mr. and Mrs. Lambert have grown similar in odd ways.

   a. They both love to have a cup of warm apple juice just before bed.

   b. _____

   c. _____

4. *Topic sentence:* It is a special time for me when my brother is in town.

   a. We always catch the latest sci-fi thriller and then stop for pizza.

   b. _____

   c. _____

5. *Topic sentence:* Our neighbor's daughter is very spoiled.

   a. When anyone else in the family has a birthday, she gets several presents too.

   b. _____

   c. _____

Providing Details in a Paragraph

ACTIVITY 14	Adding Details to a Paragraph

The following paragraph needs specific details to back up its three supporting points. In the spaces provided, write two or three sentences of convincing details for each supporting point.

A Disappointing Concert

Although I had looked forward to seeing my favorite band in concert, the experience was disappointing. For one thing, our seats were terrible, in two ways. _____

_____

_____

_____

In addition, the crowd made it hard to enjoy the music. _____

_____

_____

_____

_____

---

continued

And finally, the band members acted as if they didn't want to be there. _____

_____

_____

_____

Omitting and Grouping Details in Planning a Paragraph

One common way to develop material for a paper involves three steps: (1) Make a list of details about your point, (2) omit details that don't truly support your point, and (3) group remaining details together in logical ways. Omitting details that don't fit and grouping related details together are part of learning how to write effectively.

Grouping Details   ACTIVITY 15

See if you can figure out a way to put the following details into three groups. Write *A* in front of the details that go with one group, *B* in front of the details that go with a second group, and *C* in front of the details that make up a third group. Cross out the four details that do not relate to the topic sentence.

Topic sentence: My brother Sean caused our parents lots of headaches when he was a teenager.

_____   In constant trouble at school

_____   While playing a joke on his lab partner, nearly blew up the chemistry lab

_____   Girlfriend was eight years older than he and had been married twice

_____   Girlfriend had a very sweet four-year-old son

_____   Parents worried about people Sean spent his time with

_____   Several signs that he was using drugs

_____   Failed so many courses that he had to go to summer school in order to graduate

_____   Was suspended twice for getting into fights between classes

_____   Our father taught math at the high school we attended

_____   His money just disappeared, and he never had anything to show for it

_____   His best pal had been arrested for armed robbery

_____   Often looked glassy-eyed

_____   Hung around with older kids who had dropped out of school

_____   Until he was in eighth grade, he had always been on the honor roll

_____   No one was allowed in his room, which he kept locked whenever he was away from home

_____   Has managed to turn his life around now that he's in college

---

EXPLANATION: After thinking about the list for a while, you probably realized that the details about Sean's trouble at school form one group. He got in trouble at school for nearly blowing up the chemistry lab, failing courses, and fighting between classes. Another group of details has to do with his parents' worrying about the people he spent time with. His parents were worried because he had an older girlfriend, a best friend who was arrested for armed robbery, and older friends who were school dropouts. Finally, there are the details about signs that he was using drugs: his money disappearing, his glassy-eyed appearance, and not allowing others in his room.

The main idea—that as a teenager, the writer's brother caused their parents lots of headaches—can be supported with three kinds of evidence: the trouble he got into at school, his friends, and the signs indicating he was on drugs. The other four items in the list do not logically go with any of these three types of evidence and so should be omitted.

ACTIVITY 16	**Omitting and Grouping Details**

This activity will give you practice in omitting and grouping details. See if you can figure out a way to put the following details into three groups. Write *A* in front of the details that go with one group, *B* in front of the details that go with a second group, and *C* in front of the details that make up a third group. Cross out the four details that do not relate to the topic sentence.

Topic sentence: There are practical ways for college students to manage their time wisely.

_____A_____   Students should guard how they spend their time.

_____A_____   Students should keep track of how they spend their time.

_____B_____   College students also have a difficult time managing their money.

_____C_____   A time log will tell them how much time they spend studying, working, and so forth.

_____B_____   They should avoid distractions—the TV, the Internet, the phone, for example—when studying.

_____A_____   Students should prioritize how they spend their time.

_____C_____ A monthly calendar will allow them to record important due dates and appointments.

_____A_____ A time log will tell them how much time they waste and how they waste it.

_____B_____ Parents need to manage their time wisely.

_____A_____ Students miss deadlines because they are unable to manage their time.

_____C_____ They should ask their family members and friends to respect their regular study time.

_____B_____ A daily to-do list will allow them to prioritize what needs to be accomplished.

_____A_____ Some students even fail classes because of their poor time-management skills.

_____B_____ They should talk to their employer if their work schedule conflicts with their study time.

_____A_____ A time log can provide information on whether students are managing their time wisely.

_____A_____ Calendars and to-do lists are specific tools that students can use to prioritize their time.

Step 3: Organize the Support

You will find it helpful to learn two common ways of organizing support in a paragraph—_listing order_ and _time order._ You should also learn the signal words, known as _transitions,_ that increase the effectiveness of each method.

Transitions are words and phrases that indicate relationships between ideas. They are like signposts that guide travelers, showing them how to move smoothly from one spot to the next. Be sure to take advantage of transitions. They will help organize and connect your ideas, and they will help your readers follow the direction of your thoughts.

Listing Order

A writer can organize supporting evidence in a paper by providing a list of two or more reasons, examples, or details. Often the most important or interesting item is saved for last because the reader is most likely to remember the last thing read.

Transition words that indicate listing order include the following:

one	second	also	next	last of all
for one thing	third	another	moreover	finally
first of all	next	in addition	furthermore	

Mike's paragraph about working at the diner and truck stop (Chapter 1, p. 8) uses listing order: It lists three reasons why it was the worst job he ever had, and each of those three reasons is introduced by one of the preceding transitions. In the following spaces, write in the three transitions:

First of all _____   Second _____   Finally _____

The first reason in the paragraph about working at the plant is introduced with *first of all*, the second reason by *second*, and the third reason by *finally*.

| ACTIVITY 17 | Using Listing Order |

Use *listing order* to arrange the scrambled list of sentences below. Number each supporting sentence 1, 2, 3, . . . so that you go from the least important item to what is presented as the most important item.

Note that transitions will help by making clear the relationships between some of the sentences.

Topic sentence: I am no longer a big fan of professional sports, for a number of reasons.

_____ Basketball and hockey continue well into the baseball season, and football doesn't have its Super Bowl until the middle of winter, when basketball should be at center stage.

_____ In addition, I detest the high fives, taunting, and trash talk that so many professional athletes now indulge in during games.

_____ Second, I am bothered by the length of professional sports seasons.

_____ Also, professional athletes have no loyalty to a team or city, as they greedily sell their abilities to the highest bidder.

_____ For one thing, greed is the engine running professional sports.

_____ There are numerous news stories of professional athletes in trouble with the law because of drugs, guns, fights, traffic accidents, or domestic violence.

_____ After a good year, athletes making millions become unhappy if they aren't rewarded with a new contract calling for even more millions.

_____ But the main reason I've become disenchanted with professional sports is the disgusting behavior of so many of its athletes.

Time Order

When a writer uses time order, supporting details are presented in the order in which they occurred. *First* this happened; *next* this; *after* that, this; and so on. Many paragraphs, especially paragraphs that tell a story or give a series of directions, are organized in a time order.

Transition words that show time relationships include the following:

first	before	after	when	then
next	during	now	while	until
as	soon	later	often	finally

Read the following paragraph, which is organized in time order. See if you can underline the six transition words that show the time relationships.

Della had a sad experience while driving home last night. She traveled along the dark, winding road that led toward her home. She was only two miles from her house when she noticed a glimmer of light in the road. The next thing she knew, she heard a sickening thud and realized she had struck an animal. The light, she realized, had been its eyes reflected in her car's headlights. Della stopped the car and ran back to see what she had hit. It was a handsome cocker spaniel, with blond fur and long ears. As she bent over the still form, she realized there was nothing to be done. The dog was dead. Della searched the dog for a collar and tags. There was nothing. Before leaving, she walked to several nearby houses, asking if anyone knew who owned the dog. No one did. Finally Della gave up and drove on. She was sad to leave someone's pet lying there alone.

The main point of the paragraph is stated in its first sentence: "Della had a sad experience while driving home last night." The support for this point is all the details of Della's experience. Those details are presented in the order in which they occurred. The time relationships are highlighted by these transitions: *while, when, next, as, before,* and *finally.*

Using Time Order   ACTIVITY 18

Use *time order* to arrange the scrambled sentences below. Number the supporting sentences in the order in which they occur in time (1, 2, 3, . . .).

Note that transitions will help by making clear the relationships between sentences.

Topic sentence: If you have difficulty sleeping, the following steps should help you sleep better.

_____ Also avoid taking naps during the daytime.

_____ A good night's sleep starts by getting up early each morning.

_____ During the evening, avoid drinking caffeine, which is a stimulant.

_____ Finally, go to bed at a reasonable and regular time each evening.

_____ During the daytime, fit regular exercise into your schedule.

_____ Before you go to bed, avoid reading.

_____ First, check with your doctor to rule out medical problems such as sleep apnea.

_____ In addition, avoid watching TV before you go to bed.

More about Using Transitions

As already stated, transitions are signal words that help readers follow the direction of the writer's thoughts. To see the value of transitions, look at the two versions of the short paragraph below. Check the version that is easier to read and understand.

_____ a. There are several sources that you can use for your writing assignments. Your own experience is a major resource. For an assignment about communication skills, for instance, you can draw on your own experiences in college, at work, and in everyday life. Other people's experiences are extremely useful. You may have heard people you know or even people on TV talking about communication skills. You can also interview people. Books, magazines, and the Internet are good sources of material for assignments. Many experts, for example, have written about various aspects of communication skills.

_____ b. There are several sources that you can use for your writing assignments. First of all, your own experience is a major resource. For an assignment about communication skills, for instance, you can draw on your own experiences in college, at work, and in everyday life. In addition, other people's experiences are extremely useful. You may have heard people you know or even people on TV talking about communication skills. You can also interview people. Finally, books, magazines, and the Internet are good sources of material for assignments. Many experts, for example, have written about various aspects of communication skills.

> **EXPLANATION:** You no doubt chose the second version, *b.* The listing transitions—*first of all, in addition,* and *finally*—make it clear when the author is introducing a new supporting point. The reader of paragraph *b* is better able to follow the author's line of thinking and to note that three main sources of material for assignments are being listed: your own experience, other people's experiences, and books, magazines, and the Internet.

Using Transitions   ACTIVITY 19

The following paragraphs use listing order or time order. In each case, fill in the blanks with appropriate transitions from the box above the paragraph. Use each transition once.

1. | after | now | first | soon | while |
   |---|---|---|---|---|

My husband has developed an involving hobby, in which I, unfortunately, am unable to share. He _____ enrolled in ground flight instruction classes at the local community college. The lessons were all about air safety regulations and procedures. _____ passing a difficult exam, he decided to take flying lessons at the city airport. Every Monday he would wake at six o'clock in the morning and drive happily to the airport, eager to see his instructor. _____ he was taking lessons, he started to buy airplane magazines and talk about them constantly. "Look at that Cessna 150," he would say. "Isn't she a beauty?" _____, after many lessons, he is flying by himself. _____ he will be able to carry passengers. That is my biggest nightmare. I know he will want me to fly with him, but I am not a lover of heights. I can't understand why someone would leave the safety of the ground to be in the sky, defenseless as a kite.

2. | finally | for one thing | second |
   |---|---|---|

The karate class I took last week convinced me that martial arts may never be my strong point. _____, there is the issue of balance. The instructor asked everyone in class to stand on one foot to practice kicking. Each time I tried, I wobbled and had to spread my arms out wide to avoid falling. I even stumbled into Mr. Kim, my instructor, who glared at me. _____, there was the issue of flexibility. Mr. Kim asked us to stretch and touch our toes. Everyone did this without a problem—except me. I could barely reach my knees before pain raced up and down my back. _____, there was my lack of coordination. When everyone started practicing blocks, I got confused. I couldn't figure out where to move my arms and legs. By the time I got the first move right, the whole group had finished three more. By the end of my first lesson, I was completely lost.

3.

later	soon	when	then

At the age of thirty-one I finally had the opportunity to see snow for the first time in my life. It was in New York City on a cloudy afternoon in November. My daughter and I had gone to the American Museum of Natural History. _____ we left the museum, snow was falling gently. I thought that it was so beautiful! It made me remember movies I had seen countless times in my native Brazil. We decided to find a taxi. _____ we were crossing Central Park, snuggled in the cozy cab, watching the snow cover trees, bushes, branches, and grass. We were amazed to see the landscape quickly change from fall to winter. _____ we arrived in front of our hotel, and I still remember stepping on the crisp snow and laughing like a child who is touched by magic. _____ that day, I heard on the radio that another snowstorm was coming. I was naive enough to wait for thunder and the other sounds of a rainstorm. I did not know yet that snow, even a snowstorm, is silent and soft.

4.

last of all	another	first of all	in addition

Public school students who expect to attend school from September to June, and then have a long summer vacation, may be in for a big surprise before long. For a number of reasons, many schools are switching to a year-round calendar. _____, many educators point out that the traditional school calendar was established years ago when young people had to be available during the summer months to work on farms, but this necessity has long since passed. _____ reason is that a longer school year accommodates individual learning rates more effectively—that is, fast learners can go into more depth about a subject that interests them, while those who learn at a slower pace have more time to master the essential material. _____, many communities have gone to year-round school to relieve overcrowding, since students can be put on different schedules throughout the year. _____, and perhaps most important, educators feel that year-round schools eliminate the loss of learning that many students experience over a long summer break.

Step 4: Write Clear, Error-Free Sentences

If you use correct spelling and follow the rules of grammar, punctuation, and usage, your sentences will be clear and well written. But by no means must you have all that information in your head. Even the best writers need to use reference materials to be sure their writing is correct. So when you write your papers, keep a good dictionary and grammar handbook nearby.

In general, however, save them for after you've gotten your ideas firmly down in writing. You'll find as you write paragraphs that you will make a number of sentence errors. Simply ignore them until you get to a later draft of your paper, when there will be time enough to make the needed corrections. Part 3 of this text focuses on sentence skills.

Four Bases for Revising Writing

In this chapter, you've learned four essential steps in writing an effective paragraph. The following box shows how these steps lead to four standards, or bases, you can use in evaluating and revising paragraphs.

Four Steps ➡	Four Bases
1. If you make one point and stick to that point,	➡ your writing will have *unity*.
2. If you back up the point with specific evidence,	➡ your writing will have *support*.
3. If you organize and connect the specific evidence,	➡ your writing will have *coherence*.
4. If you write clear, error-free sentences,	➡ your writing will demonstrate effective *sentence skills*.

Base 1: Unity

Understanding Unity

To achieve unity is to have all the details in your paper related to the single point expressed in the topic sentence, the first sentence. Each time you think of something to put in, ask yourself whether it relates to your main point. If if does not, leave it out. For example, if you were writing about a certain job as the worst job you ever had and then spent a couple of sentences talking about the interesting people you met there, you would be missing the first and most essential base of good writing.

> **TIP** To check a paragraph for unity, ask yourself these questions:
> 1. Is there a clear, single point in the first sentence of the paragraph?
> 2. Is all the evidence on target in support of the opening point?

Evaluating a Paragraph for Unity

ACTIVITY 20	**Omitting Off-Target Sentences**

The following paragraph contains two sentences that are off target—sentences that do not support the opening point—and so the paragraph is not unified. In the interest of paragraph unity, such sentences must be omitted.

Cross out the off-target sentences and write the numbers of those sentences in the spaces provided.

How to Prevent Plagiarism

[1]Instructors should take steps to prevent students from cheating on exams. [2]To begin with, instructors should stop reusing old tests. [3]A test that has been used even once is soon known on the student grapevine. [4]Students will check with their friends to find out, for example, what was on Dr. Patel's biology final last term. [5]They may even manage to find a copy of the test itself, "accidentally" not turned in by a former student of Dr. Patel's. [6]Instructors should also take some commonsense precautions at test time. [7]They should make students separate themselves—at least by one seat—during an exam. [8]They should also ban cell phones during an exam. [9]If a student is found using a cell phone, that instructor should take it away. [10]Last of all, instructors must make it clear to students that there will be stiff penalties for cheating. [11]One of the problems with our school systems is a lack of discipline. [12]Instructors never used to give in to students' demands or put up with bad behavior, as they do today. [13]Anyone caught cheating should immediately receive a zero for the exam. [14]A person even suspected of cheating should be forced to take an alternative exam in the instructor's office. [15]Because cheating is unfair to honest students, it should not be tolerated.

The numbers of the off-target sentences: _____ _____

Base 2: Support

Understanding Support

The second base of effective writing, *support,* provides specific examples that illustrate the main point of a paragraph. Readers want to see and judge for ourselves whether a writer is making a valid point about a subject, but without specific details we cannot do so. After realizing the importance of specific supporting details, one student writer revised a paper she had done on a restaurant job as the worst job she ever had. In the revised paper, instead of talking about "unsanitary conditions in the kitchen," she referred to such specifics as "green mold on the bacon" and "ants in the potato salad." All your paragraphs should include many vivid details! Using ample support will help you communicate more clearly and effectively in your writing.

 To check a paragraph for support, ask yourself these questions:

1. Is there *specific* evidence to support the opening point?
2. Is there *enough* specific evidence?

Evaluating Paragraphs for Support

Checking for Specific Details	ACTIVITY 21

The paragraph that follows lacks sufficient supporting details. Identify the spot or spots where more specific details are needed.

Culture Conflict

[1]I am in a constant tug-of-war with my parents over conflicts between their Vietnamese culture and American culture. [2]To begin with, my parents do not like me to have American friends. [3]They think that I should spend all my time with other Vietnamese people and speak English only when necessary. [4]I get into an argument whenever I want to go to a fast-food restaurant or a movie at night with my American friends. [5]The conflict with my parents is even worse when it comes to plans for a career. [6]My parents want me to get a degree in science and then go on to medical school. [7]On the other hand, I think I want to become a teacher. [8]So far I have been taking both science and education courses, but soon I will have to concentrate on one or the other. [9]The other night my father made his attitude about what I should do very clear. [10]The most difficult aspect of our cultural differences is the way our family is structured. [11]My father is the center of our family, and he expects that I will always listen to him. [12]Although I am twenty-one years old, I still have a nightly curfew at an hour which I consider insulting. [13]Also, I am expected to help

continued

my mother perform certain household chores that I've really come to hate. **14**My father expects me to live at home until I am married to a Vietnamese man. **15**When that happens, he assumes I will obey my husband just as I obey him. **16**I do not want to be a bad daughter, but I want to live like my American female friends.

Fill in the blanks: The first spot where supporting details are needed occurs after sentence number _____. The second spot occurs after sentence number _____. The third spot occurs after sentence number _____.

Base 3: Coherence

Understanding Coherence

Once you have determined that a paragraph is unified and supported, check to see if the writer has a clear and consistent way of organizing the material.

The third base of effective writing is *coherence*. The supporting ideas and sentences in a composition must be organized in a consistent way so that they cohere, or "stick together." Key techniques for tying material together are choosing a clear method of organization (such as time order or emphatic order) and using transitions and other connecting words as signposts.

> **TIP** To check a paragraph for coherence, ask yourself these questions:
> 1. Does the paragraph have a clear method of organization?
> 2. Are transitions and other connecting words used to tie the material together?

Evaluating Paragraphs for Coherence

ACTIVITY 22 **Looking for Organization and Coherence**

Answer the questions about coherence that follow the paragraph below.

Why I Bought a Handgun

1I bought a handgun to keep in my house for several reasons. **2**Most important, I have had a frightening experience with an obscene phone caller. **3**For several weeks, a man has called me once or twice a day, sometimes as late as three in the morning. **4**As soon as I pick up the phone, he whispers something obscene or threatens me by saying, "I'll get you." **5**I decided to buy a gun because crime is increasing in my neighborhood. **6**One neighbor's house was burglarized while she was at work; the thieves not only stole her appliances but also threw

continued

paint around her living room and slashed her furniture. [7]Not long after this incident, an elderly woman from the apartment house on the corner was mugged on her way to the supermarket. [8]The man grabbed her purse and threw her to the ground, breaking her hip. [9]Buying a gun was my response to listening to the nightly news. [10]It seemed that every news story involved violence of some kind—rapes, murders, muggings, and robberies. [11]I wondered if some of the victims in the stories would still be alive if they had been able to frighten the criminal off with a gun. [12]As time passed, I became more convinced that I should keep a gun in the house.

a. The paragraph should use emphatic order. Write *1* before the reason that seems slightly less important than the other two, *2* before the second-most-important reason, and *3* before the most important reason.

_____ Obscene phone caller

_____ Crime increase in neighborhood

_____ News stories about crime

b. Before which of the three reasons should the transitional words *first of all* be added? _____

c. Before which of the three reasons could the transition *in addition* be added? _____

d. Which words show emphasis in sentence 2? _____

e. In sentence 8, to whom does the pronoun *her* refer? _____

_____

f. How often does the key word *gun* appear in the paragraph? _____

_____

g. What is a synonym for *burglarized* in sentence 6? _____

Base 4: Sentence Skills

Understanding Sentence Skills

Errors in grammar, punctuation, sentence structure, mechanics, and even formatting can detract greatly from your writing; the fourth base, **sentence skills**, requires that you identify, fix, and avoid these types of mistakes. Error-free sentences allow readers to focus on the content of a paragraph as a whole. Poor grammar and sentence skills can be merely distracting, or they can change the meaning of a sentence entirely; they also lessen a writer's credibility. For instance, a potential employer might think, "If he can't spell the word *political,* does he really have an interest in working on my campaign?"

Part 3 of this book focuses on a wide range of sentence skills. You should review all the skills carefully. Doing so will ensure that you know the most important rules of grammar, punctuation, and usage—rules needed to write clear, error-free sentences.

Checking for Sentence Skills

Sentence skills and the other bases of effective writing are summarized in the following chart and on the inside back cover of the book.

A Summary of the Four Bases of Effective Writing

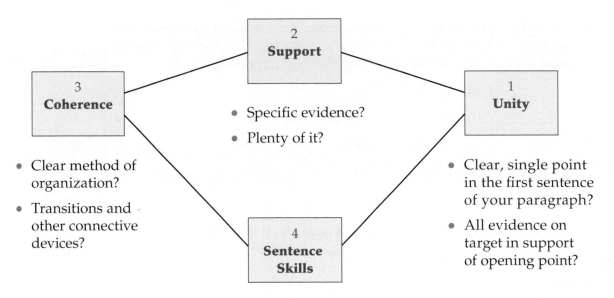

- Fragments eliminated? (162–178)
- Run-ons eliminated? (179–194)
- Correct verb forms? (210–230, 241–251)
- Subject and verb agreement? (231–240)
- Faulty modifiers and faulty parallelism eliminated? (283–288, 295–303)
- Faulty pronouns eliminated? (252–262, 263–274)
- Capital letters used correctly? (324–333)
- Punctuation marks where needed?

  (a) Apostrophe (342–353)   (d) Semicolon; colon (379–381)

  (b) Quotation marks (354–364)   (e) Hyphen; dash (381–382)

  (c) Comma (365–378)   (f) Parentheses (382–383)

- Correct paper format? (319–323)
- Needless words eliminated? (423–434)

Evaluating Paragraphs for Sentence Skills

Identifying Sentence Errors

Working with a partner, identify the sentence-skills mistakes at the under-lined spots in the paragraph that follows. From the box below, choose the letter that describes each mistake and write it in the space provided. The same mistake may appear more than once. Use Part 3: Sentence Skills (pp. 150–435) as a reference.

---

a. fragment (162–178)

b. run-on (179–194)

c. mistake in subject-verb agreement (231–240)

d. apostrophe mistake (342–353)

e. faulty parallelism (295–303)

Looking Out for Yourself

It's sad but true: "If you don't look out for yourself, no one else will." For example, some people have a false idea about the power of a college degree, they think that once they possesses the degree, the world will be waiting on their doorstep. In fact, nobody is likely to be on their doorstep unless, through advance planning, they has prepared themselves for a career. The kind in which good job opportunities exist. Even after a person has landed a job, however, a healthy amount of self-interest is needed. People who hide in corners or with hesitation to let others know about their skills doesn't get promotions or raises. Its important to take credit for a job well done, whether the job involves writing a report, organized the office filing system, or calming down an angry customer. Also, people should feel free to ask the boss for a raise. If they work hard and really deserve it. Those who look out for themselves get the rewards, people who depend on others to help them along get left behind.

---

1. _____d_____ 2. _____a_____ 3. _____b_____ 4. _____a_____ 5. _____e_____

6. _____c_____ 7. _____b_____ 8. _____a_____ 9. _____c_____ 10. _____e_____

ACTIVITY 24   **Evaluating Paragraphs for All Four Bases: Unity, Support, Coherence, and Sentence Skills**

In this activity, you will evaluate paragraphs in terms of all four bases: unity, support, coherence, and sentence skills. Evaluative comments follow each paragraph below. Circle the letter of the statement that best applies in each case.

1.

Looks Shouldn't Matter, But They Do

Often, job applicants are discriminated against based on physical appearance. First of all, some employers will not hire a man who wears an earring even though a woman who wears earrings is not singled out. In addition, someone with a facial piercing on the lip, nose, or eyebrow is often treated unfairly in the job market. Finally, some employers will not hire a person who has a visible tattoo yet they hire people whose tattoos are hidden.

---

a. The paragraph is not unified.
b. The paragraph is not adequately supported.
c. The paragraph is not well organized.
d. The paragraph does not show a command of sentence skills.
e. The paragraph is well written in terms of the four bases.

2.

Getting Better Gas Mileage

There is several ways to get better gas mileage from your car. First of all, properly maintain your car. Regularly check the air pressure in the tires owing to the fact that under-inflated tires can use up more gas. A dirty air filter will also cause your car to consume more fuel. Next, driving efficiently. When on the roadway, drive at no more than sixty miles per our. The faster you drive the more gas will be guzzled by your car. At stop signs and traffic lights, avoid sudden starts and stops. Lastly, lighten your car load. Clean out the trunk of your car and avoid hauling items unnecessarily. Added weight decrease fuel economy. Even though someone cannot control the price at the gas pump; we can control how we use the gas in our fuel tank.

---

a. The paragraph is not unified.
b. The paragraph is not adequately supported.
c. The paragraph is not well organized.
d. The paragraph does not show a command of sentence skills.
e. The paragraph is well written in terms of the four bases.

3.

Tips on Bringing Up Children

In some ways, children should be treated as mature people. Adults should not use baby talk with children. Using real words with children helps them develop language skills more quickly. Baby talk makes children feel patronized, frustrated, and confused, for they want to understand and communicate with adults by learning their speech. So animals should be called cows and dogs, not "moo-moos" and "bow-wows." Parents should be consistent when disciplining children. If a parent tells a child, "You cannot have dessert unless you put away your toys," it is important that the parent follow through on the warning. By being consistent, parents will teach children responsibility and give them a stable center around which to grow. Children should be allowed and encouraged to make simple decisions. At a restaurant, children should be allowed to decide what to order. Regarding finances, they should be able to choose if and how they want to spend their money. Parents will thus be helping their children prepare for the complex decisions that they will have to deal with later in life.

a.   The paragraph is not unified.
b.   The paragraph is not adequately supported.
c.   The paragraph is not well organized.
d.   The paragraph does not show a command of sentence skills.
e.   The paragraph is well written in terms of the four bases.

4.

Gambling My Life Away

I see now that my compulsive gambling hurt my family life. First of all, I argued constantly with my wife. When we first married, she did not seem to mind that I would bet on football and basketball games, but she began to mind when bookies started calling our home. In addition, we were always short of money for bills. I am not proud to say that my wife had to get a second job just to pay for daily expenses, such as gas and groceries. Most regrettably, I ignored my children. I spent most nights at sports bars watching the games I had placed bets on. When I was home, I preferred to play online poker rather than help my children with their homework or play with them at the park. In hindsight, I see that I gambled away not only my money but my family.

a.   The paragraph is not unified.
b.   The paragraph is not adequately supported.
c.   The paragraph is not well organized.
d.   The paragraph does not show a command of sentence skills.
e.   The paragraph is well written in terms of the four bases.

5.

> ### Children Are Expensive
>
> The cost of raising a child keeps increasing. Many families know this fact all too well. For one thing, child care costs are getting higher every year. Parents pay more today for a babysitter or for day care. Teachers' salaries, however, are not going up. For another thing, children's clothing costs more. A pair of children's athletic shoes can easily cost over fifty dollars. Budget-conscious parents should shop at discount and outlet garment stores. In addition, food also costs more. Providing nutritious food is more costly because of rising grocery prices. Sadly, a Happy Meal at McDonald's is often cheaper, but not as nutritious, as a freshly prepared sandwich at home. Health care costs are also getting higher. If a parent is fortunate to have health insurance, that parent may find more of his or her paycheck going toward the monthly premium. Other health-care expenses, such as prescription and over-the-counter drugs, are getting more expensive too.

   a.   The paragraph is not unified.
   b.   The paragraph is not adequately supported.
   c.   The paragraph is not well organized.
   d.   The paragraph does not show a command of sentence skills.
   e.   The paragraph is well written in terms of the four bases.

WRITING ASSIGNMENT

Write a paragraph about a valued material possession. Here are some suggestions:

Car	Appliance
Computer	Cell phone
TV	Photo album
iPod	Piece of clothing
Piece of furniture	Stereo system
Piece of jewelry	Piece of hobby equipment
Camera	Video game console

Your topic sentence should center on the idea that there are several reasons this possession is so important to you. Provide specific examples and details to develop each reason.

Use the following checklist as a guide while you are working on your paragraph:

Yes   No

_____   _____   Do you begin with a point?

_____   _____   Do you provide relevant, specific details that support the point?

_____   _____   Do you use the words *first of all, second,* and *finally* to introduce your three supporting details?

_____   _____   Do you have a closing sentence?

_____   _____   Are your sentences clear and free of obvious errors?

EXPLORING WRITING ONLINE

Visit a favorite Web site of yours and evaluate it for unity, support, coherence, and sentence skills. Then write a paragraph in which you present your evaluation. Use the following questions to help you:

Unity: *Can you easily identify what the Web site's goals are?*

Support: *Does the site contain valuable information, and is that information presented in an effective way?*

Coherence: *Is the site organized and easy to navigate?*

Sentence Skills: *Can you find typos, spelling mistakes, or awkward sentences?*

RESPONDING TO IMAGES

Focusing on the third base, *coherence*, describe the organizing principles of this site, as introduced on its home page, shown here.

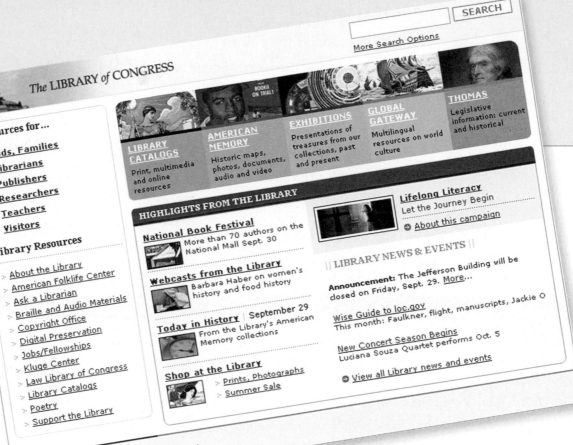

For additional materials on Chapter 3, visit www.mhhe.com/langan.

Nine Patterns of Paragraph Development

RESPONDING TO IMAGES

These photographs capture life before and after Hurricane Katrina hit the Gulf Coast. Compare or contrast these photographs, paying attention to which specific details changed or stayed constant after the hurricane struck.

Important Considerations in Paragraph Development

Before you begin work on particular types of paragraphs, there are several general considerations about writing to keep in mind.

Knowing Your Subject

Whenever possible, write on a subject that interests you. You will then find it easier to put more time into your work. Even more important, try to write on a subject that you already know something about. If you do not have direct experience with the subject, you should at least have indirect experience—knowledge gained through thinking, prewriting, reading, or talking about the subject.

If you are asked to write on a topic about which you have no experience or knowledge, you should do whatever research is required to gain the information you need. Without direct or indirect experience, or the information you gain through research, you may not be able to provide the specific evidence needed to develop whatever point you are trying to make. Your writing will be starved for specifics.

Knowing Your Purpose and Audience

The three most common purposes of writing are to inform, to persuade, and to entertain. Each is described briefly below.

- To **inform**—to give information about a subject. Authors who are writing to inform want to provide facts that will explain or teach something to readers. For example, an informative paragraph about sandwiches might begin, "Eating food between two slices of bread—a sandwich—is a practice that has its origins in eighteenth-century England."

- To **persuade**—to convince the reader to agree with the author's point of view on a subject. Authors who are writing to persuade may give facts, but their main goal is to argue or prove a point to readers. A persuasive paragraph about sandwiches might begin, "There are good reasons why every sandwich should be made with whole-grain bread."

- To **entertain**—to amuse and delight; to appeal to the reader's senses and imagination. Authors write to entertain in various ways, through fiction and nonfiction. An entertaining paragraph about sandwiches might begin, "What I wanted was a midnight snack, but what I got was better—the biggest, most magical sandwich in the entire world."

Your audience will be primarily your instructor and sometimes other students. Your instructor is really a symbol of the larger audience you should see yourself writing for—an audience of educated adults who expect you to present your ideas in a clear, direct, organized way. If you can learn to write to persuade or inform such a general audience, you will have accomplished a great deal.

A Note on Tone

It will also be helpful for you to write some paragraphs for a more specific audience. By so doing, you will develop an ability to choose words and adopt a tone of voice that is just right for a given purpose and a given group of people. *Tone* reveals the attitude that a writer has toward a subject. It is expressed through the words and details the writer selects. Just as a speaker's voice can project a range of feelings, a writer's voice can project one or more tones, or feelings: anger, sympathy, hopefulness, sadness, respect, dislike, and so on.

Patterns of Development

Traditionally, writing has been divided into the following patterns of development:

- Exposition
  Exemplification
  Process
  Cause and effect
  Comparison or contrast
  Definition
  Division-Classification

- Description

- Narration

- Argumentation

In *exposition*, the writer provides information about and explains a particular subject. Patterns of development within exposition include giving examples (*exemplification*), detailing a *process* of doing or making something, analyzing *causes and effects*, *comparing* or *contrasting*, *defining* a term or concept, and *dividing* something into parts or *classifying* it into categories.

In addition to exposition, three other patterns of development are common: description, narration, and argumentation. A *description* is a verbal picture of a person, place, or thing. In *narration*, a writer tells the story of something that happened. Finally, in *argumentation*, a writer attempts to support a controversial point or defend a position on which there is a difference of opinion.

Each pattern has its own internal logic and provides its own special strategies for imposing order on your ideas.

> **TIP** As you practice each pattern, you should remember the following:
>
> - Although each paragraph that you write will involve one predominant pattern, very often one or more additional patterns may be involved as well. For instance, the paragraph "My Job at the Crescent Falls Diner and Truck Stop" that you have already read (page 8) presents a series of examples showing why Mike disliked his job. There is also an element of narration, as the writer recounts his experience as a story.
> - Additionally, the paragraph shows how conditions caused this negative effect. No matter which pattern or patterns you use, each paragraph will probably involve some form of argumentation. You will advance a point and then go on to support your point. To convince the reader that your point is valid, you may use a series of examples, or narration, or description, or some other pattern of organization. For instance, a writer could advance the opinion that good horror movies can be easily distinguished from bad horror movies and then supply comparative information about both to support her claim. Much of your writing, in short, will have the purpose of persuading your reader that the idea you have advanced is valid.

1. Exemplification

In our daily conversations, we often provide *examples*—that is, details, particulars, and specific instances—to explain statements that we make. Consider the several statements and supporting examples in the following box:

Statement	Examples
Wal-Mart was crowded today.	There were at least four carts waiting at each of the checkout counters, and it took me forty-five minutes to get through a line.
The corduroy shirt I bought is poorly made.	When I washed it, the colors began to fade, one button cracked and another fell off, a shoulder seam opened, and the sleeves shrank almost two inches.
My son Peter is unreliable.	If I depend on him to turn off a pot of beans in ten minutes, the family is likely to eat burned beans. If I ask him to turn down the thermostat before he goes to bed, the heat is likely to stay on all night.

In each case, the examples help us *see for ourselves* the truth of the statement that has been made. In paragraphs, too, explanatory examples help the audience fully understand a point. Lively, specific examples also add interest to a piece of writing.

A Paragraph to Consider

> **Walking Billboards**
>
> ¹Many I Americans have turned into driving, walking billboards. ²As much as we all claim to hate commercials on television, we don't seem to have any qualms about turning ourselves into commercials. ³Our car bumpers, for example, advertise lake resorts, underground caverns, and amusement parks. ⁴Also, we wear clothes marked with other people's initials and slogans. ⁵Our fascination with the names of designers shows up on the backs of our sneakers and the pockets of our shirts and blue jeans. ⁶Furthermore, we wear T-shirts filled with all kinds of advertising messages. ⁷For instance, people are willing to wear shirts that read "Dillon Construction," "Nike," or even "I Got Crabs at Ed's Seafood Palace." ⁸These messages belong on highway billboards. ⁹In conclusion, we say we hate commercials, but we actually pay people for the right to advertise their products.

QUESTIONS

About Unity

1. Which sentence in "Walking Billboards" is irrelevant to the point that Americans are walking billboards? (*Write the sentence number here.*)

_____

About Support

2. How many specific examples are given that show that Americans are walking billboards?

_____ two _____ three _____ four _____ five _____ six

About Coherence

3. What transition words and phrases are used in "Walking Billboards"?

_____   _____   _____   _____   _____

Writing an Exemplification Paragraph

WRITING ASSIGNMENT

Complete this unfinished paragraph (in the following box), which has as its topic sentence, "My husband Roger is a selfish person." Provide the supporting details needed to develop the examples of Roger's selfishness. The first example has been done for you.

A Selfish Person

My husband Roger is a selfish person. For one thing, he refuses to move out of the city, even though it is a bad place to raise the children. *We inherited some money when my parents died, and it might be enough for a down payment on a small house in a nearby town. But Roger says he would miss his buddies in the neighborhood.*

_____

Also, when we go on vacation, we always go where Roger wants to go. _____

_____

_____

_____

Another example of Roger's selfishness is that he always spends any budget money that is left over. _____

_____

_____

_____

_____

Finally, Roger leaves all the work of caring for the children to me.

_____

_____

_____

_____

PREWRITING

a. On a separate piece of paper, jot down a couple of answers for each of the following questions:

- What specific vacations did the family go on because Roger wanted to go? Write down particular places, length of stay, time of year. What vacations has the family never gone on (for example, to visit the wife's relatives), even though the wife wanted to?

- What specific items has Roger bought for himself (rather than for the whole family's use) with leftover budget money?

- What chores and duties involved in the everyday caring for the children has Roger never done?

Your instructor may ask you to work with one or two other students in generating the details needed to develop the three examples in the paragraph. The groups may then be asked to read their details aloud, with the class deciding which details are the most effective for each example.

Here, and in general in your writing, try to generate *more* supporting material than you need. You are then in a position to choose the most convincing details for your paper.

b. Read over the details you have generated and decide which sound most effective. Jot down additional details as they occur to you.

c. Take your best details, reshape them as needed, and use them to complete the paragraph about Roger.

REVISING: PEER REVIEW

Read the paragraph to a classmate or friend with these questions in mind to make sure you have covered the four bases of effective writing:

CHECKLIST FOR EXEMPLIFICATION: THE FOUR BASES

ABOUT *UNITY*

✔ Do all of the examples I provide support the central idea that Roger is selfish?

ABOUT *SUPPORT*

✔ Are there enough examples to make my point about Roger and convince others to agree with me?

✔ Do I appeal to my readers' senses with vivid, specific examples?

ABOUT *COHERENCE*

✔ Have I presented the examples in my paragraph in the most effective order?

ABOUT *SENTENCE SKILLS*

✔ Have I used specific rather than general words?

✔ Are my sentences varied in length and structure?

✔ Have I checked for spelling and other sentence skills, as listed on the inside back cover of the book?

Continue revising your work until you and your reader can answer *yes* to all these questions.

BEYOND THE CLASSROOM

Exemplification

Imagine that you are a restaurant manager who needs to write a paragraph-long article for the training manual about high-quality customer service. Explain this concept by providing specific examples so that your employees understand how important customer service is in the competitive food service industry.

Paint a picture
So your outside
read can
Come in.

2. Description "

When you describe something or someone, you give your readers a picture in words. To make this "word picture" as vivid and real as possible, you must observe and record specific details that appeal to your readers' senses (sight, hearing, taste, smell, and touch). More than any other type of writing, a descriptive paragraph needs sharp, colorful details.

Here is a description in which only the sense of sight is used:

A rug covers the living-room floor.

In contrast, here is a description rich in sense impressions:

A thick, reddish-brown shag rug is laid wall to wall across the living-room floor. The long, curled fibers of the shag seem to whisper as you walk through them in your bare feet, and when you squeeze your toes into the deep covering, the soft fibers push back at you with a spongy resilience.

Sense impressions include sight (*thick, reddish-brown shag rug; laid wall to wall; walk through them in your bare feet; squeeze your toes into the deep covering; push back*), hearing (*whisper*), and touch (*bare feet, soft fibers, spongy resilience*). The sharp, vivid images provided by the sensory details give us a clear picture of the rug and enable us to share the writer's experience.

A Paragraph to Consider

My Teenage Son's Room

[1]I push open the door with difficulty. [2]The doorknob is loose and has to be jiggled just right before the catch releases from the doorjamb. [3]Furthermore, as I push at the door, it runs into a basketball shoe lying on the floor. [4]I manage to squeeze in through the narrow opening. [5]I am immediately aware of a pungent odor in the room, most of which is coming from the closet, to my right. [6]That's the location of a white wicker clothes hamper, heaped with grass-stained jeans, sweat-stained T-shirts, and smelly socks. [7]But the half-eaten burrito, lying dried and unappetizing on the bedside table across the room, contributes a bit of aroma, as does the glass

continued

of curdled, sour milk sitting on the sunny windowsill. **8**To my left, the small wire cage on Greg's desk is also fragrant, but pleasantly. **9**From its nest of sweet-smelling cedar chips, the gerbil peers out at me with its bright eyes, its tiny claws scratching against the cage wall. **10**The floor around the wastebasket that is next to the desk is surrounded by what appears to be a sprinkling of snowballs. **11**They're actually old wadded-up school papers, and I can picture Greg sitting on his bed, crushing them into balls and aiming them at the "basket"—the trash can. **12**I glance at the bed across from the desk and chuckle because pillows stuffed under the tangled nest of blankets make it look as if someone is still sleeping there, though I know Greg is in history class right now. **13**I step carefully through the room, trying to walk through the obstacle course of science-fiction paperbacks, a wristwatch, sports magazines, and a dust-covered computer on which my son stacks empty soda cans. **14**I leave everything as I find it, but tape a note to Greg's door saying, "Isn't it about time to clean up?"

QUESTIONS

About Unity

1. Does this paragraph have a topic sentence?

    _____

About Support

2. Label as *sight, touch, hearing,* or *smell* all the sensory details in the following sentences.

    That's the location of a white wicker clothes hamper, heaped with

    grass-stained jeans, sweat-stained T-shirts, and smelly socks.

About Coherence

3. Spatial signals (*above, next to, to the right,* and so on) are often used to help organize details in a descriptive paragraph. List four space signals that appear in "My Teenage Son's Room":

    _____

Writing a Descriptive Paragraph

WRITING ASSIGNMENT

Write a paragraph describing a certain person's room. Use as your topic sentence "I could tell by looking at the room that a _____ lived there." There are many kinds of people who could be the focus for such a paragraph. You can select any one of the following, or think of another type of person.

Photographer	Music lover	Carpenter
Cook	TV addict	Baby
Student	Camper	Cat or dog lover
Musician	Hacker	World traveler
Hunter	Cheerleader	Drug addict
Slob	Football player	Little boy or girl
Outdoors person	Actor	Alcoholic
Doctor	Dancer	Swimmer

PREWRITING

a. After choosing a topic, spend a few minutes making sure it will work. Prepare a list of all the details you can think of that support the topic. For example, a student who planned to describe a soccer player's room made this list:

soccer balls

shin guards

posters of professional soccer teams

soccer trophies

shirt printed with team name and number

autographed soccer ball

medals and ribbons

photos of player's own team

sports clippings

radio that looks like soccer ball

soccer socks

soccer shorts

If you don't have enough details, choose another type of person. Check your new choice by listing details before committing yourself to the topic.

b. You may want to use other prewriting techniques, such as freewriting or questioning, to develop more details for your topic. As you continue prewriting, keep the following in mind:

- Everything in the paragraph should support your point. For example, if you are writing about a soccer player's room, every detail should serve to show that the person who lives in that room plays and loves soccer. Other details—for example, the person's computer, tropical fish tank, or daily "to-do" list—should be omitted.

- Description depends on the use of specific rather than general descriptive words. For example:

General	Specific
Mess on the floor	The obstacle course of science-fiction paperbacks, a wristwatch, sports magazines, and a dust-covered computer on which my son stacks empty soda cans
Ugly turtle tub	Large plastic tub of dirty, stagnant-looking water containing a few motionless turtles
Bad smell	Unpleasant mixture of strong chemical deodorizers, urine-soaked newspapers, and musty sawdust
Nice skin	Soft, velvety brown skin

Remember that you want your readers to experience the room vividly. Your words should be as detailed as a clear photograph, giving readers a real feel for the room. Appeal to as many senses as possible. Most of your description will involve the sense of sight, but you may be able to include details about touch, hearing, and smell as well.

- Spatial order is a good way to organize a descriptive paragraph. Move as a visitor's eye might move around the room, from right to left or from larger items to smaller ones. Here are a few transition words of the sort that show spatial relationships.

to the left	across from	on the opposite side
to the right	above	nearby
next to	below	

Such transitions will help prevent you—and your reader—from getting lost as the description proceeds.

c. Before you write, see if you can make a scratch outline based on your list. Here is one possible outline of the paragraph about the soccer player's room. Note that the details are organized according to spatial order—from the edges of the room in toward the center.

Topic sentence: I could tell by looking at the room that a soccer player lived there.

1. Walls
2. Bookcase
3. Desk
4. Chair
5. Floor

d. Then proceed to write a first draft of your paragraph.

REVISING: PEER REVIEW

Read your descriptive paragraph slowly out loud to a friend or classmate. Ask the friend to close his or her eyes and try to picture the room as you read. Read it out loud a second time. To ensure you have covered the four bases of effective writing, ask your friend to answer these questions:

CHECKLIST FOR DESCRIPTION: THE FOUR BASES

ABOUT *UNITY*

✔ Does every detail in the paragraph support the topic sentence? Here's one way to find out: Ask your friend to imagine omitting the key word or words (in the case of our example, *soccer player*) in your topic sentence. Would readers know what word should fit in that empty space?

ABOUT *SUPPORT*

✔ Are the details specific and vivid rather than general?

✔ Has the writer included details that appeal to as many senses as possible?

ABOUT *COHERENCE*

✔ Does the paragraph follow a logical spatial order?

✔ Has the writer used transitions (such as *on top of*, *beside*, and *to the left of*) to help the reader follow that order?

ABOUT *SENTENCE SKILLS*

✔ Has the writer carefully proofread his or her paragraph, using the list on the inside back cover of the book, and corrected all sentence-skills mistakes, including spelling?

Continue revising your work until you and your reader can answer *yes* to all these questions.

BEYOND THE CLASSROOM

Description

Imagine that you are an interior designer. Write a paragraph describing a design for one of the following: a child's bedroom, a kitchen, a small restaurant, a porch, or a bakery. In your prewriting, you might list all the relevant needs of the people who live or work in the space you are designing. Consider issues such as storage space, appropriate lighting and colors, and the first thing people should or would notice when they walk in. Then put all the parts together so that they work well as a whole. Use a spatial order in your paragraph to help readers "see" your room.

3. Narration

At times we make a statement clear by relating in detail something that has happened. In the story we tell, we present the details in the order in which they happened. A person might say, for example, "I was embarrassed yesterday," and then go on to illustrate the statement with the following narrative:

> I was hurrying across campus to get to a class. It had rained heavily all morning, so I was hopscotching my way around puddles in the pathway. I called to two friends ahead to wait for me, and right before I caught up to them, I came to a large puddle that covered the entire path. I had to make a quick choice of either stepping into the puddle or trying to jump over it. I jumped, wanting to seem cool, since my friends were watching, but didn't clear the puddle. Water splashed everywhere, drenching my shoe, sock, and pants cuff, and spraying the pants of my friends as well. "Well done, Dave!" they said. My embarrassment was all the greater because I had tried to look so casual.

The speaker's details have made his moment of embarrassment vivid and real for us, and we can see and understand just why he felt as he did.

A Paragraph to Consider

Detail

Deceptive Appearance

[1]Outward appearance can be deceptive. [2]Eric, a friendly and good-humored college student, is a prime example. [3]On the days when Eric is absent from classes, his professors seem to miss his lively personality. [4]One day after psychology class, Eric asked his classmate Mona if she wanted to have lunch with him, and she felt happy that Eric wanted to be her friend. [5]Later, while they were sitting at a booth together eating double cheeseburgers and home fries, Eric took out a small brown envelope with several kinds of colorful pills inside. [6]"Which one?" he asked. [7]"They're great because you'll be so amped up that you won't need to sleep for a week." [8]Mona must have looked surprised because Eric said, "Don't worry." [9]He went on to say, "They're not very expensive, and I'll even cut you a break this time." [10]Mona told him that she didn't want any pills. [11]Finally, Eric said, "Your loss," and then got up and walked away without even saying good-bye or paying for his portion of the lunch bill. [12]Mona felt very disappointed. [13]Eric didn't want to be her friend. [14]He only wanted to find more people to buy his drugs.

QUESTIONS

About Unity

1. Which sentence in this paragraph should be omitted in the interest of unity? (*Write the sentence number here.*)

_____

About Support

2. What do you think is the best (most real and vivid) detail or image in the paragraph "Deceptive Appearance"?

_____

About Coherence

3. Does the paragraph use time order or emphatic order to organize details?

_____

4. What are at least three transitions words used in this paragraph?

_____

Writing a Narrative Paragraph

WRITING ASSIGNMENT

Write a paragraph about an experience in which a certain emotion was predominant. The emotion might be fear, pride, satisfaction, embarrassment, or any of these:

Frustration	Sympathy	Shyness
Love	Bitterness	Disappointment
Sadness	Violence	Happiness
Terror	Surprise	Jealousy
Shock	Nostalgia	Anger
Relief	Loss	Hate
Envy	Silliness	Nervousness

The experience you write about should be limited in time. Note that the paragraph presented in this chapter details an experience that occurred within a relatively short period of time: one frustrating night of babysitting.

A good way to bring an event to life for your readers is to include some dialogue, as the writers of two of the three paragraphs in this chapter have done. Words that you said, or that someone else said, help make a situation come alive. First, though, be sure to check the section on quotation marks on pages 354–364.

PREWRITING

a. Begin by freewriting. Think of an experience or event that caused you to feel a certain emotion strongly. Then spend ten minutes writing freely about the experience. Do not worry at this point about spelling or grammar or putting things in the right order. Instead, just try to get down all the details you can think of that seem related to the experience.

b. This preliminary writing will help you decide whether your topic is promising enough to develop further. If it is not, choose another emotion and repeat step *a*. If it does seem promising, do two things:

- First, write your topic sentence, underlining the emotion you will focus on. For example, "My first day in kindergarten was one of the *scariest* days of my life."

- Second, make up a list of all the details involved in the experience. Then number these details according to the order in which they occurred.

c. Referring to your list of details, write a rough draft of your paragraph. Use time signals such as *first, then, after, next, while, during,* and *finally* to help connect details as you move from the beginning to the middle to the end of your narrative. Be sure to include not only what happened but also how you felt about what was going on.

REVISING: PEER REVIEW

Put your first draft away for a day or so. When you return to your paragraph, share it with a friend or classmate whose judgment you trust. Go over the following questions with your reader to make sure you have covered the four bases of effective writing:

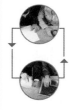

CHECKLIST FOR NARRATION: THE FOUR BASES

ABOUT *UNITY*

✔ Does my topic sentence clearly state what emotion the experience made me feel?

✔ Are there any off-topic sentences I should eliminate for the sake of paragraph unity?

ABOUT *SUPPORT*

✔ Have I included some dialogue to make the experience come alive?

✔ Have I explained how I felt as the experience occurred?

ABOUT *COHERENCE*

✔ Have I used time order to narrate the experience from beginning to end?

✔ Have I used time signals to connect one detail to the next?

ABOUT *SENTENCE SKILLS*

✔ Have I carefully proofread my paragraph, using the list on the inside back cover of the book, and corrected all sentence-skills mistakes, including spelling?

✔ Is the first-person point of view (I) in my paragraph consistent?

✔ Did I use verb tenses consistently and correctly? (This is especially important when relaying a story.)

Continue revising your work until you and your reader can answer *yes* to all these questions.

BEYOND THE CLASSROOM

Narration

Imagine that one of your oldest friends has to make a difficult decision of some kind. Narrate a relevant story from your own experience (or the experience of someone you know) that will help your friend carefully weigh the decision he or she must make. In your paragraph, include a comment or two about how your story relates to your friend's situation. Throughout, try to be helpful without being condescending. You can also be entertaining, as long as you are careful to stay sensitive to the problem at hand.

4. Process

Every day we perform many activities that are *processes*—that is, series of steps carried out in a definite order. Many of these processes are familiar and automatic: for example, tying shoelaces, changing bed linen, using a vending machine, and starting a car. We are thus seldom aware of the sequence of steps making up each activity. In other cases, such as when we are asked for directions to a particular place, or when we try to read and follow the directions for a new table game, we may be painfully conscious of the whole series of steps involved in the process.

> **TIP**   In process writing, you are often giving instruction to the reader, so the pronoun *you* can appropriately be used. As a general rule, though, do not use *you* in your writing.

A Paragraph to Consider

How to Harass an Instructor

[1]There are several steps you can take to harass an instructor during a class. [2]First of all, show up late so that you can interrupt the beginning of the instructor's presentation. [3]Saunter in nonchalantly and try to find a seat next to a friend. [4]In a normal tone of voice, speak some words of greeting to your friends as you sit down, and scrape your chair as loudly as possible while you make yourself comfortable in it. [5]Then just sit there and do anything but pay attention. [6]When the instructor sees that you are not involved in the class, he or she may pop a quick question, probably hoping to embarrass you. [7]You should then say, in a loud voice, "I DON'T KNOW THE ANSWER." [8]This declaration of ignorance will throw the instructor off guard. [9]If the instructor then asks you why you don't know the answer, say, "I don't even know what page we're on" or "I thought the assignment was boring,

continued

so I didn't do it." **10**After the instructor calls on someone else, get up loudly from your seat, walk to the front of the classroom, and demand to be excused for an emergency visit to the washroom. **11**Stay there at least fifteen minutes and take your time coming back. **12**On your way back, find a vending machine and buy yourself a snack; this class is boring, so you deserve a pick-me-up. **13**If the instructor asks you where you've been when you reenter the room, simply ignore the question and go to your seat. **14**Flop into your chair, slouching back and extending your legs as far out as possible. **15**When the instructor informs you of the assignment that the class is working on, heave an exaggerated sigh and very slowly open up your book and start turning the pages. **16**About a half hour before class is over, begin to look at the clock every few minutes. **17**Ten minutes before dismissal time, start noisily packing up your books and papers. **18**Then get up and begin walking to the door a couple of minutes before the class is supposed to end. **19**The instructor will look at you and wonder whether it wouldn't have been better to go into business instead of education.

QUESTIONS

About Unity

1. Which sentence should be eliminated in the interest of paragraph unity? (*Write the sentence number here.*)

    _____

About Support

2. After which sentence in "How to Harass an Instructor" are supporting details (examples) needed?

    _____

About Coherence

3. Does this paragraph use time order or emphatic order?

    _____

Writing a Process Paragraph

Choose one of the following topics to write about in a process paragraph.

WRITING ASSIGNMENT

> How to feed a family on a budget
>
> How to break up with a boyfriend or girlfriend
>
> How to balance a checkbook
>
> How to change a car or bike tire

How to get rid of house or garden pests, such as mice, roaches, or wasps

How to play a simple game, such as checkers

How to parallel park

How to shorten a skirt or pants

How to meet new people, for either dating or friendship

How to plant a garden

How to get started on Facebook

How to fix a leaky faucet, a clogged drain, or the like

How to build a campfire or start a fire in a fireplace

How to study for an important exam

How to conduct a yard or garage sale

How to wash dishes efficiently, clean a bathroom, or do laundry

How to create the perfect online dating profile

PREWRITING

a. Begin by freewriting on your topic for ten minutes. Do not worry about spelling, grammar, organization, or other matters of form. Just write whatever comes into your head regarding the topic. Keep writing for more than ten minutes if ideas keep coming to you. This freewriting will give you a base of raw material to draw from during the next phase of your work on the paragraph. After freewriting, you should have a sense of whether there is enough material available for you to write a process paragraph about the topic. If so, continue as explained below. If there is not enough material, choose another topic and freewrite about *it* for ten minutes.

b. Write a clear, direct topic sentence stating the process you are going to describe. For instance, if you are going to describe a way to study for major exams, your topic sentence might be "My study-skills instructor has suggested a good way to study for major exams." Or you can state in your topic sentence the process and the number of steps involved: "My technique for building a campfire involves four main steps."

c. List all the steps you can think of that may be included in the process. At this point, don't worry about how each step fits or whether two steps overlap. Here, for example, is the list prepared by a student who is writing about how to sneak into the house at night.

Quiet on stairs

Come in after Dad's asleep

House is freezing at night

Bring key

Know which steps to avoid

Lift up front door

Late parties on Saturday night

Don't turn on bathroom light

Avoid squeaky spots on floor

Get into bed quietly

Undress quietly

d. Number your items in the order in which they occur; strike out items that do not fit in the list; add others that come to mind. The student writer did this step as follows:

~~Quiet on stairs~~

2   Come in after Dad's asleep

~~House is freezing at night~~

1   Bring key

5   Know which steps to avoid

3   Lift up front door

~~Late parties on Saturday night~~

6   Don't turn on bathroom light

4   Avoid squeaky spots on floor

8   Get into bed quietly

7   Undress quietly

e. Use your list as a guide to write the first draft of your paragraph. As you write, try to think of additional details that will support your opening sentence. Do not expect to finish your paragraph in one draft. After you complete your first rough draft, in fact, you should be ready to write a series of drafts as you work toward the goals of unity, support, and coherence.

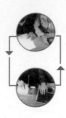

REVISING: PEER REVIEW

After you have written the first draft of your paragraph, set it aside for a while if you can. Then read it out loud, either to yourself or (better yet) to a friend or classmate who will be honest with you about how it sounds. Reexamine your paragraph with these questions in mind to make sure you have covered the four bases of effective writing:

CHECKLIST FOR PROCESS: THE FOUR BASES

ABOUT *UNITY*

✔ An effective process composition describes a series of events in a way that is clear and easy to follow. Are the steps in your paragraph described in a clear, logical way?

ABOUT *SUPPORT*

✔ Does your paragraph explain every necessary step so that a reader could perform the task described?

ABOUT *COHERENCE*

✔ Have you used transitions such as *first*, *next*, *also*, *then*, *after*, *now*, *during*, and *finally* to make the paper move smoothly from one step to another?

ABOUT *SENTENCE SKILLS*

✔ Is the point of view consistent? For example, if you begin by writing "This is how I got rid of mice" (first person), do not switch to "You must buy the right traps" (second person). Write this paragraph either from the first-person point of view (using *I* and *we*) or from the second-person point of view (*you*)—do not jump back and forth between the two.

✔ Have you corrected any sentence-skills mistakes that you noticed while reading the paragraph out loud? Have you checked the composition for sentence skills, including spelling, as listed on the inside back cover of this book?

Continue revising your work until you and your reader can answer *yes* to all these questions.

Imagine that you have to train someone to take your place in any job you've held (or currently hold); if you have never held a job, you can train this person to take your place as a student. Write a process paragraph that describes what a day on the job entails. Break the day's activities down into steps, making sure to include what advance preparation your replacement might need.

5. Cause and Effect

What caused Pat to drop out of school? Why are soap operas so popular? Why does our football team do so poorly each year? How has retirement affected Dad? What effects does divorce have on children? Every day we ask such questions and look for answers. We realize that situations have causes and effects—good or bad. By examining causes and effects, we seek to understand and explain things.

A Paragraph to Consider

New Puppy in the House

[1]Buying a new puppy can have significant effects on a household. [2]For one thing, the puppy keeps the entire family awake for at least two solid weeks. [3]Every night when the puppy is placed in its box, it begins to howl, yip, and whine. [4]Even after the lights go out and the house quiets down, the puppy continues to moan. [5]A second effect is that the puppy tortures the family by destroying material possessions. [6]Every day something different is damaged. [7]Family members find chewed belts and shoes, gnawed table legs, and ripped sofa cushions leaking stuffing. [8]In addition, the puppy often misses the paper during the paper-training stage of life, thus making the house smell like the public restroom at a city bus station. [9]Maybe the most serious problem, though, is that the puppy causes family arguments. [10]Parents argue with children about who is supposed to feed and walk the dog. [11]Children argue about who gets to play with the puppy first. [12]Puppies are adorable, and no child can resist their charm. [13]Everyone argues about who left socks and shoes around for the puppy to find. [14]These continual arguments, along with the effects of sleeplessness and the loss of valued possessions, can really disrupt a household. [15]Only when the puppy gets a bit older does the household settle back to normal.

QUESTIONS

About Unity

1. Which sentence does not support the opening idea and should be omitted? (*Write the sentence number here.*)

   _15_

About Support

2. How many effects of bringing a new puppy into the house are given in this paragraph?

   _____ one _____ two _____ three __9__ four

About Coherence

3. What words signal the effect that the author feels may be the most important? *nurturer make it clear, the points and unity everthing must support what the writer is talking about*

Writing a Cause-and-Effect Paragraph

WRITING ASSIGNMENT

Choose one of the following three topic sentences and brief outlines. Each is made up of three supporting points (causes or effects). Your task is to turn the topic sentence and outline into a cause-and-effect paragraph.

Option 1
Topic sentence: There are several reasons why parenthood makes people more responsible.
(1) Ensure that children's needs are met (*cause*)
(2) Cannot think only of themselves (*cause*)
(3) Provide children with a better life (*cause*)

Option 2
Topic sentence: My divorce has changed my life in positive ways.
(1) Enrolled in college (*effect*)
(2) More quality time with children (*effect*)
(3) Began exercising regularly (*effect*)

Option 3
Topic sentence: Lack of sleep makes daily life more difficult.
(1) Difficulty focusing on homework (*cause*)
(2) Irritable all the time (*cause*)
(3) More prone to colds and the flu (*cause*)

PREWRITING

a. After you've chosen the option that appeals to you most, jot down all the details you can think of that might go under each of the supporting points. Use separate paper for your lists. Don't worry yet about whether you can use all the items—your goal is to generate more material than you need. Here, for example, are some of the details generated by the author of "New Puppy in the House" to back up her supporting points.

Topic sentence: Having a new puppy disrupts a household.

1. Keeps family awake
   a. Whines at night
   b. Howls
   c. Loss of sleep
2. Destroys possessions
   a. Chews belts and shoes
   b. Chews furniture
   c. Tears up toys it's supposed to fetch
3. Has accidents in house
   a. Misses paper
   b. Disgusting cleanup
   c. Makes house smell bad
4. Causes arguments
   a. Arguments about walking dog
   b. Arguments about feeding dog
   c. Arguments about who gets to play with dog
   d. Arguments about vet bills

b. Now go through the details you have generated and decide which are most effective. Strike out the ones you decide are not worth using. Do other details occur to you? If so, jot them down as well.

c. Now you are ready to write your paragraph. Begin the paragraph with the topic sentence you chose. Make sure to develop each of the supporting points from the outline into a complete sentence, and then back it up with the best of the details you have generated.

REVISING: PEER REVIEW

Review your paragraph with a friend or classmate. The two of you should keep these questions in mind to make sure you have covered the four bases of effective writing:

CHECKLIST FOR CAUSE AND EFFECT: THE FOUR BASES

ABOUT *UNITY*

✔ Have you begun the paragraph with the topic sentence provided?

✔ Are any sentences in your paragraph not directly relevant to this topic sentence?

ABOUT *SUPPORT*

✔ Is each supporting point stated in a complete sentence?

✔ Have you provided effective details to back up each supporting point?

ABOUT *COHERENCE*

✔ Have you used transitions such as *in addition*, *another thing*, and *also* to make the relationships between the sentences clear?

ABOUT *SENTENCE SKILLS*

✔ Have you avoided wordiness?

✔ Have you proofread the paragraph for sentence-skills errors, including spelling, as listed on the inside back cover of the book?

Continue revising your work until you and your reader can answer *yes* to all these questions.

BEYOND THE CLASSROOM

Cause and Effect

Imagine that you are a retail store manager and must write a letter to one of your employees. Not only is this person a poor salesperson but also he or she has a negative attitude and lacks leadership qualities. Write a paragraph that explains three ways in which this person has negatively impacted the company, and then write another paragraph in which you ask this person to help you understand the causes of his or her behavior and attitude.

---

6. Comparison or Contrast

Comparison and contrast are two everyday thought processes. When we *compare* two things, we show how they are similar; when we *contrast* two things, we show how they are different. We might compare or contrast two brand-name products (for example, Nike versus Adidas running shoes), two television shows, two instructors, two jobs, two friends, or two courses of action we could take in a given situation. The purpose of comparing and contrasting is to understand each of the two things more clearly and, at times, to make judgments about them.

There are two common methods, or formats, of development in a comparison or contrast paper. One format presents the details *one side at a time.* The other presents the details *point by point.*

Two Paragraphs to Consider

Read these sample paragraphs of comparison or contrast and then answer the questions that follow.

Two Views on Toys

[1]Children and adults have very different preferences. [2]First, there is the matter of taste. [3]Adults pride themselves on taste, while children ignore the matter of taste in favor of things that are fun. [4]Adults, especially grandparents, pick out tasteful toys that go unused, while children love the cheap playthings advertised on television. [5]Second, of course, there is the matter of money. [6]The new games on the market today are a case in point. [7]Have you ever tried to lure a child away from some expensive game in order to get him or her to play with an old-fashioned game or toy? [8]Finally, there is a difference between an adult's and a child's idea of what is educational. [9]Adults, filled with memories of their own childhood, tend to be fond of the written word. [10]Today's children, on the other hand, concentrate on anything electronic. [11]These things mean much more to them than to adults. [12]Next holiday season, examine the toys that adults choose for children. [13]Then look at the toys the children prefer. [14]You will see the difference.

Mike and Helen

[1]Mike and Helen, a married couple we know, look very much alike. [2]They are both short, dark-haired, and slightly pudgy. [3]Like his wife, Mike has a good sense of humor. [4]Both Mike and Helen can be charming when they want to be, and they seem to handle small crises in a calm, cool way. [5]A problem such as an overflowing washer, a stalled car, or a sick child is not a cause for panic; they seem to take such events in stride. [6]In contrast to Helen, though, Mike tends to be disorganized. [7]He is late for appointments and unable to keep important documents—bank records, receipts, and insurance papers—where he can find them. [8]Also unlike Helen, Mike tends to hold a grudge. [9]He is slow to forget a cruel remark, a careless joke, or an unfriendly slight. [10]Another difference between these two is how they like to spend their free time; while Mike enjoys swimming, camping, and fishing, Helen prefers to stay inside and read or play chess.

QUESTIONS

About Unity

1. Which paragraph lacks a topic sentence?

    _____

2. Which paragraph has a topic sentence that is too broad?

    _____

About Support

3. Which paragraph contains almost no specific details?

    _____

4. Which paragraph provides more complete support?

    _____

About Coherence

5. What method of development (one side at a time or point by point) is used in "Mike and Helen"?

    _____

6. What method of development is used in "Two Views in Toys"?

    _____

RESPONDING TO IMAGES

Compare or contrast these two photographs of men cooking:

Writing a Comparison or Contrast Paragraph

Write a comparison or contrast paragraph on one of the following topics:

Two holidays	Two characters in the same movie or TV show
Two instructors	
Two children	Two homes
Two kinds of eaters	Two neighborhoods
Two drivers	Two cartoon strips
Two coworkers	Two cars
Two members of a team (or two teams)	Two friends
Two singers or groups	Two crises
Two pets	Two bosses or supervisors
Two parties	Two magazines
Two jobs	

WRITING ASSIGNMENT

PREWRITING

a. Choose your topic, the two subjects you will write about.

b. Decide whether your paragraph will *compare* the two subjects (discuss their similarities), *contrast* them (discuss their differences), or do both. If you choose to write about differences, you might write about how a musical group you enjoy differs from a musical group you dislike. You might discuss important differences between two employers you have had or between two neighborhoods you've lived in. You might contrast a job you've had in a car factory with a job you've had as a receptionist.

c. Write a direct topic sentence for your paragraph. Here's an example: "My job in a car-parts factory was very different from my job as a receptionist."

d. Come up with at least three strong points to support your topic sentence. If you are contrasting two jobs, for example, your points might be that they differed greatly (1) in their physical setting, (2) in the skills they required, and (3) in the people they brought you into contact with.

e. Use your topic sentence and supporting points to create a scratch outline for your paragraph. For the paragraph about jobs, the outline would look like this:

Topic sentence: My job in a car-parts factory was very different from my job as a receptionist.

1. The jobs differed in physical setting.
2. The jobs differed in the skills they required.
3. The jobs differed in the people they brought me into contact with.

f. Under each of your supporting points, jot down as many details as occur to you. Don't worry yet about whether the details all fit perfectly or whether you will be able to use them all. Your goal is to generate a wealth of material to draw on. An example:

Topic sentence: My job in a car-parts factory was very different from my job as a receptionist.

1. The jobs differed in physical setting.
    Factory loud and dirty
    Office clean and quiet
    Factory full of machines, hunks of metal, tools
    Office full of desks, files, computers
    Factory smelled of motor oil
    Office smelled of new carpet
    Windows in factory too high and grimy to look out of
    Office had clean windows onto street

2. The jobs differed in the skills and behavior they required.
    Factory required physical strength
    Office required mental activity
    Didn't need to be polite in factory
    Had to be polite in office
    Didn't need to think much for self in factory
    Constantly had to make decisions in office

3. The jobs differed in the people they brought me into contact with.
    In factory, worked with same crew every day
    In office, saw constant stream of new customers
    Most coworkers in factory had high school education or less
    Many coworkers and clients in office well educated
    Coworkers in factory spoke variety of languages
    Rarely heard anything but English in office

g. Decide which format you will use to develop your paragraph: one side at a time or point by point. Either is acceptable; it is up to you to decide which you prefer. The important thing is to be consistent: Whichever format you choose, be sure to use it throughout the entire paragraph.

h. Write the first draft of your paragraph.

REVISING: PEER REVIEW

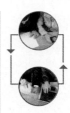

Put your composition away for a day or so. You will return to it with a fresh perspective and a better ability to critique what you have written. Share your paragraph with a friend or fellow classmate. Together, read your paragraph with these questions in mind to make sure you have covered the four bases of effective writing:

CHECKLIST FOR COMPARISON OR CONTRAST: THE FOUR BASES

ABOUT *UNITY*

✔ Does your topic sentence make it clear what two things you are comparing or contrasting?

✔ Do all sentences in the paragraph stay on topic?

ABOUT *SUPPORT*

✔ Have you compared or contrasted the subjects in at least three important ways?

✔ Have you provided specific details that effectively back up your supporting points?

ABOUT *COHERENCE*

✔ If you have chosen the point-by-point format, have you consistently discussed a point about one subject, then immediately discussed the same point about the other subject before moving on to the next point?

✔ If you have chosen the one-side-at-a-time format, have you discussed every point about one of your subjects, then discussed the same points *in the same order* about the second subjects?

✔ Have you used appropriate transitions, such as *first, in addition, also,* and *another way,* to help readers follow your train of thought?

ABOUT *SENTENCE SKILLS*

✔ Have you carefully proofread your paragraph, using the guidelines on the inside back cover of the book, and corrected all sentence-skills mistakes, including spelling?

Continue revising your work until you and your reader can answer *yes* to all these questions.

BEYOND THE CLASSROOM

Comparison or Contrast

Imagine that a new club has opened in the building next to your house/apartment/dorm. At first, you were thrilled—but then loud music and screaming patrons started making it nearly impossible for you to study or sleep. Seven days a week, the club stays open until 2:00 A.M.

1. Write a paragraph-long letter of complaint to the club owners, contrasting life before and after the club opened.

2. Write an e-mail on the same topic to one of your friends.

3. How do the two pieces of writing (for two different purposes/audiences) differ from each other? How are they similar?

7. Definition

In talking with other people, we sometimes offer informal definitions to explain just what we mean by a particular term. Suppose, for example, we say to a friend, "Karen can be so clingy." We might then expand on our idea of "clingy" by saying, "You know, a clingy person needs to be with someone every single minute. If Karen's best friend makes plans that don't include her, she becomes hurt. And when she dates someone, she calls him several times a day and gets upset if he even goes to the grocery store without her. She hangs on to people too tightly." In a written definition, we make clear in a more complete and formal way our own personal understanding of a term. Such a definition typically starts with one meaning of a term. The meaning is then illustrated with a series of examples or a story.

A Paragraph to Consider

Absent-Minded Professor

¹My English teacher is an absent-minded professor. ²For example, when she lectures on a given subject one day, she forgets where she left off and asks us to tell her the next day. ³Then there are our papers. ⁴She gives us topics to write about and gives us a due date, but when the due date comes around, we have to remind her that they're due. ⁵Furthermore, it sometimes takes weeks before we get our papers back. ⁶One time, I worked really hard on an assignment on dolphins. ⁷These animals have always fascinated me. ⁸After I turned it in, it took her a month to return it, and then the grade was only a B. ⁹She had made no corrections, just a couple of check marks on the margins. ¹⁰I felt so frustrated and powerless. ¹¹Some students like having absent-minded professors because they do not have to work as hard and feel that they're getting away with something. ¹²But they're getting the short end of their education. ¹³Absent-minded professors do not know how much harm they're doing to their students, and it's just plain not fair to us.

About Unity

1. Which sentence in the "Absent-Minded Professor" is irrelevant to the unity of the paragraph and should be eliminated? (*Write the sentence number here.*)

_____

About Support

2. Which four sentences provide extended examples for one of the supporting points in "Absent-Minded Professor"? (*Write the sentence numbers here.*)

_____

About Coherence

3. What are the four transitions used within the "Absent-Minded Professor" paragraph?

_____   _____   _____   _____

Writing a Definition Paragraph

Write a paragraph that defines the term *TV addict*. Base your paragraph on the topic sentence and three supporting points provided below.

Topic sentence: Television addicts are people who will watch all the programs they can, for as long as they can, without doing anything else.

(1) TV addicts, first of all, will watch anything on the tube, no matter how bad it is. . . .

(2) In addition, addicts watch more hours of TV than normal people do. . . .

(3) Finally, addicts feel that TV is more important than other people or any other activities that might be going on. . . .

PREWRITING

a. Generate as many examples as you can for each of the three qualities of a TV addict. You can do this by asking yourself the following questions:

- What are some truly awful shows that I (or TV addicts I know) watch just because the television is turned on?

- What are some examples of the large amounts of time that I (or TV addicts I know) watch television?

- What are some examples of ways that I (or TV addicts I know) neglect people or give up activities in order to watch TV?

    Write down every answer you can think of for each question. At this point, don't worry about writing full sentences or even about grammar or spelling. Just get your thoughts down on paper.

DEFINE "GOOD."

RESPONDING TO IMAGES
Explain to someone who doesn't know what "good" means why this cartoon is funny.

b. Look over the list of examples you have generated. Select the strongest examples you have thought of. You should have at least two or three for each quality. If not, ask yourself the questions in step *a* again.

c. Write out the examples you will use, this time expressing them in full, grammatically correct sentences.

d. Start with the topic sentence and three points provided in the assignment. Fill in the examples you've generated to support each point and write a first draft of your paragraph.

REVISING: PEER REVIEW

Put your first draft away for a day or so. When you come back to it, reread it critically and ask a friend or classmate to read it as well. The two of you should keep these questions in mind to make sure you have covered the four bases of effective writing:

CHECKLIST FOR DEFINITION: THE FOUR BASES

ABOUT *UNITY*

✔ Have you used the topic sentence and the three supporting points that were provided?

✔ Does every sentence in the paragraph help define the term *TV addict?*

ABOUT *SUPPORT*

✔ Have you backed up each supporting point with at least two examples?

✔ Does each of your examples effectively illustrate the point that it backs up?

ABOUT *COHERENCE*

✔ Have you used appropriate transitional language (*another*, *in addition*, *for example*) to tie your thoughts together?

✔ Are all transitional words correctly used?

ABOUT *SENTENCE SKILLS*

✔ Have you carefully proofread your paragraph, using the guidelines on the inside back cover of the book, and corrected all sentence-skills mistakes, including spelling?

✔ Have you used a consistent point of view throughout the paragraph?

Continue revising your work until you and your reader can answer *yes* to all these questions.

Imagine that you are applying for a grant from your town or city government to build a community garden in an urban area or a community theater in a rural/suburban one. To make such an appeal effective, you will need to define *community*; such a definition will help you to show that the garden or theater will enhance the lives of everyone in this particular community. Use examples or one extended example to illustrate each of your general points.

**BEYOND THE
CLASSROOM**

Definition

8. Division-Classification

If you were doing the laundry, you might begin by separating the clothing into piles. You would then put all the whites in one pile and all the colors in another. Or you might classify the laundry, not according to color, but according to fabric—putting all cottons in one pile, polyesters in another, and so on. *Classifying* is the process of taking many things and separating them into categories. We generally classify to better manage or understand many things. Librarians classify books into groups (novels, travel, health, etc.) to make them easier to find. A scientist sheds light on the world by classifying all living things into two main groups: animals and plants.

Dividing, in contrast, is taking one thing and breaking it down into parts. We often divide, or analyze, to better understand, teach, or evaluate something. For instance, a tinkerer might take apart a clock to see how it works; a science text might divide a tree into its parts to explain their functions. A music reviewer may analyze the elements of a band's performance—for example, the skill of the various players, rapport with the audience, selections, and so on.

In short, if you are classifying, you are sorting *numbers of things* into categories. If you are dividing, you are breaking *one thing* into parts. It all depends on your purpose—you might classify flowers into various types or divide a single flower into its parts.

Two Paragraphs to Consider

Types of E-Mail

[1]As more and more people take advantage of e-mailing, three categories of e-mail have emerged. [2]One category of e-mail is junk mail. [3]When most people sign on to their computers, they are greeted with a flood of get-rich-quick schemes, invitations to pornographic Web sites, and ads for a variety of unwanted products. [4]E-mail users quickly become good at hitting the "delete" button to get rid of this garbage. [5]The second category that clogs most people's electronic mailbox is forwarded mail, most of which also gets deleted without being read. [6]The third and best category of e-mail is genuine personal e-mail from genuine personal friends. [7]Getting such real, thoughtful e-mail can almost make up for the irritation of the other two categories.

Planning a Trip

¹Designating a destination where the political and societal conditions are healthy and secure is the first and most important step in planning a trip. ²Unstable governments very often lead to social unrest and violence. ³Once settling on a general location, devising a budget is the next step. ⁴The cost of living in some countries can be drastically higher than others. ⁵When the destination is settled on, becoming familiar with the religious and cultural customs of the country is highly recommended. ⁶What is accepted in the United States may be considered illegal or insulting in a foreign country. ⁷For example, in Islamic countries, women are expected to cover their entire body and head. ⁸In many instances, women wear veils across the face with a small slit positioned in front of the eyes. ⁹Showing up in a tank top and shorts will very likely jeopardize one's sense of security and safety. ¹⁰Now it is time to purchase an airline ticket and again, research is strongly advised in order to obtain the best possible deal. ¹¹Depending on one's idea of fun, planning an itinerary can be exceedingly complicated or relatively simple. ¹²If lying on a lounge chair and sipping a cocktail by the water's edge is the desired activity, then planning the itinerary will be quite effortless. ¹³But if a traveler is interested in involving himself or herself in some rigorous activities such as mountain climbing, scuba diving, or kayaking, planning the itinerary will probably require a lot more time. ¹⁴Many people do not realize that there is in fact a lot of research involved in planning a trip. ¹⁵These people should not be so careless, as they could expose themselves to extremely dangerous situations. ¹⁶It is frustrating that so few people take research seriously.

QUESTIONS

About Unity

1. Which paragraph lacks a topic sentence?

   _____

2. Which sentence(s) in "Planning a Trip" should be eliminated in the interest of paragraph unity? (*Write the sentence number[s] here.*)

   _____

About Support

3. Which aspect of "Planning a Trip" lacks specific details?

   _____

4. After which sentence in "Types of E-Mail" are supporting details needed? (*Write the sentence number here.*)

   _____

About Coherence

5. Which paragraph uses emphatic order to organize its details?

_____

6. Which words in "Types of E-mail" signal the most important detail?

_____

Writing a Division-Classification Paragraph

Below are four options to develop into a classification paragraph. Each one presents a topic to classify into three categories. Choose one option to develop into a paragraph.

Option 1
Casino gambling
(1) Blackjack
(2) Poker
(3) Slot machine

Option 2
Movies
(1) Action
(2) Comedy
(3) Horror

Option 3
Home gym equipment
(1) Treadmill
(2) Elliptical machine
(3) Stationary bicycle

Option 4
House pets
(1) Dogs
(2) Cats
(3) Birds

PREWRITING

a. Begin by doing some freewriting on the topic you have chosen. For five or ten minutes, simply write down everything that comes into your head when you think about "casino gambling," "house pets," or whichever option you choose. Don't worry about grammar, spelling, or organization—just write.

b. Now that you've "loosened up your brain" a little, try asking yourself questions about the topic and writing down your answers. If you are writing about house pets, for instance, you might ask questions like these:

• What are some unique qualities for each kind of house pet?

• How do these house pets differ? How are they similar?

• What would dog owners say about their dogs? What would cat owners say about their cats? What would bird owners say about their birds?

Write down whatever answers occur to you for these and other questions. Again, do not worry at this stage about writing correctly. Instead, concentrate on getting down all the information you can think of that supports your three points.

c. Reread the material you have accumulated. If some of the details you have written make you think of even better ones, add them. Select the details that best support your three points. Number them in the order you will present them.

d. Restate your topic as a grammatically complete topic sentence. For example, if you're writing about home gym equipment, your topic sentence might be "Home gym equipment can be divided into three categories." Turn each of your three supporting points into a full sentence as well.

e. Using your topic sentence and three supporting sentences and adding the details you have generated, write the first draft of your paragraph.

REVISING: PEER REVIEW

Put your work away for a couple of days. Then reread it with a critical eye and have a friend or classmate read it as well. Ask your reader to give you honest feedback as the two of you answer the following questions.

> ## CHECKLIST FOR DIVISION-CLASSIFICATION: THE FOUR BASES
>
> ### ABOUT *UNITY*
>
> ✔ Does the paragraph include a complete topic sentence and three supporting points?
>
> ### ABOUT *SUPPORT*
>
> ✔ Have you backed up each supporting point with strong, specific details?
>
> ### ABOUT *COHERENCE*
>
> ✔ Does the paragraph successfully classify types of casino gambling, movies, home gym equipment, or house pets?
>
> ### ABOUT *SENTENCE SKILLS*
>
> ✔ Have you carefully proofread the paragraph, using the list on the inside back cover of the book, and corrected all sentence-skills mistakes, including spelling?
>
> ✔ Have you used specific rather than general words?

Continue revising your work until you and your reader can answer *yes* to all these questions.

BEYOND THE CLASSROOM

Division-Classification

Imagine that you are a real estate agent and someone new to the area has asked you for suggestions about where to look for a home. Write a paragraph classifying local neighborhoods into three or more types. For each type, include an explanation with one or more examples.

9. Argument

Most of us know someone who enjoys a good argument. Such a person usually challenges any sweeping statement we might make. "Why do you say that?" he or she will ask. "Give your reasons." Our questioner then listens carefully as we cite our reasons, waiting to see if we really do have solid evidence to support our point of view. In an argument, the two parties each present their supporting evidence. The goal is to determine who has the more solid evidence to support his or her point of view. A questioner may make us feel a bit nervous, but we may also appreciate the way he or she makes us think through our opinions.

The ability to advance sound, compelling arguments is an important skill in everyday life. We can use argument to get an extension on a term paper, obtain a favor from a friend, or convince an employer that we are the right person for a job. Understanding persuasion based on clear, logical reasoning can also help us see through the sometimes faulty arguments advanced by advertisers, editors, politicians, and others who try to bring us over to their side.

A Paragraph to Consider

Living Alone

¹Living alone is quite an experience. ²People who live alone, for one thing, have to learn to do all kinds of tasks by themselves. ³They must learn—even if they have had no experience—to change fuses, put up curtains and shades, temporarily dam an overflowing toilet, cook a meal, and defrost a refrigerator. ⁴When there is no father, husband, mother, or wife to depend on, a person can't fall back on the excuse, "I don't know how to do that." ⁵Those who live alone also need the strength to deal with people. ⁶Alone, singles must face noisy neighbors, unresponsive landlords, dishonest repair people, and aggressive bill collectors. ⁷Because there are no buffers between themselves and the outside world, people living alone have to handle every visitor—friendly or unfriendly—alone. ⁸Finally, singles need a large dose of courage to cope with occasional panic and unavoidable loneliness. ⁹That weird thump in the night is even more terrifying when there is no one in the next bed or the next room. ¹⁰Frightening weather or unexpected bad news is doubly bad when the worry can't be shared. ¹¹Even when life is going well, little moments of sudden loneliness can send shivers through the heart. ¹²Struggling through such bad times taps into reserves of courage that people may not have known they possessed. ¹³Facing everyday tasks, confronting all types of people, and handling panic and loneliness can shape singles into brave, resourceful, and more independent people.

QUESTIONS

About Unity

1. The topic sentence in "Living Alone" is too broad. Circle the topic sentence that states accurately what the paragraph is about.

    a. Living alone can make one a better person.
    b. Living alone can create feelings of loneliness.
    c. Living alone should be avoided.

2. How many reasons are given to support the topic sentence in this paragraph?

    _____ one _____ two _____ three _____ four

About Coherence

3. What are the three main transition words in this paragraph?

    _____   _____   _____

Writing an Argument Paragraph

WRITING ASSIGNMENT

Develop an argument paragraph based on one of these statements:

Condoms should (*or* should not) be made available in schools.

_____ (*name a specific athlete*) is the athlete most worthy of admiration in his *or* her sport.

Television is one of the best (*or* worst) inventions of this century.

_____ make the best (*or* worst) pets.

Cigarette and alcohol advertising should (*or* should not) be banned.

Teenagers make poor parents.

_____ is one public figure today who can be considered a hero.

This college needs a better _____ (cafeteria *or* library *or* student center *or* grading policy *or* attendance policy).

PREWRITING

a. Make up brief outlines for any three of the preceding statements. Make sure you have three separate and distinct reasons for each statement. Below is an example of a brief outline for a paragraph making another point.

Large cities should outlaw passenger cars.
1. Cut down on smog and pollution
2. Cut down on noise
3. Make more room for pedestrians

b. Decide, perhaps through discussion with your instructor or classmates, which of your outlines is the most promising for development into a paragraph. Make sure your supporting points are logical by asking yourself in each case, "Does this item truly support my topic sentence?"

c. Do some prewriting. Prepare a list of all the details you can think of that might actually support your point. Don't limit yourself; include more details than you can actually use. Here, for example, are details generated by the writer of "Living Alone":

Deal with power failures	Noisy neighbors
Nasty landlords	Develop courage
Scary noises at night	Do all the cooking
Spiders	Home repairs
Bill collectors	Obscene phone calls
Frightening storms	Loneliness

d. Decide which details you will use to develop your paragraph. Number the details in the order in which you will present them. Because presenting the strongest reason last (emphatic order) is the most effective way to organize an argument paragraph, be sure to save your most powerful reason for last. Here is how the author of "Living Alone" made decisions about details:

1   Deal with power failures

4   Nasty landlords

7   Scary noises at night

~~Spiders~~

6   Bill collectors

8   Frightening storms

5   Noisy neighbors

10   Develop courage

2   Do all the cooking

3   Home repairs

~~Obscene phone calls~~

9   Loneliness

e. Write the first draft of your paragraph. As you write, develop each reason with specific details. For example, in "Living Alone," notice how the writer makes the experience of living alone come alive with phrases like "That weird thump in the night" or "little moments of sudden loneliness can send shivers through the heart."

REVISING: PEER REVIEW

Put your paragraph away for a day or so. Then, share your paragraph with a partner and refer to the following questions to make sure you have covered the four bases of effective writing:

CHECKLIST FOR ARGUMENT: THE FOUR BASES

ABOUT *UNITY*

✔ Imagine that your audience is a jury who will ultimately render a verdict on your argument. Have you presented a convincing case? If you were on the jury, would you both understand and be favorably impressed by this argument?

✔ Does every one of your supporting points help prove the argument stated in your topic sentence?

ABOUT *SUPPORT*

✔ Have you backed up your points of support with specific details?

✔ Have you appealed to your readers' senses with these details?

ABOUT *COHERENCE*

✔ Have you used emphatic order in your paragraph, saving the most important, strongest detail for last?

ABOUT *SENTENCE SKILLS*

✔ Have you used strong verbs (rather than *is* and *to be*) throughout?

✔ Have you written your argument in the active, rather than passive, voice? (see pages 249–250)

✔ Have you checked your paper for sentence-skills mistakes, including spelling?

Continue revising your work until you and your partner can answer *yes* to all these questions.

BEYOND THE CLASSROOM

Argument

Imagine that you have implemented a new procedure at work, one that will make your workplace more efficient. For example, if you work at a retail store, you may have reorganized the customer files by zip code rather than by last name. Write a one-paragraph memo to your supervisor explaining in detail why you chose to implement this procedure and why he or she would approve or endorse this change. Do your best to convince your supervisor that your idea brings more efficiency.

REFLECTIVE ACTIVITY

1. Reread two or three paragraphs you have written in response to the writing assignments in this chapter. Are these paragraphs unified? Do any contain off-target sentences?

2. Are the paragraphs coherent, or do you need to add transitions? Which ones?

3. Does each paragraph contain enough support?

EXPLORING WRITING ONLINE

Examine your college's home page and consider what patterns of development it uses—and for what purposes. In your response, consider some of the following questions: How does the home page describe and/or define your school, and does it serve to narrate your college's story? As a prospective student, what kind of first impression does this page (not the site as a whole) offer? How is it an *argument* or advertisement for you school? How does it use *classification* and/or *division* as organizing principles? Does the site seem easy to navigate? What might you, as a current student, use the site for?

RESPONDING TO IMAGES

The following images address the topic of same-sex marriage. Why do you think the photographs were taken? Consider issues of purpose and audience. What patterns of development are at work in each image? How might the reason a photograph is taken differ from how it is used in a textbook?

For additional materials on Chapter 4, visit www.mhhe.com/langan.

5 CHAPTER

Moving from Paragraph to Essay

RESPONDING TO IMAGES

Italian artist Leonardo da Vinci focused on different aspects of the human form in Mona Lisa (pictured here). What can an artist learn about drawing the human form by focusing on one particular aspect of it, such as a hand?

What Is an Essay?

Differences between an Essay and a Paragraph

An essay is simply a paper composed of several paragraphs, rather than one paragraph. In an essay, subjects can and should be treated more fully than they would be in a single-paragraph paper.

The main idea or point developed in an essay is called the *thesis statement* or *thesis sentence* (rather than, as in a paragraph, the *topic sentence*). The thesis statement appears in the introductory paragraph, and it is then developed in the supporting paragraphs that follow. A short concluding paragraph closes the essay.

The Form of an Essay

The following diagram shows the form of an essay.

Introductory Paragraph

Introduction

Thesis statement

Plan of development:

Points 1, 2, 3

The *introduction* attracts the reader's interest.

The *thesis statement* (or *thesis sentence*) states the main idea advanced in the paper.

The *plan of development* is a list of points that support the thesis. The points are presented in the order in which they will be developed in the paper.

First Supporting Paragraph

Topic sentence (point 1)

Specific evidence

The *topic sentence* advances the first supporting point for the thesis, and the *specific evidence* in the rest of the paragraph develops that first point.

Second Supporting Paragraph

Topic sentence (point 2)

Specific evidence

The *topic sentence* advances the second supporting point for the thesis, and the *specific evidence* in the rest of the paragraph develops that second point.

Third Supporting Paragraph

Topic sentence (point 3)

Specific evidence

The *topic sentence* advances the third supporting point for the thesis, and the *specific evidence* in the rest of the paragraph develops that third point.

Concluding Paragraph

Summary, Conclusion, or both

A *summary* is a brief restatement of the thesis and its main points. A *conclusion* is a final thought or two stemming from the subject of the paper.

A Model Essay

Mike, the writer of the paragraph on working in a diner and truck stop (page 8), later decided to develop his subject more fully. Here is the essay that resulted.

Introductory paragraph

First supporting paragraph

Second supporting paragraph

Third supporting paragraph

Concluding paragraph

My Job at the Crescent Falls Diner and Truck Stop

[1]In the course of working my way through school, I have taken many jobs I would rather forget. [2]I have spent nine hours a day lifting heavy automobile and truck batteries off the end of an assembly belt. [3]I have risked the loss of eyes and fingers working a punch press in a textile factory. [4]I have served as a ward aide in a mental hospital, helping care for brain-damaged men who would break into violent fits at unexpected moments. [5]But none of these jobs was as dreadful as my job at the Crescent Falls Diner and Truck Stop. [6]The work was physically hard; the pay was poor; and, most of all, the working conditions were dismal.

[7]First, the job made enormous demands on my strength and energy. [8]For ten hours, I waited on tables, carried heavy trays of food and dirty dishes, cleaned bathrooms, and unloaded heavy cartons from delivery trucks. [9]The trays weighed from twenty to fifty pounds. [10]The cartons of food and restaurant supplies could weigh as much as 75 pounds, and I sometimes unloaded full truck trailers by myself.

[11]I would not have minded the difficulty of the work so much if the pay had not been so poor. [12]I was paid minimum wage, plus tips. [13]At first, I thought this would be fine, but then I learned that I would have to share my tips with the kitchen staff and cashiers. [14]The first night, I made over $50 in tips, but I brought home less than $8. [15]To make enough money for the following semester's college tuition, I had to work about sixty hours per week. [16]If I worked overtime, I was paid my regular hourly salary. [17]There was no overtime bonus.

[18]But even more than the low pay, what upset me about my job was the working conditions. [19]Sometimes, I had to wash dishes in a corner of the kitchen that was extremely hot and steamy. [20]Once, when unloading a large delivery truck, I strained my back and was laid up for about a week—without pay, of course! [21]Finally, the manager was a tyrant. [22]I never seemed to get my orders out quickly enough for him, nor could I ever clean the tables to his satisfaction. [23]He disliked and envied college students, and he went out of his way to favor other employees over me. [24]For example, while some of my co-workers got off for holidays, I was expected to work. [25]When I asked for two days off to attend a wedding in Georgia, he threatened to fire me. [26]He made negative comments about the way I combed my hair and the clothes I wore. [27]Once he even made a slur about my race.

[28]I stayed on the job for five months, all the while hating the difficulty of the work, the low pay, and the conditions under which I worked. [29]By the time I quit, I was determined never to do such degrading work again.

Important Points about the Essay

Introductory Paragraph

An introductory paragraph has certain purposes or functions and can be constructed using various methods.

Purposes of the Introduction

An introductory paragraph should do three things:

1. Attract the reader's *interest*. Using one of the suggested methods of introduction described under "Common Methods of Introduction" can help draw the reader into your paper.

2. Present a *thesis sentence*—a clear, direct statement of the central idea that you will develop in your paper. The thesis statement, like a topic sentence, should have a keyword or keywords reflecting your attitude about the subject. For example, in the essay on the Crescent Diner and Truck Stop job, the keyword is *dreadful*.

3. Indicate a *plan of development*—a preview of the major points that will support your thesis statement, listed in the order in which they will be presented. In some cases, the thesis statement and plan of development may appear in the same sentence. In other cases, the plan of development may be omitted.

Introductory Paragraphs	**ACTIVITY 1**

1. In "My Job at the Crescent Falls Diner and Truck Stop," which sentences are used to attract the reader's interest?

    _____ sentences 1 to 3   _____ 1 to 4   _____ 1 to 5

2. The thesis in "My Job at the Crescent Falls Diner and Truck Stop" is presented in

    _____ sentence 4   _____ sentence 5   _____ sentence 6

3. Is the thesis followed by a plan of development?

    _____ Yes   _____ No

4. Which words in the plan of development announce the three major supporting points in the essay? Write them below.

    a. _____

    b. _____

    c. _____

Common Methods of Introduction

Four common methods of introducing an essay are as follows:

a. Begin with a broad statement and narrow it down to your thesis statement.

b. Present an idea or situation that is the opposite of the one you will develop.

c. Tell a brief story.

d. Ask one or more questions.

| **ACTIVITY 2** | **Identifying Methods of Introduction** |

Following are four introductions. In the space provided, write the letter of the method of introduction used in each case. You may work with a partner to complete this activity.

_____ 1. Last week I was in the kitchen preparing dinner when I heard my nine-year-old daughter shriek from behind the computer. I was so startled that I dropped the knife onto the floor. As I ran to where she was doing her homework, she looked up, obviously stunned, and uttered, "That's *too* gross, Mom!" When I looked at the screen, I too was shocked to find an image that was clearly pornographic. Even though I thought I carefully monitored how my children used the computer, I did not realize that one wrong click could bring them to one of the million "adult" sites on the Internet. As a concerned parent, I urge all parents to install software on their home computers that blocks access to pornographic Web sites.

_____ 2. We Americans love our fast food. Instead of picking up groceries on the way home, we pick up a bucket of crispy fried chicken and a side of mashed potatoes and gravy. Instead of making a sandwich on whole-grain bread, we order a three-topping pizza with extra cheese. If fast food were nutritious, there would not be a problem, but most of the fast food we love is loaded with too much fat, sodium, and sugar. The sad reality is that at least a third of all Americans are battling obesity, and fast food is a leading culprit. If we prepare our meals at home, we can control the food we eat. We Americans, therefore, should say no to fast food and yes to home-cooked meals.

_____ 3. Most college students are hard working. They regularly attend classes and labs, they diligently take notes and ask questions, and they do their homework and study for exams. Even if a class is boring or an instructor is annoying, they still make an effort to learn. After all, these students are paying for their education. Some students, however, think that they are still in high school and carry over the mentality that "getting by" is good enough. Instructors should be able to dis-enroll slacker students—those who skip classes, borrow lecture notes, use paper mills, and cheat on exams—because they are taking up valuable seats that could be occupied by those students who truly want to learn.

_____ 4. What are your vices? Do you need your cigarettes even though you know that smoking causes lung cancer? Do you have one too many "cold ones" after a long day of work even though you know that you shouldn't? Do you find yourself lying even though you know that "honesty is the best policy"? Do you gamble? Do you do drugs? Have you cheated on someone? Most of us have bad habits that we know we should stop doing but don't until something terrible happens.

Supporting Paragraphs

Most essays have three supporting points, developed in three separate paragraphs. (Some essays will have two supporting points; others will have four or more.) Each of the supporting paragraphs should begin with a topic sentence that states the point to be detailed in that paragraph. Just as the thesis provides a focus for the entire essay, topic sentences provide a focus for each supporting paragraph.

Supporting Paragraphs	ACTIVITY 3

1. What is the topic sentence for the first supporting paragraph of "My Job at the Crescent Falls Diner and Truck Stop"? (*Write the sentence number here.*) _____

2. What is the topic sentence for the second supporting paragraph? _____

3. What is the topic sentence for the third supporting paragraph? _____

Transitional Sentences

In paragraphs, transitions and other connective devices (pages 67–73) are used to help link sentences. Similarly, in an essay, *transitional sentences* are used to help tie the supporting paragraphs together. Such transitional sentences usually occur near the end of one paragraph or the beginning of the next.

In "My Job at the Crescent Falls Diner and Truck Stop," the first transitional sentence is

I would not have minded the difficulty of the work so much if the pay had not been so poor.

In this sentence, the keyword *difficulty* reminds us of the point of the first supporting paragraph, while *pay* tells us the point to be developed in the second supporting paragraph.

| ACTIVITY 4 | **Transitional Sentences** |

Here is the other transitional sentence in "My Job at the Crescent Falls Diner and Truck Stop":

> But even more than the low pay, what upset me about my job was the working conditions.

Complete the following statement: In the preceding sentence, the key-words _____ echo the point of the second supporting para-graph, and the keywords _____ announce the topic of the third supporting paragraph.

Concluding Paragraph

The concluding paragraph often summarizes the essay by briefly restating the thesis and, at times, the main supporting points. Also, the conclusion brings the paper to a natural and graceful end, sometimes leaving the reader with a final thought on the subject.

| ACTIVITY 5 | **The Concluding Paragraph** |

1. Which sentence in the concluding paragraph of "My Job at the Crescent Falls Diner and Truck Stop" restates the thesis and supporting points of the essay? _____

2. Which sentence contains the concluding thought of the essay? _____

Essays to Consider

Read the following two student essays and then answer the questions that follow.

Definition of a Football Fan

[1]What is a football fan? [2]The word "fan" is an abbreviation of "fanatic," meaning "an insane or crazy person." [3]In the case of football fans, the term is appropriate. [4]They behave insanely, they are insane about the past, and they are insanely loyal.

[5]First of all, football fans just plain behave insanely. [6]They wear their official team T-shirts and warm-up jackets to the mall, the supermarket, the classroom, and even—if they can get away with it—to work. [7]If the team offers a giveaway item, the fans rush to the stadium to claim the hat or sports bag or water bottle that is being handed out that day. [8]Even the fact that fans spend the coldest months of

---

continued

the year huddled on icy metal benches in places like Chicago proves that fans behave insanely. [9]When they go to a game, which they do as often as possible, they also decorate their bodies. [10]True football fans not only put on their team jackets and grab their pennants, but they also paint their heads to look like helmets. [11]At the game, these fans devote enormous energy to trying to get a "wave" going.

[12]In addition, football fans are insanely fascinated by the past. [13]They talk about William "Refrigerator" Perry's 1985 Super Bowl touchdown as though it had happened last week. [14]They describe the "Fog Bowl" as if dense fog blanketed yesterday's game, not 1988's playoff match between the Philadelphia Eagles and the Chicago Bears. [15]They excitedly discuss John Elway's final game before retiring—when he won the 1999 Super Bowl and received MVP honors—as if it were current news. [16]If you can't manage to get excited about such ancient history, they look at you as though you were the insane one.

[17]Most of all, football fans are insanely loyal to the team of their choice, often dangerously so. [18]Should their beloved team lose three in a row, fans may begin to react negatively as a way to hide their broken hearts. [19]They still obsessively watch each game and spend the entire day afterward listening to the postgame commentary on TV. [20]Furthermore, this intense loyalty makes fans dangerous. [21]To anyone who dares to say to a loyal fan that another team has better players or coaches, or God forbid, to anyone wandering near the home cheering section wearing the jacket of the opposing team, physical injuries such as bloody noses, black eyes, and broken bones are real possibilities.

[22]From February through August, football fans act like any other human beings. [23]They pay their taxes, take out the garbage, and complain about the high cost of living. [24]However, when September rolls around, the team's colors are displayed, the sports record books come off the shelves, and the devotion returns. [25]For the true football fan, another season of insanity has begun.

An Interpretation of Lord of the Flies

[1]Modern history has shown us the evil that exists in human beings. [2]Assassinations are common, governments use torture to discourage dissent, and six million Jews were exterminated during World War II. [3]In Lord of the Flies, William Golding describes a group of schoolboys shipwrecked on an island with no authority figures to control their behavior. [4]One of the boys soon yields to dark forces within himself, and his corruption symbolizes the evil in all of us. [5]First, Jack Merridew kills a living creature; then, he rebels against the group leader; and finally, he seizes power and sets up his own murderous society.

[6]The first stage in Jack's downfall is his killing of a living creature. [7]In Chapter 1, Jack aims at a pig but is unable to kill. [8]His upraised arm

continued

pauses "because of the enormity of the knife descending and cutting into living flesh, because of the unbearable blood," and the pig escapes. [9]Three chapters later, however, Jack leads some boys on a successful hunt. [10]He returns triumphantly with a freshly killed pig and reports excitedly to the others, "I cut the pig's throat." [11]Yet Jack twitches as he says this, and he wipes his bloody hands on his shorts as if eager to remove the stains. [12]There is still some civilization left in him.

[13]After the initial act of killing the pig, Jack's refusal to cooperate with Ralph shows us that this civilized part is rapidly disappearing. [14]With no adults around, Ralph has made some rules. [15]One is that a signal fire must be kept burning. [16]But Jack tempts the boys watching the fire to go hunting, and the fire goes out. [17]Another rule is that at a meeting, only the person holding a special seashell has the right to speak. [18]In Chapter 5, another boy is speaking when Jack rudely tells him to shut up. [19]Ralph accuses Jack of breaking the rules. [20]Jack shouts: "Bollocks to the rules! We're strong—we hunt! If there's a beast, we'll hunt it down! We'll close in and beat and beat and beat—!" [21]He gives a "wild whoop" and leaps off the platform, throwing the meeting into chaos. [22]Jack is now much more savage than civilized.

[23]The most obvious proof of Jack's corruption comes in Chapter 8, when he establishes his own murderous society. [24]Insisting that Ralph is not a "proper chief" because he does not hunt, Jack asks for a new election. [25]After he again loses, Jack announces, "I'm going off by myself. . . . Anyone who wants to hunt when I do can come too." [26]Eventually, nearly all the boys join Jack's "tribe." [27]Following his example, they paint their faces like savages, sacrifice to "the beast," brutally murder two of their schoolmates, and nearly succeed in killing Ralph as well. [28]Jack has now become completely savage—and so have the others.

[29]Through Jack Merridew, then, Golding shows how easily moral laws can be forgotten. [30]Freed from grown-ups and their rules, Jack learns to kill living things, defy authority, and lead a tribe of murdering savages. [31]Jack's example is a frightening reminder of humanity's potential for evil. [32]The "beast" the boys try to hunt and kill is actually within every human being.

QUESTIONS

1. In which essay does the thesis statement appear in the last sentence of the introductory paragraph?

   _____

2. In the essay on <u>Lord of the Flies</u>, which sentence of the introductory paragraph contains the plan of development? __ _____

3. Which method of introduction is used in "Definition of a Football Fan"?

   a. General to narrow   c. Incident or story
   b. Stating importance of topic   d. One or more questions

4. Complete the following outline of "Definition of a Football Fan":

   a. _____

   b. _____

   c. _____

5. How does the essay "An Interpretation of <u>Lord of the Flies</u>" connect the first supporting paragraph with the second one?

   _____

6. *Complete the following statement:* Emphatic order is shown in the last supporting paragraph of "Definition of a Football Fan" with the words *most of all;* and in the last supporting paragraph of "An Interpretation of <u>Lord of the Flies</u>" with the words _____

7. Which essay uses time order as well as emphatic order to organize its three supporting paragraphs? _____

8. List four major transitions used in the supporting paragraphs of "An Interpretation of <u>Lord of the Flies</u>."

   a. _____   c. _____

   b. _____   d. _____

Planning the Essay

Outlining the Essay

When you write an essay, planning is crucial for success. You should plan your essay by outlining in two ways:

1. Prepare a scratch outline. This should consist of a short statement of the thesis followed by the main supporting points for the thesis. Here is Mike's scratch outline for his essay on the diner and truck stop:

Working at the Crescent Falls Diner and Truck Stop was my worst job.

1. Hard work

2. Poor pay

3. Bad working conditions

Do not underestimate the value of this initial outline—or the work involved in achieving it. Be prepared to do a good deal of plain hard thinking at this first and most important stage of your paper.

2. Prepare a more detailed outline. The outline form that follows will serve as a guide. Your instructor may ask you to submit a copy of this form either before you actually write an essay or along with your finished essay.

Form for Planning the Essay

To write an effective essay, use a form such as the one that follows.

Opening remarks

Thesis statement _____

_____

Plan of development

Topic sentence 1 _____

_____

Specific supporting evidence

Topic sentence 2 _____

_____

Specific supporting evidence

Topic sentence 3 _____

_____

Specific supporting evidence

Summary, closing remarks, or both

Practice in Writing the Essay

In this section, you will expand and strengthen your understanding of the essay form as you work through the following activities.

Understanding the Two Parts of a Thesis Statement

In this chapter, you have learned that effective essays center on a thesis, or main point, that a writer wishes to express. This central idea is usually presented as a *thesis statement* in an essay's introductory paragraph.

A good thesis statement does two things. First, it tells readers an essay's *topic*. Second, it presents the *writer's attitude, opinion, idea,* or *point* about that topic. For example, look at the following thesis statement:

> Celebrities are often poor role models.

In this thesis statement, the topic is *celebrities;* the writer's main point is that *celebrities are often poor role models.*

Topics and Main Points	ACTIVITY 6

For each thesis statement, single-underline the topic and double-underline the main point that the writer wishes to express about it.

1. My roommate Chang-Yoon helped me overcome prejudice.

2. Raising a family as a single parent can actually have certain benefits.

3. Being the eldest child has its own rewards.

4. Those who want to quit smoking should pledge to do so, throw away all their cigarettes, and ask their friends and family to support their brave efforts.

5. Internet advertisers use several media-savvy techniques to interact directly with online customers.

6. Jealousy often results from lack of self-confidence, lack of self-fulfillment, and lack of trust.

7. Parents should teach their children at an early age how to protect themselves from online predators.

8. My sales techniques benefitted greatly from a weekend seminar on customer needs, customer relationships, and customer negotiation.

9. Adults should feel free to engage in fun activities that they enjoyed as children.

10. Teachers should take certain steps to communicate more openly with their students.

Supporting the Thesis with Specific Evidence

The first essential step in writing a successful essay is to form a clearly stated thesis. The second basic step is to support the thesis with specific reasons or details.

To ensure that your essay will have adequate support, you may find an informal outline very helpful. Write down a brief version of your thesis idea, and then work out and jot down the three points that will support your thesis.

Here is the scratch outline that was prepared for one essay:

> The college cafeteria is poorly managed.
>
> The checkout lines are always long.
>
> The floor and tables are often dirty.
>
> Food choices are often limited.

A scratch outline like the previous one looks simple, but developing it often requires a good deal of careful thinking. The time spent on developing a logical outline is invaluable, though. Once you have planned the steps that logically support your thesis, you will be in an excellent position to go on to write an effective essay.

ACTIVITY 7	Using Specific Evidence

Following are five informal outlines in which two points (*a* and *b*) are already provided. Complete each outline by adding a third logical supporting point (*c*).

1. Success in college can be attributed to several reasons.
    a. Regularly attend classes
    b. Devote enough time to studying
    c. _____

2. *MySpace.com* is an important part of my life.
    a. Keep in touch with friends and family
    b. Share life's ups and downs
    c. _____

3. My "significant other" has three qualities I admire.
    a. Sense of humor
    b. Charming personality
    c. _____

4. A break-up is always filled with mixed feelings.
    a. Anger
    b. Sadness
    c. _____

5. Being promoted to shift manager was a mistake.
    a. Difficult to supervise employees who still see you as their equal
    b. Difficult to monitor employees who steal from the company
    c. _____

Identifying Introductions

The following box lists the six common methods for introducing an essay that are discussed in this chapter.

1. Broad statement	4. Incident or story
2. Contrast	5. Question
3. Relevance	6. Quotation

Methods of Introduction

ACTIVITY 8

Review the methods of introduction on pages 129–131 with a partner. Next, refer to the box preceding and read the following six introductory paragraphs. Together, in the space provided, write the number of the kind of introduction used in each paragraph. Each kind of introduction is used once.

Paragraph A _____

Is bullying a natural, unavoidable part of growing up? Is it something that everyone has to endure as a victim, practice as a bully, or tolerate as a bystander? Does bullying leave deep scars on its victims, or is it fairly harmless? Does being a bully indicate some deep-rooted problems, or is it not a big deal? These and other questions need to be looked at as we consider the three forms of bullying: physical, verbal, and social.

Paragraph B _____

In a perfect school, students would treat each other with affection and respect. Differences would be tolerated, and even welcomed. Kids would become more popular by being kind and supportive. Students would go out of their way to make sure one another felt happy and comfortable. But most schools are not perfect. Instead of being places of respect and tolerance, they are places where the hateful act of bullying is widespread.

Paragraph C _____

Students have to deal with all kinds of problems in schools. There are the problems created by difficult classes, by too much homework, or by personality conflicts with teachers. There are problems with scheduling the classes you need and still getting some of the ones you want. There are problems with bad cafeteria food, grouchy principals, or overcrowded classrooms. But one of the most difficult problems of all has to do with a terrible situation that exists in most schools: bullying.

Paragraph D _____

Eric, a new boy at school, was shy and physically small. He quickly became a victim of bullies. Kids would wait after school, pull out his shirt, and punch and shove him around. He was called such names as "Mouse Boy" and "Jerk Boy." When he sat down during lunch hour, others would leave his table. In gym games he was never thrown the ball, as if he didn't exist. Then one day he came to school with a gun. When the police were called, he told them he just couldn't take it anymore. Bullying had hurt him badly, just as it hurts many other students. Every member of a school community should be aware of bullying and the three hateful forms that it takes: physical, verbal, and social bullying.

Paragraph E _____

A British prime minister once said, "Courage is fire, and bullying is smoke." If that is true, there is a lot of "smoke" present in most schools today. Bullying in schools is a huge problem that hurts both its victims and the people who practice it. Physical, verbal, and social bullying are all harmful in their own ways.

Paragraph F _____

A pair of students bring guns and homemade bombs to school, killing a number of their fellow students and teachers before taking their own lives. A young man hangs himself on Sunday evening rather than attend school the following morning. A junior high school girl is admitted to the emergency room after cutting her wrists. What do all these horrible reports have to do with each other? All were reportedly caused by a terrible practice that is common in schools: bullying.

Revising an Essay for All Four Bases: Unity, Support, Coherence, and Sentence Skills

You know from your work on paragraphs that there are four bases a paper must cover to be effective. In the following activity, you will evaluate and revise an essay in terms of all four bases: *unity, support, coherence,* and *sentence skills.*

ACTIVITY 9   **Revising an Essay**

Comments follow each supporting paragraph and the concluding paragraph. Circle the letter of the *one* statement that applies in each case.

Paragraph 1: Introduction

A Group of People Who Should Be Helped

One day walking to class, I ran into a homeless man. He was dirty and disheveled. It looked and smelled like he hadn't bathed in days. My college is located downtown near a homeless shelter, and I guess the homeless like to stay close to the facility. He asked me for some change. At first I thought about how much pocket money I had, then quickly I thought about a comment I had heard on the news or in some magazine. It was about how some homeless ask for money so they can purchase drugs. So I offered to buy him a breakfast combo at the nearby fast-food place. I still remember what he told me: "Man, I just want some money. You gonna give me some or not?" I realized then he did not want my money for food, but for alcohol or drugs. That incident made me think about how much help these people need. A group of people that I believe should be helped is the homeless.

Paragraph 2: First Supporting Paragraph

Many homeless men are veterans of the United States. If we help them get back on their feet by providing them shelters and veterans' assistance, they would be able to become productive citizens once again. Many require medical attention that they can receive free through the local VA hospital. They can receive their monthly stipends from the government, so they can take care of their daily needs, like food and transportation. The VA hospitals and clinics can provide them with the necessary drug rehabilitation program that would allow them to take back their lives and no longer live on the streets begging for money to support their habits.

a. Paragraph 2 contains an irrelevant sentence.
b. Paragraph 2 lacks transition words.
c. Paragraph 2 lacks supporting details at one key spot.
d. Paragraph 2 contains a fragment and a run-on.

Paragraph 3: Second Supporting Paragraph

Another reason the homeless should be helped is that many homeless women are mothers too. These homeless mothers with children should be able to live in a safe and clean shelter while their children attend school. They should be provided with job training courses and also get any social service resource available from the local government. Often, these women can qualify for housing assistance, food stamps, and other free services. The only thing they need is to be steered in the right direction. This is important, for they are the role models for their children, and providing a stable environment for them is part of the American dream.

a. Paragraph 3 contains an irrelevant sentence.
b. Paragraph 3 lacks transition words.
c. Paragraph 3 lacks supporting details at one key spot.
d. Paragraph 3 contains a fragment and a run-on.

Paragraph 4: Third Supporting Paragraph

Finally, the most important reason why we should help the homeless is that they are living in the United States of America. We are the richest country in the world, and we should be able to provide for individuals when they can't provide for themselves. We spend countless dollars on objects like cars, houses, pets, and clothing. The communities in which they live should have volunteer efforts like food and clothing drives to aid those in need.

a. Paragraph 4 contains an irrelevant sentence.

b. Paragraph 4 lacks transition words.

c. Paragraph 4 lacks supporting details at one key spot.

d. Paragraph 4 contains a fragment and a run-on.

Paragraph 5: Concluding Paragraph

> Therefore, there are many reasons why a group of people I believe should be helped is the homeless. If we all make an effort to care for one another as a community. Help each other the best way we can, we can eliminate or ease some of the social ills in our communities.

a. Paragraph 5 contains an irrelevant sentence.

b. Paragraph 5 lacks transition words.

c. Paragraph 5 lacks supporting details at one key spot.

d. Paragraph 5 contains a fragment and a run-on.

Essay Assignments

WRITING ASSIGNMENT 1

Balancing School, Work, and Family Demands

Many college students struggle to balance school, work, and family. Write an essay about how you are able to balance the many demands in your life. In your introduction, you might begin with a brief story about a particular incident that illustrates your roles as a student, an employee, a spouse, a parent, a mentor, and/or a community member. End your introductory paragraph with your thesis statement and plan of development.

Here are some thesis statements that may help you think about and develop your own essay.

Thesis statement: Time management is the key to balancing my life as a college student, a single mom, and a full-time pharmacy technician.

(A *supporting* paragraph on managing your time as a college student, for example, might focus on the fact that you use a personal organizer and Post-it notes to keep track of your due dates.)

Thesis statement: The only way that I can juggle school, a girlfriend, and coaching is by taking good care of my health.

(A *supporting* paragraph on taking care of your health might explain how you and your girlfriend work out together at the gym and then cook a healthy—and romantic—meal together at home afterward.)

Thesis statement: I learned the hard way that I need at least seven hours of sleep each night if want to be a student on the dean's list, a loving parent to my three-year-old son, and a caregiver for my aging dad.

(A *supporting* paragraph on the need for adequate sleep could begin with this topic sentence: "If I get adequate sleep, I'm able to pay attention in class." Such a sentence might then be followed with some specific examples to support the main point of your paragraph.)

> **HINT**   Listing transitions such as *first of all, second, another, also, in addition, finally,* and so on may help you introduce your supporting paragraphs as well as set off different supporting details within those paragraphs.

WRITING ASSIGNMENT 2

Life Improvement

If you were given the time and resources to improve your life, what would you do and how would this change make your life better? Write an essay in which you describe what you would do, and then explain how this change would improve your life in three specific ways. Here are some examples:

> If I could pay off all my outstanding debts, I would improve my credit score, rent a larger apartment, and ask my girlfriend to marry me.

> If I had the time to go to school full-time, I would finish my college degree, apply for a full-time accountant job, and study for the CPA exam.

> If I didn't have to work the night shift, I would pick up my kids right after school, help them with their homework, and take them to the neighborhood park to play basketball before dinner.

To develop support for this essay, make a list of all the possible changes that you would like to make in your life. Don't worry about the practical details, such as cost. Then go back to your list and brainstorm all the benefits that each of these changes would bring to you. Alternatively, you could do some freewriting about the changes that you would like to see in your life. Use the ideas you generated to select one change and three positive effects. These prewriting techniques—listing and freewriting—are both helpful ways of getting started with an essay and thinking about it on paper.

WRITING ASSIGNMENT 3

Something Special

Imagine that your apartment or house is burning down. Of course, the best strategy would be to get yourself and others out of the building as quickly as possible. But suppose you knew for sure that you had time to rescue three of your possessions. Which three would you choose? Write an essay in which you discuss the three things in your home that you would most want to save from a fire.

Begin by doing some prewriting to find the items you want to write about. You could, for instance, try making a list and then choosing several of the most likely candidates. Then you could freewrite about each of those candidates. In this way, you are likely to find three possessions that will make strong subjects for this essay. Each will be the basis of a supporting paragraph. Each supporting paragraph will focus on why the object being discussed is so important to you. Make your support as specific and colorful as possible, perhaps using detailed descriptions, anecdotes, or quotations to reveal the importance of each object.

In planning your introduction, consider beginning with a broad, general idea and then narrowing it down to your thesis statement. Here, for example, is one such introduction for this paper:

> I have many possessions that I would be sad to lose. Because I love to cook, I would miss various kitchen appliances that provide me with

so many happy cooking adventures. I would also miss the wonderful electronic equipment that entertains me every day, including my large flat-screen TV and my Nintendo Wii. I would miss the various telephones on which I have spent many interesting hours chatting in every part of my apartment, including the bathtub. But if my apartment were burning down, I would most want to rescue three things that are irreplaceable and hold great meaning for me—the silverware set that belonged to my grandmother, my mother's wedding gown, and my giant photo album.

WRITING ASSIGNMENT 4

Teaching the Basics

What are you experienced in? Fixing cars? Growing flowers? Baking? Waiting on customers? Solving math problems? Write an essay teaching readers the basics of an activity in which you have some experience. If you're not sure about which activity to choose, use prewriting to help you find a topic you can support strongly. Once you've chosen your topic, continue to prewrite as a way to find your key points and organize them into three supporting paragraphs. The key details of waiting on customers in a diner, for instance, might be divided according to time order, as seen in the following topic sentences:

Topic sentence for supporting paragraph 1: Greeting customers and taking their orders should not be done carelessly.

Topic sentence for supporting paragraph 2: There are right and wrong ways to bring customers their food and to keep track of them during their meal.

Topic sentence for supporting paragraph 3: The final interaction with customers may be brief, but it is important.

HINT   To make your points clear, be sure to use detailed descriptions and concrete examples throughout your essay. Also, you may want to use transitional words such as *first, then, also, another, when, after, while,* and *finally* to help organize your details.

WRITING ASSIGNMENT 5

Advantages or Disadvantages of Single Life

More and more people are remaining single longer, and almost half of the people who marry eventually divorce and become single again. Write an essay on the advantages or disadvantages of single life. Each of your three supporting paragraphs will focus on one advantage or one disadvantage. To decide which approach to take, begin by making two lists. A list of advantages might include:

More freedom of choice

Lower expenses

Fewer responsibilities

Dating opportunities

A list of disadvantages could include:

Loneliness

Depression on holidays

Lack of support in everyday decisions

Disapproval of parents and family

Go on to list as many specific details as you can think of to support your advantages and disadvantages. Those details will help you decide whether you want your thesis to focus on benefits or drawbacks. Then create a scratch outline made up of your thesis statement and each of your main supporting points. Put the most important or most dramatic supporting point last.

In your introduction, you might gain your reader's interest by asking several questions or by telling a brief, revealing story about single life. As you develop your supporting paragraphs, make sure that each paragraph begins with a topic sentence and focuses on one advantage or disadvantage of single life. While writing the essay, continue developing details that vividly support each of your points.

In a concluding paragraph, provide a summary of the points in your paper as well as a final thought to round off your discussion. Your final thought might be in the form of a prediction or a recommendation.

Detailed writing assignments follow each of the twenty readings in Part 4. As you work on those assignments, you will find it helpful to turn back to the writing activities in this chapter.

REFLECTIVE ACTIVITY

1. Reread one of the essays you wrote for an assignment in this chapter. Does your essay have a thesis that states both a topic and a main point? If not, does that affect the effectiveness of the essay? In what way(s)? How might you rewrite this thesis to make it stronger?

2. Is the evidence you provided to support the thesis specific or is it vague and general? How can you make this detail more specific? What other detail might you add to improve the paragraph?

3. Is each of the essay's paragraphs unified and coherent? If not, what ways have you learned so far to correct the problem?

EXPLORING WRITING ONLINE

Visit a favorite Web site of yours and think about how its home page is like an introductory paragraph. Specifically, examine how the home page attracts readers' interest, presents a central idea, and provides an overview of the entire site. Then write an essay in which you present your analysis.

RESPONDING TO IMAGES

These three photographs of the Sistine Chapel's ceiling zoom in closer and closer to focus on Michelangelo's famous depiction of God's finger touching Adam's. Write a paragraph describing any one of these images. Then make an outline for a larger essay that compares and contrasts the three photographs.

For additional materials on Chapter 5, visit www.mhhe.com/langan.

In college, you may want to ask your classmates to give you feedback on your writing, and you may want to help them with their writing. As you are reading the following paragraph written by Deepak for a geology class, think about what advice you would offer him as he prepares to write his final draft by using the questions that follow.

The Sun's Effect

[1]The sun has an effect on the weather. [2]First, the sun warms the surface of the earth. [3]Some parts of land warm faster than others. [4]A parking lot, for instance, absorbs the sun's heat more quickly than a forest. [5]All land, however, absorbs the sun's heat faster than a body of water. [6]A forest, therefore, warms more quickly than a large lake or ocean. [7]The warmed land and water give off heat to the air above them. [8]The hot air rises, and it goes up, cooler air moves in to replace it. [9]In addition to the sun, clouds affect the weather.

QUESTIONS FOR DISCUSSION

1. The topic sentence (see above) states the paragraph's main point, which is a little broad. How could Deepak narrow and focus his topic sentence?

   _____

2. Does any sentence stray from the main point? If so, indicate the sentence.

   _____

3. What are some transitional words and phrases that Deepak uses in his paragraph?

   _____ _____ _____ _____ _____

EXPLORE WRITING FURTHER

4. Write a revision of this paragraph, using the checklist that follows as a guide.

5. How might this paragraph be turned into an essay? Make an outline that shows how Deepak might expand and develop his point.

A CHECKLIST: Four Bases

Unity

✔ Every sentence in my paragraph is relevant to my main point or topic sentence, which is _____ _____ .

✔ A sentence, detail, or word that I have omitted for the sake of unity is _____ _____ .

✔ The pattern or patterns of development I'm using serve my topic and point well because _____ _____ .

Support

✔ My main idea is supported by several supporting points or by one extended example, which are/is _____ .

✔ Several examples of specific evidence for this point/these points are:

_____

_____ .

✔ I appeal to my readers' five senses with vivid descriptions, such as _____ and _____ .

Coherence

✔ I use one or more patterns of development, which is/are _____ _____, to organize my paragraph.

✔ I use the following transition words or signals to make my paragraph easy for readers to follow:

_____ .

Sentence Skills

Grammar

✔ I use parallelism to balance my words and ideas. (pp. 295–303)

✔ I use pronouns and their antecedents correctly. (pp. 252–274)

✔ My paragraph includes no misplaced or dangling modifiers. (pp. 283–294)

✔ I read my paragraph out loud to help catch typos and awkward or grammatically incorrect sentences.

Style

✔ I use active verbs, rather than "is" and "to be." Some examples of active verbs I use are _____ and _____ . (pp. 249–250)

✔ I use a consistent point of view throughout the paragraph. It is written in the _____ person. (pp. 258–262)

✔ I use specific, concrete language throughout, avoiding vague or abstract words.

Notes

_____

_____

_____

_____

_____

_____

_____

_____

_____

_____

_____

_____

_____

_____

_____

_____

_____

_____

_____

_____

Sentence Skills

PART 3 WILL

- explain the basic skills needed to write clear, error-free sentences

- provide numerous activities so that you can practice these skills enough to make them habits

- In addition, each chapter in Part 3 concludes with one or more review tests, allowing you to immediately test your understanding of each skill

EXPLORING WRITING PROMPT:

We see short bits of writing on traffic signs, in restaurant menus, on flyers posted in hallways, on highway billboards, or in captions rolling along the bottom of our television screens. Sometimes, such writing is done quickly with little attention paid to editing for

SAT

FRIED CHICEN

correctness. During the next week, be particularly alert to such items. In a notebook or journal, keep a record of examples containing errors in spelling, punctuation, word choice, and other sentence skills—the areas covered in Part 3. You can start with the sign pictured above.

I

Sentences

RESPONDING TO IMAGES

1. *Why is the writing in the child's drawing a fragment? How might you make it a complete sentence? For more on fragments, see pp. 162–178.*

2. *This sign features a comma splice, which is a type of run-on sentence. What are two ways in which you could fix this error? For more on comma splices, see p. 180.*

3. *Would you pay less attention to a sign that was confusing or grammatically incorrect? Why or why not?*

Subjects and Verbs

INTRODUCTORY ACTIVITY

Understanding subjects and verbs is a major step toward mastering many sentence skills. As a speaker of English, you already have an instinctive feel for these basic building blocks of English sentences. See if you can insert an appropriate word in each space that follows. The answer will be a subject.

1. _Google_ is one of my favorite Web sites.

2. _Natasha_ told me a secret.

3. A _Drink_ is all I need to make me happy.

4. _My dad_ appeared in my dreams.

Now insert an appropriate word in the following spaces. Each answer will be a verb.

5. The student _Study_ for the exam.

6. My children _Learns_ much faster than I do.

7. Every night, I _TEXTS_ my friends.

8. Kalani _ran_ home right after class.

Finally, insert appropriate words in the following spaces. Each answer will be a subject in the first space and a verb in the second.

9. A _Man_ slowly _ran_ into the room.

10. Many _People_ today _use_ the Internet.

11. The _Doctor_ never _Called_ me.

12. The _Women_ nervously _Asked_ you for help.

The basic building blocks of English sentences are subjects and verbs. Understanding them is an important first step toward mastering a number of sentence skills.

Every sentence has a subject and a verb. Who or what the sentence speaks about is called the *subject*; what the sentence says about the subject is called the *verb*. In the following sentences, the subject is underlined once and the verb twice:

People gossip.

The truck belched fumes.

He waved at me.

Alaska contains the largest wilderness area in the United States.

That woman is a millionaire.

The pants feel itchy.

A Simple Way to Find a Subject

To find a subject, ask *who* or *what* the sentence is about. As shown below, your answer is the subject.

Who is the first sentence about? People

What is the second sentence about? The truck

Who is the third sentence about? He

What is the fourth sentence about? Alaska

Who is the fifth sentence about? That woman

What is the sixth sentence about? The pants

It helps to remember that the subject of a sentence is always a *noun* (any person, place, or thing) or a pronoun. A *pronoun* is simply a word like *he, she, it, you,* or *they* used in place of a noun. In the preceding sentences, the subjects are persons (*People, He, woman*), a place (*Alaska*), and things (*truck, pants*). And note that one pronoun (*He*) is used as a subject.

A Simple Way to Find a Verb

To find a verb, ask what the sentence *says about* the subject. As shown below, your answer is the verb.

What does the first sentence *say about* people? They gossip.

What does the second sentence *say about* the truck? It belched (fumes).

What does the third sentence *say about* him? He waved (at me).

What does the fourth sentence *say about* Alaska? It contains (the largest wilderness area in the United States).

What does the fifth sentence *say about* that woman? She is (a millionaire).

What does the sixth sentence *say about* the pants? They feel (itchy).

A second way to find the verb is to put *I, you, he, she, it,* or *they* in front of the word you think is a verb. If the result makes sense, you have a verb. For example, you could put *they* in front of *gossip* in the first sentence in the preceding list, with the result, *they gossip,* making sense. Therefore, you know that *gossip* is a verb. You could use the same test with the other verbs as well.

Finally, it helps to remember that most verbs show action. In "People gossip," the action is *gossiping*. In "The truck belched fumes," the action is *belching*. In "He waved at me," the action is *waving*. In "Alaska contains the largest wilderness area in the United States," the action is *containing*.

Certain other verbs, known as *linking verbs,* do not show action. They do, however, give information about the subject of the sentence. In "That woman is a millionaire," the linking verb *is* tells us that the woman is a millionaire. In "The pants feel itchy," the linking verb *feel* gives us the information that the pants are itchy.

Finding Subjects and Verbs

ACTIVITY 1

In each of the following sentences, draw one line under the subject and two lines under the verb.

> **HINT**   To find the subject, ask *who* or *what* the sentence is about. Then to find the verb, ask what the sentence *says about* the subject.

1. Rachel poured extra-virgin olive oil into the skillet.

2. The company offered a fifty-dollar rebate on every energy-efficient refrigerator bought during the month of June.

3. The talk show host introduced ten-year-old Drake as a future *American Idol* star.

4. Taryn adjusted the volume on her iPod as she entered the library.

5. The discarded cigarette butt burned a hole in the upholstery.

6. The bathroom upstairs is infested with cockroaches.

7. Royden tripped over the tangled cables behind my office desk.

8. The sports drink quenched my thirst.

9. The lawn trimmer tossed small rocks and other debris into the air.

10. Volunteers collected canned meats, beans, and peanut butter for the food bank.

ACTIVITY 2   Subjects and Linking Verbs

Follow the directions given for Activity 1. Note that all the verbs here are linking verbs.

> **HINT**   Who is item 1 about? What linking verb gives us information about them?

1. My parents are not very sociable.
2. I am always nervous on the first day of classes.
3. Tri Lee was the first person to finish the exam.
4. Our dog becomes friendly after a few minutes of growling.
5. Liz seems ready for a nervous breakdown.
6. That plastic hot dog looks good enough to eat.
7. Most people appear slimmer in clothes with vertical stripes. *sub ~~ver~~*
8. Many students felt exhausted after finishing the placement exam. *sub verb*
9. A cheeseburger has more than seven times as much sodium as French fries. *sub verb   sub verb*
10. Yesterday, my phone seemed to be ringing constantly. *sub verb*

ACTIVITY 3   Subjects and Verbs

Follow the directions given for Activity 1.

> **HINT**   What is item 1 about? What did they do?

1. The rabbits ate more than their share of my garden.
2. My father prefers his well-worn jeans to new ones.
3. A local restaurant donated food for the homeless.
4. Stanley always looks ready for a fight.
5. An elderly couple relaxed on a bench in the shopping mall.
6. Lightning brightened the dark sky for a few seconds.
7. Our town council voted for a curfew on Halloween.
8. Lynn's sore throat kept her home from work today.
9. Surprisingly, Charlotte's little sister decided not to go to the circus.
10. As usual, I chose the slowest checkout line in the supermarket.

More about Subjects and Verbs

Distinguishing Subjects from Prepositional Phrases

The subject of a sentence never appears within a prepositional phrase. A *prepositional phrase* is simply a group of words beginning with a preposition and ending with the answer to the question *what, when,* or *where.* Here is a list of common prepositions.

Common Prepositions				
about	before	by	inside	over
above	behind	during	into	through
across	below	except	of	to
among	beneath	for	off	toward
around	beside	from	on	under
at	between	in	onto	with

When you are looking for the subject of a sentence, it is helpful to cross out prepositional phrases.

In the middle of the night, we heard footsteps on the roof.

The magazines on the table belong in the garage.

Before the opening kickoff, a brass band marched onto the field.

The hardware store across the street went out of business.

In spite of our advice, Sally quit her job at Burger King.

Subjects and Prepositional Phrases	**ACTIVITY 4**

Cross out prepositional phrases. Then draw a single line under subjects and a double line under verbs.

> **HINT** What are the two prepositional phrases in item 1? What is the subject? What does the sentence say about her?

1. By accident, my girlfriend dropped her set of keys into the toilet at the public restroom.

2. Before the trial, the defense attorney quickly read through her trial notes.

3. My two-year-old daughter Olivia sleeps in my bed on stormy nights.

4. I applied for a pre-approved credit card from my bank.

5. On Friday nights, my family watches movies on our newly purchased LCD TV.

6. Over the weekend, Patrice wrote a five-page research paper on indigenous rights for her political science class.

7. The wireless connection from my neighbor's apartment allows me access to the Internet for free.

8. On Thursday, several foreign-born soldiers received U.S. citizenship during the naturalization ceremony at the Federal Building.

9. All my friends, except Nino, play the video game *Grand Theft Auto* on their home computers.

10. The spicy horseradish beneath the raw tuna in my *nigiri* sushi roll burned the back of my tongue.

Verbs of More Than One Word

Many verbs consist of more than one word. Here, for example, are some of the many forms of the verb *help*:

Some Forms of the Verb *Help*		
helps	should have been helping	will have helped
helping	can help	would have been helped
is helping	would have been helping	has been helped
was helping	will be helping	had been helped
may help	had been helping	must have helped
should help	helped	having helped
will help	have helped	should have been helped
does help	has helped	had helped

The following are sentences that contain verbs of more than one word:

Yolanda is working overtime this week.

Another book has been written about the Kennedy family.

We should have stopped for gas at the last station.

The game has just been canceled.

Words such as *not, just, never, only,* and *always* are not part of the verb, although they may appear within the verb.

Yolanda is not working overtime next week.

The boys should just not have stayed out so late.

The game has always been played regardless of the weather.

No verb preceded by *to* is ever the verb of a sentence.

Sue wants to go with us.

The newly married couple decided to rent a house for a year.

The store needs extra people to help out at Christmas.

No *-ing* word by itself is ever the verb of a sentence. (It may be part of the verb, but it must have a helping verb in front of it.)

We planning the trip for months. (This is not a sentence because the verb is not complete.)

We were planning the trip for months. (This is a complete sentence.)

Verbs of More than One Word ACTIVITY 5

Draw a single line under subjects and a double line under verbs. Be sure to include all parts of the verb.

HINT Who or what is item 1 about? What does it say about him, her, or them? What two words make up the verb?

1. Ellen has chosen blue dresses for her bridesmaids.
2. You should plan your weekly budget more carefully.
3. Felix has been waiting in line for tickets all morning.
4. We should have invited Terri to the party.
5. I would have preferred a movie with a happy ending.
6. Classes were interrupted three times today by a faulty fire alarm.
7. Sam can touch his nose with his tongue.
8. I have been encouraging my mother to quit smoking.
9. Joe has just agreed to feed his neighbor's fish over the holiday.
10. Many students have not been giving much thought to selecting a major.

Compound Subjects and Verbs

A sentence may have more than one verb:

The dancer stumbled and fell.

Eva washed her hair, blew it dry, and parted it in the middle.

A sentence may have more than one subject:

Cats and dogs are sometimes the best of friends.

The striking workers and their bosses could not come to an agreement.

A sentence may have several subjects and several verbs:

<u>Holly</u> and <u>I</u> <u>read</u> the book and <u>reported</u> on it to the class.

<u>Pete</u>, <u>Nick</u>, and <u>Fran</u> <u>caught</u> the fish in the morning, <u>cleaned</u> them in the afternoon, and <u>ate</u> them that night.

ACTIVITY 6   Compound Subjects and Verbs

Draw a single line under subjects and a double line under verbs. Be sure to mark *all* the subjects and verbs.

> **HINT**   What two things is item 1 about? What does it say about them?

1. Boards and bricks make a nice bookcase. *verb*
2. We bought a big bag of peanuts and finished it by the movie's end.
3. A fly and a bee hung lifelessly in the spider's web.
4. The twins look alike but think, act, and dress quite differently.
5. Canned salmon and tuna contain significant amounts of calcium.
6. I waited for the bubble bath to foam and then slipped into the warm tub.
7. The little girl in the next car waved and smiled at me.
8. The bird actually dived under the water and reappeared with a fish.
9. Singers, dancers, and actors performed at the heart-association benefit.
10. The magician and his assistant bowed and disappeared in a cloud of smoke. *Sub*

REVIEW TEST 1

Draw one line under the subjects and two lines under the verbs. To help find subjects, cross out prepositional phrases as necessary. Underline all the parts of a verb.

> **HINT**   You may find more than one subject and verb in a sentence.

1. Most noodle soups at the Vietnamese restaurant contain beef broth, flat rice noodles, and fresh basil leaves.
2. The security guard on duty at my workplace noticed a suspicious person lurking behind the warehouse.
3. The credit counseling center may be able to help me with my late payments.

4. After several minutes, the Chihuahua yelped loudly and scratched on the screen door.

5. Wireless carriers should not charge an early termination fee to cell phone users.

6. The project manager looked at the blueprints before visiting the job site.

7. Before the end of the day, Royce needs to call his son's teacher at school.

8. Between you and me, none of the children should have been running in the hall.

9. Thunderstorms and hurricanes swept through the northern part of the state.

10. Alberto used his employee discount to purchase a washing machine for his mom.

REVIEW TEST 2

Follow the directions given for Review Test 1.

1. Gasoline from the broken fuel line dripped onto the floor of the garage.

2. All the carrot tops in the garden had been eaten by rabbits.

3. An old man with a plastic trash bag collected aluminum cans along the road.

4. The majority of people wait until April 15 to file their income tax.

5. My brother became a college freshman at the age of forty-two.

6. At the delicatessen, Linda and Paul ate corned beef sandwiches and drank root beer.

7. The window fan made a clanking sound during the night and kept us from sleeping.

8. An umbrella tumbled across the street in the gusty wind and landed between two cars.

9. Telephones in the mayor's office rang continuously with calls from angry citizens about the city tax increase.

10. A teenager pushed a woman, grabbed her purse, and ran off through the crowd.

For additional material on Chapter 6, visit www.mhhe.com/langan.

Fragments

INTRODUCTORY ACTIVITY

Every sentence must have a subject and a verb and must express a complete thought. A word group that lacks a subject or a verb and does not express a complete thought is a *fragment*.

What follows are a number of fragments and sentences. See if you can complete the statement that explains each fragment.

1. Telephones. *Fragment*

    Telephones ring. *Sentence*

"Telephones" is a fragment because, although it has a subject (*Telephones*), it lacks a ___Verb___ (*ring*) and so does not express a complete thought.

2. Explains. *Fragment*

    Darrell explains. *Sentence*

"Explains" is a fragment because, although it has a verb (*Explains*), it lacks a _____ (*Darrell*) and does not express a complete thought.

3. Scribbling notes in class. *Fragment*

    Jayne was scribbling notes in class. *Sentence*

"Scribbling notes in class" is a fragment because it lacks a _____ (*Jayne*) and also part of the _____ (*was*). As a result, it does not express a complete thought.

4. When the dentist began drilling. *Fragment*

    When the dentist began drilling, I closed my eyes. *Sentence*

"When the dentist began drilling" is a fragment because we want to know *what happened when* the dentist began drilling. The word group does not follow through and _____.

Answers are on page 620.

What Fragments Are

Every sentence must have a subject and a verb and must express a complete thought. A word group that lacks a subject or a verb and does not express a complete thought is a *fragment.* Following are the most common types of fragments that people write:

- Dependent-word fragments

- *-ing* and *to* fragments

- Added-detail fragments

- Missing-subject fragments

Once you understand the specific kind or kinds of fragments that you might write, you should be able to eliminate them from your writing. The following pages explain all four types of fragments.

Dependent-Word Fragments

Some word groups that begin with a dependent word are fragments. Here is a list of common dependent words:

Common Dependent Words	
after	unless
although, though	until
as	what, whatever
because	when, whenever
before	where, wherever
even though	whether
how	which, whichever
if, even if	while
in order that	who
since	whose
that, so that	

Whenever you start a sentence with one of these dependent words, you must be careful that a dependent-word fragment does not result. The word group beginning with the dependent word *After* in the following selection is a fragment.

<u>After I stopped drinking coffee.</u> I began sleeping better at night.

A *dependent statement*—one starting with a dependent word such as *After*—cannot stand alone. It depends on another statement to complete the thought. "After I stopped drinking coffee" is a dependent statement. It leaves us hanging. We expect in the same sentence to find out *what happened after* the writer stopped drinking coffee. When a writer does not follow through and complete a thought, a fragment results.

To correct the fragment, simply follow through and complete the thought:

After I stopped drinking coffee, I began sleeping better at night.

Remember, then, that *dependent statements by themselves* are fragments. They must be attached to a statement that makes sense standing alone.

Here are two other examples of dependent-word fragments that need to be corrected.

Brian sat nervously in the dental clinic. <u>While waiting to have his wisdom tooth pulled.</u>

Maria decided to throw away the boxes. <u>That had accumulated for years in the basement.</u>

EXPLANATION: "While waiting to have his wisdom tooth pulled" is a fragment; it does not make sense standing by itself. We want to know in the same statement *what Brian did* while waiting to have his tooth pulled. The writer must complete the thought. Likewise, "That had accumulated for years in the basement" is not in itself a complete thought. We want to know in the same statement what *that* refers to.

How to Correct Dependent-Word Fragments

In most cases, you can correct a dependent-word fragment by attaching it to the sentence that comes after it or to the sentence that comes before it:

After I stopped drinking coffee, I began sleeping better at night.

(The fragment has been attached to the sentence that comes after it.)

Brian sat nervously in the dental clinic while waiting to have his wisdom tooth pulled.

(The fragment has been attached to the sentence that comes before it.)

Maria decided to throw away the boxes that had accumulated for years in the basement.

(The fragment has been attached to the sentence that comes before it.)

Another way of correcting a dependent-word fragment is to eliminate the dependent word and make a new sentence:

I stopped drinking coffee.

He was waiting to have his wisdom tooth pulled.

They had accumulated for years in the basement.

Do not use this second method of correction too frequently, however, because it may cut down on interest and variety in your writing style.

Use a comma if a dependent-word group comes at the *beginning* of a sentence:

After I stopped drinking coffee, I began sleeping better at night.

Identifying and Correcting Fragments

ACTIVITY 5

Underline the fragment in each selection that follows. Then make it a sentence by rewriting it, using the method described in parentheses.

EXAMPLE

My husband and I share the household chores. <u>Including meals.</u> I do the cooking and he does the eating.

(Add the fragment to the preceding sentence.)

My husband and I share the household chores, including meals.

1. Denise puts things off until the last minute. For example, waiting until the night before a test to begin studying.

   (Add the subject *she* and change *waiting* to the proper form of the verb, *waits*.)

   _____

   _____

2. My eleventh-grade English teacher picked on everybody. Except the athletes. They could do no wrong.

   (Add the fragment to the preceding sentence.)

   _____

   _____

3. Bernardo always buys things out of season. For example, an air conditioner in December. He saves a lot of money this way.

   (Add the subject and verb *he bought.*)

   _____

   _____

Identifying and Correcting Added-Detail Fragments

ACTIVITY 6

Underline the added-detail fragment in each selection. Then rewrite that part of the selection needed to correct the fragment. Use one of the three methods of correction described on page 170.

HINT   In item 1, attach the added-detail fragment to the preceding sentence.

1. My daughter faithfully watches the programs on the Disney Channel. Including *Hannah Montana, Wizards of Waverly Place,* and *The Suite Life of Zack and Cody.* She has never missed a single episode.

   _____

   _____

   _____

2. There are certain snacks I love to eat when I watch TV. Especially micro-wave popcorn. So I always try to keep several bags in the cupboard.

_____

_____

3. Some of the printers in the computer lab are unreliable. The ink-jet one, for instance. It often needs a new printer cartridge.

_____

_____

4. By noon, the stadium parking lot was packed with tailgaters. With some of them grilling barbeque ribs and drinking ice-cold beer.

_____

_____

5. Some Web sites contain annoying pop-up advertisements. For example, free online game Web sites. These sites are filled with distracting marketing messages.

_____

_____

Missing-Subject Fragments

In each example, underline the word group in which the subject is missing.

EXAMPLE 1

One example of my grandfather's generosity is that he visits sick friends in the hospital. <u>And takes along get-well cards with a few dollars folded in them.</u>

EXAMPLE 2

The weight lifter grunted as he heaved the barbells into the air. <u>Then, with a loud groan, dropped them.</u>

> **TIP** People write missing-subject fragments because they think the subject in one sentence will apply to the next word group as well. But the subject, as well as the verb, must be in *each* word group to make a sentence.

How to Correct Missing-Subject Fragments

1. Attach the fragment to the preceding sentence. Example 1 could read: "One example of my grandfather's generosity is that he visits sick friends in the hospital and takes along get-well cards with a few dollars folded in them."

» OR «

2. Add a subject (which can often be a pronoun standing for the subject in the preceding sentence). Example 2 could read: "Then, with a loud groan, he dropped them."

Correcting Missing-Subject Fragments

Underline the missing-subject fragment in each selection. Then rewrite that part of the selection needed to correct the fragment. Use one of the two methods of correction previously described.

 In item 1, the missing subject is *he*.

1. Jack tripped on his shoelace. Then looked around to see if anyone had noticed.

    HE (handwritten)

    _____

2. I started the car, And quickly turned down the blaring radio.

    I (handwritten)

    _____

3. The fire in the fireplace crackled merrily. Its orange-red flames shot high in the air, And made strange shadows all around the dark room.

    Then (handwritten)

    _____

    _____

4. The receptionist at that office is not very well trained. She was chewing gum and talking with a coworker at the same time she took my call. And forgot to take my name.

    EVEN (handwritten)

    _____

    _____

5. My elderly aunt never stands for long on a bus ride. She places herself in front of a seated young man. And stands on his feet until he gets up.

    _____

    _____

TIP   How to Check for Fragments

1. Read your paper aloud from the *last* sentence to the *first*. You will be better able to see and hear whether each word group you read is a complete thought.
2. If you think any word group is a fragment, ask yourself: Does this contain a subject and a verb and express a complete thought?
3. More specifically, be on the lookout for the most common fragments.
    *   Dependent-word fragments (starting with words such as *after*, *because*, *since*, *when*, and *before*)
    *   *-ing* and *to* fragments (*-ing* or *to* at or near the start of a word group)
    *   Added-detail fragments (starting with words such as *for example*, *such as*, *also*, and *especially*)
    *   Missing-subject fragments (a verb is present but not the subject)

ACTIVITY 8   Editing and Rewriting

Working with a partner, read the following short paragraph and underline the five fragments. Then use the space provided to correct the fragments. Feel free to discuss the rewrite quietly with your partner and refer back to the chapter when necessary.

---

¹Did you know that one in every five children is overweight? ²If you think that these kids will simply outgrow their "baby fat." ³You're wrong. ⁴The number of overweight children in this country has doubled in the past twenty years. ⁵Creating a health epidemic. ⁶Too many children spend hours watching television. ⁷And playing video games when they should be outside playing. ⁸They consume sugary, high-calorie snacks. ⁹When they should be eating fresh fruits and low-fat yogurt. ¹⁰These children are at a higher risk for high cholesterol, high blood pressure, and type 2 diabetes. ¹¹They are also more likely to be teased at school, miss school, and develop low self-esteem. ¹²These problems often follow them through adolescence and into adulthood. ¹³Sadly, overweight kids have a 70 percent greater chance of becoming overweight adults. ¹⁴Everyone, however, can make a difference. ¹⁵For example, being a positive role model. ¹⁶So, live a healthy life. ¹⁷Turn off your television and take a twenty-minute walk.

---

1. _____

    _____

2. _____

    _____

3. _____

    _____

4. _____

    _____

5. _____

ACTIVITY 9   Creating Sentences

Working with a partner, make up your own short fragments test as directed.

1. Write a dependent-word fragment in the space below. Then correct the fragment by making it into a complete sentence. You may want to begin your fragment with the word *before, after, when, because,* or *if.*

    Fragment _____

    Sentence _____

2. In the space below, write a fragment that begins with a word that has an *-ing* ending. Then correct the fragment by making it into a complete sentence. You may want to begin your fragment with the word *laughing, walking, shopping,* or *talking.*

   Fragment _____

   Sentence _____

3. Write an added-detail fragment in the space below. Then correct the fragment by making it into a complete sentence. You may want to begin your fragment with the word *also, especially, except,* or *including.*

   Fragment _____

   Sentence _____

REFLECTIVE ACTIVITY

1. Look at the paragraph that you revised in Activity 8. How has correcting fragments improved the paragraph? Is it clearer? Easier to read? Explain.

2. Explain what it is about fragments that you find most difficult to remember and apply. Use an example to make your point clear. Feel free to refer to anything in this chapter.

REVIEW TEST 1

Turn each of the following word groups into a complete sentence. Use the space provided.

EXAMPLES

Wanting to impress everyone
Wanting to impress everyone, I told a white lie.

Until the semester begins
Until the semester begins, I plan to work forty hours a week.

1 After we left the classroom

   _____

2. Whenever the weather is bad

   _____

3. Behind the TV stand

   _____

4. If I am late for my class

   _____

5. Tyler, who is extremely successful

_____

6. To get to trust each other better

_____

7. Which was surprising

_____

8. Will see me tomorrow

_____

9. Texting a message on my phone

_____

10. Guessing the answer

_____

REVIEW TEST 2

Underline the fragment in each item that follows. Then correct the fragment in the space provided.

EXAMPLE

Sam received all kinds of junk mail. <u>Then complained to the post office.</u> Eventually, some of the mail stopped coming.

Then he complained to the post office.

1. Fascinated, Nina stared at the stranger. Who was standing in the door-way. She wondered if she could convince him they had met before.

_____

_____

2. Trees can survive on a steep mountain slope if they obey two rules. They must grow low to the ground. And bend with the wind.

_____

_____

3. While waiting in line at the supermarket. I look in people's baskets. Their food choices give hints about their personalities.

_____

_____

4. I saw spectacular twin rainbows through the kitchen window. So I rushed to get my camera. To take a picture before they vanished.

_____

_____

5. Whenever you buy cotton clothes, get them one size too large. By allowing for shrinkage. You will get a longer life out of them.

_____

_____

6. My nutty cousin cuts the address labels off his magazines. Then pastes them on envelopes. This way, he doesn't have to write his return address.

_____

_____

7. Marian never has to buy ketchup or mustard. Because she saves the extra packets that come with fast-food orders.

_____

_____

8. The soccer players were amazing. Using their feet as well as most people use their hands.

_____

_____

9. My husband climbed his first mountain yesterday. Now he's calling all our friends. To tell them about his peak experience.

_____

_____

10. The trivia book listed some interesting facts about Babe Ruth. For instance, he spoke German fluently. Also, kept cool on hot days by putting wet cabbage leaves under his cap.

_____

_____

REVIEW TEST 3

In the space provided, write *C* if a word group is a complete sentence; write *frag* if it is a fragment. The first two are done for you.

*frag* 1. When the bus drivers went on strike.

_C_ 2. I saw many people giving rides to strangers.

_____ 3. Some even drove out of their way for others.

Frag   4. Especially when the weather was bad.

_C_   5. One rainy day, I saw an elderly woman pull her cab over to the curb.

Frag   6. Yelling and waving for five shivering students to get into her car.

Frag   7. Until the strike finally ended.

_C_   8. Scenes like that were not uncommon.

_C_   9. It seems that community problems bring people together.

Frag   10. By weakening the feeling that we live very separate lives.

Now correct the *fragments* you have found. Attach each fragment to the sentence that comes before or after it, or make whatever other change is needed to turn the fragment into a sentence. Use the space provided. The first one is corrected for you.

1. *When the bus drivers went on strike, I saw many people giving rides to strangers.*

2. _____

   _____

3. _____

   _____

4. _____

5. _____

   _____

REVIEW TEST 4

On separate paper, write quickly for five minutes about the town or city where you live. Don't worry about spelling, punctuation, finding exact words, or organizing your thoughts. Just focus on writing as many words as you can without stopping.

After you have finished, go back and make whatever changes are needed to correct any fragments in your writing.

For additional materials on Chapter 7, visit www.mhhe.com/langan.

Run-Ons

INTRODUCTORY ACTIVITY

A run-on occurs when two sentences are run together with no adequate sign given to mark the break between them. Shown below are four run-on sentences, each followed by a correct sentence. See if you can complete the statement that explains how each run-on is corrected.

1. A man coughed in the movie theater, the result was a chain reaction of copycat coughing.

    A man coughed in the movie theater. The result was a chain reaction of copycat coughing.

The run-on has been corrected by using a _Period_ and a capital letter to separate the two complete thoughts.

2. I heard laughter inside the house, no one answered the bell.

    I heard laughter inside the house, but no one answered the bell.

The run-on has been corrected by using a joining word, _but_ , to connect the two complete thoughts.

3. A car sped around the corner, it sprayed slush all over the pedestrians.

    A car sped around the corner; it sprayed slush all over the pedestrians.

The run-on has been corrected by using a _Semicolon_ to connect the two closely related thoughts.

4. I had a campus map, I still could not find my classroom building.

    Although I had a campus map, I still could not find my classroom building.

The run-on has been corrected by using the subordinating word _Although_ to connect the two closely related thoughts.

Answers are on page 620.

What Are Run-Ons?

A *run-on* is two complete thoughts that are run together with no adequate sign given to mark the break between them. As a result of the run-on, the reader is confused, unsure of where one thought ends and the next one begins. Two types of run-ons are fused sentences and comma splices.

Some run-ons have no punctuation at all to mark the break between two or more thoughts. Such run-ons are known as *fused sentences:* They are fused or joined together as if they were only one thought.

Fused Sentence

Rita decided to stop smoking she didn't want to die of lung cancer.

Fused Sentence

The exam was postponed the class was canceled as well.

In other run-ons, known as *comma splices,* a comma is used to connect or "splice" together the two complete thoughts. However, a comma alone is *not enough* to connect two complete thoughts. Some connection stronger than a comma alone is needed.

Comma Splice

Rita decided to stop smoking, she didn't want to die of lung cancer.

Comma Splice

The exam was postponed, the class was canceled as well.

Comma splices are the most common kind of run-on. Students sense that some kind of connection is needed between thoughts, so they put a comma at the dividing point. But the comma alone is *not sufficient.* A stronger, clearer mark is needed between the two thoughts.

TIP   Some instructors refer to each complete thought in a run-on as an *independent clause*. A *clause* is simply a group of words having a subject and a verb. A clause may be *independent* (expressing a complete thought and able to stand alone) or *dependent* (not expressing a complete thought and not able to stand alone). A run-on is two independent clauses that are run together with no adequate sign given to mark the break between them.

Some instructors believe that the term *run-ons* should be applied only to fused sentences, not to comma splices. But for many other instructors, and for our purposes in this book, the term *run-on* applies equally to fused sentences and comma splices. The bottom line is that you do not want either fused sentences or comma splices in your writing.

A Warning: Words That Can Lead to Run-Ons

People often write run-ons when the second complete thought begins with one of the following words. Be on the alert for run-ons whenever you use these words:

Common Dependent Words		
after	before	unless
although	even though	until
as	if	when
because	since	while

Using Dependent Words   ACTIVITY 9

Choose a logical dependent word from the preceding box and write it in the space provided.

EXAMPLE

_____Until_____ I was six, I thought chocolate milk came from brown cows.

HINT In item 1, which dependent word best signals that something extends from the past (July 4, 2008) to the present?

1. Will hasn't had a cigarette __Since__ July 4, 2008.
2. __Until__ you're willing to work hard, don't sign up for Professor Dunn's class.
3. The lines at that supermarket are so long __because__ there are too few cashiers.
4. __When__ reading the scary novel, my sister had nightmares for days.
5. My boss gave me smoked salmon for my birthday __even though__ he knows I'm a vegetarian.

Using Subordination   ACTIVITY 10

Rewrite the five sentences that follow (all taken from this chapter) so that one idea is subordinate to the other. Use one of the dependent words from the box "Common Dependent Words."

EXAMPLE

Auto races no longer use gasoline; spectators have nothing to fear from exhaust fumes.

Since auto races no longer use gasoline, spectators have nothing to fear from

exhaust fumes.

HINT For item 1, select a dependent word that logically connects the two ideas (a wish to stop smoking and a wish not to gain weight).

Even though)

Since

~~1.~~ I want to stop smoking; I don't want to gain weight.

_____

_____

Since

Even though

2. It was too hot indoors to study; I decided to go down to the shopping center for ice cream.

_____

_____

Although)   *Although,*

3. He had hair implants; it looked very natural.

_____

_____

When)   *While*

4. Professor Williams scowled at the class; her facial expression told the story.

_____

_____

Although)

5. This world map was published only three years ago; the names of some countries are already out of date.

_____

_____

ACTIVITY 11   Editing and Rewriting

Working with a partner, read carefully the short paragraph that follows and underline the five run-ons. Then use the space provided to correct the five run-ons. Feel free to discuss the rewrite quietly with your partner and refer back to the chapter when necessary.

¹When Mark began his first full-time job, he immediately got a credit card. A used sports car was his first purchase. ²Then he began to buy expensive clothes that he could not afford. He also bought impressive gifts for his parents and his girlfriend. ³Several months passed before Mark realized that he owed an enormous amount of money. ⁴To make matters worse, his car broke down. A stack of bills suddenly seemed to be due at once. ⁵Mark tried to cut back on his purchases. He soon realized he had to cut up his credit card to prevent himself from using it. ⁶He also began keeping a careful record of his spending. He had no idea where his money had gone till then. ⁷He hated to admit to his family and friends that he had to get his budget under control. ⁸However, his girlfriend said she did not mind inexpensive dates, and his parents were proud of his growing maturity.

2. Then he began to buy expensive clothes, *stop here* That he could not afford, he also bought impressive gifts for his parent, and his girlfriends.

6.

Creating Sentences

ACTIVITY 12

Working with a partner, make up your own short run-ons test as directed.

1. Write a run-on sentence. Then rewrite it, using a period and a capital letter to separate the thoughts into two sentences.

   Run-on

   _____

   Rewrite

   _____

2. Write a sentence that has two complete thoughts. Then rewrite it, using a comma and a joining word to correctly join the complete thoughts.

   Two complete thoughts

   _____

   Rewrite

   _____

3. Write a sentence that has two complete thoughts. Then rewrite it, using a semicolon to correctly join the complete thoughts.

   Two complete thoughts

   _____

   Rewrite

   _____

REFLECTIVE ACTIVITY

1. Look at the paragraph that you revised in Activity 11. Explain how run-ons affect the paragraph.

2. In your own written work, which type of run-on are you most likely to write: comma splices or fused sentences? Why do you tend to make this kind of mistake?

3. Which method for correcting run-ons are you most likely to use in your own writing? Which are you least likely to use? Why?

REVIEW TEST 1

In the space provided, write *R-O* beside run-on sentences. Write *C* beside the one sentence that is punctuated correctly. Some of the run-ons have no punctuation between the two complete thoughts; others have only a comma.

Correct each run-on by using (1) a period and a capital letter; (2) a comma and a joining word *and, but, for, so*; or (3) a semicolon. Do not use the same method of correction for every sentence.

EXAMPLE

_____R-O_____ Sam never saved his work, so he lost his paper when his computer crashed.

_____R-O_____ 1. Americans spend millions of dollars each year on bottled water, but critics argue that tap water is equally safe to drink.

_____R-O_____ 2. Isaiah is confident that the trucking company will hire him, and he has a valid CDL license and a clean traffic abstract.

_____R-O_____ 3. The mechanic said that many hybrid cars have transmission problems, so I am glad that I purchased a gasoline-powered subcompact car, which is equally fuel efficient.

_____R-O_____ 4. This summer brought record-breaking drought conditions, so many farmers are being forced to plant fewer crops or irrigate water into their fields.

_____R-O_____ 5. Sydney decided to use recycled plastic to build an outdoor deck, her children asked her to build a doghouse with the extra lumber.

_____R-O_____ 6. Mark worried that the canned chili sauce he ate while on his camping trip was recalled for botulism, but he did not experience any symptoms of food poisoning.

_____R-O_____ 7. Parents who sign up their children for mixed martial arts, hope that the sport will provide physical exercise, self-confidence, and personal discipline, their children; however, say that they are simply having fun.

[handwritten: 2 Then he began to buy expensive clothes +r 2]

_____ 8. The Ladies Professional Golf Association (LPGA) was founded in 1950, making it the oldest female professional sports organization in the United States.

__R-O__ 9. Witnesses reported that the bank robber was a woman, *[but]* security cameras revealed that the thief was a man carrying a handbag and wearing a wig and lipstick.

__R-O__ 10. Today, the average American teenager works 16 hours per week parents and educators are concerned that these part-time jobs leave little time for homework or sleep.

REVIEW TEST 2

Correct each run-on by using subordination. Choose from among the following dependent words.

after	before	unless
although	even though	until
as	if	when
because	since	while

EXAMPLE

Tony hated going to a new barber, he was afraid of butchered hair.

Because Tony was afraid of butchered hair, he hated going to a new barber.

1. Mom was frying potatoes, the heat set off the smoke alarm.

_____

_____

2. I love animals I'm not ready to take on the responsibility of a pet.

_____

_____

3. Lani leaves a lecture class, she reviews and clarifies her notes.

_____

_____

4. Matthew jogs, he thinks over his day's activities.

_____

_____

5. My mother puts apples in the fruit bowl she first washes the wax off them.

_____

_____

6. I began to shake on the examining table the nurse reached out and held my hand.

_____

_____

7. Some pets are easy to care for, others require patience and lots of hard work.

_____

_____

8. Molly forgot to turn the oven off her homemade bread looked like burned toast.

_____

_____

9. A wheel hit a crack in the sidewalk the skateboard shot out from under Dan.

_____

_____

10. John Grisham and Stephen King make huge fortunes with their novels most writers barely make a living.

_____

_____

REVIEW TEST 3

On a separate piece of paper, write six sentences, each of which has two complete thoughts. In two of the sentences, use a period and a capital letter between the thoughts. In another two sentences, use a comma and a joining word (*and, but, or, nor, for, so, yet*) to join the thoughts. In the final two sentences, use a semicolon to join the thoughts.

REVIEW TEST 4

Write for five minutes about something that makes you angry. Don't worry about spelling, punctuation, finding exact words, or organizing your thoughts. Just focus on writing as many words as you can without stopping.

After you have finished, go back and make whatever changes are needed to correct any run-on sentences in your writing.

For additional materials on Chapter 8, visit www.mhhe.com/langan.

CHAPTER 9

Sentence Variety I

Four Traditional Sentence Patterns

Sentences in English are traditionally described as *simple, compound, complex,* or *compound-complex.*

The Simple Sentence

A simple sentence has a single subject-verb combination.

Children play.

The game ended early.

My car stalled three times last week.

The lake has been polluted by several neighboring streams.

A simple sentence may have more than one subject:

Lola and Tony drove home.

The wind and heat dried my hair.

or more than one verb:

The children smiled and waved at us.

The lawn mower smoked and sputtered.

or several subjects and verbs:

Manny, Kira, and Jack lubricated my car, replaced the oil filter, and cleaned the spark plugs.

The Simple Sentence	ACTIVITY 1

On separate paper, write:

Three sentences, each with a single subject and verb

Three sentences, each with a single subject and a double verb

Three sentences, each with a double subject and a single verb

In each case, underline the subject once and the verb twice. (See pages 150–161 if necessary for more information on subjects and verbs.)

The Compound Sentence

A compound, or "double," sentence is made up of two (or more) simple sentences. The two complete statements in a compound sentence are usually connected by a comma plus a joining word (*and, but, for, or, nor, so, yet*).

A compound sentence is used when you want to give equal weight to two closely related ideas. The technique of showing that ideas have equal importance is called *coordination.*

Following are some compound sentences. Each sentence contains two ideas that the writer considers equal in importance.

The rain increased, so the officials canceled the game.

Denise wanted to go shopping, but Fred refused to drive her.

Hollis was watching television in the family room, and April was upstairs on the phone.

I had to give up wood carving, for my arthritis had become very painful.

ACTIVITY 2   **The Compound Sentence**

Combine the following pairs of simple sentences into compound sentences. Use a comma and a logical joining word (*and, but, for, so*) to connect each pair.

> **HINT**   If you are not sure what *and, but, for,* and *so* mean, review
> page 184.

EXAMPLE

- The children wanted to eat pizza.
- I picked up fried chicken on the way home.
  The children wanted to eat pizza, but I picked up fried chicken on the way
  home.

1. • I am majoring in digital media arts.
   • I hope to find a job doing video-game animation.
   I am majoring in digital media arts and

2. • My children were spending too much time in front of the TV and computer, so I
   • I signed up my entire family for a one-year gym membership.

3.   • Nicole's skin was blemished and sun damaged, *so*

   • She consulted with a plastic surgeon about a chemical face peel.

   _____

   _____

4.   • Riley insists on buying certified-organic fruits and vegetables, ~~so~~ *but*

   • I cannot distinguish organic from conventionally grown produce.

   _____

   _____

5.   • I was recently promoted to shift manager at work, *so*

   • I need to drop down to part-time status at school next semester.

   _____

   _____

Writing Compound Sentences   ACTIVITY 3

On a separate piece of paper, write five compound sentences of your own.
Use a different joining word (*and, but, for, or, nor, so, yet*) to connect the two
complete ideas in each sentence.

The Complex Sentence

A complex sentence is made up of a simple sentence (a complete statement) and a statement that begins with a dependent word. Here is a list of
common dependent words:

Dependent Words		
after	if, even if	when, whenever
although, though	in order that	where, wherever
as	since	whether
because	that, so that	which, whichever
before	unless	while
even though	until	who
how	what, whatever	whose

> **TIP**   The two parts of a complex sentence are sometimes called an
> *independent clause* and a *dependent clause*. A *clause* is simply a word group that
> contains a subject and a verb. An *independent clause* expresses a complete
> thought and can stand alone. A *dependent clause* does not express a complete
> thought in itself and "depends on" the independent clause to complete its mean-
> ing. Dependent clauses always begin with a dependent or subordinating word.

A complex sentence is used when you want to emphasize one idea over another in a sentence. Look at the following complex sentence:

Because I forgot the time, I missed the final exam.

The idea that the writer wants to emphasize here—*I missed the final exam*—is expressed as a complete thought. The less important idea—*Because I forgot the time*—is subordinated to the complete thought. The technique of giving one idea less emphasis than another is called *subordination*.

Following are other examples of complex sentences. In each case, the part starting with the dependent word is the less emphasized part of the sentence.

While Aisha was eating breakfast, she began to feel sick.

I checked my money *before* I invited Pedro for lunch.

When Jerry lost his temper, he also lost his job.

Although I practiced for three months, I failed my driving test.

ACTIVITY 4	**Creating Complex Sentences**

Use logical dependent words to combine the following pairs of simple sentences into complex sentences. Place a comma after a dependent statement when it starts the sentence.

EXAMPLE

- I applied for a low-interest student loan.
- I spoke to a financial aid counselor about my options.

    After I spoke to a financial aid counselor about my options, I applied for a

    low-interest student loan.

> **HINT**   In item 1, use the dependent word *while*.

while

1. • Lydia read the quarterly reports,
   • Her assistant drove them to a regional sales meeting.

   _____

2. *While* Keiko laughed hysterically,
   after • She heard the punch line to the joke.

   _____

   _____

3. • I wanted to order the chef's seafood special. *, before*

   • The kitchen ran out of fresh prawns.

   _____

   _____

4. • Raymond refuses to drink from a public water fountain. *Since*

   • He is afraid that he will catch an infectious disease.

   _____

   _____

5. *because* • I want to register for a calculus class. *, ~~but~~*

   • I need to take the math placement exam.

   _____

   _____

Using Subordination

Rewrite the following sentences, using subordination rather than coordination. Include a comma when a dependent statement starts a sentence.

EXAMPLE

The hair dryer was not working right, so I returned it to the store.

Because the hair dryer was not working right, I returned it to the store.

_____

HINT   In item 1, use the dependent word *as*.

1. Carlo set the table, *~~and~~* *as* his wife finished cooking dinner.

   _____

   _____

2. Maggie could have gotten good grades, *Although* ~~but~~ she did not study enough.

   _____

   _____

3. I watered my drooping African violets, ~~and~~ they perked right up.

   Apply or Because

   _____

CONNECT WRITING

Meet Emilio. He and his family just returned home from a trip where they received incredibly poor service at their hotel. He is writing a letter to the hotel manager about the experience. He has all the facts listed, but his ideas don't seem to connect in any clear way. Help Emilio connect his ideas by creating complex sentences using subordination.

mhconnectwriting.com

Even though

4. The little boy kept pushing the "down" button, but the elevator didn't come any more quickly.

_____

_____

5. I never really knew what pain was, and then I had four impacted wisdom teeth pulled at once.

_____

_____

ACTIVITY 6 | **Using *Who*, *Which*, or *That***

Combine the following simple sentences into complex sentences. Omit repeated words. Use the dependent words *who, which,* or *that.*

> **HINT**
> - The word *who* refers to persons.
> - The word *which* refers to things.
> - The word *that* refers to persons or things.

Use commas around the dependent statement only if it seems to interrupt the flow of thought in the sentence. (See pages 365–378 for more about commas.)

EXAMPLES

- Clyde picked up a hitchhiker.
- The hitchhiker was traveling around the world.

  Clyde picked up a hitchhiker who was traveling around the world.

  _____

- Larry is a sleepwalker.
- Larry is my brother.

  Larry, who is my brother, is a sleepwalker.

  _____

1. - Karen just gave birth to twins.
   - Karen is an old friend of mine. *Who*

   _____

2. • The tea burned the roof of my mouth. *Which*

   • The tea was hotter than I expected.

   _____

   _____

3. • I dropped the camera. *that*

   • My sister had just bought the camera.

   _____

   _____

4. • Ashaki brought us some enormous oranges.

   • Ashaki *who* is visiting from California,

   _____

   _____

5. • Liz used a steam cleaner to shampoo her rugs. *Which*

   • The rugs were dirtier than she had expected.

   _____

   _____

Writing Complex Sentences   ACTIVITY 7

On a separate piece of paper, write eight complex sentences, using, in turn, the dependent words *unless, if, after, because, when, who, which,* and *that.*

The Compound-Complex Sentence

A compound-complex sentence is made up of two (or more) simple sentences and one or more dependent statements. In the following examples, there is a solid line under the simple sentences and a dotted line under the dependent statements.

> When the power line snapped, Jack was listening to the stereo, and Linda was reading in bed.

> After I returned to school following a long illness, the math teacher gave me makeup work, but the history teacher made me drop her course.

Using Joining Words and Dependent Words   ACTIVITY 8

Read through each sentence to get a sense of its overall meaning. Then insert a logical joining word (*and, or, but, for,* or *so*) and a logical dependent word (*because, since, when,* or *although*).

HINT In item 1, use *after* and *for.*

1. _____ you listen to our professor's lecture, read the assigned pages in the textbook, _____ the information will be much more relevant.

2. _____ I ride the bus to work, I always intend to read the newspaper, _____ I usually end up listening to new songs on my iPod.

3. My daughter told the truth _____ I asked her about skipping classes, _____ she also explained why she hates junior high school.

4. _____ I am on a strict budget now, I am trying to resist buying lattes at Starbucks, _____ I brew myself coffee before leaving the house.

5. Daniel wanted to attend the event, _____ he had to work a double shift _____ several of his coworkers called in sick.

| ACTIVITY 9 | Writing Compound-Complex Sentences |

On a separate piece of paper, write five compound-complex sentences.

Review of Subordination and Coordination

Subordination and coordination are ways of showing the exact relationship of ideas within a sentence. Through **subordination,** we show that one idea is less important than another. When we subordinate, we use dependent words such as *when, although, while, because,* and *after.* (See the list of common dependent words on page 197.) Through **coordination,** we show that ideas are of equal importance. When we coordinate, we use the words *and, but, for, or, nor, so,* and *yet.*

| ACTIVITY 10 | Using Subordination or Coordination |

Working with a fellow classmate, use subordination or coordination to combine the following groups of simple sentences into one or more longer sentences. Be sure to omit repeated words. Since various combinations are possible, you might want to jot down several combinations on a separate piece of paper. Then read them aloud to find the combination that sounds best.

Keep in mind that, very often, the relationship among ideas in a sentence will be clearer when subordination rather than coordination is used.

EXAMPLE

- My car does not start on cold mornings.

- I think the battery needs to be replaced.

- I already had it recharged once.
- I don't think charging it again would help.

Because my car does not start on cold mornings, I think the battery needs

to be replaced. I already had it recharged once, so I don't think charging it

again would help.

> **HINT** Use a comma at the end of a word group that starts with a dependent word (as in "Because my car does not start on cold mornings, . . .").

> **HINT** Use a comma between independent word groups connected by *and, but, for, or, nor, so,* and *yet* (as in "I already had it recharged once, so . . ."). In item 1, use *although*, two commas, and the joining word *so*.

1. • Jaylen likes loud music.
   • His parents can't stand it.
   • He wears earphones.

   _____

   _____

   _____

2. • The volcano erupted.
   • The sky turned black with smoke.
   • Nearby villagers were frightened.
   • They clogged the roads leading to safety.

   _____

   _____

   _____

3. • Min-Yeng had a haircut today.
   • She came home and looked in the mirror.
   • She decided to wear a hat for a few days.
   • She thought she looked like a bald eagle.

   _____

   _____

   _____

CONNECT WRITING

Meet Vickie. She's opening an account on a social networking site so that she can keep in touch with her daughter and son who are soldiers in the US Army. She's filling out the profile page, but feels a lot of her sentences are too short and choppy. Help Vickie add compound sentences to her writing by using coordination correctly.

mhconnectwriting.com

4. • I ran out of gas on the way to work.

   • I discovered how helpful strangers can be. (~)

   • A passing driver saw I was stuck.

   • He drove me to the gas station and back to my car.

   _____

   _____

   _____

5. • Our dog often rests on the floor in the sunshine.

   • He waits for the children to get home from school.

   • The sunlight moves along the floor.

   • He moves with it.

   _____

   _____

   _____

6. • My father was going to be late from work.

   • We planned to have a late dinner.

   • I was hungry before dinner.

   • I ate a salami and cheese sandwich.

   • I did this secretly.

   _____

   _____

   _____

7. • A baseball game was scheduled for early afternoon.

   • It looked like rain.

   • A crew rolled huge tarps to cover the field.

   • Then the sun reappeared.

   _____

   _____

   _____

8. • Cassy worries about the pesticides used on fruit.

   • She washes apples, pears, and plums in soap and water.

   • She doesn't rinse them well.

   • They have a soapy flavor.

   _____

   _____

   _____

   _____

9. • Charlene needed to buy stamps.

   • She went to the post office during her lunch hour.

   • The line was long.

   • She waited there for half an hour.

   • She had to go back to work without stamps.

   _____

   _____

   _____

   _____

10. • The weather suddenly became frigid.

    • Almost everyone at work caught a cold.

    • Someone brought a big batch of chicken soup.

    • She poured it into one of the office coffeepots.

    • The pot was empty by noon.

    _____

    _____

    _____

    _____

REVIEW TEST 1

Combine each group of short sentences into one sentence. Various combinations are possible. Choose the combination that reads most smoothly and clearly and that sounds most appropriate in the context of surrounding sentences. Use a separate piece of paper.

Here is an example of a group of sentences and some possible combinations:

EXAMPLE

- Carly moved in the desk chair.
- Her moving was uneasy.
- The chair was hard.
- She worked at the assignment.
- The assignment was for her English class.

Carly moved uneasily in the hard desk chair, working at the assignment for her English class.

Moving uneasily in the hard desk chair, Carly worked at the assignment for her English class.

Carly moved uneasily in the hard desk chair as she worked at the assignment for her English class.

While she worked at the assignment for her English class, Carly moved uneasily in the hard desk chair.

H I N T   In combining short sentences into one sentence, omit repeated words where necessary.

Doctor's Waiting Room

- People visit the doctor.
- Their ordeal begins.

- A patient has an appointment for 2:00.
- He is told he will have to wait.
- The wait will be at least one hour.

- Other people arrive.
- Everyone takes a seat.
- Soon the room becomes crowded.

- Some people read old magazines.
- Others count the stripes.
- The stripes are in the wallpaper.

- Some people look at each other.
- Some people may smile.
- No one talks to anyone else.

- Some people are very sick.
- They cough a lot.
- They hold tissues to their noses.

- The people around them turn away.
- They hold their breath.
- They are afraid of becoming infected.

- Time passes.
- It passes slowly.
- All the people count.
- They count the number of people ahead of them.

- The long-awaited moment finally arrives.
- The receptionist comes into the waiting area.

- She looks at the patient.
- She says the magic words.
- "The doctor will see you now."

Combine each group of short sentences into one sentence. Various combinations are possible. Choose the combination that reads most smoothly and clearly and that sounds most appropriate in the context of surrounding sentences. Use a separate piece of paper.

H I N T   In combining short sentences into one sentence, omit repeated words where necessary.

A Remedy for Shyness

- Linda Nelson was shy.
- She seldom met new people.
- She spent a lot of time alone.

- Too often Linda avoided speaking.
- She did not want to take a risk.
- The risk was embarrassing herself.

- Luckily, Linda got some advice.
- The advice was good.
- She got the advice from her cousin Rose.
- Linda decided to try to change.
- She would change her behavior.

- Rose told Linda not to blame herself for being shy.
- She told her the shyness made her seem attractive.
- She told her the shyness made her seem modest.

- Rose encouraged her to talk to others.
- Linda began to join conversations at school.
- Linda began to join conversations at work.

- Gradually, Linda learned something.
- She could start conversations.
- She could start them herself.
- She could do this even though her heart pounded.
- She could do this even though her stomach churned.

- Linda still feels uncomfortable sometimes.
- She is doing things that once seemed impossible.

- Linda joined a bowling league.
- She did this recently.
- Some of her new friends invited her to join.
- The friends were from work.

- She is not the best bowler on the team.
- She is winning a victory over shyness.
- She is winning, thanks to her cousin's help.
- She is winning, thanks to her own determination.

- Linda is a happier person today.
- She has taken charge of her life.
- She has made herself a more interesting person.

REFLECTIVE ACTIVITY

1.　Read your answers to Activity 10 in this chapter. When did you use subordination? When did you use coordination? Which of the two methods do you find easier to use?

2.　Read what you wrote for Review Tests 1 and 2 in this chapter. What methods for creating variety did you use when combining sentences? Why do you think your sentences are better than the originals?

For additional materials on Chapter 9, visit **www.mhhe.com/langan**.

Verbs, Pronouns, and Agreement

LOVER'S LEAP

1827 ——•—— 1973

The poetic lines inscribed on the boulder below is a replica of those carved in 1827 by Thomas W. Farrar.
Thomas W. Farrar was the Founder and first Grand Master of the Masonic Lodge in Alabama 1821-22-24.
This historical site donated to the public by Jonas W. Schwab in 1935.
The work was done and fence provided by Thomas W. Martin and George B. Ward.

ERECTED BY SHADES CREST GARDEN CLUB, JEFFERSON COUNTY, BIRMINGHAM, ALABAMA
APRIL 18, 1973

RESPONDING TO IMAGES

How could you change this sign's wording to make it grammatically correct? What specific errors have been made?

Standard English Verbs

INTRODUCTORY ACTIVITY

Underline what you think is the correct form of the verb in each pair of sentences that follows.

That radio station once (play, played) top-forty hits.

It now (play, plays) classical music.

When Jean was a little girl, she (hope, hoped) to become a movie star.

Now she (hope, hopes) to be accepted at business school.

At first, my father (juggle, juggled) with balls of yarn.

Now that he is an expert, he (juggle, juggles) raw eggs.

On the basis of the previous examples, see if you can complete the following statements.

1. The first sentence in each pair refers to an action in the (past time, present time), and the regular verb has an _Past time_ ending.

2. The second sentence in each pair refers to an action in the (past time, present time), and the regular verb has an _Present_ ending.

Answers are on page 622.

Many people have grown up in communities where nonstandard verb forms are used in everyday life. Such nonstandard forms include *they be, it done, we has, you was, she don't,* and *it ain't.* Community dialects have richness and power, but in college and the world at large, Standard English verb forms must be used. Standard English helps ensure clear communication among English-speaking people everywhere, and it is especially important in the world of work.

This chapter compares the community dialect and the Standard English forms of a regular verb and three common irregular verbs.

Regular Verbs: Dialect and Standard Forms

The following chart compares community dialect (nonstandard) and Standard English forms of the regular verb *talk.*

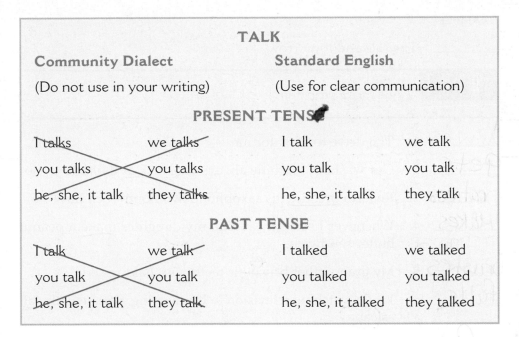

TALK			
Community Dialect		**Standard English**	
(Do not use in your writing)		(Use for clear communication)	
PRESENT TENSE			
I talks	we talks	I talk	we talk
you talks	you talks	you talk	you talk
he, she, it talk	they talks	he, she, it talks	they talk
PAST TENSE			
I talk	we talk	I talked	we talked
you talk	you talk	you talked	you talked
he, she, it talk	they talk	he, she, it talked	they talked

One of the most common nonstandard forms results from dropping the endings of regular verbs. For example, people might say "Rose work until ten o'clock tonight" instead of "Rose works until ten o'clock tonight." Or they'll say "I work overtime yesterday" instead of "I worked overtime yesterday." To avoid such nonstandard usage, memorize the forms shown above for the regular verb *talk.* Then do the activities that follow. These activities will help you make it a habit to include correct verb endings in your writing.

Present Tense Endings

The verb ending *-s* or *-es* is needed with a regular verb in the present tense when the subject is *he, she, it,* or any one person or thing.

He	He lifts weights.
She	She runs.
It	It amazes me.
One person	Their son Ted swims.
One person	Their daughter Terri dances.
One thing	Their house jumps at night with all the exercise.

Using Standard Verb Forms   ACTIVITY 1

All but one of the ten sentences that follow need *-s* or *-es* endings. Cross out the nonstandard verb forms and write the standard forms in the spaces provided. Mark with a *C* the one sentence that needs no change.

EXAMPLE

_____ends_____ The sale ~~end~~ tomorrow.

HINT Add *s* to *drive* in item 1.

drives 1. Tim ~~drive~~ too fast for me.

gets 2. Our washing machine always ~~get~~ stuck at the rinse cycle.

pratices 3. Roberto <u>practice</u> his saxophone two hours each day.

Makes 4. Whenever I serve meat loaf, my daughter <u>make</u> a peanut butter sandwich.

brushes 5. My grandfather ~~brush~~ his teeth with baking soda.

falls 6. While watching television in the evening, Sara usually <u>fall</u> asleep.

C 7. Mom always wakes me by saying, "Get up, the day is growing older."

Comes 8. On my old car radio, a static sound <u>come</u> from every station but one.

Watches 9. My little sister <u>watch</u> fireworks with her hands over her ears.

buzzes 10. The broken cell phone <u>buzz</u> like an angry wasp.

ACTIVITY 2 | **Using Present Tense -s Verb Endings**

Rewrite the short selection that follows, adding present tense -*s* verb endings in the ten places where they are needed.

> My little sister want to be a singer when she grow up. She constantly hum and sing around the house. Sometimes she make quite a racket. When she listen to music on the radio, for example, she sing very loudly in order to hear herself over the radio. And when she take a shower, her voice ring through the whole house because she think nobody can hear her from there.

_____

_____

_____

_____

_____

Past Tense Endings

The verb ending -*d* or -*ed* is needed with a regular verb in the past tense.

Yesterday we finished painting the apartment.

I completed the paper an hour before class.

Ty's car stalled on his way to work this morning.

Using Standard Verb Forms: -*d* and -*ed* Endings	**ACTIVITY 3**

All but one of the ten sentences that follow need -*d* or -*ed* endings. Cross out the nonstandard verb forms and write the standard forms in the spaces provided. Mark with a *C* the one sentence that needs no change.

EXAMPLE

___jumped___   The cat ~~jump~~ onto my lap when I sat down.

> **HINT**   In item 1, add *ed* to *spill.*

Spilled 1. A waiter at the new restaurant accidentally spill~~ed~~ ice water into Phil's lap.

Jailed 2. In a prim Indiana town, a couple was actually jail~~ed~~ for kissing in public.

burned 3. While ironing my new shirt this morning, I burn~~ed~~ a hole right through it.

tied 4. Fran wrapped the gag gift in waxed paper and tie~~d~~ it with dental floss.

Measured 5. Pencil marks dotted Matt's bedroom wall where he measure~~d~~ his height each month.

C 6. My brother was eating too fast and almost choked on a piece of bread.

Smashed 7. Last summer, a burglar smash~~ed~~ my car window and stole my jacket.

Constructed 8. The kids construct~~ed~~ an obstacle course in the basement out of boxes and toys.

leveled 9. The rain came down so hard it level~~ed~~ the young cornstalks in our garden.

Relized 10. As Alfonso pulled up to the red light, he suddenly realize~~d~~ his brakes were not working.

| ACTIVITY 4 | **Using Past Tense Verb Endings** |

Rewrite this selection, adding past tense -*d* or -*ed* verb endings where needed.

> Brad hate working long hours, but he need money to support his growing family and to pay for school. He start working at the auto body shop when he graduate from high school because he like cars, but now the job bore him. He wish that he could spend more time at home with his wife and new baby girl. He also want to dedicate more time to his homework. Brad knew that he had made his own choices, so he decide to appreciate his job, his family, and his chance to move ahead in life.

_____

_____

_____

_____

_____

_____

Three Common Irregular Verbs: Dialect and Standard Forms

The following charts compare the community dialect (nonstandard) and Standard English forms of the common irregular verbs *be, have,* and *do.*

| **TIP** | For more on irregular verbs, see Chapter 11, beginning on page 220. |

BE			
Community Dialect		**Standard English**	
(Do not use in your writing)		(Use for clear communication)	
PRESENT TENSE			
I be (*or* is)	we be	I am	we are
you be	you be	you are	you are
he, she, it be	they be	he, she, it is	they are
PAST TENSE			
I were	we was	I was	we were
you was	you was	you were	you were
he, she, it were	they was	he, she, it was	they were

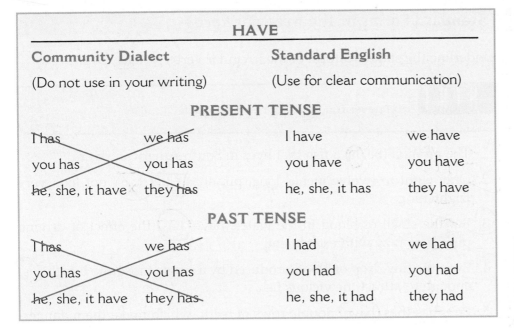

HAVE

Community Dialect		Standard English	
(Do not use in your writing)		(Use for clear communication)	

PRESENT TENSE

Community Dialect		Standard English	
~~I has~~	~~we has~~	I have	we have
~~you has~~	~~you has~~	you have	you have
~~he, she, it have~~	~~they has~~	he, she, it has	they have

PAST TENSE

Community Dialect		Standard English	
~~I has~~	~~we has~~	I had	we had
~~you has~~	~~you has~~	you had	you had
~~he, she, it have~~	~~they has~~	he, she, it had	they had

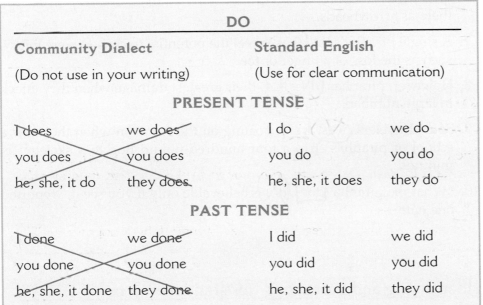

DO

Community Dialect		Standard English	
(Do not use in your writing)		(Use for clear communication)	

PRESENT TENSE

Community Dialect		Standard English	
~~I does~~	~~we does~~	I do	we do
~~you does~~	~~you does~~	you do	you do
~~he, she, it do~~	~~they does~~	he, she, it does	they do

PAST TENSE

Community Dialect		Standard English	
~~I done~~	~~we done~~	I did	we did
~~you done~~	~~you done~~	you did	you did
~~he, she, it done~~	~~they done~~	he, she, it did	they did

CONNECT WRITING

Meet Sergey. He's writing a Wiki posting for his culinary arts class. They're putting together a Wiki cookbook and he wants to explain how to cook perfectly steamed white rice. He's unsure how to use all the different verb forms and is worried that his cooking instructions are unclear. Help Sergey recognize all the different verb forms for regular and irregular verbs in his writing.

mhconnectwriting.com

TIP Many people have trouble with one negative form of *do*. They will say, for example, "She don't listen" instead of "She doesn't listen," or they will say "This pen don't work" instead of "This pen doesn't work." Be careful to avoid the common mistake of using *don't* instead of *doesn't*.

ACTIVITY 5 — Standard Forms of the Irregular Verbs

Underline the standard form of the irregular verbs *be*, *have*, or *do*.

> **HINT** *Be* never functions as a verb by itself.

1. The piranha (be, is) a fish that lives in South American rivers.

2. Only eight to twelve inches long, piranhas (do, does) not look very frightening.

3. But the smell of blood in the water (have, has) the effect of driving piranhas crazy with excitement.

4. Even the tiny drop of blood produced by a single mosquito bite (be, is) enough to attract the vicious fish.

5. Piranhas (has, have) double rows of teeth, which make them dangerous hunters.

6. Those teeth (be, are) so sharp that some Native American tribes use them as arrowheads.

7. A single piranha's bite (has, have) the potential to cause severe injury, such as the loss of a finger or toe.

8. However, piranhas (does, do) their greatest damage when they attack in large numbers.

9. Some travelers (was, were) boating on the Amazon when they saw a school of piranhas strip a four-hundred-pound hog to a skeleton in minutes.

10. "What the piranha (does, do) is believable only if you see it," reported one witness.

ACTIVITY 6 — Identifying and Correcting Nonstandard Verbs

Cross out the nonstandard verb form in each sentence. Then write the standard form of *be*, *have*, or *do* in the space provided.

> **HINT** *You does* is never a correct form.

do / is   1. If you does your assignments on time, you may not understand my friend Albert.

have   2. Albert be the world's worst procrastinator.

is/are ~~is~~ 3. Procrastinators ~~be~~ _are_ people who always put things off.

are ~~have~~ 4. They ~~has~~ _have_ problems with deadlines of all kinds.

was 5. Albert ~~were~~ _was_ a procrastinator at the age of six.

had 6. The boy next door ~~have~~ _had_ a few friends over for lunch one day.

were 7. Albert's parents ~~was~~ _were_ upset when they learned Albert got there three hours late.

~~have~~ 8. They ~~done~~ _did_ the neighbors a favor by taking Albert home at once.

does Ø 9. Today, Albert still ~~do~~ _es_ everything at the last minute or even later.

 10. He ~~have~~ _has_ plans to join Procrastinators Anonymous—when he gets around to it.

Using Standard Forms of _be_, _have_, and _do_

Fill in each blank with the standard form of _be_, _have_, or _do_.

My cousin Rita ~~have~~ _has_ decided to lose thirty pounds, so she ~~have~~ _has_ put herself on a rigid diet that _does_ not allow her to eat anything that she enjoys. Last weekend, while the family ~~be~~ _were_ _was_ at Aunt Jenny's house for dinner, all Rita _have_ to eat _were_ a can of Diet Delight peaches. We _were_ convinced that Rita meant business when she joined an exercise club whose members _had_ to work out on enormous machines and _do_ twenty sit-ups just to get started. If Rita _does_ reach her goal, we _are_ all going to be very proud of her. But I would not be surprised if she _is_ not succeed, because this _is_ her fourth diet this year.

REVIEW TEST 1

Underline the standard verb form.

1. A double-shot espresso (help, helps) me start the day.

2. Jordan carefully (choose, chooses) his classes according to his major.

3. My current supervisor (don't, doesn't) know that I was fired from my last job.

4. After I left work, I (remember, remembered) that I forgot to shut down my computer.

5. The receptionist at the counter will probably (ask, asked) me to make an appointment first.

6. If we (was, were) quicker, we could have bought tickets to the concert, which is sold out now.

7. Leanne's sister (is, are) adopting a child from Kazakhstan.

8. A police officer (stop, stopped) me on the highway for driving five miles over the speed limit.

9. When the applicant (answer, answered) the interview questions, she impressed everyone.

10. *Newsweek* (did, done) a cover story on childhood obesity.

REVIEW TEST 2

Cross out the nonstandard verb form in each of the sentences that follow. Then write the Standard English verb form in the space at the left, as shown.

EXAMPLE

played Yesterday morning, the children ~~play~~ quietly in the sandbox.

_____ 1. Making promises be easier than keeping them.

_____ 2. Baked potatoes doesn't have as many calories as I thought.

_____ 3. The game were lost when the other team scored a fourth-quarter touchdown.

_____ 4. Our psychology professor ride a motorcycle to school.

_____ 5. The mayor cover his face from photographers as he was escorted to jail.

_____ 6. The large dog growl fiercely when I approached my neighbor's house.

_____ 7. Lightning struck a nearby building last night and cause a major fire.

_____ 8. Many childhood diseases, such as scarlet fever and whooping cough, has almost vanished in the United States.

_____ 9. Natalie turned the television on during the day because the house sound too quiet without it.

_____ 10. That restaurant offers free nonalcoholic drinks to the person who be the driver for a group.

For additional materials on Chapter 10, visit www.mhhe.com/langan.

Irregular Verbs

INTRODUCTORY ACTIVITY

You may already have a sense of which common English verbs are regular and which are not. To test yourself, fill in the past tense and past participle of each verb below. Five are regular verbs and so take -d or -ed in the past tense and past participle. For these verbs, write R under *Verb Type* and then write their past tense and past participle verb forms. Five are irregular verbs and will probably not sound right when you try to add -d or -ed. For these verbs, write I under *Verb Type*. Also, see if you can write in their irregular verb forms.

Present	Verb Type	Past	Past Participle
hide	*I*	*hid*	*hidden*
1. talk	I	Talked	Talked
2. read	I	read	Read
3. sing	R	sang	Sung
4. taste	R	tasted	tasted
5. pick	I	picked	picked
6. make	I	made	made
7. feel	I	Picked	Picked
8. type	R	typed	typed
9. become	I	became	become
10. mail	R	mailed	mailed

Answers are on page 623.

A Brief Review of Regular Verbs

Every verb has four principal forms: present, past, past participle, and present participle. These forms can be used to build all the verb tenses (the times shown by a verb).

Most verbs in English are regular. The past and past participle of a regular verb are formed by adding *-d* or *-ed* to the present. The *past participle* is the form of the verb used with the helping verbs *have, has,* or *had* (or some form of *be* with passive verbs, which are explained on page 249). The *present participle* is formed by adding *-ing* to the present.

Here are the principal forms of some regular verbs:

Present	Past	Past Participle	Present Participle
laugh	laughed	laughed	laughing
ask	asked	asked	asking
touch	touched	touched	touching
decide	decided	decided	deciding
explode	exploded	exploded	exploding

List of Irregular Verbs

Irregular verbs have irregular forms in the past tense and past participle. For example, the past tense of the irregular verb *grow* is *grew*; the past participle is *grown*.

Almost everyone has some degree of trouble with irregular verbs. When you are unsure about the form of a verb, you can check the following list of irregular verbs. (The present participle is not shown on this list because it is formed simply by adding *-ing* to the base form of the verb.) Or you can check a dictionary, which gives the principal forms of irregular verbs.

Present	Past	Past Participle
arise	arose	arisen
awake	awoke *or* awaked	awoke *or* awaked
be (am, are, is)	was (were)	been
become	became	become
begin	began	begun
bend	bent	bent
bite	bit	bitten
blow	blew	blown
break	broke	broken
bring	brought	brought
build	built	built
burst	burst	burst
buy	bought	bought

Present	Past	Past Participle
catch	caught	caught
choose	chose	chosen
come	came	come
cost	cost	cost
cut	cut	cut
do (does)	did	done
draw	drew	drawn
drink	drank	drunk
drive	drove	driven
eat	ate	eaten
fall	fell	fallen
feed	fed	fed
feel	felt	felt
fight	fought	fought
find	found	found
fly	flew	flown
freeze	froze	frozen
get	got	got or gotten
give	gave	given
go (goes)	went	gone
grow	grew	grown
have (has)	had	had
hear	heard	heard
hide	hid	hidden
hold	held	held
hurt	hurt	hurt
keep	kept	kept
know	knew	known
lay	laid	laid
lead	led	led
leave	left	left
lend	lent	lent
let	let	let
lie	lay	lain
light	lit	lit

Present	Past	Past Participle
lose	lost	lost
make	made	made
meet	met	met
pay	paid	paid
ride	rode	ridden
ring	rang	rung
rise	rose	risen
run	ran	run
say	said	said
see	saw	seen
sell	sold	sold
send	sent	sent
shake	shook	shaken
shrink	shrank	shrunk
shut	shut	shut
sing	sang	sung
sit	sat	sat
sleep	slept	slept
speak	spoke	spoken
spend	spent	spent
stand	stood	stood
steal	stole	stolen
stick	stuck	stuck
sting	stung	stung
swear	swore	sworn
swim	swam	swum
take	took	taken
teach	taught	taught
tear	tore	torn
tell	told	told
think	thought	thought
wake	woke *or* waked	woken *or* waked
wear	wore	worn
win	won	won
write	wrote	written

ACTIVITY 1   Identifying Incorrect Verb Forms

Cross out the incorrect verb form in the following sentences. Then write the correct form of the verb in the space provided.

EXAMPLE

_____began_____   When the mud slide started, the whole neighborhood ~~begun~~ going downhill.

> **HINT**   In item 1, use the past tense of *come*.

Came 1. The coach caught Otto when he ~~come~~ in two hours after curfew.

Stood 2. We ~~standed~~ out in the rain all night to buy tickets to the concert.

built 3. The Romans had ~~builded~~ a network of roads so the army could travel more quickly from place to place.

Swum 4. Our championship team has ~~swam~~ in every important meet this year.

held 5. The nervous mother ~~holded~~ her child's hand tightly as they crossed the busy street.

drove 6. Hakeem ~~drived~~ in circles for an hour before he admitted that he was lost.

Written 7. He had ~~wrote~~ the answers to all the questions before anyone else had finished the first page.

blew 8. The tornado ~~blowed~~ the sign from the top of the bank, and it landed five blocks away in the motel swimming pool.

bought 9. Kathy ~~buyed~~ school clothes with the money she earned from her summer job.

Knew 10. The poker players ~~knowed~~ they were in trouble when the stranger shuffled the cards with one hand.

ACTIVITY 2   Using Present Tense, Past Tense, and Past Participle Verbs

For each of the italicized verbs in the following sentences, fill in the three missing forms in the order shown in the box:

> a. Present tense, which takes an *-s* ending when the subject is *he, she, it,* or any *one person or thing* (see page 211)
>
> b. Past tense
>
> c. Past participle—the form that goes with the helping verb *have, has,* or *had*

EXAMPLE

My nephew loves to *break* things. Every Christmas he (a) _____breaks_____ his new toys the minute they're unwrapped. Last year he (b) _____broke_____ five toys in seven minutes and then went on to smash his family's new china platter. His mother says he won't be happy until he has (c) _____broken_____ their hearts.

> **HINT**   In item 1, add an *s* to *sleep* in choice a. Use the past tense of *sleep* for b and c.

1. Did you ever go to *sleep* on a water bed? My cousin Ysabel (a) _____sleep_____ on one. Last year I spent the weekend at Ysabel's apartment, and I (b) _____slept_____ on it. Since then I have (c) _____slept_____ on it several more times, without once getting seasick.

2. A dreadful little boy in my neighborhood loves to *ring* my doorbell and run away. Sometimes he (a) _____Rings_____ it several times a day. The last time it (b) _____Rang_____ over and over, I finally refused to answer the door. Then I found out that the mail carrier had (c) _____Rung_____ the doorbell to deliver a gift from my boyfriend.

3. Why does every teacher ask us to *write* about our summer vacations? Most students (a) _____Write_____ about what really happened, but that is usually too dull. I (b) _____Wrote_____ an essay about being taken aboard an alien spacecraft. I bet it was the most interesting essay anybody has ever (c) _____Written_____ for my teacher's English class.

4. My sister never has to *stand* in line for a movie very long. She always (a) _____Stands_____ for a few minutes and then walks straight to the entrance. "I (b) _____stood_____ in line as long as I could," she tells the ticket taker. "In fact," she continues in a weak voice, "I have (c) _____stood_____ in line too long already. I feel faint." She is always ushered inside immediately.

5. As usual, Ron planned to *swim* at least a hundred laps before breakfast. He knew that an Olympic hopeful (a) _____Swims_____ while others sleep. That morning he (b) _____Swam_____ with a deliberate stroke, counting the rhythm silently. He had (c) _____Swam_____ this way daily for the last two years. It was a price he was willing to pay to be one of the best.

6. I know a woman who likes to *buy* things and return them after she uses them. For example, she always (a) _buy_ new shoes to wear for special occasions. Then she wears them for the event and returns them the next day. Once she (b) _bought_ a complete outfit, wore it twice, and returned it a week later. Whenever I shop, I worry that I have (c) _bought_ something that she has used and returned.

7. Craig sat in his car at the rural crossroads and wondered which direction to *choose*. Should he (a) _Choose_ left or right? He sighed and turned right, knowing that if he (b) _Chose_ the wrong way, he would run out of gas before finding his way back to the highway. After several anxious minutes, he spotted an Exxon sign. He pulled into the service station, grateful that he had (c) _Chosen_ the right direction after all.

8. My friend Alice loves to *eat*. But no matter how much she (a) _eat_, she stays thin. Her husband, on the other hand, is fat. "Why?" he jokingly complains. "I (b) _ate_ very little today. In fact," he adds with a grin, "all my life I have (c) _eaten_ just one meal a day. Of course, it usually lasts from morning till night."

9. All the kids in the neighborhood waited each winter for Mahoney's pond to *freeze*. They knew that a sudden cold snap (a) _freezes_ only the surface. It took at least a week of low temperatures before the pond (b) _frozen_ more than a few inches deep. Mr. Mahoney checked the ice each day. When it had finally (c) _frozen_ to a depth of six inches, he gave his permission for the children to skate on it.

10. It is important for people to *give* blood. A healthy person can (a) _give_ a pint of blood in less than fifteen minutes with little or no discomfort. The first time I (b) _gave_ blood, I was afraid the needle would hurt, but all I felt was a slight pinch. I have (c) _given_ blood many times since then. Each time I do, I feel good, knowing that my gift will help other people.

Troublesome Irregular Verbs

Three common irregular verbs that often give people trouble are *be, have,* and *do*. See pages 214–215 for a discussion of these verbs. Three sets of other irregular verbs that can lead to difficulties are *lie-lay, sit-set,* and *rise-raise*.

Lie-Lay

The principal forms of *lie* and *lay* are as follows:

Present	Past	Past Participle
lie	lay	lain
lay	laid	laid

> **TIP** *To lie* means *to rest* or *recline*. *To lay* means *to put something down*.

To Lie	**To Lay**
Anthony *lies* on the couch.	I *lay* the mail on the table.
This morning he *lay* in the tub.	Yesterday I *laid* the mail on the counter.
He has *lain* in bed all week with the flu.	I have *laid* the mail where everyone will see it.

Using *lie* and *lay*

ACTIVITY 3

Underline the correct verb.

> **HINT** Use a form of *lie* if you can substitute *recline*. Use a form of *lay* if you can substitute *place*.

> **HINT** Since the kitten is resting, what is the correct answer?

1. On warm sunny days, Serena's kitten often (lies, lays) on the bedroom windowsill.

2. (Lying, Laying) too long in bed in the morning can give me a headache.

3. The Magna Carta (lay, laid) the foundation for the establishment of the English Parliament.

4. He was certain he had (lain, laid) the tiles in a straight line until he stepped back to look.

5. I (lay, laid) down on the couch and pressed my face into the pillow.

Sit-Set

The principal forms of *sit* and *set* are as follows:

Present	Past	Past Participle
sit	sat	sat
set	set	set

> **TIP**   To *sit* means *to take a seat* or *to rest*. To *set* means *to put* or *to place*.

To Sit	To Set
I *sit* down during work breaks.	Antonio *sets* out the knives, forks, and spoons.
I *sat* in the doctor's office for three hours.	His sister already *set* out the dishes.
I have always *sat* in the last desk.	They have just *set* out the dinner ware.

ACTIVITY 4 — Using *set* and *sit*

Underline the correct form of the verb.

> **HINT**   Use a form of *sit* if you can substitute *rest*. Use a form of *set* if you can substitute *place*. Since Dillon placed the Shuffle, what is the correct verb?

1. Dillon had (sat, **set**) his iPod Shuffle on the counter for only a few seconds before someone walked off with it.

2. Zena (sat, **set**) her heavy backpack down on the floor, and then she proceeded to take out her calculus textbook, graphing calculator, and class notes.

3. The cardiologist told me to (**sit**, set) down before she went over my x-ray results.

4. I (sat, **set**) a candle on the mantel in the living room to remember my younger sister, who died of leukemia last month.

5. Jackson was (sitting, **setting**) the box down on the floor when he heard his spine crack.

Rise-Raise

The principal forms of *rise* and *raise* are as follows:

Present	Past	Past Participle
rise	rose	risen
raise	raised	raised

> **TIP**   To *rise* means *to get up* or *to move up*. To *raise* (which is a regular verb with simple -*ed* endings) means *to lift up* or *to increase in amount*.

To Rise	To Raise
The soldiers *rise* at dawn.	I'm going to *raise* the stakes in the card game.
The crowd *rose* to applaud the batter.	I *raised* the shades to let in the sun.
Dracula has *risen* from the grave.	I would have quit if the company had not *raised* my salary.

Using *rise* and *raise*

ACTIVITY 5

Underline the correct verb.

> **HINT** Use a form of *rise* if you can substitute *get up* or *move up*. Use a form of *raise* if you can substitute *lift up* or *increase*. Since heat moves upward, what is the correct verb?

1. It is usually warmer upstairs because heat (*rises*, raises).
2. The new owner (rose, *raised*) the rent, so now I will have to look for another apartment.
3. We (*rose*, raised) at three o'clock in the morning to watch the meteor shower.
4. After four days of rain, the river had (*risen*, raised) over its banks and threatened to flood the highway.
5. A single sailboat made them (rise, *raise*) the drawbridge, stopping traffic in both directions for fifteen minutes.

REFLECTIVE ACTIVITY

1. Reread some paragraphs or essays you have written in this course (see Chapters 4 and 5 for writing assignments). Underline all of the verbs you used in this work.
2. Check that the present and past tense endings of all regular verbs are correct, as explained in Chapter 10. Pay special attention to forms of *be*, *have*, and *do*.
3. Check that the present and past tense endings of all irregular verbs are correct, as explained in this chapter. If not, correct them.

REVIEW TEST 1

Cross out the incorrect verb form in each sentence. Then write the correct form of the verb in the space provided.

_____ 1. The sound of the lawnmower in the front yard waked up my baby from her late morning nap.

_____ 2. Your two pairs of cotton cargo pants may have shrinked because I accidentally ran them through the dryer on the high setting.

_____ 3. No one thinked to ask the woman at the bus stop if she was waiting for the express route, which was delayed at the bus terminal.

_____ 4. Rob selled his Honda motorcycle for a good price on Craigslist.

_____ 5. This morning's earthquake might have shook the picture frames and figurines on the shelf.

_____ 6. The invitation indicated that casual attire should be wore to the event, but most of the guests came in formal wear.

_____ 7. During final exam week, I sleeped under three hours a night.

_____ 8. Few people spoken up at the neighborhood board meeting about the proposed legislation.

_____ 9. The breakfast meeting at the hotel costed the company over five hundred dollars.

_____ 10. I flown on standby to save on the cost of airfare.

REVIEW TEST 2

Write short sentences using the form noted for the following irregular verbs.

EXAMPLE

Past of *ride* _The Lone Ranger rode into the sunset._

1. Present of *shake* _I shook his hand_
2. Past participle of *write* _I written him yesterday_
3. Past participle of *begin* _I begun to give out treats_
4. Past of *go* _I went to Daniel yesterday_
5. Past participle of *grow* _She grown up fast._
6. Present of *speak* _I spoke to Sanya earlyer._
7. Past of *bring* _I brought that home._
8. Present of *do* _does that hurt_
9. Past participle of *give* _Tony given me that_
10. Past of *drink* _You drank all the kool-aide_

For additional materials on Chapter 11, visit www.mhhe.com/langan.

Subject-Verb Agreement

INTRODUCTORY ACTIVITY

As you read each pair of sentences, write an *X* beside the sentence that you think uses the underlined word correctly.

The postings on the college gossip site <u>is</u> very cruel. _~~X~~_

The postings on the college gossip site <u>are</u> very cruel. _X_

There <u>was</u> many résumés for the supervisor to read. _____

There <u>were</u> many résumés for the supervisor to read. _X_

Everybody <u>want</u> wireless Internet access on campus. _____

Everybody <u>wants</u> wireless Internet access on campus. _X_

On the basis of the above examples, see if you can complete the following statements.

1. In the first two pairs of sentences, the subjects are _posting_ and _Resumes_. Since both these subjects are plural, the verb must be plural.

2. In the last pair of sentences, the subject, *Everybody*, is a word that is always (<u>singular</u>, plural), so its accompanying verb must be (<u>singular</u>, plural).

Answers are on page 624.

Answers are on page 624.

CHAPTER PREVIEW

Words between the Subject and the Verb

Verb before the Subject

Indefinite Pronouns

Compound Subjects

Who, Which, and *That*

A verb must agree with its subject in number. A *singular subject* (one person or thing) takes a singular verb. A *plural subject* (more than one person or thing) takes a plural verb. Mistakes in subject-verb agreement are sometimes made in the following situations:

*   When words come between the subject and the verb
*   When a verb comes before the subject
*   With indefinite pronouns
*   With compound subjects
*   With *who, which,* and *that*

Each situation is explained in depth on the following pages.

Words between the Subject and the Verb

Words that come between the subject and the verb do not change subject-verb agreement. In the following sentence

> The breakfast cereals in the pantry are made mostly of sugar.

the subject (*cereals*) is plural, so the verb (*are*) is plural. The words *in the pantry* that come between the subject and the verb do not affect subject-verb agreement. To help find the subject of certain sentences, cross out prepositional phrases (explained on page 157):

> One of the crooked politicians was jailed for a month.

> The boxes in my grandmother's attic contained old family photos and long-forgotten toys.

Following is a list of common prepositions.

COMMON PREPOSITIONS				
about	before	by	inside	over
above	behind	during	into	through
across	below	except	of	to
among	beneath	for	off	toward
around	beside	from	on	under
at	between	in	onto	with

ACTIVITY 1   Words between Subjects and Verbs

Draw one line under the subject. Then lightly cross out any words that come between the subject and the verb. Finally, draw two lines under the correct verb in parentheses.

EXAMPLE

The price ~~of the stereo speakers~~ (is, are) too high for my wallet.

> **HINT**   In item 1, cross out the preposition between the subject and verb.

1. A trail of bloodstains (leads, lead) to the spot where the murder was committed.

2. The winter clothes in the hall closet (takes, take) up too much room.

3. A basket of fancy fruit and nuts (was, were) delivered to my house.

4. The garbled instructions for assembling the bicycle (was, were) almost impossible to follow.

5. Smoke from the distant forest fires (is, are) visible from many miles away.

6. Workers at that automobile plant (begins, begin) each day with a period of exercise.

7. The earliest date on any of the cemetery gravestones (appears, appear) to be 1804.

8. The line of cars in the traffic jam (seems, seem) to extend for miles.

9. Several boxes in the corner of the attic (contains, contain) old family pictures.

10. Sleeping bags with the new insulation material (protects, protect) campers even in subzero temperatures.

Verb before the Subject

A verb agrees with its subject even when the verb comes *before* the subject. Words that may precede the subject include *there, here,* and, in questions, *who, which, what,* and *where*.

Inside the storage shed are the garden tools.

At the street corner were two panhandlers.

There are times when I'm ready to quit my job.

Where are the instructions for assembling the bed?

> **TIP**   If you are unsure about the subject, ask *who* or *what* of the verb. With the first sentence above, you might ask, "What is inside the storage shed?" The answer, garden *tools,* is the subject.

Verbs That Precede Subjects | ACTIVITY 2

Draw one line under the subject. Then draw two lines under the correct verb in parentheses.

> **HINT**   To find the subject in item 1, ask "What is coming from behind the wall?"

1. There (is, are) a scratching noise coming from behind this wall.

2. On the bottom of the jar of preserves (is, are) the berries.

3. Floating near the base of the dock (was, were) several discarded aluminum cans.

4. In the middle of the woods behind our home (sits, sit) an abandoned cabin.

5. There (was, <u>were</u>) so many students talking ~~at once that the instructor shouted for quiet.~~

6. Outside the novelty shop ~~at the mall~~ (<u>stands</u>, stand) a life-size cutout of W. C. Fields.

7. Coming out ~~of the fog~~ toward the frightened boys (was, <u>were</u>) the menacing shape ~~of a large dog~~.

8. In the rear of the closet (was, <u>were</u>) the basketball sneakers that I thought I had lost.

9. On the table in the doctor's office (is, <u>are</u>) some magazines that are five years old.

10. Lining one wall of the gym (<u>was,</u> were) a <u>row</u> of <u>lockers</u> for the team members.

Indefinite Pronouns

The following words, known as *indefinite pronouns*, always take singular verbs.

<table>
<tr><td colspan="4" align="center">**INDEFINITE PRONOUNS**</td></tr>
<tr><td>(*-one* words)</td><td>(*-body* words)</td><td>(*-thing* words)</td><td></td></tr>
<tr><td>one</td><td>nobody</td><td>nothing</td><td>each</td></tr>
<tr><td>anyone</td><td>anybody</td><td>anything</td><td>either</td></tr>
<tr><td>everyone</td><td>everybody</td><td>everything</td><td>neither</td></tr>
<tr><td>someone</td><td>somebody</td><td>something</td><td></td></tr>
</table>

> **TIP** *Both* always takes a plural verb.

| **ACTIVITY 3** | **Using Verbs with Indefinite Pronouns** |

Write the correct form of the verb in the space provided.

> **HINT** The indefinite pronoun *something* requires a singular verb.

keeps, keep
1. Something always __Keeps__ me from getting to bed on time.

works, work
2. Nobody that I know __Works__ as hard as Manuel.

pays, pay
3. Neither of the jobs offered to me __pays__ more than eight dollars an hour.

has, have
4. Both of the speakers _____ told us more than we care to know about the dangers of water pollution.

lips, slip

5. Someone in Inez's apartment house _slips_ an unsigned valentine under her door every year.

eans, lean

6. Anything sitting on the old wooden floor _____ to one side.

xpects, xpect

7. Each of my friends _____ to be invited to my new in-ground pool.

vas, were

8. Not one of the three smoke detectors in the house _____ working properly.

tops, stop

9. Only one of all the brands of waxes _____ the rust on my car from spreading.

as, have

10. Just about everybody who hates getting up early for work _____ jumped out of bed at 6:00 a.m. to go on vacation.

Compound Subjects

Subjects joined by *and* generally take a plural verb.

Yoga and biking are Lola's ways of staying in shape.

Ambition and good luck are the keys to his success.

When subjects are joined by *either . . . or, neither . . . nor,* or *not only . . . but also,* the verb agrees with the subject closer to the verb.

Either the restaurant manager or his assistants deserve to be fired for the spoiled meat used in the stew.

> **EXPLANATION:** The nearer subject, *assistants*, is plural, and so the verb is plural.

Using Verbs with Compound Subjects   ACTIVITY 4

Write the correct form of the verb in the space provided.

seem, seems

1. The pilates and spinning classes _____ to help me stay in shape, but the key to fitness is a sensible diet.

is, are

2. Either the tongue ring or dragon tattoo _____ responsible for Zack's appeal.

is, are

3. A double shot of espresso and two pumps of hazelnut syrup _____ all I need to start my morning.

help, helps

4. The lecture podcasts and study guides _____ me prepare for exams.

impress, impresses

5. Neither Mick Jagger nor my favorite rock band, The Rolling Stones, _____ my ten-year old daughter, who prefers Disney's Hannah Montana.

Who, Which, and That

When *who, which,* and *that* are used as subjects of verbs, they take singular verbs if the word they stand for is singular, and they take plural verbs if the word they stand for is plural. For example, in the sentence

Gary is one of those people who are very private.

the verb is plural because *who* stands for *people,* which is plural. On the other hand, in the sentence

Gary is a person who is very private.

the verb is singular because *who* stands for *person,* which is singular.

ACTIVITY 5	Using *who, which,* or *that* with Verbs

Write the correct form of the verb in the space provided.

> **HINT**   *Who* stands for a singular subject and requires a singular verb.

has, have

1. The young man who _____ mowed my grass for years just left for college.

goes, go

2. The jacket that _____ with those pants is at the cleaners.

becomes, become

3. Women who _____ police officers often have to prove themselves more capable than do their male coworkers.

tastes, taste

4. The restaurant serves hamburgers that _____ like dry cereal.

is, are

5. The ceiling in Kevin's bedroom is covered with stars, which _____ arranged in the shape of the constellations.

ACTIVITY 6	Editing and Rewriting

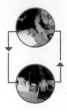

Working with a partner, read the short paragraph below and see if you can underline the five mistakes in subject-verb agreement. Then use the space provided to correct these five errors. Feel free to discuss the rewrite quietly with your partner and refer back to the chapter when necessary.

> When most people think about cities, they do not thinks about wild animals. But in my city apartment, there is enough creatures to fill a small forest. In the daytime, I must contend with the pigeons.

continued

These unwanted guests ~~at my apartment~~ makes a loud feathery mess ~~on my bedroom windowsill~~. In the evening, my apartment is visited by roaches. These large insects creep ~~onto my kitchen floor~~ and walls ~~after dark~~ and frighten me ~~with their shiny glistening bodies~~. Later at night, my apartment is invaded by mice. Waking from sleep, I can hear their little feet tapping as they scurry ~~behind walls~~ and ~~above my ceiling~~. Everybody I know think I should move ~~into a new apartment~~. What I really need is to go somewhere that have fewer wild creatures—maybe a forest!

_____

_____

_____

_____

_____

CONNECT WRITING

Meet Devon. He has created a family Web site with his wife and two children. They have each written an entry for the Web site and Devon has noticed that each one contains errors in subject-verb agreement. Help Devon locate and correct all the subject-verb agreement mistakes before posting his family's entries.

mhconnectwriting.com

Creating Sentences

ACTIVITY 7

Working with a partner, write sentences as directed. Use a separate piece of paper. For each item, pay special attention to subject-verb agreement.

1. Write a sentence in which the words *in the cafeteria* or *on the table* come between the subject and verb. Underline the subject of your sentence and circle the verb.

2. Write a sentence that begins with the words *There is* or *There are*. Underline the subject of your sentence and circle the verb.

3. Write a sentence in which the indefinite pronoun *nobody* or *anything* is the subject.

4. Write a sentence with the compound subject *manager and employees*. Underline the subject of your sentence and circle the verb.

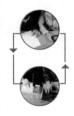

REFLECTIVE ACTIVITY

1. Look at the paragraph about the apartment that you revised in Activity 6. Which rule involving subject-verb agreement gave you the most trouble? How did you figure out the correct answer?

2. Five situations involving subject-verb agreement have been discussed in this chapter. Explain which one is most likely to cause you problems.

REVIEW TEST 1

Complete each of the following sentences using *is, are, was, were, have,* or *has.* Underline the subject of each of these verbs. In some cases you will need to provide that subject.

EXAMPLE

The <u>hot dogs</u> in that luncheonette _____ *are hazardous to your health.* _____

1. In my glove compartment _____

2. The cat and her three kittens _____

3. I frequently see people who _____

4. Neither of the wrestlers _____

5. Scattered across the parking lot _____

6. The dust under my bed _____

7. There are _____

8. My friend and his brother _____

9. The newspapers that accumulate in my garage _____

_____

10. It was one of those movies that _____

_____

REVIEW TEST 2

Underline the correct verb in the parentheses. Note that you will first have to determine the subject of each sentence. To find subjects in certain sentences, you may find it helpful to cross out prepositional phrases.

1. Sadly, none of the food at weddings (is, are) particularly good.

2. One of my roommates in college (wants, want) to become a software engineer so that she can create cutting-edge video and computer games.

3. The cost of all my utilities, which include electricity, water, cable, and phone, (is, are) ridiculous.

4. High-speed chases and grisly car accidents (seems, seem) to be the focus on many reality television shows.

5. Not one of the red-tag specials advertised in yesterday's newspaper (was, were) on the shelf when I arrived at the discount department store this morning.

6. Once a year, Jackie and her girlfriends (takes, take) a weekend trip to Las Vegas for shopping, dining, and gambling.

7. The online articles that the librarian located for the student (was, were) originally published in print.

8. Squeaking from underneath the refrigerator (was, were) a tiny mouse caught in a forgotten spring-based trap.

9. The nurses on strike at the metropolitan hospital (wants, want) safe staffing ratios and retirement security.

10. Neither Dad nor my brother Miguel (wants, want) to talk about their experiences as combat soldiers in the Iraq War.

11. There (was, were) a laptop computer left in one of the carrels at the library.

12. A kleptomaniac will steal anything that (is, are) not nailed down.

13. A few girls at my daughter's high school (plans, plan) to try out for the football team.

14. There is rarely a person among the political candidates who (is, are) humble yet confident.

15. Not only the air ducts but also the plumbing in the abandoned building (is, are) infested with rats.

16. Everyone in my history class (believes, believe) that the professor grades unfairly, but nobody is willing to approach her.

17. Homebuyers should be warned that "fixer-upper" houses on the market often (requires, require) costly repairs.

18. The private e-mail message that I sent in confidence to a few coworkers (was, were) forwarded to my supervisor.

19. Economics (is, are) a subject that requires strong analytic skills.

20. The most popular car colors in the United States (is, are) silver and pearl white.

REVIEW TEST 3

There are ten mistakes in subject-verb agreement in the following passage. Cross out each incorrect verb and write the correct form above it. In addition, underline the subject of each of the verbs that must be changed.

After almost forty years on television, there is few honors that *Sesame Street* has not won. The awards are deserved, for *Sesame Street* is a show that treat children with respect. Most children's programs consists of cheaply made cartoons that is based on the adventures of a superhero or a video-game character. Unfortunately,

continued

children's TV programs are generally so poor because quality kids' shows does not make the profits that the networks demand. Both the superhero story and the video-game story is easy to slap together. By contrast, the producers of *Sesame Street* spends enormous amounts of time and money researching how children learn. Another reason for the low profits are the nature of the audience. Because children have little money to spend on sponsors' products, each of the networks charge bottom rates for advertising during children's programs. *Sesame Street,* a nonprofit show, does not even accept ads. And income from the sale of *Sesame Street* products are used to do an even better job of producing the show.

For additional materials on Chapter 12, visit **www.mhhe.com/langan**.

Consistent Verb Tense

INTRODUCTORY ACTIVITY

CHAPTER PREVIEW
Keeping Tenses
Consistent

See if you can find and underline the two mistakes in verb tense in the following selection.

> When Computer Warehouse had a sale, Alex decided to buy a new computer. He planned to set up the machine himself and hoped to connect to the Internet right away. When he arrived home, however, Alex discovers that setting up a wireless hub could be complicated and confusing. The directions sounded as if they had been written for engineers. After two hours of frustration, Alex gave up and calls a technician for help.

Now try to complete the following statement:

Verb tenses should be consistent. In the selection above, two verbs have to be changed because they are mistakenly in the (*present, past*) _____ tense while all the other verbs in the selection are in the (*present, past*) _____ tense.

Answers are on page 624.

Keeping Tenses Consistent

Do not shift tenses unnecessarily. If you begin writing a paper in the present tense, don't shift suddenly to the past. If you begin in the past, don't shift without reason to the present. Notice the inconsistent verb tenses in the following example:

incorrect   Smoke <u>spilled</u> from the front of the overheated car. The driver <u>opens</u> up the hood, then <u>jumped</u> back as steam <u>billows</u> out.

The verbs must be consistently in the present tense:

correct   Smoke <u>spills</u> from the front of the overheated car. The driver <u>opens</u> up the hood, then <u>jumps</u> back as steam <u>billows</u> out.

Or the verbs must be consistently in the past tense:

correct   Smoke <u>spilled</u> from the front of the overheated car. The driver <u>opened</u> up the hood, then <u>jumped</u> back as steam <u>billowed</u> out.

| ACTIVITY 1 | **Avoiding Unnecessary Tense Shifts** |

In each item, one verb must be changed so that it agrees in tense with the other verbs. Cross out the incorrect verb and write the correct form in the space at the left.

EXAMPLE

confused   I rewrote my essay after the tutor told me that my introduction ~~confuse~~ him.

HINT Change *answer* to past tense to agree with the rest of the sentence.

_____ 1. The salesperson at the electronics store showed me several home theater systems and answer all my questions.

_____ 2. On Tuesday, I skipped lunch so that I could study for an exam, and later I grab a bag of chips from the vending machine.

_____ 3. The judges thanked the contestants and then announce the winner of the contest.

_____ 4. Before I began college, I work full-time as a data entry clerk for a supply company.

_____ 5. When Serena was late for dinner, I call her workplace and her home.

_____ 6. The apartment I rented in the city was ideal. The landlord allow me to make minor improvements, which included painting the kitchen and installing new window blinds.

_____ 7. The dental hygienist show my children how to brush their teeth properly.

_____ 8. Last night, Todd impulsively stop at the convenience store to buy a pack of cigarettes.

_____ 9. While in Las Vegas, my neighbor place twelve quarters into a Megabucks slot machine and won an impressive jackpot.

_____ 10. The campus seemed busy on the first day of school; the parking lot was packed with cars, the bookstore was crammed with students buying textbooks, and the cafeteria was crowd with students buying coffee before their first class.

REVIEW TEST 1

Change the verbs where needed in the following selection so that they are consistently in the past tense. Cross out each incorrect verb and write the correct form above it, as shown in the example. You will need to make ten corrections.

Years ago, I live in an old apartment building where I got little peace and quiet. For one thing, I often heard the constant fights that went on in the adjoining apartment. The husband yells about killing his wife, and she screamed right back about leaving him or having him arrested. In addition, the people in the apartment above me have four noisy kids. Sometimes it seem as if football games were going on upstairs. The noise reach a high point when I got home from work, which also happened to be the time the kids return from school. If the kids and neighbors were not disturbing me, I always had one other person to depend on—the superintendent, who visits my apartment whenever he felt like it. He always had an excuse, such as checking the water pipes or caulking the windows. But each time he came, I suspect he just wants to get away from his noisy family, which occupied the basement apartment. I move out of that apartment as soon as I was able to.

REVIEW TEST 2

Change verbs as necessary in the following selection so that they are consistently in the past tense. Cross out each incorrect verb and write the correct form above it. You will need to make ten corrections in all.

As a kid, I never really enjoyed the public swimming pool. First, there were all sorts of rules that prevent me from having much fun in the water. One was that children under the age of fourteen had to be accompanied by an adult. I didn't like having to beg a parent or a

continued

neighbor to take me swimming every time I want to go. Another rule was that girls are not allowed in the water without bathing caps. The required bathing cap was so tight that it cause a heavy pressure mark on my forehead. Also, it often gives me a headache. Second, I wasn't a very good swimmer then. Most of the time I find myself hanging on to the side of the pool. And whenever I attempted a graceful dive, I end up doing a belly flop. Finally, many of the kids tease me. Some of them liked splashing water into my face, which force me to swallow chlorine and a dead bug or two. Even worse was the boy who sneaks up behind me all summer long to dump ice cubes down the back of my swimsuit.

For additional materials on Chapter 13, visit **www.mhhe.com/langan**.

15 | CHAPTER | Pronoun Reference, Agreement, and Point of View

INTRODUCTORY ACTIVITY

Read each pair of sentences below, noting the underlined pronouns. Then see if you can circle the correct letter in each of the statements that follow.

1. a. None of my daughters gave <u>their</u> teacher a difficult time in kindergarten.

    b. None of my daughters gave <u>her</u> teacher a difficult time in kindergarten.

2. a. At the library, <u>they</u> helped me find online journal articles.

    b. At the library, <u>the librarians</u> helped me find online journal articles.

3. a. I want to apply for that job because <u>you</u> will have the opportunity to seek promotions.

    b. I want to apply for that job because <u>I</u> will have the opportunity to seek promotions.

In the first pair, (a, b) uses the underlined pronoun correctly because the pronoun refers to *None*, which is a singular word.

In the second pair, (a, b) is correct because otherwise the pronoun reference would be unclear.

In the third pair, (a, b) is correct because the pronoun point of view should not be shifted unnecessarily.

Answers are on page 625.

Pronouns are words that take the place of nouns (persons, places, or things). In fact, the word *pronoun* means *for a noun*. Pronouns are shortcuts that keep you from unnecessarily repeating words in writing. Here are some examples of pronouns:

> Melinda shampooed *her* dog. (*Her* is a pronoun that takes the place of *Melinda*.)

> As the door swung open, *it* creaked. (*It* replaces *door*.)

> When the motorcyclists arrived at McDonald's, *they* removed *their* helmets. (*They* and *their* replace *motorcyclists*.)

This section presents rules that will help you avoid three common mistakes people make with pronouns. The rules are as follows:

1. A pronoun must refer clearly to the word it replaces.

2. A pronoun must agree in number with the word or words it replaces.

3. Pronouns should not shift unnecessarily in point of view.

Pronoun Reference

A sentence may be confusing and unclear if a pronoun appears to refer to more than one word, as in this sentence:

> I locked my suitcase in my car, and then it was stolen.

(*What* was stolen? It is unclear whether the suitcase or the car was stolen.)

> I locked my suitcase in my car, and then my car was stolen.

A sentence may also be confusing if the pronoun does not refer to any specific word. Look at this sentence:

> We never buy fresh vegetables at that store because they charge too much.

(*Who* charges too much? There is no specific word that *they* refers to. Be clear.)

> We never buy fresh vegetables at that store because the owners charge too much.

Here are additional sentences with unclear pronoun reference. Read the explanations of why they are unclear and look carefully at the ways they are corrected.

Unclear	**Clear**
Amy told Gina that she had gained weight.	Amy told Gina, "You've gained weight."
(*Who* had gained weight: Amy or Gina? Be clear.)	(Quotation marks, which can sometimes be used to correct an unclear reference, are explained in Chapter 27.)
My older brother is an electrician, but I'm not interested in it. (There is no specific word that *it* refers to. It does not make sense to say, "I'm not interested in electrician.")	My older brother is an electrician, but I'm not interested in becoming one.
Our instructor did not explain the assignment, which made me angry. (Does *which* mean that the instructor's failure to explain the assignment made you angry, or that the assignment itself made you angry? Be clear.)	I was angry that our instructor did not explain the assignment.

| ACTIVITY 1 | Pronoun Reference |

Rewrite each of the following sentences to make clear the vague pronoun reference. Add, change, or omit words as necessary.

EXAMPLE

Lana thanked Maggie for the gift, which was very thoughtful of her.

Lana thanked Maggie for the thoughtful gift.

> In item 1, what does *it* stand for?

1. Sienna removed the blanket from the sofa bed and folded it up.

   _____

   _____

2. The defendant told the judge he was mentally ill.

   _____

3. Before the demonstration, they passed out signs for us to carry.

   _____

   _____

4. Kristy complained to Rachel that her boyfriend was being dishonest.

   _____

   _____

5. Because I didn't rinse last night's dishes, it smells like a garbage can.

   _____

   _____

6. The students watched a film on endangered species, which really depressed them.

   _____

   _____

7. The veterinarian said that if I find a tick on my dog, I should get rid of it immediately.

   _____

   _____

8. My sister removed the curtains from the windows so that she could wash them.

   _____

   _____

7. Neither one of the injured basketball players on the girls' team wanted to give up (her, their) spot on the team.

8. When Trevor visited the hospital, (they, the nurses) told him that his brother was discharged that morning.

9. Even if you want to socialize with your friends on the weekend, (you, I) need to finish your homework first.

10. Not one of the students in the class knew what (his or her, their) midterm grade was.

Cross out the pronoun error in each sentence and write the correction in the space provided. Then circle the letter that correctly describes the type of error that was made.

EXAMPLES

~~Anyone~~ turning in their papers late will be penalized.

_____Students_____

Mistake in: a. pronoun reference   (b.) pronoun agreement

When Clyde takes his son Paul to the park, ~~he~~ enjoys himself.

_____Paul (or Clyde)_____

Mistake in: (a.) pronoun reference   b. pronoun point of view

From where we stood, ~~you~~ could see three states.

_____we_____

Mistake in: a. pronoun agreement   (b.) pronoun point of view

1. A good salesperson knows that ~~you~~ They should be courteous to customers.

_____They_____

Mistake in: (a.) pronoun agreement   b. pronoun point of view

2. Neither of the girls who flunked bothered to bring their grades home.

_____

Mistake in: a. pronoun reference   b. pronoun agreement

3. When the shabbily dressed woman walked into the fancy hotel, they weren't very polite to her.

_____

Mistake in: a. pronoun agreement   b. pronoun reference

4. Nobody seems to add or subtract without ~~their~~ calculator anymore.

_____

Mistake in: a. pronoun agreement   b. pronoun point of view

5. Denise went everywhere with Nina until she moved to Texas last year.

   Mistake in: a. pronoun agreement   b. pronoun reference

6. Everyone on my street believes they saw a strange glow in the sky last night.

   Mistake in: a. pronoun agreement   b. pronoun point view

7. In baking desserts, people should follow the directions carefully or you are likely to end up with something unexpected.

   Mistake in: a. pronoun reference   b. pronoun point of view

8. When Jerry added another card to the delicate structure, it fell down.

   Mistake in: a. pronoun reference   b. pronoun point of view

9. Anyone who wants to join the car pool should leave their name with me.

   Mistake in: a. pronoun agreement   b. pronoun reference

10. Any working mother knows that you need at least a twenty-five-hour day.

    Mistake in: a. pronoun agreement   b. pronoun point of view

H I N T   In item 10, you will also need to correct a verb form.

For additional materials on Chapter 15, visit **www.mhhe.com/langan**.

Misplaced Modifiers

CHAPTER 18

INTRODUCTORY ACTIVITY

Because of misplaced words, each of the sentences below has more than one possible meaning. In each case, see if you can explain both the intended meaning and the unintended meaning.

1. The grocery clerk won the Mega Millions lottery working at the supermarket.

   Intended meaning: _____

   Unintended meaning: _____

   _____

2. The social worker met with the terminally ill patient's family who works for the hospital.

   Intended meaning:_____

   Unintended meaning: _____

   _____

Answers are on page 626.

What Misplaced Modifiers Are and How to Correct Them

Misplaced modifiers are words that, because of awkward placement, do not describe the words the writer intended them to describe. Misplaced modifiers often confuse the meaning of a sentence. To avoid them, place words as close as possible to what they describe.

Misplaced Words

They could see the Goodyear blimp *sitting on the front lawn*.
(The *Goodyear blimp* was sitting on the front lawn?)

We had a hamburger after the movie, *which was too greasy for my taste*.
(The *movie* was too greasy for my taste?)

Correctly Placed Words

Sitting on the front lawn, they could see the Goodyear blimp.
(The intended meaning—that the Goodyear blimp was visible from the front lawn—is now clear.)

After the movie, we had a hamburger, which was too greasy for my taste.
(The intended meaning—that the hamburger was greasy—is now clear.)

Our phone *almost rang* fifteen times last night.
(The phone *almost rang* fifteen times, but in fact did not ring at all?)

Our phone rang almost fifteen times last night.
(The intended meaning—that the phone rang a little under fifteen times—is now clear.)

Other single-word modifiers to watch out for include *only, even, hardly, nearly,* and *often.* Such words should be placed immediately before the word they modify.

ACTIVITY 1   **Fixing Misplaced Modifiers**

Underline the misplaced word or words in each sentence. Then rewrite the sentence, placing related words together to make the meaning clear.

EXAMPLE

Anita returned the hamburger to the supermarket <u>that was spoiled</u>.

Anita returned the hamburger that was spoiled to the supermarket.

> **H I N T**   Who is *at the back of the cage* in item 1?

1. The tiger growled at a passerby at <u>the back of his cage</u>.

   at the back of his cage the tiger

2. Lee hung colorful scarves over her windows <u>made of green and blue silk</u>.

   _____

   _____

3. We watched the fireworks <u>standing on our front porch</u>.

   _____

   _____

4. Jason almost has two hundred friends on Facebook.

   _____

   _____

5. The salesclerk exchanged the blue sweater for a yellow one with a smile.

   the saleclerk with a smile   ex change

   the blue sweater for a yellow one.

6. We all stared at the man in the front row of the theater with curly purple hair.

_____

_____

7. I love the cookies from the bakery with the chocolate frosting.

I love the chocolate frosting cookies from the bakery.

8. The faculty decided to strike during their last meeting.

During their last meeting

_____

9. Larry looked on as his car burned with disbelief.

Larry looked on as his car burned on with disbelief

10. My cousin sent me instructions on how to get to her house in a letter.

My cousin sent instructions on in a letter how to get her house

Placing Modifiers Correctly

ACTIVITY 2

Rewrite each sentence, adding the *italicized* words. Make sure that the intended meaning is clear and that two different interpretations are not possible.

EXAMPLE

I use a flash drive to store my computer files. (Insert *that I keep on my key chain*.)

I use a flash drive that I keep on my key chain to store my computer files.

HINT   Who is *using caution* in item 1?

1. I rolled down my car window only a few inches for the police officer. (Insert *using caution*.)

I caution use Rolled down my windows only a few inches for the police

2. Tabloids publish unflattering photos of celebrities who are arrested for drunk driving or possession of illicit drugs. (Insert *all over the world*.)

_____

_____

3. The mongoose was brought to Hawaii to kill rats but has since destroyed much of the native plant life. (Insert *which resembles the ferret*.)

    _____

    _____

4. Led Zeppelin's fourth album has sold 22 million copies. (Insert *almost*.)

    _____

    _____

5. Elisa decided to undergo laser eye surgery to correct her astigmatism. (Insert *at the university medical center*).

    Surgery University Medical Center

REFLECTIVE ACTIVITY

Review your answers to Activity 1 in this chapter. Explain why your corrections make the sentences clearer and more logical.

REVIEW TEST 1

Write *M* for *misplaced* or *C* for *correct* in front of each sentence.

M   1. I keep a twenty-dollar bill under the car seat for emergencies.

C   2. I keep a twenty-dollar bill for emergencies under the car seat.

M   3. This morning, I planned my day in the shower.

C   4. In the shower this morning, I planned my day.

M   5. While skating, Ben ran over a dog's tail.

C   6. Ben ran over a dog's tail skating.

M   7. I could hear my neighbors screaming at each other through the apartment wall.

C   8. Through the apartment wall, I could hear my neighbors screaming at each other.

C   9. For the family reunion, we cooked hamburgers and hot dogs on an outdoor grill.

_M_ 10. For the family reunion on an outdoor grill we cooked hamburgers and hot dogs.

_M_ -11. Virgil visited the old house, still weak with the flu.

_C_ 12. Virgil, still weak with the flu, visited the old house.

_C_ 13. While still weak with the flu, Virgil visited the old house.

_M_ 14. My teenage son nearly grew three inches last year.

_C_ 15. My teenage son grew nearly three inches last year.

_M_ 16. The instructor explained how to study for the final exam at the end of her lecture.

_C_ 17. The instructor explained how to study at the end of her lecture for the final exam.

_C_ 18. At the end of her lecture, the instructor explained how to study for the final exam.

_MC_ 19. In the library, I read that a deadly virus was spread through an air-conditioning system.

_CM_ 20. I read that a deadly virus was spread through an air-conditioning system in the library.

-4

80%

REVIEW TEST 2

Underline the five misplaced modifiers in the following passage. Then, in the spaces that follow, show how you would correct them.

¹The young teenagers who almost hang out in our town library every night are becoming a major nuisance. ²They show up on weeknights and infuriate the otherwise mild librarians throwing spitballs and paper airplanes. ³Some of the kids hide out behind stacks of bookcases; others indulge in continual adolescent flirting games. ⁴The noise many of these teenagers make is especially offensive to some of the older library patrons, who often give looks to the clusters of young people that are disapproving. ⁵One time there was so much noise that a librarian lost her temper and yelled at some boys to be quiet or leave the library at the top of her lungs. ⁶The worst recent offense took place when a soaking-wet dog was led into the middle of the library by a junior high school boy with a stubby tail and the meanest-looking face one could ever imagine.

Sentence number: _____

Correction:

_____

Sentence number: _____

Correction:

_____

Sentence number: _____

Correction:

_____

Sentence number: _____

Correction:

_____

Sentence number: _____

Correction:

_____

_____

 For additional materials on Chapter 18, visit www.mhhe.com/langan.

Dangling Modifiers

INTRODUCTORY ACTIVITY

Because of dangling modifiers, each of the sentences below has more than one possible meaning. In each case, see if you can explain both the intended meaning and the unintended meaning.

1. Sizzling, the customer at the restaurant enjoyed her grilled T-bone steak.

    Intended meaning: _____

    _____

    Unintended meaning: _____

    _____

2. Arriving home from college, Eric's parents threw a huge barbeque party for him.

    Intended meaning: _____

    _____

    Unintended meaning: _____

Answers are on page 627.

What Dangling Modifiers Are and How to Correct Them

A modifier that opens a sentence must be followed immediately by the word it is meant to describe. Otherwise, the modifier is said to be *dangling,* and the sentence takes on an unintended meaning. For example, look at this sentence:

While sleeping in his backyard, a Frisbee hit Bill on the head.

The unintended meaning is that the *Frisbee* was sleeping in his backyard. What the writer meant, of course, was that *Bill* was sleeping in his backyard. The writer should have placed *Bill* right after the modifier, revising the rest of the sentence as necessary:

While sleeping in his backyard, *Bill* was hit on the head by a Frisbee.

The sentence could also be corrected by adding the missing subject and verb to the opening word group:

> While *Bill* was sleeping in his backyard, a Frisbee hit him on the head.

Other sentences with dangling modifiers follow. Read the explanations of why they are dangling and look carefully at how they are corrected.

Dangling	**Correct**
Having almost no money, my survival depended on my parents. (*Who* has almost no money? The answer is not *survival* but *I*. The subject *I* must be added.)	Having almost no money, *I* depended on my parents for survival. *Or:* Since I had almost no money, I depended on my parents for survival.
Riding his bike, a German shepherd bit Tony on the ankle. (*Who* is riding the bike? The answer is not *German shepherd,* as it unintentionally seems to be, but *Tony*. The subject *Tony* must be added.)	Riding his bike, *Tony* was bitten on the ankle by a German shepherd. *Or:* While *Tony* was riding his bike, a German shepherd bit him on the ankle.
When trying to lose weight, all snacks are best avoided. (*Who* is trying to lose weight? The answer is not *snacks* but *you*. The subject *you* must be added.)	When trying to lose weight, *you* should avoid all snacks. *Or:* When *you* are trying to lose weight, avoid all snacks.

CONNECT WRITING

Meet Ajay. He's having trouble writing a letter to his daughter's principal about her food allergies. He's worried that some of his ideas are unclear because of where he's placed them in his sentences. Help Ajay locate and correct the misplaced and dangling modifiers in his letter to make it more readable.

mhconnectwriting.com

These examples make clear two ways of correcting a dangling modifier. Decide on a logical subject and do one of the following:

1. Place the subject *within* the opening word group:

   > Since *I* had almost no money, I depended on my parents for survival.

> **TIP**   In some cases an appropriate subordinating word such as *since* must be added, and the verb may have to be changed slightly as well.

2. Place the subject right *after* the opening word group:

   > Having almost no money, *I* depended on my parents for survival.

Sometimes even more rewriting is necessary to correct a dangling modifier. What is important to remember is that a modifier must be placed as close as possible to the word that it modifies.

Correcting Dangling Modifiers

Rewrite each sentence to correct the dangling modifier. Mark the one sentence that is correct with a C.

> **HINT**   What is *hanging safely on a wall* in item 1?

1. Hanging safely on a wall, a security guard pointed to the priceless painting. *The security guard pointed to the priceless painting, hanging safely on the wall.*

2. At the age of five, my mother bought me a chemistry set. *My mother bought me a chemistry set at the age of five.*

3. While it was raining, shoppers ran into the stores. *Shoppers ran into the stores, while it was raining.*

4. Having turned sour, I would not drink the milk. *Since the milk had turned sour, I would not drink it.*

5. Updating my Facebook profile, my hot tea turned cold. *While I was*

6. Piled high with dirty dishes, Pete hated to look at the kitchen sink. *Pete hated to look at the kitchen sink, piled high with dirty dishes.*

7. Having locked my keys in the car, the police had to open it for me. *C Because I locked my key in the car,*

8. Drooping and looking all dried out, the children watered the plants. *The children watered all the drooping dried out looking plants.*

9. After sitting through a long lecture, my foot was asleep.

[handwritten: I was] *[handwritten: feel]*

_____

_____

10. Being late, stopping at Starbucks was out of the question.

[handwritten: Sinice I was late]

_____

| ACTIVITY 2 | **Placing Modifiers Correctly** |

Complete the following sentences. In each case, a logical subject should follow the opening words.

EXAMPLE

Checking my monthly credit card statement, <u>I discovered that the</u> restaurant had charged me twice for my meal.

1. Since starting college, _____.

2. After finishing the first semester, _____.

3. While listening to music downloads, _____.

4. Before starting a family, _____.

5. At the age of sixteen, _____.

REFLECTIVE ACTIVITY

Review your answers to Activity 1. Explain why your corrections make the sentences clearer and more logical.

REVIEW TEST 1

Write *D* for *dangling* or *C* for *correct* in front of each sentence. Remember that the opening words are a dangling modifier if they are not followed immediately by a logical subject.

[handwritten: D] 1. Burning quickly, the firefighters turned several hoses on the house.

[handwritten: C] 2. Because the house was burning quickly, firefighters turned several hoses on it.

[handwritten: D] 3. While focusing the camera, several people wandered out of view.

_____ C 4. While I focused the camera, several people wandered out of view.

_____ D 5. When I peered down from the thirtieth floor, the cars looked like toys.

_____ D 6. Peering down from the thirtieth floor, the cars looked like toys.

_____ C 7. The cars looked like toys peering down from the thirtieth floor.

_____ D 8. Riding in the rear of the bus, the sudden starts and stops were sickening.

_____ C 9. For passengers riding in the rear of the bus, the sudden starts and stops were sickening.

_____ D 10. Speaking excitedly, the phone seemed glued to Sara's ear.

_____ C 11. The phone seemed glued to Sara's ear as she spoke excitedly.

_____ D 12. In a sentimental frame of mind, the music brought tears to Beth's eyes.

_____ C 13. As Beth was in a sentimental frame of mind, the music brought tears to her eyes.

_____ C 14. When Helen suddenly became sick, I drove her to the doctor's office.

_____ D 15. Suddenly sick, I drove Helen to the doctor's office.

_____ C 16. The pancake was browned on one side, so Mark flipped it over.

_____ D 17. Browned on one side, Mark flipped the pancake over.

_____ D 18. Hanging by her teeth, the acrobat's body swung back and forth.

_____ D 19. Hanging by her teeth, the acrobat swung back and forth.

_____ C 20. While hanging by her teeth, the acrobat's body swung back and forth.

REVIEW TEST 2

Underline the five dangling modifiers in this passage. Then correct them in the spaces provided.

¹Have you ever thought about what life was like for the first generation of your family to come to America? ²Or have you wondered what your grandparents did for fun when they were your age?

continued

³Family stories tend to be told for two or three generations and then disappear because no one ever records them. ⁴Using a camcorder, these stories can be saved for the future. ⁵Here are some hints for conducting interviews with older members of your family. ⁶Thinking hard about what you really want to know, good questions can be prepared in advance. ⁷Try to put the people you interview at ease by reassuring them that you value what they have to say. ⁸Nervous about the camera, stories might not come so easily to them otherwise. ⁹Remember that most people have never been interviewed before. ¹⁰Listening carefully to everything the person says, your interview will be more successful. ¹¹By respecting their feelings, your older relatives will be delighted to share their stories. ¹²The videos you record will be valued by your family for many years to come.

Sentence number: _____

Correction:

_____

_____

Sentence number: _____

Correction:

_____

_____

Sentence number: _____

Correction:

_____

_____

Sentence number: _____

Correction:

_____

Sentence number: _____

Correction:

_____

_____

For additional materials on Chapter 19, visit www.mhhe.com/langan.

Faulty Parallelism

INTRODUCTORY ACTIVITY

Read aloud each pair of sentences below. Write a check mark beside the sentence that reads more smoothly and clearly and sounds more natural.

Pair 1

_____ I use my TV remote control to change channels, to adjust the volume, and for turning the set on and off.

___✓___ I use my TV remote control to change channels, to adjust the volume, and to turn the set on and off.

Pair 2

_____ One option the employees had was to take a cut in pay; the other was longer hours of work.

___✓___ One option the employees had was to take a cut in pay; the other was to work longer hours.

Pair 3

_____ The refrigerator has a cracked vegetable drawer, one of the shelves is missing, and a strange freezer smell.

___✓___ The refrigerator has a cracked vegetable drawer, a missing shelf, and a strange freezer smell.

Answers are on page 627.

CHAPTER PREVIEW

Parallelism Explained

Homework

Parallelism Explained

Words in a pair or series should have parallel structure. By balancing the items in a pair or series so that they have the same kind of structure, you will make the sentence clearer and easier to read. Notice how the parallel sentences that follow read more smoothly than the nonparallel ones.

Nonparallel (Not Balanced)

Brit spends her free time reading, listening to music, and she works in the garden.

Parallel (Balanced)

Brit spends her free time reading, listening to music, and working in the garden.

(A balanced series of *-ing* words: *reading, listening, working.*)

Nonparallel (Not Balanced)	Parallel (Balanced)
After the camping trip I was exhausted, irritable, and wanted to eat.	After the camping trip I was exhausted, irritable, and hungry. (A balanced series of descriptive words: *exhausted, irritable, hungry.*)
My hope for retirement is to be healthy, to live in a comfortable house, and having plenty of money.	My hope for retirement is to be healthy, to live in a comfortable house, and to have plenty of money. (A balanced series of *to* verbs: *to be, to live, to have.*)
Nightly, Fred puts out the trash, checks the locks on the doors, and the burglar alarm is turned on.	Nightly, Fred puts out the trash, checks the locks on the doors, and turns on the burglar alarm. (Balanced verbs and word order: *puts out the trash, checks the locks, turns on the burglar alarm.*)

Balanced sentences are not a skill you need to worry about when you are writing first drafts. But when you rewrite, you should try to put matching words and ideas into matching structures. Such parallelism will improve your writing style.

ACTIVITY 1 | Using Parallelism

The one item in each list that is not parallel in form to the other items is crossed out. In the space provided, rewrite that item in parallel form. The first one has been done for you as an example.

1. fresh food

   attractive setting

   ~~service that is fast~~

   fast service

2. screaming children

   ~~dogs that howl~~

   blaring music

   howling dogs

3. slow

   ~~speaks rudely~~

   careless

   rude

4. ~~to hike~~

   swimming

   boating

   hiking

5. noisy neighbors

   high rent

   ~~security that is poor~~

   Poor security

6. ~~cleaning of the apartment~~

   paid the bills

   did the laundry

   Cleaned the apartment

7. looking good

~~to have fun~~

feeling fine

have fun

8. healthy soups

tasty sandwiches

~~desserts that are inexpensive~~

inexpensive desserts

9. under the desk drawers

~~the floor of the closet~~

behind the bedroom curtains

on the closet floor

10. works at the supermarket

~~singer in the church choir~~

coaches the Little League team

Singing in the church choir

Correcting Nonparallel Sentences

ACTIVITY 2

The unbalanced part of each sentence is *italicized*. Rewrite this part so that it matches the rest of the sentence.

EXAMPLE

In the afternoon, I changed two diapers, ironed several shirts, and *was studying* for two exams. _studied_

1. Taiyaba dropped a coin into the slot machine, pulled the lever, and *~~was waiting~~* to strike it rich.

   waited

2. Studying a little each day is more effective than *to cram.*

   cramming

3. Many old people fear loneliness, *~~becoming ill~~,* and poverty.

   illness

4. My pet peeves are screeching chalk, *buses that are late,* and dripping sinks.

   late buses

5. The magazine cover promised stories on losing weight quickly, *how to attract a* rich spouse, and finding the perfect haircut.

   attracting

6. As smoke billowed around her, Paula knew her only choices were to jump or *suffocation.*

   to suffocate

7. The principal often pestered students, yelled at teachers, and *was interrupting* classes.

   interrupted

8. People immigrate to America with hopes of finding freedom, happiness, and *~~in order to become financially secure~~.*

   financial security

CONNECT WRITING

Meet Yelina. She's very impressed with the slides her classmate put together for his class presentation, but thinks a few of his ideas could be presented more clearly. Some of the words paired together in his sentences do not have a parallel structure. Help Yelina and her classmate locate and correct the parallelism mistakes in the class presentation.

mhconnectwriting.com

9. Once inside the zoo gates, Julio could hear lions roaring, *the chirping of birds*, and elephants trumpeting.

   bird chirping

10. As a child, I had nightmares about a huge monster that came out of a cave, *was breathing fire*, and wanted to barbecue me.

    breathed fire

REFLECTIVE ACTIVITY

Review your answers to Activity 2. Explain why your corrections make the sentences clearer and more logical.

ACTIVITY 3   **Writing Parallel Sentences**

Complete the following statements. The first two parts of each statement are parallel in form; the part that you add should be parallel in form as well.

EXAMPLE

Three things I could not live without are my cell phone, my laptop, and <u>my morning coffee.</u>

1. The new reality TV show is disappointing: The premise is absurd, the cast members are uninteresting, and *it uneducation*

2. As a parent, I promise to love my child unconditionally, to provide for my child's needs, and *To*

3. As the students waited for the professor to arrive for class, they rummaged through their backpacks, silenced their phones, and *pepared for class, finish there paper*

4. During my first year in my own apartment, I learned how to fix leaky toilets and torn screens, how to survive on instant ramen and frozen pizzas, and *pay bills on time.*

5. Online dating is popular, unpredictable, and *dangerous*

Editing and Rewriting

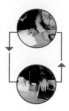

Working with a partner, read carefully the short paragraph below and cross out the five instances of faulty parallelism. Then use the space provided to correct the instances of faulty parallelism. Feel free to discuss the rewrite quietly with your partner and refer back to the chapter when necessary.

> Running is an exercise that can be good for you mentally, physically, and also be helpful for your emotions. A beginning runner should keep three things in mind: the warm-up session, the actual time that you are running, and the cool-down period. Never start a run without first having warmed up through stretching exercises. Stretching reduces muscle stiffness, decreases the possibility of injury, and it's a good method to gradually increase the heart rate. During the run itself, move at a comfortable pace. Your breathing should be steady and with depth. Finally, remember to cool down after a run. An adequate cool-down period allows time for the body to relax and the normalizing of the heart rate.

REFLECTIVE ACTIVITY

1. Look at the paragraph that you revised in Activity 4. How does parallel form improve the paragraph?

2. How would you evaluate your own use of parallel form? When you write, do you use it almost never, at times, or often? How would you benefit from using it more?

| ACTIVITY 5 | Creating Sentences |

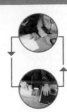

Working with a partner, make up your own short test on faulty parallelism, as directed.

1. Write a sentence that includes three things you want to do tomorrow. One of those things should not be in parallel form. Then correct the faulty parallelism.

    Nonparallel _____

    _____

    Parallel _____

    _____

2. Write a sentence that names three positive qualities of a person you like or three negative qualities that you don't like.

    Nonparallel _____

    _____

    Parallel _____

    _____

3. Write a sentence that includes three everyday things that annoy you.

    Nonparallel _____

    _____

    Parallel _____

    _____

| REVIEW TEST 1 |

Cross out the unbalanced part of each sentence. Then rewrite the unbalanced part so that it matches the other item or items in the sentence.

EXAMPLE

I enjoy texting my friends and ~~to chat~~ online.

chatting _____

1. Andreas is known to skip classes, make excuses, and then he borrows his classmates' notes.

    _____ Borrow _____

2. Before my blind date, I bought a new outfit, got a haircut, ~~and to work~~ out at the gym.

   _____worked out_____ *[margin: work out]*

3. The children at the preschool had fingerpaint-stained hands, jelly-smudged lips, and th~~eir faces were~~ smiling.

   _____Smiling faces_____ *[margin: smiling faces]*

4. Zach listened to his iPod, was text messaging his friends, and surfed online ~~all at the same time.~~

   _____Surfing Online_____ *[margin: surfing online]*

5. My homemade pesto recipe calls for extra-virgin olive oil, several sprigs of fresh basil, and ~~pine nuts that were roasted.~~

   _____roasted pine nuts_____ *[margin: and roasted pine nuts]*

6. When I want to relax, I grab a cold soda, open a bag of chips, turn on the TV, and ~~I like to watch whatever sports game is on.~~

   _____Watch Sports_____ *[margin: watch sports]*

7. The mail brought utility bills, monthly statements from the bank, and credit card applications.

   _____Credit application_____ *[margin: credit application]*

8. Samantha goes to Las Vegas every year with her friends to gamble, to eat at the buffets, and ~~she sees at least one show.~~

   _____Sees a show_____

9. This summer, Kalani will travel to Samoa, Tahiti, and ~~he is going to~~ Guam.

   _____and Guam_____

10. My baby enjoys her mechanical swing, her gym mat, and ~~her bouncer that plays music.~~

    _____Music bouncer_____

REVIEW TEST 2

Each group of sentences contains two errors in parallelism. Underline these errors. Then, on the lines below, rewrite each item that doesn't match to make it parallel with the other item or items in the sentence.

1. When Phil left for work, he felt bright and cheerful. But by midafternoon he was coughing, wheezing, and shivers ran throughout his body. He left work, drove home, and was crawling into bed, where he stayed for the next four days.

   a. _____

   b. _____

2. I never spend money on fancy wrapping paper. When people get a present, they generally want to rip off the paper and be looking at what's inside. So I wrap my gifts in either plain brown grocery bags or Sunday comics that are colorful.

    a. _____

    b. _____

3. Failing students can be kinder than to pass them. There is little benefit to passing a student to a level of work he or she can't do. In addition, it is cruel to graduate a student from high school who has neither the communication skills nor the ~~skills at math needed~~ to get along in the world. *math skills*

    a. _____

    b. _____

4. The little boy drew back from his new babysitter. Her long red nails, black eye makeup, and jewelry that jangled all frightened him. He was sure she was either a bad witch or a queen who was evil.

    a. *a bad or Queen or* _____

    b. *evil witch* _____

5. An actress stopped in the middle of a Broadway show and scolded flash photographers in the audience. She said they can either have a photo session or they can be enjoying the show, but they can't do both. The photographers *sat* ~~sank down~~ in their seats, their cameras *put* ~~were put~~ away, and quietly watched the show.

    a. *Put away* _____

    b. _____

REVIEW TEST 3

Cross out the five nonparallel parts in the following passage. Correct them in the spaces between the lines.

> When a few people in one community decided to form a homeowners' association, many of their neighbors were skeptical. Some objected to stirring things up, and others were feeling the dues were too high. But many neighbors joined, and their first big success was a garage sale. They scheduled a day for everybody in the neighborhood to bring unwanted items to a community center. Big appliances and other items that are heavy were picked up by

continued

volunteers with trucks. The association promoted the sale by placing ads in newspapers and ~~with the~~ distribution ~~of~~ fliers at local shopping centers. Dozens of families took part. After that, the association helped plant trees, start*ed* a Crime Watch Program, and ~~in~~ repairing cracked sidewalks. Members now receive discounts from local merchants and theater owners. This association's success has inspired many more neighbors to join and people in other ~~neighborhood~~ neighborhoods, who ~~are~~ *to* start*ed* their own organizations.

For additional materials on Chapter 20, visit **www.mhhe.com/langan**.

Paper Format

INTRODUCTORY ACTIVITY

Check the paper opening below that seems clearer and easier to read.

____ A

	Dangers of Prescription Drugs
	Careless consumers can harm themselves with
	prescription drugs. To begin with, consumers should always
	be aware of the possible side effects of a prescription drug.

____ B

	"dangers of prescription drugs"
	Careless consumers can harm themselves with prescription drugs.
	To begin with, consumers should always be aware of the possible
	side effects of a prescription drug. They should take the time.

What are four reasons for your choice?

_____

_____

_____

_____

Answers are on page 628.

CHAPTER PREVIEW

Guidelines for Preparing a Paper

Guidelines for Preparing a Paper

Here are guidelines to follow in preparing a paper for an instructor.

1. Use standard letter-sized 8½ by 11 paper.

2. Leave wide margins (1 to 1½ inches) all around the paper. In particular, do not crowd the right-hand or bottom margin. This white space makes your paper more readable and leaves the instructor room for comments.

3. Always use black as your font color, and choose a font style that is easy to read, such as Times New Roman. Avoid fancy or distracting colors and fonts. Make sure the type is large enough to be readable but not overwhelming. Most instructors prefer fonts in the 10–12 point range.

4. If you write by hand (check whether your instructor permits it):

   - Use a pen with blue or black ink (*not* a pencil).

   - Be careful not to overlap letters and not to make decorative loops on letters.

   - On narrow-ruled paper, write on every other line.

   - Make all your letters distinct. Pay special attention to *a, e, i, o,* and *u*—five letters that people sometimes write illegibly.

5. Center the title of your paper on the first line of the first page. Do not put quotation marks around the title. Do not underline the title. Capitalize all the major words in a title, including the first word. Short connecting words within a title, such as *of, for, the, in, to,* and all prepositions, are not capitalized.

6. Skip a line between the title and the first line of your text. Indent the first line of each paragraph about five spaces (half an inch) from the left-hand margin.

7. Make commas, periods, and other punctuation marks firm and clear. Leave a slight space after each period.

8. If you break a word at the end of a line, break only between syllables. Do not break words of one syllable.

9. Put your name, date, and course number where your instructor asks for them.

Remember these points about the title and the first sentence of your paper.

10. The title should be one or several words that tell what the paper is about. It should usually *not* be a complete sentence. For example, if you are writing a paper about your jealous sister, the title could simply be "My Jealous Sister."

11. Do not rely on the title to help explain the first sentence of your paper. The first sentence must be independent of the title. For instance, if the title of your paper is "My Jealous Sister," the first sentence should *not* be, "She has been this way as long as I can remember." Rather, the first sentence might be, "My sister has always been a jealous person."

Correcting Formatting Errors

Identify the mistakes in format in the following lines from a student composition. Explain the mistakes in the spaces provided. One mistake is described for you as an example.

	"Being a younger sister"
	When I was young, I would gladly have donated my older sister to ano-
	ther family. First of all, most of my clothes were hand-me-downs. I ra-
	rely got to buy anything new to wear. My sister took very good care
	of her clothes, which only made the problem worse. Also, she was always
	very critical of everything.

1. Break words at correct syllable divisions (an-other).

2. Do not quations mark around the title

3. capátlizé the major words in the title Begin Young sister

4. Skip a line Between title and the Frist line

5. Indent the frist line

6. Keep margins on both side of the paper

Writing Titles

As already stated, a title should tell in several words what a paper is about. Often a title can be based on the sentence that expresses the main idea of a paper.

Following are five main-idea sentences from student papers. Write a suitable specific title for each paper, basing the title on the main idea.

EXAMPLE

Title: Aging Americans as Outcasts

Our society treats aging Americans as outcasts in many ways.

HINT What is a three-word subject for the paper in item 1?

1. Title: Benifit of pets

Pets offer a number of benefits to their owners.

2. Title: Leaning How to budget

Since I have learned to budget carefully, I no longer run out of money at the end of the week.

3. Title: _The Vaulabe of a study group_

Studying regularly with a study group has helped me raise my grades.

4. Title: _____

Grandparents have a special relationship with their grandchildren.

5. Title: _a Special relationship or grandparent and Grand child_

My decision to eliminate junk food from my diet has been good for my health and my budget.

| ACTIVITY 3 | **Rewriting Dependent Sentences** |

In four of the five following sentences, the writer has mistakenly used the title to help explain the first sentence. But as previously noted, you must *not* rely on the title to explain your first sentence. Rewrite the sentences so that they are independent of the title. Write *Correct* under the one sentence that is independent.

EXAMPLE

Title: Flunking an Exam

First sentence: I managed to do this because of several bad habits.

Rewritten: I managed to flunk an exam because of several bad habits.

> **HINT**   Indicate the words that *this* stands for in item 1.

EXAMPLE

Title: Finishing a Marathon

First sentence: I managed to do this because I followed a strict training schedule.

Rewritten: I managed to finish a marathon because I followed a strict training schedule.

1. Title: Effective Communication

First sentence: This is often the key to a healthy relationship.

Rewritten: _____

_____

2. Title: Reality TV Shows

First sentence: They are popular for several reasons.

Rewritten: _____

_____

3. Title: My First Day of College

First sentence: My first day of college was the most nervous day of my adult life.

Rewritten: _____

4. Title: The Best Vacation I Ever Had

    First sentence: It began when my friends from high school booked a one-week trip to Cancun, Mexico.

    Rewritten: _____

    _____

5. Title: Professional Athletes on Steroids

    First sentence: Most of them say that they don't use it to enhance athletic performance.

    Rewritten: _____

    _____

Use the space below to rewrite the following sentences from a student paper, correcting the mistakes in format.

teachers should encourage cheating
Teachers warn students about the dangers of it, but they should encourage the-
ir students to cheat at least once. When I was a senior in high school, I cheated on a
take-home history test. Although I studied, I was not able to answer all the questions,
so I looked online and copied down information from a few Web sites. I was so worried
that I would be caught that I could not look directly at my teacher when I turned in my
test. All week, I thought that he would confront me about my cheating. Instead, my
teacher gave me an "A" on the test. I felt so guilty that I vowed never to cheat again,
and I have never cheated since.

For additional materials on Chapter 22, visit **www.mhhe.com/langan**.

23 CHAPTER | Capital Letters

INTRODUCTORY ACTIVITY

You probably know a good deal about the uses of capital letters. Answering the questions below will help you check your knowledge.

1. Write the full name of a person you know: _____

2. In what city and state were you born? _____

3. What is your present street address? _____

4. Name a country where you would like to travel: _____

5. Name a school that you attended: _____

6. Give the name of a store where you buy food: _____

7. Name a company where you or anyone you know

   works: _____

8. Which day of the week is the busiest for you? _____

9. What holiday is your favorite? _____

10. Which brand of toothpaste do you use? _____

11. Give the brand name of a candy you like: _____

12. Name a song or a television show you enjoy: _____

13. Write the title of a magazine or newspaper you

    read: _____

Items 14–16

Three capital letters are needed in the example below. Underline the words you think should be capitalized. Then write them, capitalized, in the spaces provided.

> on Super Bowl Sunday, my roommate said, "let's buy some snacks and invite a few friends over to watch the game." i knew my plans to write a term paper would have to be changed.

14. _____   15. _____   16. _____

Answers are on page 629.

Main Uses of Capital Letters

Capital letters are used with:

1. First word in a sentence or direct quotation

2. Names of persons and the word *I*

3. Names of particular places

4. Names of days of the week, months, and holidays

5. Names of commercial products

6. Titles of books, magazines, articles, films, television shows, songs, poems, stories, papers that you write, and the like

7. Names of companies, associations, unions, clubs, religious and political groups, and other organizations

Each use is illustrated on the pages that follow.

First Word in a Sentence or Direct Quotation

Our company has begun laying people off.

The doctor said, "This may hurt a bit."

"My husband," said Martha, "is a light eater. When it's light, he starts to eat."

EXPLANATION: In the third example above, *My* and *When* are capitalized because they start new sentences. But *is* is not capitalized because it is part of the first sentence.

Names of Persons and the Word *I*

At the picnic, I met Tony Curry and Lola Morrison.

Names of Particular Places

After graduating from Gibbs High School in Houston, I worked for a summer at a nearby Holiday Inn on Clairmont Boulevard.

But   Use small letters if the specific name of a place is not given.

After graduating from high school in my hometown, I worked for a summer at a nearby hotel on one of the main shopping streets.

Names of Days of the Week, Months, and Holidays

This year, Memorial Day falls on the last Thursday in May.

But   Use small letters for the seasons—summer, fall, winter, and spring.

In the early summer and fall, my hay fever bothers me.

Names of Commercial Products

The consumer magazine gave high ratings to Cheerios breakfast cereal, Breyer's ice cream, and Progresso chicken noodle soup.

But Use small letters for the *type* of product (breakfast cereal, ice cream, chicken noodle soup, and the like).

Titles of Books, Magazines, Articles, Films, Television Shows, Songs, Poems, Stories, Papers That You Write, and the Like

My oral report was on *The Diary of a Young Girl,* by Anne Frank.

While watching *All My Children* on television, I thumbed through *Cosmopolitan* magazine and the *New York Times.*

Names of Companies, Associations, Unions, Clubs, Religious and Political Groups, and Other Organizations

A new bill before Congress is opposed by the National Rifle Association.

My wife is Jewish; I am Roman Catholic. We are both members of the Democratic Party.

My parents have life insurance with Prudential, auto insurance with Allstate, and medical insurance with United Healthcare.

ACTIVITY 1	**Capitalizing Names and Titles**

In the sentences that follow, cross out the words that need capitals. Then write the capitalized forms of the words in the space provided. The number of spaces tells you how many corrections to make in each case.

EXAMPLE

Rhoda said, "~~why~~ should I bother to *eat* this ~~hershey~~ bar? I should just apply it directly to my hips." <u>Why</u>   <u>Hershey</u>

> The word *I* and names of organizations are capitalized.

1. Sometimes i still regret not joining the boy scouts when I was in grade school.

   _____ _____ _____

2. On the friday after thanksgiving, Carole went to target to buy gifts for her family.

   _____ _____ _____

3. In the box office of the regal cinema is a sign saying, "if you plan to see an R-rated movie, be ready to show your ID."

   _____   _____   _____

4. In many new england towns, republicans outnumber democrats five to one.

   _____   _____   _____   _____

5. Nelson was surprised to learn that both state farm and nationwide have insurance offices in the prudential building.

   _____   _____   _____   _____   _____

6. Magazines such as *time* and *newsweek* featured articles about the fires that devastated part of southern california.

   _____   _____   _____

7. The rose grower whom Steve works for said that the biggest rose-selling holidays are valentine's day and mother's day.

   _____   _____   _____   _____

8. With some pepsis and fritos nearby, the kids settled down to play a game on the macintosh computer.

   _____   _____   _____

9. Bob's ford taurus was badly damaged when he struck a deer last saturday.

   _____   _____   _____

10. Though Julie Andrews excelled in the broadway version of *my fair lady*, Audrey Hepburn was cast as the female lead in the movie version.

   _____   _____   _____   _____

Other Uses of Capital Letters

Capital letters are also used with:

- Names that show family relationships
- Titles of persons when used with their names
- Specific school courses
- Languages
- Geographic locations
- Historic periods and events
- Races, nations, and nationalities
- Opening and closing of a letter

Each use is illustrated on the pages that follow.

Names That Show Family Relationships

Aunt Sally and Uncle Jack are selling their house.

I asked Grandfather to start the fire.

Is Mother feeling better?

But   Do not capitalize words such as *mother, father, grandmother, grandfather, uncle, aunt,* and so on when they are preceded by *my* or another possessive word.

My aunt and uncle are selling their house.

I asked my grandfather to start the fire.

Is my mother feeling better?

Titles of Persons When Used with Their Names

I wrote an angry letter to Senator Blutt.

Can you drive to Dr. Stein's office?

We asked Professor Bushkin about his attendance policy.

But   Use small letters when titles appear by themselves, without specific names.

I wrote an angry letter to my senator.

Can you drive to the doctor's office?

We asked our professor about his attendance policy.

Specific School Courses

My courses this semester include Accounting I, Introduction to Computer Science, Business Law, General Psychology, and Basic Math.

But   Use small letters for general subject areas.

This semester I'm taking mostly business courses, but I have a psychology course and a math course as well.

Languages

Lydia speaks English and Spanish equally well.

Geographic Locations

I lived in the South for many years and then moved to the West Coast.

But   Use small letters in giving directions.

Go south for about five miles and then bear west.

Historic Periods and Events

One essay question dealt with the Battle of the Bulge in World War II.

Races, Nations, and Nationalities

The census form asked whether I was African American, Native American, Hispanic, or Asian.

Last summer I hitchhiked through Italy, France, and Germany.

The city is a melting pot for Koreans, Vietnamese, and Mexican Americans.

But   Use small letters when referring to *whites* or *blacks*.

Both whites and blacks supported our mayor in the election.

Opening and Closing of a Letter

Dear Sir:	Sincerely yours,
Dear Madam:	Truly yours,

Capitalize only the first word in a closing.

Where Is Capitalization Needed?	ACTIVITY 2

Cross out the words that need capitals in the following sentences. Then write the capitalized forms of the words in the spaces provided. The number of spaces tells you how many corrections to make in each case.

1. My uncle david, who has cirrhosis of the liver, added his name to the national waiting list for organ transplants.

   _____   _____

2. My daughter asked me to buy her a magenta pink motorola razr phone and bluetooth headset for her sixteenth birthday.

   _____   _____   _____

3. Former united states president jimmy carter received the nobel peace prize in 2002.

   _____   _____   _____   _____   _____

   _____   _____   _____

4. Terisa spoke to the class about her experience as a pacific islander from samoa who is now living on the east coast.

   _____   _____   _____   _____

   _____

5. Next semester, I want to register for principles of marketing and two other business courses.

   _____   _____

Unnecessary Use of Capitals

| ACTIVITY 3 | **Where Is Capitalization Unnecessary?** |

Many errors in capitalization are caused by adding capitals where they are not needed. Cross out the incorrectly capitalized letters in the following sentences and write the correct forms in the spaces provided. The number of spaces tells you how many corrections to make in each sentence.

1. Everyone waits for Mariko's Husband, who is from Texas, to make his famous Barbeque Ribs.

   _____ _____ _____

2. One of Stuart's English professors at his Community College worked for Google as a Technical Writer.

   _____ _____ _____ _____

3. The Electronics Store at Meadowland Mall is having a sale on Televisions and DVD Players.

   _____ _____ _____ _____

4. Several Community Organizations are sponsoring a Food Drive at the neighborhood homeless shelter.

   _____ _____ _____ _____

5. Bridget spoke to her daughter's Science Teacher about the upcoming field trip to the Tidal Pools at Sunset Grove Beach.

   _____ _____ _____ _____

| ACTIVITY 4 | **Editing and Rewriting** |

Working with a partner, read the short paragraph below and mark off the fifteen spots where capital letters are missing. Then use the space provided to rewrite the passage, adding capital letters where needed. Feel free to discuss the passage quietly with your partner and refer back to the chapter when necessary.

The morning that I visited the lincoln memorial, it was raining. It was a quiet thursday in late october, and the air was cold. I was with uncle walt, and we had spent the morning visiting the smithsonian institution together. After lunch, my uncle said to me, "now we're going to go someplace that you'll never forget." When we arrived, I was overwhelmed by lincoln's massive statue, which dwarfed everything around it—just as the man had done in life. To my left I was aware of the silently flowing potomac river. Engraved

continued

on one of the marble walls was the gettysburg address. I read those familiar words and remained there for a time in silence, touched by the simple eloquence of that speech. I then snapped just one picture with my kodak camera and walked down the stone steps quietly.   The photograph still sits on my desk today as a reminder of that special visit.

_____

_____

_____

_____

_____

_____

_____

_____

Creating Sentences

ACTIVITY 5

Working with a partner, write a sentence (or two) as directed. Pay special attention to capital letters.

1. Write about a place you like (or want) to visit. Be sure to give the name of the place, including the city, state, or country where it is located.

2. Write a sentence (or two) in which you state the name of your elementary school, your favorite teacher or subject, and your least favorite teacher or subject.

3. Write a sentence (or two) that includes the names of three brand-name products that you often use. You may begin the sentence with the words, "Three brand-name products I use every day are . . ."

4. Think of the name of your favorite musical artist or performer. Then write a sentence in which you include the musician's name and the title of one of his or her songs.

5. Write a sentence in which you describe something you plan to do two days from now. Be sure to include the date and day of the week.

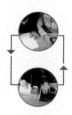

REFLECTIVE ACTIVITY

1. What would writing be like without capital letters? Use an example or two to help show how capital letters are important to writing.

2. What three uses of capital letters are most difficult for you to remember? Explain, giving examples.

REVIEW TEST 1

Cross out the words that need capitals in the following sentences. Then write the capitalized forms of the words in the spaces provided. The number of spaces tells you how many corrections to make in each sentence.

EXAMPLE

During halftime of the ~~saturday~~ afternoon football game, my sister said, "~~let's~~ get some hamburgers from ~~wendy~~'s or put a pizza in the oven."

Saturday   _Let's_   _Wendy's_

1. When he saw the commercial that said "just do it," Lance put on his nike running shoes and went to the store to get some ice cream.

   _____   _____

2. Millions of years ago, america's midwest was covered by a great inland sea.

   _____   _____

3. One of our thanksgiving traditions is sending a check to an organization such as greenpeace, which helps protect the environment.

   _____   _____

4. If you drive onto route 10 in tallahassee, florida, and stay on that road, you'll eventually end up in california.

   _____   _____   _____   _____

5. Just before english class this morning, Arlene titled her final paper "my argument for an A."

   _____   _____   _____

6. I read in the book *royal lives* that when an ancient egyptian king died, his servants were often killed and buried with him.

   _____   _____   _____

7. dear mr. Bradford:
   This is the third and final time I will write to complain about the leak
   in my bathroom.
   sincerely,
   Anne Morrison

   _____   _____   _____

8. "After age eighty," grandma ida would say, "time passes very quickly.
   it seems as though it's time for breakfast every fifteen minutes."

   _____   _____   _____

9. Dr. Green, who teaches a course called cultural anthropology, spent
   last summer on an archaeological dig in israel.

   _____   _____   _____

10. During the singing of "the star-spangled banner," many fans at
    yankee stadium drank sodas, read their programs, or chatted with each
    other.

    _____   _____   _____

    _____   _____   _____

REVIEW TEST 2

On a separate piece of paper, write:

- seven sentences demonstrating the seven main uses of capital letters.

- eight sentences demonstrating the eight other uses of capital letters.

For additional materials on Chapter 23, visit www.mhhe.com/langan.

24 CHAPTER | Numbers and Abbreviations

INTRODUCTORY ACTIVITY

Write a check mark beside the item in each pair that you think uses numbers correctly.

I left the gym at 7:30, but I only completed 75 percent of my workout routine. _____

I left the gym at seven-thirty, but I only completed seventy-five percent of my workout routine. _____

85 people applied for the government job, but there are only 15 permanent positions. _____

Eighty-five people applied for the government job, but there are only fifteen permanent positions. _____

Write a check mark beside the item in each pair that you think uses abbreviations correctly.

My daughter's preschool teacher, Mrs. Landry, likes to start class at 9 am sharp. _____

My daughter's preschool teacher, Mrs. Landry, likes to start class at 9 a.m. sharp. _____

I waited one hr. to see Dr. Lee, but my exam only took five mins. _____

I waited one hour to see Dr. Lee, but my exam only took five minutes. _____

Answers are on page 629.

Numbers

Keep the following three rules in mind when using numbers.

Rule 1

Spell out numbers that take no more than two words. Otherwise, use numerals—the numbers themselves.

Last year Tina bought nine new CDs.

Ray struck out fifteen batters in Sunday's softball game.

But

Tina now has 114 CDs in her collection.

Already this season Ray has recorded 168 strikeouts.

You should also spell out a number that begins a sentence.

One hundred fifty first-graders throughout the city showed flu symptoms today.

Rule 2

Be consistent when you use a series of numbers. If some numbers in a sentence or paragraph require more than two words, then use numbers themselves throughout the selection.

That executive who tried to cut 250 employees' salaries owns 8 cars, 4 homes, 3 boats, and 1 jet.

Rule 3

Use numbers to show dates, times, addresses, percentages, exact sums of money, and parts of a book.

John F. Kennedy was killed on November 22, 1963.

My job interview was set for 10:15. (*But:* Spell out numbers before *o'clock*. For example: The time was then changed to eleven o'clock.)

Janet's new address is 118 North 35 Street.

Almost 40 percent of my meals are eaten at fast-food restaurants.

The cashier rang up a total of $18.35. (*But:* Round amounts may be expressed as words. For example: The movie has an eight-dollar admission charge.)

Read Chapter 6 in your math textbook and answer questions 1 to 5 on page 250.

CONNECT WRITING

Meet Ronit. She's very excited to be adopting a baby girl from Kazakhstan and is throwing a party to celebrate the adoption. She's almost finished writing out the invitations, but keeps stumbling over how to write numbers correctly. Help Ronit locate and correct all the number mistakes in her adoption party invitation.

mhconnectwriting.com

Using Numbers

ACTIVITY 1

Working with a partner, use the three rules to make the corrections needed in these sentences.

 HINT In item 1, use numerals to show time.

1. During the summer, I like to stay up until two thirty a.m. playing video games and chatting online with my gamer friends.

2. This semester, Mohammed is taking 5 classes and two labs.

3. My dog Missy, an adorable Maltese, is 11 years old—that's 77 in people years.

4. Every day Mike gets up at 5 o'clock to run 4 miles.

5. Americans waste over fifteen percent of the food that they purchase from supermarkets and restaurants.

6. An adult human body has two hundred and six bones.

7. Dr. Martin Luther King Jr. was born on January fifteenth.

8. Someone ate over 200 pickled jalapeño peppers at the State Fair of Texas.

9. My cousin went to Las Vegas to get married on July seventh, two thousand and seven, supposedly the luckiest day of the year.

10. Akira Kurosawa's film The 7 *Samurai* was nominated for an Academy Award in 1954.

Abbreviations

While abbreviations are a helpful time-saver in note-taking, you should avoid most abbreviations in formal writing. Listed below are some of the few abbreviations that are acceptable in compositions. Note that a period is used after most abbreviations.

- Mr., Mrs., Ms., Jr., Sr., Dr., when used with proper names:

  Mr. Rollin   Ms. Peters   Dr. Coleman

- Time references:

  A.M. or AM or a.m.   P.M. or PM or p.m.   BC/AD or B.C./A.D.

- First or middle initial in a name:

  T. Alan Parker   Linda M. Evans

- Organizations, technical words, and trade names known primarily by initials:

  ABC   CIA   UNESCO   GM   AIDS   DNA

| ACTIVITY 2 | **Using Abbreviations** |

Cross out the words that should not be abbreviated and correct them in the spaces provided.

 No words should be abbreviated in item 1.

1. After I placed the "bike for sale" ad in the newsp., the tele. rang nonstop for a week.

   _____   _____

2. Sharon bought two bush. of ripe tomatoes at the farm mkt. on Rt. 73.

   _____   _____   _____

3. On Mon., NASA will announce its plans for a Sept. flight to Mars.

   _____   _____

4. The psych class was taught by Dr. Aronson, a noted psychiatrist from Eng.

   _____   _____

5. The best things on the menu are the chick. pot pie and the mac. and cheese.

   _____   _____

6. Several baby opossums (each of which weighs less than an oz.) can fit into a tbsp.

   _____   _____

7. I didn't have time to study for my chem. test on Sun., but I studied for four hrs. yesterday.

   _____   _____   _____

8. Every Jan., our co. gives awards for the best employee suggestions of the previous yr.

   _____   _____   _____

9. Lawrence T. Johnson lost his lic. to practice medicine when the state board discovered he never went to med. school.

   _____   _____

10. Mick, a vet. who served in Iraq, started his own photography bus. after graduating from a community coll.

    _____   _____   _____

CONNECT WRITING

Meet Scott. His dad is recovering from surgery and Scott wants to let the nurses at the hospital know how grateful he is that they took such good care of his dad. He's writing a letter to thank them, but is worried that his writing contains mistakes. After looking over his first draft, he believes he's made several abbreviation mistakes. Help Scott locate and correct the abbreviation mistakes in his letter.

mhconnectwriting.com

REVIEW TEST

Cross out the mistake or mistakes in numbers and abbreviations and correct them in the spaces provided.

1. Best Buy's 4-day sale starts this coming Thurs.

   _____   _____

2. One suspect had blue eyes and brn. hair and was over 6 ft. tall.

   _____   _____   _____

3. Answers to the chpt. questions start on p. two hundred and ninety-three.

   _____   _____   _____

4. With Dec. twenty-fifth only hrs. away, little Abby couldn't eat or sleep.

   _____   _____   _____

5. Over 200 children helped in the collection of seven hundred and thirty-two dollars for UNICEF.

   _____   _____

6. My growing 15-year-old son wears sz. 11 shoes that look like boats.

   _____   _____

7. My 3 years of Spanish in h.s. helped me to get a job in the city health clinic.

   _____   _____   _____

8. The robber was sentenced to 10 yrs. in prison for holding up a bank on Pacific Blvd.

   _____   _____   _____

9. I canceled my appt. when I got an emerg. call that my mother had been taken to the hosp.

   _____   _____   _____

10. When city employees staged a strike on Mon., more than 70 pct. of them didn't show up for work.

   _____   _____

For additional materials on Chapter 24, visit www.mhhe.com/langan.

26 CHAPTER | Apostrophes

INTRODUCTORY ACTIVITY

Look carefully at the three items below. Then see if you can answer the questions that follow each item.

1. the desk of the manager   = the manager's desk

    the car of Hakim   = Hakim's car

    the teeth of my dog   = my dog's teeth

    the smile of the woman   = the woman's smile

    the briefcase of my mother   = my mother's briefcase

    What is the purpose of the apostrophe in each example above?

    _____

2. He is my best friend.   = He's my best friend.

    I am afraid of spiders.   = I'm afraid of spiders.

    Do not watch too much TV.   = Don't watch too much TV.

    They are an odd couple.   = They're an odd couple.

    It is a wonderful movie.   = It's a wonderful movie.

    What is the purpose of the apostrophe in each example above?

    _____

3. Several buildings were damaged by the severe storm. One building's roof was blown off and dropped in a nearby field.

    Why does the apostrophe belong in the second sentence but not the first?

    _____

    _____

Answers are on page 630.

The two main uses of the apostrophe are:

- To show the omission of one or more letters in a contraction
- To show ownership or possession

Each use is explained on the pages that follow.

Apostrophes in Contractions

A contraction is formed when two words are combined to make one word. An apostrophe is used to show where letters are omitted in forming the contraction. Here are two contractions:

have + not   = haven't (the *o* in *not* has been omitted)

I   + will = I'll (the *wi* in *will* has been omitted)

The following are some other common contractions:

I	+ am	= I'm	it	+ is	= it's
I	+ have	= I've	it	+ has	= it's
I	+ had	= I'd	is	+ not	= isn't
who	+ is	= who's	could	+ not	= couldn't
do	+ not	= don't	I	+ would	= I'd
did	+ not	= didn't	they	+ are	= they're
let	+ us	= let's	there	+ is	= there's

> **TIP** The combination *will* + *not* has an unusual contraction: *won't.*

Combining Words   ACTIVITY 1

Combine the following words into contractions. One is done for you.

she	+ is	= <u>she's</u>	you	+ will	= <u>you'll</u>
you	+ have	= <u>you've</u>	we	+ would	= <u>we'd</u>
have	+ not	= <u>haven't</u>	could	+ not	= <u>couldn't</u>
he	+ has	= <u>he's</u>	they	+ will	= <u>they'll</u>
we	+ are	= <u>we're</u>	does	+ not	= <u>doesn't</u>

Forming Contractions   ACTIVITY 2

Write the contraction for the words in parentheses.

EXAMPLE

He (could not) <u>couldn't</u> come.

> **HINT** An apostrophe replaces the letter *o* in both answers in item 1.

1. I (did not) _didn't_ like the movie, but the popcorn (was not) _wasn't_ bad.

2. Tara (does not) _doesn't_ hide her feelings well, so if (she is) _She's_ angry, you will know it.

3. (You are) _You're_ taking the wrong approach with Len, as he (cannot) _Can't_ stand being lectured.

4. This (is not) _isn't_ the first time (you have) _you've_ embarrassed me in public.

5. (We would) _We'd_ love to have you stay for dinner if you (do not) _don't_ mind eating leftovers.

> **TIP** Even though contractions are common in everyday speech and in written dialogue, usually it is best to avoid them in formal writing.

ACTIVITY 3	Using the Apostrophe

Write five sentences using the apostrophe in different contractions.

1. _____
2. _____
3. _____
4. _____
5. _____

Four Contractions to Note Carefully

Four contractions that deserve special attention are *they're*, *it's*, *you're*, and *who's*. Sometimes these contractions are confused with the possessive words *their*, *its*, *your*, and *whose*. The following list shows the difference in meaning between the contractions and the possessive words.

Contractions	Possessive Words
they're (means *they are*)	their (means *belonging to them*)
it's (means *it is* or *it has*)	its (means *belonging to it*)
you're (means *you are*)	your (means *belonging to you*)
who's (means *who is*)	whose (means *belonging to whom*)

Whose

| T I P | Possessive words are explained further below. |

Using Apostrophes Correctly

ACTIVITY 4

Underline the correct form (the contraction or the possessive word) in each of the following sentences. Use the contraction whenever the two words of the contraction (*they are, it is, you are, who is*) would also fit.

| H I N T | The sentence in item 1 contains one contraction and one possessive word. |

1. (Your, You're) hunger for knowledge means that (you're, your) a good student.

2. I listened to (you're, your) advice and bought a Toyota Prius because (it's, its) hybrid engine should save me money at the gas pump.

3. At the Super Bowl party, Ron wondered (who's, whose) Coke he accidentally drank, so he asked his friends, "(Who's, Whose) without a drink?"

4. (They're, There) are a few pieces of leftover pizza in the refrigerator, but I would ask your roommates if (they're, there) planning to eat any first.

5. (It's, Its) unfortunate that (they're, there) closing the only mom-and-pop grocery store in the neighborhood.

Apostrophes to Show Ownership or Possession

To show ownership or possession, we can use such words as *belongs to, owned by,* or (most commonly) *of.*

the computer *that belongs to* Uwem

the grades *possessed by* Travis

the house *owned by* my mother

the sore arm *of* the pitcher

But the apostrophe plus *s* (if the word is singular or does not end in -*s*) is often the quickest and easiest way to show possession. Thus we can say:

Uwem's computer

Travis's grades

my mother's house

the pitcher's sore arm

Points to Remember

1. The *'s* goes with the owner or possessor (in the examples given, *Uwem*, *Travis*, *mother*, and *pitcher*). What follows is the person or thing possessed (in the examples given, *computer*, *grades*, *house*, and *sore arm*). An easy way to determine the owner or possessor is to ask the question "Who owns it?" In the first example, the answer to the question "Who owns the computer?" is *Uwem*. Therefore, the *'s* goes with *Uwem*.

2. In handwriting, there should always be a break between the word and the *'s*.

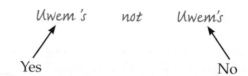

    Uwem 's   *not*   *Uwem's*

    Yes   No

3. A singular word ending in *-s* (such as *Travis* in the earlier example) also shows possession by adding an apostrophe plus *s* (Travis's).

ACTIVITY 5	**Using 's to Show Possession**

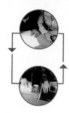

Working with a partner, rewrite the italicized part of each sentence below, using *'s* to show possession. Remember that the *'s* goes with the owner or possessor.

EXAMPLES

The motorcycle owned by Jordan is a frightening machine.

  Jordan's motorcycle

The roommate of my brother is a sweet and friendly person.

  My brother's roommate

> ## HINT
> In item 1, who owns the *voice*?

1. The *voice of the singer* had a relaxing effect on the crowd.

    Singers

2. *The garage of Dawn* has so much furniture stored in it that there's no room for her car.

    Dawn Garage

3. *The law of Murphy* states, "Anything that can go wrong will go wrong."

    Murphy Law

4. All the financial-planning information has been stored in the *memory of the computer*.

    Computers Memory

5. Because *the mother of my wife* is in jail for forgery, I call her my motheroutlaw.

My wife Mother

6. Where is the rest of *the meat loaf of yesterday*, which I was planning to eat for lunch?

yesterday meat loaf

7. *The promotion of my sister* to vice president of the company was well earned.

my sister promotions

8. *The bratty little brother of Alexis* has grown up to become a charming young man.

Alexis's has brother

9. The judges reversed *the call of the referee* after they viewed the replay.

Referee's Call

10. Thousands of gallons of crude oil spilled into the ocean when *the hull of the tanker* ruptured in the storm.

Tanker's hull

Indentifying Possessive Nouns

Underline the word in each sentence that needs *'s*. Then write the word correctly in the space at the left.

HINT In item 1, the hoof belongs to the horse.

horse's 1. The trainer removed a nail from the <u>horse</u> hoof.

brother's 2. My <u>brother's</u> appetite is like a bottomless pit.

Son's 3. Jamal pulled his young <u>son</u> hand away from the kerosene heater.

_____ 4. The <u>comedian's</u> trademarks were long cigars and red socks.

_____ 5. No matter when you dial the <u>landlord's</u> number, nobody answers the phone.

_____ 6. The assistant manager always takes credit for <u>Ted's</u> ideas.

_____ 7. We all froze when the bank <u>teller's</u> wig fell off.

_____ 8. Some people never feel other <u>people's</u> problems are their concern.

_____ 9. Nita hires an accountant to prepare her dance <u>studio's</u> tax's returns each year.

_____ 10. The screen door slammed on the little <u>girl's</u> fingers.

| ACTIVITY 7 | **Making Words Possessive** |

Add 's to each of the following words to make it the possessor or owner of something. Then write sentences using the words. Your sentences can be serious or playful. One is done for you as an example.

1. Aaron _____Aaron's_____

   Aaron's girlfriend sends him over forty text messages a day.

2. bus _____

   _____

3. computer _____

   _____

4. Ross _____

   _____

5. pizza _____

   _____

Apostrophes versus Possessive Pronouns

Do not use an apostrophe with possessive pronouns. They already show ownership. Possessive pronouns include *his, hers, its, yours, ours,* and *theirs.*

Incorrect	**Correct**
The bookstore lost its' lease.	The bookstore lost its lease.
The racing bikes were theirs'.	The racing bikes were theirs.
The change is yours'.	The change is yours.
His' problems are ours', too.	His problems are ours, too.
Her' cold is worse than his'.	Her cold is worse than his.

Apostrophes versus Simple Plurals

When you want to make a word plural, just add *s* at the end of the word. Do *not* add an apostrophe. For example, the plural of the word *movie* is *movies,* not *movie's* or *movies'.*

   Look at this sentence:

   When Sally's cat began catching birds, the neighbors called the police.

The words *birds* and *neighbors* are simple plurals, meaning more than one bird, more than one neighbor. The plural is shown by adding -*s* only. (More information about plurals starts on page 397.) On the other hand, the 's after *Sally* shows possession—that Sally owns the cat.

Apostrophes vs. Simple Plurals

In the spaces provided under each sentence, add the one apostrophe needed and explain why the other words ending in *s* are simple plurals.

EXAMPLE

Originally, the cuffs of mens pants were meant for cigar ashes.

cuffs: _simple plural meaning more than one cuff_

mens: _men's, meaning "belonging to men"_

ashes: _simple plural meaning more than one ash_

H I N T   In item 1, what possesses the *aromas?*

1. The pizza parlors aromas seeped through the vents to our second-floor apartment.

   parlors: _____

   aromas: _____

   vents: _____

2. A police cars siren echoed through the streets and buildings of the city.

   cars: _____

   streets: _____

   buildings: _____

3. Karens tomato plants are taller than the six-foot stakes she used to support them.

   Karens: _____

   plants: _____

   stakes: _____

4. Because of the lakes high bacteria level, officials prohibited boating, swimming, and fishing there.

   lakes: _____

   officials: _____

5. I have considered applying for many positions, but an exterminators job is not one of them.

   positions: _____

   exterminators: _____

CONNECT WRITING

Meet Malik. He is designing banners for several clients at work. He loves creating the art work, but isn't as confident about the messages he's written for the banners. His biggest problem seems to be with apostrophes. He's either put them in places they're not needed, or has left them out completely. At times, he's even used the wrong words. Help Malik locate and correct all the apostrophe mistakes in his banners.

mhconnectwriting.com

6. The candlelights glow fell gently on the pale white plates and ruby-red goblets.

candlelights: _____

plates: _____

goblets: _____

7. Crackers layered with cheese and apple slices are my fathers favorite snack.

Crackers: _____

slices: _____

fathers: _____

8. Within a day, that insects eggs will turn into glistening white worms.

insects: _____

eggs: _____

worms: _____

9. Seabirds skidding along the oceans edge at midnight looked like miniature moonlight surfers.

Seabirds: _____

oceans: _____

surfers: _____

10. My daughters prayers were answered when the heavy snow caused all the schools in the area to close for the rest of the week.

daughters: _____

prayers: _____

schools: _____

Apostrophes with Plural Words Ending in -s

Plurals that end in -s show possession simply by adding the apostrophe, rather than an apostrophe plus s.

Both of my *neighbors'* homes have been burglarized recently.

The many *workers'* complaints were ignored by the company.

All the *campers'* tents were damaged by the hailstorm.

ACTIVITY 9   **Missing Apostrophes**

Add an apostrophe where needed in each sentence that follows.

In item 1, whose *union* is it?

1. The nurse's union protested my layoff.
2. My two sisters' feet are the same size, so they share their shoes.
3. The lions' keeper has worked with those lions since birth.
4. The Tylers' new flat screen TV was mistakenly delivered to our house.
5. The photo album that was lost contained my parents' wedding pictures.

after y if more than two and before if not

Editing and Rewriting

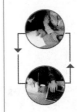

Working with a partner, read the short paragraph below. Underline ten places where you could rewrite, using apostrophes to indicate contractions and possessives. Then rewrite those parts in the spaces that follow. Feel free to discuss the rewrite quietly with your partner and refer back to the chapter when necessary.

> The dog of my neighbor is evil. For one thing, it barks constantly, even when there is nothing to bark at. Because of the constant barking of the dog, I cannot sleep at night. The dog also growls menacingly whenever it sees me. One time, it tried to charge at me through the fence of my landlord. Luckily for me, the fence was strong enough to restrain the dog. I have tried to talk to my neighbor about the problem, but he refuses to listen. He thinks there is nothing wrong with the behavior of the dog. But that is because the dog does not show its fangs to him.

_____

_____

_____

_____

_____

Creating Sentences

Working with a partner, write sentences that use apostrophes as directed.

1. Write a sentence describing something a friend owns. For instance, you might mention a pet or a material possession.

_____

2. Using an apostrophe to show a contraction, write a sentence about something at school or work that you feel is wrong and needs to be changed. The image in the accompanying photo might provide you with some ideas.

_____

_____

3. Write a sentence that correctly uses the word *teachers*. Then write a second sentence that correctly uses the word *teacher's*.

_____

REFLECTIVE ACTIVITY

1. Look at the paragraph about the dog that you just revised. How has adding apostrophes affected the paragraph?

2. Explain what it is about apostrophes that you find most difficult to remember and apply. Use an example to make your point clear.

REVIEW TEST 1

In each sentence, cross out the two words that need apostrophes. Then write the words correctly in the spaces provided.

1. That authors' latest horror novel isn't so horrifying.

   Author's   isn't

2. "I don't get it,'" I confessed after hearing Pams' long, complicated joke.

   don't   ~~Jokes~~ pam's

3. Luckily the motorcycles' gas tank <u>handn't</u> been scratched in the collision.

   Motorcycle's had'nt

4. Whos been stealing the Sunday papers from my doorsteps before Im awake?

   Who's'   I'm

5. Nadias aunts never start the day without asking an astrologers advice.

   _____   _____

6. I, too, would like to take a shower, if there's any water left by the time you're finished.

   there's you're

7. Olivia watched sadly as the highway departments bulldozer demolished the house shed grown up in.

_____ *She's*

8. Sylvia wasnt on time for her first day of work because her mothers car broke down on the highway.

Wasn't Mothers'

9. The coach said theres no room on the team for players who dont want to win.

there's don't

10. The authorities guess is that a radical protest group put the toxic chemical in the towns water supply.

_____ *town's*

Rewrite the following sentences, changing each underlined phrase into either a contraction or a possessive.

1. Joe <u>was not</u> happy to hear the high-pitched sound of the <u>drill of the dentist</u>.

_____

_____

2. The <u>weather forecast of today</u> assured us that <u>it is</u> definitely going to be sunny, cloudy, or rainy.

_____

_____

3. The <u>enthusiasm of my brother Manny</u> for baseball is so great that <u>he will</u> even wear his glove and cap when he watches a game on TV.

_____

_____

4. Many parents think <u>the influence of television</u> is to blame for <u>the poor performance of their children</u> in school.

_____

_____

For additional materials on Chapter 26, visit www.mhhe.com/langan.

27 CHAPTER | Quotation Marks

INTRODUCTORY ACTIVITY

Read the following scene and underline all the words enclosed within quotation marks. Your instructor may also have you dramatize the scene with one person reading the narration and three persons acting the speaking parts—Clyde, Charlotte, and Sam. The speakers should imagine the scene as part of a stage play and try to make their words seem as real and true-to-life as possible.

At a party that Clyde and his wife, Charlotte, recently hosted, Clyde got angry at a guy named Sam who kept bothering Charlotte. "Listen, man," Clyde said, "what's this thing you have for my wife? There are lots of other women at this party."

"Relax," Sam replied. "Charlotte is very attractive, and I enjoy talking with her."

"Listen, Sam," Charlotte said, "I've already told you three times that I don't want to talk to you anymore. Please leave me alone."

"Look, there's no law that says I can't talk to you if I want to," Sam challenged.

"Sam, I'm only going to say this once," Clyde warned. "Lay off my wife, or leave this party *now*."

Sam grinned at Clyde smugly. "You've got good liquor here. Why should I leave? Besides, I'm not done talking with Charlotte."

Clyde went to his basement and was back a minute later holding a two-by-four. "I'm giving you a choice," Clyde said. "Leave by the door or I'll slam you out the window."

Sam left by the door.

1. On the basis of the above selection, what is the purpose of quotation marks?

   Of the Quotation Mark show word of the speacker

2. Do commas and periods that come after a quotation go inside or outside the quotation marks?

   Inside

Answers are on page 631.

8. One way Joanne deals with depression is to get out her Man of La Mancha album and play the song "The Impossible Dream."

9. I read the article "How Good Is Your Breakfast?" in Consumer Reports while munching a doughnut this morning.

10. According to a Psychology Today article titled "Home on the Street," there are 36,000 people living on New York City's sidewalks.

Other Uses of Quotation Marks

Here are two more uses of quotation marks.

1. To set off special words or phrases from the rest of a sentence (italics can also be used for this purpose):

   Many people spell the words "all right" as one word, "alright," instead of correctly spelling them as two words.

   I have trouble telling the difference between "principal" and "principle."

2. To mark off a quotation within a quotation. For this purpose, single quotation marks (' ') are used:

   Ben Franklin said, "The noblest question in the world is, 'What good may I do in it?'"

   "If you want to have a scary experience," Nick told Fran, "read Stephen King's story 'The Mangler' in his book *Night Shift*."

CONNECT WRITING

Meet Craig. He's been working all month on an essay for his geography class. He's very interested in the topic, but he still needs to edit his work. One section of his essay seems incorrect and he believes it's because he's made some italics mistakes. Help Craig locate and correct all the italics mistakes in his essay.

mhconnectwriting.com

| **Editing and Rewriting** | **ACTIVITY 7** |

Working with a partner, read the short paragraph below and circle the places where quotation marks are needed. Then use the space provided to rewrite the paragraph, adding quotation marks where necessary. Feel free to discuss the rewrite quietly with your partner and refer back to the chapter if you have questions.

Harry and his friend Susan got stuck in an elevator. Another man was stuck with them. Harry turned to Susan and asked, Has this ever happened to you before?

Once, she said, About ten years ago in a department store. We weren't stuck long.

Harry took a deep breath. We're lucky only three of us are here. I don't like being closed up in small places, especially crowded ones.

Then the other man asked Is there a phone or something here so we can talk to somebody?

Susan looked around and noticed a small panel in the corner of the elevator. A sign just over the panel read Open in Case of Emergency.

I think it might be in there, she said, pointing to the sign.

The man opened the panel, found a telephone, and dialed the security number written nearby. Can anyone hear me? he asked.

continued

A voice on the phone said, Yes, and we know you're stuck.' Just wait a few minutes.'

When Harry heard that people knew about their problem, he let out a sigh. I sure hope they can fix this quickly, he said softly, wringing his hands.

Susan put her arm around him and smiled. Don't worry. We'll be out of here in no time.

_____

_____

_____

_____

_____

_____

_____

_____

_____

_____

_____

| **ACTIVITY 8** | **Creating Sentences** |

Homework

Working with a partner, write sentences that use quotation marks as directed.

1. Write a sentence in which you quote a favorite expression of someone you know. Identify the person's relationship to you.

    EXAMPLE

    My brother Sam often says after a meal, "That wasn't bad at all."

    _____

    _____

2. Write a quotation that contains the words *Ron asked Rose*. Write a second quotation that includes the words *Rose replied*.

    _____

    _____

3. Write a sentence that interests or amuses you from a book, magazine, or newspaper. Identify the title and author of the book, magazine article, or newspaper article.

EXAMPLE

> In her book <u>At Wit's End</u>, Erma Bombeck advises, "Never go to a doctor whose office plants have died."

_____

_____

REFLECTIVE ACTIVITY

1. Look at the paragraph about the elevator that you previously revised. Explain how adding quotation marks has affected the paragraph.

2. What would writing be like without quotation marks? Explain, using an example, how quotation marks are important to understanding writing.

3. Explain what it is about quotation marks that is most difficult for you to remember and apply. Use an example to make your point clear. Feel free to refer back to anything in this chapter.

Do

Write it out so you can Decused

REVIEW TEST 1

Place quotation marks around the exact words of a speaker or writer in the sentences that follow.

1. Give me a break! Charlie shouted to no one in particular.

2. My mother always says, Some are wise, and some are otherwise.

3. Why do men continue to wear ties when they serve no purpose? asked Paul.

4. Take all you want, but eat all you take, read the sign in the cafeteria.

5. One of Mark Twain's famous lines is, Man is the only animal that blushes—or needs to.

6. My friend the radio announcer loses his voice every time we drive under a bridge, said the comedian.

7. The first time my daughter had a headache, she told me, Mommy, I have a pain in my brain.

8. If your parachute doesn't open, the skydiving instructor joked, bring it back, and we'll give you a new one.

9. The novelist ended a letter to his brother by saying, I'm sorry for writing such a long letter. I didn't have time for a shorter one.

10. Work fascinates me, said the comedian. I could sit and watch it for hours.

REVIEW TEST 2

Place quotation marks around the exact words of a speaker in the sentences that follow. Three of the sentences contain indirect quotations and do not require quotation marks.

EXAMPLE

Soon after moving into their new house, Mike said to Marian,"Why don't we have a party? It'd be a good way to meet all our neighbors."

1. Nice idea, said Marian, but way too much work.

2. It won't be that bad. We'll grill hamburgers and ask everybody to bring a side dish, Mike answered.

3. Marian said that she would agree to the idea if Mike called all the guests.

4. Hi, this is Mike Josephs, your new neighbor in 44B, Mike said each time he called someone.

5. Afterward, he told Marian that everything was under control.

6. I told them we'd provide burgers and plenty of drinks, Mike explained, and they'll bring everything else.

7. When the party started, the first guests arrived saying, We brought potato salad—we hope that's all right!

8. Then guests number two, three, and four arrived, also announcing that they had brought potato salad.

9. As the sixth bowl of potato salad arrived, Mike mumbled to Marian Maybe I should have made some more suggestions about what people should bring.

10. Oh, well, I really love potato salad, Marian said.

REVIEW TEST 3

Go through the comics section of a newspaper to find a comic strip that amuses you. Be sure to choose a strip where two or more characters are speaking to each other. Write a full description that will enable people who have not read the comic strip to visualize it clearly and appreciate its humor. Describe the setting and action in each panel and enclose the words of the speakers in quotation marks.

For additional materials on Chapter 27, visit www.mhhe.com/langan.

Commas

CHAPTER 28

INTRODUCTORY ACTIVITY

Commas often (though not always) signal a minor break or pause in a sentence. Each of the six pairs of sentences below illustrates one of six main uses of the comma. Read each pair of sentences aloud and place a comma wherever you feel a slight pause occurs. Then choose the rule that applies from the box at the bottom of the page, and write its letter on the line provided.

__A__ 1. You can use a credit card, write out a check, or provide cash.

The old house was infested with red ants, roaches, and mice.

__B__ 2. To start the car, depress the accelerator and turn the ignition key.

Before you go hiking buy a comfortable pair of shoes.

__C__ 3. Leeches, creatures that suck human blood, are valuable to medical science.

George Derek, who was just arrested, was a classmate of mine.

__D__ 4. Our professor said the exam would be easy, but I thought it was difficult.

Wind howled through the trees, and rain pounded against the window.

__E__ 5. Emily asked, "Why is it so hard to remember your dreams the next day?"

"I am so tired after work," Lily said, "that I fall asleep right away."

__F__ 6. Bert has driven 1,500,000 accident-free miles in his job as a trucker.

The Gates Trucking Company of Newark, New Jersey, gave Bert an award on August 26, 2009, for his superior safety record.

a.	separate items in a list
b.	separate introductory material from the sentence
c.	separate words that interrupt the sentence
d.	separate complete thoughts in a sentence
e.	separate direct quotations from the rest of the sentence
f.	separate numbers, addresses, and dates in everyday writing

Answers are on page 632.

CHAPTER PREVIEW

Six Main Uses of the Comma

- Commas between Items in a Series
- Commas after Introductory Material
- Commas around Words Interrupting the Flow of Thought
- Commas between Complete Thoughts Connected by Joining Words
- Commas with Direct Quotations
- Commas with Everyday Material

Unnecessary Use of Commas

Six Main Uses of the Comma

Commas are used mainly as follows:

- To separate items in a series

- To set off introductory material

- On both sides of words that interrupt the flow of thought in a sentence

- Between two complete thoughts connected by *and, but, for, or, nor, so, yet*

- To set off a direct quotation from the rest of a sentence

- To set off certain everyday material

You may find it helpful to remember that the comma often marks a slight pause, or break, in a sentence. These pauses or breaks occur at the points where the six main comma rules apply. Sentence examples for each of the comma rules are given on the following pages; read these sentences aloud and listen for the minor pauses or breaks that are signaled by commas.

However, you should keep in mind that commas are far more often overused than underused. As a general rule, you should *not* use a comma unless a given comma rule applies or unless a comma is otherwise needed to help a sentence read clearly. A good rule of thumb is that "when in doubt" about whether to use a comma, it is often best to "leave it out."

After reviewing each of the comma rules that follow, you will practice adding commas that are needed and omitting commas that are not needed.

Commas between Items in a Series

Use a comma to separate items in a series.

Magazines, paperback novels, and textbooks crowded the shelves.

Hard-luck Sam needs a loan, a good-paying job, and a close friend.

Pat sat in the doctor's office, checked her watch, and flipped nervously through a magazine.

Mira bit into the ripe, juicy apple.

More and more people entered the crowded, noisy stadium.

> **TIP**   A comma is used between two descriptive words in a series only if the word *and* inserted between the words sounds natural. You could say:
>
> Mira bit into the ripe *and* juicy apple.
> More and more people entered the crowded *and* noisy stadium.
>
> But notice in the following sentences that the descriptive words do not sound natural when *and* is inserted between them. In such cases, no comma is used.
>
> The model wore a classy black dress. ("A classy *and* black dress" doesn't sound right, so no comma is used.)
>
> Dr. Van Helsing noticed two tiny puncture marks on the patient's neck. ("Two *and* tiny puncture marks" doesn't sound right, so no comma is used.)

Commas between Items in a Series   ACTIVITY 1

Place commas between items in each series.

1. Mae-Lin tossed her sunglasses, a bottle of water, and a recent issue of *Every Day with Rachel Ray*, into her tote bag.

2. Steve uses the computer to check email, play games, surf the Internet, download music, and send instant messages.

3. In the Williams' backyard are an igloo-shaped doghouse, several plastic toys, trampled flowers, and a cracked ceramic gnome.

Necessary and Unnecessary Commas   ACTIVITY 2

For each item, cross out the one comma that is not needed. Add the one comma that is needed between items in a series.

1. I discovered gum wrappers, pennies, and a sock hidden, under the seats when I vacuumed my car.

2. Squirrels, Canada geese, two white swans, and clouds of mosquitoes, populate Farwell Park.

3. Lewis dribbled twice, spun to his left, and lofted his patented hook shot over the outstretched arms, of the Panthers' center.

Commas after Introductory Material

Use a comma to set off introductory material.

Fearlessly, Jessie picked up the slimy slug.

Just to annoy Steve, she let it crawl along her arm.

Although, I have a black belt in karate, I decided to go easy on the demented bully who had kicked sand in my face.

Mumbling under her breath, the woman picked over the tomatoes.

> **TIP**   If the introductory material is brief, the comma is sometimes omitted. In the activities here, you should include the comma.

ACTIVITY 3   ## Commas after Introductory Clauses

Place commas after introductory material.

> **HINT**   In item 1, the last introductory word is *airport*.

1. Before, I left for the airport I turned off my water heater and unplugged my appliances.
2. If you left your backpack at the library, you should call Campus Security.
3. Wanting to help others, Brian volunteers at the Meals on Wheels program.

ACTIVITY 4   ## More Neccessary and Unnecessary Commas

For each item, cross out the one comma that is not needed. Add the one comma that is needed after introductory material.

> **HINT**   In item 1, add a comma to the first sentence and omit the comma in the second.

1. Using metallic cords from her Christmas presents, young Ali made several bracelets for herself. After that, she took a long ribbon, and, tied a bow around her dog's head.
2. As the bride smiled and strolled past me down the aisle, I saw a bead of sweat roll, from her forehead down her cheek. Remembering my own wedding, I knew she wasn't sweating from the heat.
3. When my children were young, I wrote interesting anecdotes about them in a notebook. For example, I wrote a note to remind me, that my son once wanted to be a yo-yo maker.

Commas around Words Interrupting the Flow of Thought

Use a comma before and after words that interrupt the flow of thought in a sentence.

The car, cleaned and repaired, is ready to be sold.

Martha, our new neighbor, used to work as a bartender at Rexy's Tavern.

Taking long walks, especially after dark, helps me sort out my thoughts.

Usually you can "hear" words that interrupt the flow of thought in a sentence. However, when you are not sure if certain words are interrupters, remove them from the sentence. If it still makes sense without the words, you know that the words are interrupters and that the information they give is nonessential. Such nonessential information is set off with commas. In the following sentence

Susie Hall, who is my best friend, won a new car in the *Reader's Digest* sweepstakes.

the words *who is my best friend* are extra information, not needed to identify the subject of the sentence, *Susie Hall.* Put commas around such nonessential information. On the other hand, in the sentence

The woman who is my best friend won a new car in the *Reader's Digest* sweepstakes.

The words *who is my best friend* supply essential information that we need to identify the woman. If the words were removed from the sentence, we would no longer know which woman won the sweepstakes. Commas are not used around such essential information.

Here is another example:

The Shining, a novel by Stephen King, is the scariest book I've ever read.

Here the words *a novel by Stephen King* are extra information, not needed to identify the subject of the sentence, *The Shining.* Commas go around such nonessential information. On the other hand, in the sentence

Stephen King's novel *The Shining* is the scariest book I've ever read.

the words *The Shining* are needed to identify the novel because he has written more than one. Commas are not used around such essential information.

Most of the time you will be able to "hear" words that interrupt the flow of thought in a sentence and will not have to think about whether the words are essential or nonessential.

CONNECT WRITING

Meet Amy. She has been keeping track of current events in a journal for her Political Science class. She's written some very detailed notes, but is struggling with how to use commas correctly. Help Amy find and correct the comma mistakes in her notes.

mhconnectwriting.com

TIP Some instructors refer to nonessential or extra information that is set off by commas as a *nonrestrictive clause*. Essential information that interrupts the flow of thought is called a *restrictive clause*. No commas are used to set off a restrictive clause.

| ACTIVITY 5 | **Commas That Set Off Interrupters** |

Add commas to set off interrupting words.

 In item 1, the interrupting words are *assisted by no one.*

1. The supply control clerk assisted by no one conducted a quarterly inventory on Tuesday.

2. Jo Ann and Craig who were engaged for a year married last July at a winery in Sonoma.

3. The lawn furniture rusted beyond repair needs to be thrown out.

| ACTIVITY 6 | **More Necessary and Unnecessary Commas** |

For each item, cross out the one comma that is not needed. Add the comma that is needed to completely set off the interrupting words.

 In item 1, the interrupting words are *even the most gigantic.*

1. All trees, even the most gigantic are only 1 percent living tissue; the rest, is deadwood.

2. The city council in a rare fit, of wisdom, established a series of bicycle paths around town.

3. John Adams and Thomas Jefferson, the second and third presidents, of the United States died on the same day in 1826.

4. My aunt, a talkative, woman married a patient man who is a wonderful listener.

Commas between Complete Thoughts Connected by Joining Words

Use a comma between two complete thoughts connected by *and, but, for, or, nor, so,* or *yet* (joining words).

My parents threatened to throw me out of the house, so I had to stop playing the drums.

The polyester bedsheets had a gorgeous design, but they didn't feel as comfortable as plain cotton sheets.

The teenage girls walked along the hot summer streets, and the teenage boys drove by in their shiny cars.

TIP   The comma is optional when the complete thoughts are short:
Hunter relaxed but Bob kept working.
The soda was flat so I poured it away.
We left school early for the furnace had broken down.

Be careful not to use a comma in sentences having *one* subject and a *double* verb. The comma is used only in sentences made up of two complete thoughts (two subjects and two verbs). In the sentence

Mary lay awake that stormy night and listened to the thunder crashing.

there is only one subject (*Mary*) and a double verb (*lay* and *listened*). No comma is needed. Likewise, the sentence

The quarterback kept the ball and plunged across the goal line for a touchdown.

has only one subject (*quarterback*) and a double verb (*kept* and *plunged*); therefore, no comma is needed.

Commas That Connect Complete Thoughts

ACTIVITY 7

Place a comma before a joining word that connects two complete thoughts (two subjects and two verbs). Remember, do *not* place a comma within sentences that have only one subject and a double verb. Mark sentences that are correct with a *C*.

> **H I N T**   In item 1, *but* connects two complete thoughts.

1. The apartment Kate looked at was clean and spacious, but the rent was too expensive for her budget.

2. Our power went out during the thunderstorm, so we decided to eat dinner by candlelight.

3. Eddie is building a kayak in his garage and plans to take it down the Columbia River next year.

4. I desperately need more storage space for I can't seem to throw anything away.

5. The helicopter hovered overhead and lowered a rescue line to the downed pilot.

6. Travis was going to quit his job at the supermarket, but he changed his mind after getting a raise.

7. One of the men got ready to leave work at four but put his coat away upon seeing his boss.

8. The family expected Valerie to go to college, but she went to work after eloping with her boyfriend.

9. Bobby pleaded with his parents to buy him a computer for his schoolwork, but he spends most of his time playing games on it.

10. The doctor examined me for less than ten minutes and then presented me with a bill for two hundred dollars.

Commas with Direct Quotations

Use a comma or commas to set off a direct quotation from the rest of a sentence.

"Please take a number," said the deli clerk.

Chris told Sophia, "I've just signed up for a course on Web-page design."

"Those who sling mud," a famous politician once said, "usually lose ground."

"Reading this book," complained Stan, "is about as interesting as watching paint dry."

> **TIP**   Commas and periods at the end of a quotation go inside quotation marks. See also page 355.

ACTIVITY 8   **Setting Off Quotations with Commas**

In each sentence, add the one or more commas needed to set off the quoted material.

> **HINT**   In item 1, add a comma after the quoted material.

1. "Think before you speak," said my dad.

2. "A child miseducated," said John F. Kennedy, "is a child lost."

3. "Before you leave the building," muttered the night patrol officer, "be sure to sign out."

ACTIVITY 9   **More Necessary and Unnecessary Commas**

In each item, cross out the one comma that is not needed to set off a quotation. Add the comma(s) needed to set off a quotation from the rest of the sentence.

> **HINT**   In item 1, add a comma before the quoted material.

1. "If you're looking for a career change," read the poster, in the subway station, "consider the US Armed Forces."

2. "Your arms look fine," said the swimming instructor, "but you keep forgetting, to kick."

3. "Did you really think," the judge asked, the defendant, "you could kill both your parents and, then ask for mercy because you're an orphan?"

Commas with Everyday Material

Use commas to set off certain everyday material, as shown in the following sections.

Persons Spoken to

I think, Bella, that you should go to bed.

Please turn down the stereo, Mark.

Please, sir, can you spare a dollar?

Dates

Our house was burglarized on June 28, 2009, and two weeks later on July 11, 2009.

Addresses

Robyn's sister lives at 342 Red Oak Drive, Los Angeles, California 90057. She is moving to Manchester, Vermont, after her divorce.

 TIP No comma is used before a zip code.

Openings and Closings of Letters

Dear Marilyn,   Sincerely,

Dear John,   Truly yours,

In formal letters, a colon is used after the opening:

Dear Sir:

Dear Madam:

Numbers

Government officials estimate that Americans spend about 785,000,000 hours a year filling out federal forms.

Adding Commas   **ACTIVITY 10**

Place commas where needed.

 HINT Two commas are needed in item 1.

1. Excuse me madam but your scarf is in my soup.

2. Before age eighteen, the average child spends 6000 hours in school and 15000 hours watching television.

3. The famous ocean liner *Titanic* sank in the Atlantic Ocean on April 151912.

4. Teresa
   What do you think of this psychology lecture? Will you meet me for lunch after class? I'll treat. Text me your answer right away.

   > Love
   > Jeff

5. The zoo in Washington D.C. purchases 50000 pounds of meat; 6 500 loaves of bread; 114000 live crickets; and other foods for its animals each year.

Unnecessary Use of Commas

Remember that if no clear rule applies for using a comma, it is usually better not to use one. As stated previously, "When in doubt, leave it out." Following are some typical examples of unnecessary commas.

Incorrect

Sharon told me, that my socks were different colors.

(A comma is not used before *that* unless the flow of thought is interrupted.)

The union negotiations, dragged on for three days.

(Do not use a comma between a simple subject and verb.)

I waxed all the furniture, and cleaned the windows.

(Use a comma before *and* only with more than two items in a series or when *and* joins two complete thoughts.)

Liz carried, the baby into the house.

(Do not use a comma between a verb and its object.)

I had a clear view, of the entire robbery.

(Do not use a comma before a prepositional phrase.)

ACTIVITY 11	Eliminating Unnecessary Commas

Cross out commas that do not belong. Some commas are correct. Do not add any commas.

1. We grew a pumpkin last year, that weighed over one hundred pounds.

2. Anyone with a failing grade, must meet with the instructor during office hours.

3. Last weekend a grizzly bear attacked a hiker, who got too close to its cubs.

4. After watching my form, on the high-diving board, Mr. Riley, my instructor, asked me if I had insurance.

5. Rosa flew first to Los Angeles, and then she went to visit her parents, in Mexico City.

6. The tall muscular man wearing the dark sunglasses, is a professional wrestler.

7. Onions, radishes, and potatoes, seem to grow better in cooler climates.

8. Whenever Vincent is in Las Vegas, you can find him at the blackjack table, or the roulette wheel.

9. While I watched in disbelief, my car rolled down the hill, and through the front window of a Chinese restaurant.

10. The question, sir, is not, whether you committed the crime, but, when you committed the crime.

Editing and Rewriting

Working with a partner, read carefully the short paragraph below and cross out the five misplaced commas. Then insert the ten additional commas needed. Feel free to discuss the rewrite quietly with your partner and refer back to the chapter when necessary.

Dear Olivia,

On Tuesday, May 5, 2009, my husband, and I were unable to sleep because of the loud music coming from your apartment. When I first heard the music I didn't say anything to you because it was still early. But the music, along with loud, laughter and talking, continued until around four o'clock in the morning. At midnight, my husband went into the hallway to see what was happening and he ran into one of your guests. The man who seemed very drunk stared at him, and said "Go back to bed, old man," The next morning, we found beer, cans pizza boxes, and cigarette butts, piled outside our door. This is unacceptable. We have written this letter to you as a warning. The next time something like this happens we will call the police, and the building manager. We don't want to cause trouble with you but we will not tolerate another incident like what happened that night.

Sincerely,

Rose Connelly

ACTIVITY 13	**Creating Sentences**

Working with a partner, write sentences that use commas as directed.

1. Write a sentence mentioning three items you want to get the next time you go to the store.

    _____

    _____

2. Write two sentences describing how you relax after getting home from school or work. Start the first sentence with *After* or *When*. Start the second sentence with *Next*.

    _____

    _____

3. Write a sentence that tells something about your favorite movie, book, television show, or song. Use the words *which is my favorite movie* (or *book, television show,* or *song*) after the name of the movie book, television show, or song.

    _____

    _____

4. Write two complete thoughts about a person you know. The first thought should mention something that you like about the person. The second thought should mention something you don't like. Join the two thoughts with *but.* Do not use the name of a classmate.

    _____

    _____

5. Invent a line that Lola might say to Tony. Use the words *Lola said* in the sentence. Then include Tony's reply, using the words *Tony responded.*

    _____

    _____

6. Write a sentence about an important event in your life. Include the day, month, and year of the event.

    _____

    _____

REFLECTIVE ACTIVITY

1. Look at the letter that you revised on page 375. Explain how adding commas has affected the paragraph.

2. What would writing be like without the comma? How do commas help writing?

3. What is the most difficult comma rule for you to remember and apply? Explain, giving an example.

REVIEW TEST 1

Do three things: (1) Cross out the one comma that is not needed; (2) add the one comma that is needed; and (3) in the space provided, write the letter of the rule that applies for each comma you added.

a. Between items in a series

b. After introductory material

c. Around interrupters

d. Between complete thoughts

e. With direct quotations

_____ 1. *Harry Potter and the Deathly Hallows*, the seventh and final book in the *Harry Potter* series sold over eight million copies, on the first day of its release.

_____ 2. Pretending to be a babysitter the shoplifter slipped several CDs, into her baby stroller.

_____ 3. Emmett, who recently adopted a baby girl, rushed to the super-market, to buy infant formula, baby wipes and disposable diapers.

_____ 4. "Before I leave on my business trip", Emily told her two children, "I want both of you to promise me that you will *not* torment the dog or Dad."

_____ 5. Brandie, a breast cancer survivor religiously wears her pink "awareness bracelet" to remember her victory over the disease.

_____ 6. Recognizing the deadly effects of cigarette smoking the Walt Disney Company has banned depictions of smoking in its films.

_____ 7. Kurt rehearsed the exact moment for months but he still stumbled over his own words when he asked Keisha to marry him.

_____ 8. Everyone at the barbeque party enjoyed the mustard-coated oil-drizzled Alaskan Copper River sockeye salmon fillets roasted on cedar planks.

_____   9. Mahatma Gandhi, was wise when he said,"We must be the change we wish to see."

_____ 10. The substitute teacher tried to enforce the class rules, yet students misbehaved by sending text messages, and playing games on their cell phones.

REVIEW TEST 2

Insert commas where needed. One sentence does not need commas. Mark it with a C.

1. Some people believe that television can be addictive, but I think they're wrong.

2. While there are people who turn on their TVs upon waking up in the morning I don't do that.

3. I turn on my TV only upon sitting down for breakfast, and then I watch the *Today Show.*

4. I don't need to watch game shows, soap operas, and situation comedies to get through the day.

5. Instead, I watch all these programs simply because I enjoy them.

6. I also keep the TV turned on all evening because, thanks to cable and On Demand, there is always something decent to watch.

7. If I did not have good viewing choices I would flick off the TV without hesitation.

8. Lots of people switch channels rapidly to preview what is on.

9. I, on the other hand turn immediately, to the channel I know I want.

10. In other words, I am not addicted; I am a selective viewer who just happens to select a lot of shows.

REVIEW TEST 3

On a separate piece of paper, write six sentences, with each sentence demonstrating one of the six main comma rules.

For additional materials on Chapter 28, visit www.mhhe.com/langan.

Other Punctuation Marks

INTRODUCTORY ACTIVITY

Each sentence below needs one of the following punctuation marks.

See if you can insert the correct mark(s) in each case.

1. The following items were on my son's Christmas list an iPod, a PlayStation, and a skateboard.

2. An admirer gave me chocolate dipped strawberries for Valentine's Day.

3. Everyone in the household misses Indy, our pet cat who lived for fourteen years 1994–2008 .

4. As students, we need to take college seriously we are now responsible for our own learning.

5. The stray dog was malnourished, dirty, abused   but happy to have been rescued.

Answers are on page 633.

Colons (:)

The colon is a mark of introduction. Use the colon at the end of a complete statement to do the following:

- Introduce a list:

    My little brother has three hobbies: playing video games, racing his Hot Wheels cars all over the floor, and driving me crazy.

- Introduce a long quotation:

    Janet's paper was based on a passage from George Eliot's novel *Middlemarch*: "If we had a keen vision and feeling of all ordinary human life, it would be like hearing the grass grow and the squirrel's heart beat, and we should die of that roar which lies on the other side of silence. As it is, the quickest of us walk about well wadded with stupidity."

> **TIP** In formal writing, indent long quotations, and do not set them off with quotation marks; a "long quotation" is generally four lines or longer.

CONNECT WRITING

Meet Sofia. She's working on two letters for a non-profit organization that sponsors women's shelters. She feels pretty good about her writing skills, but is not sure if she's using colons and semicolons correctly. Help Sofia locate and correct all the colon and semicolon mistakes in her two letters.

mhconnectwriting.com

- Introduce an explanation:

    There are two ways to do this job: the easy way and the right way.

Two minor uses of the colon are after the opening in a formal letter (*Dear Sir or Madam:*) and between the hour and the minute in writing the time (*The bus will leave for the game at 11:45*).

ACTIVITY 1	Using Colons

Place colons where needed.

 HINT   Add a colon before the explanation in item 1.

1. Roger is on a "see-food" diet if he sees food, he eats it.

2. Brenda had some terrible problems last summer her mother suffered a heart attack, her husband lost his job, and one of her children was arrested for shoplifting.

3. Andy Rooney wrote in one of his columns "Doctors should never talk to ordinary people about anything but medicine. When doctors talk politics, economics, or sports, they reveal themselves to be ordinary mortals, idiots just like the rest of us. That isn't what any of us wants our doctors to be."

Semicolons (;)

The semicolon signals more of a pause than the comma alone but not quite the full pause of a period. Use a semicolon to do the following:

- Join two complete thoughts that are not already connected by a joining word such as *and, but, for,* or *so:*

    The chemistry lab blew up; Professor Thomas was fired.

    I once stabbed myself with a pencil; a black mark has been under my skin ever since.

- Join two complete thoughts that include a transitional word such as *however, otherwise, moreover, furthermore, therefore,* or *consequently:*

    I changed and made the bed; moreover, I cleaned the entire bedroom.

    Tara finished typing the paper; however, she forgot to bring it to class.

TIP   The first two uses of the semicolon are treated in more detail on pages 186–188.

- Separate items in a series when the items themselves contain commas:

   This fall I won't have to work on Labor Day, September 7; Veterans Day, November 11; or Thanksgiving Day, November 26.

   At the final Weight Watchers' meeting, prizes were awarded to Sally Johnson, for losing 20 pounds; Irving Ross, for losing 26 pounds; and Betty Mills, the champion loser, who lost 102 pounds.

Using Semicolons	**ACTIVITY 2**

Place semicolons where needed.

 Add a semicolon before the transitional word in item 1.

1. Christina returned the wallet that she had found at the library consequently, she felt proud of herself for being honest.

2. My friends could tell that I had been crying my eyes were puffy and bloodshot.

3. I invited Vida, who's my roommate, Rami, who's Vida's boyfriend, and Rachel, who's my best friend.

Dashes (—)

A dash signals a degree of pause longer than a comma but not as complete as a period. Use the dash to set off words for dramatic effect.

   I suggest—no, I insist—that you stay for dinner.

   The prisoner walked toward the electric chair—grinning.

   A meaningful job, a loving wife, and a car that wouldn't break down all the time—these are the things he wanted in life.

CONNECT WRITING

Meet Li Mei. She has purchased postcards from the college bookstore, which she plans to send to family and friends back home in China. She's glad she's written out her messages on Post-it notes first when she realizes she's made several dash mistakes in her writing. Help Li Mei locate and correct all the dash mistakes in her messages before she adds them to the postcards.

mhconnectwriting.com

Using the Dash	**ACTIVITY 3**

Place dashes where needed.

 One dash is needed in item 1.

1. The members of the Polar Bear Club marched into the icy sea shivering.

2. The actress's wedding her third in three years included a dozen bridesmaids and a flock of white doves.

3. My sociology class meets at the worst possible time eight o'clock on Monday morning.

Hyphens (-)

Use a hyphen in the following ways:

- With two or more words that act as a single unit describing a noun:

    The society ladies nibbled at the deep-fried grasshoppers.

    A white-gloved waiter then put some snails on their table.

    Your dictionary will often help when you are unsure about whether to use a hyphen between words.

- To divide a word at the end of a line of writing or typing:

    Although it was raining, the teams decided to play the cham-pionship game that day.

TIPS
1. Divide a word only between syllables. Use your dictionary (see page 387) to be sure of correct syllable divisions.
2. Do not divide words of one syllable.
3. Do not divide a word if you can avoid dividing it.

ACTIVITY 4   **Using Hyphens**

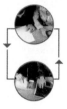

Working with a partner, place hyphens where needed.

HINT   Two hyphens are needed in item 1.

1. Grandpa needs to throw out his console TV and rabbit ear antenna and buy a new high definition TV.
2. Sideway Inn, a hole in the wall diner located downtown, serves both comfort food and upscale, hoity toity dishes.
3. The people in my hometown are honest, hard working folks, but they aren't very friendly to out of towners.

Parentheses ( )

Use parentheses to do the following:

- Set off extra or incidental information from the rest of a sentence:

    The chapter on drugs in our textbook (pages 234–271) contains some frightening statistics.

    The normal body temperature of a cat (101° to 102°) is 3° higher than the temperature of its owner.

- Enclose letters or numbers that signal items in a series:

    Three steps to follow in previewing a textbook are to (1) study the title, (2) read the first and last paragraphs, and (3) study the headings and subheadings.

Do not use parentheses too often in your writing.

Using Parentheses

Working in pairs, add parentheses where needed.

 Put the extra information in item 1 in parentheses.

1. According to the 2000 Census, a majority of Americans (80 percent) had earned a high school diploma.

2. That instructor's office hours (3:00 to 4:00 p.m.) are impossible for any student (with an afternoon job).

3. Since I am forgetful, I often (1) make a list and then (2) check off items I have done. Now, where did I put my list?

At the appropriate spot or spots, insert the punctuation mark shown in the margin.

EXAMPLE

The speed dating event was a success; I met several people I wanted to see again.   ;

1. That catalog lists some unusual items: a sausage stuffer, an electric foot warmer, and a remote-control car starter.   :

2. My brother's jokes—none of which I can repeat—are unfunny and tasteless.   —

3. These days, many two-career couples have decided not to have children.   -

4. The section on space travel in my daughter's science book Chapters (10–11) is sadly out of date.   ()

5. Anne Frank wrote in her diary: "It's a wonder I haven't abandoned all my ideals; they seem so absurd and impractical. Yet I cling to them because I still believe, in spite of everything, that people are truly good at heart."   :

6. The frightened hamster darted from room to room; finally, it crawled under a dresser.   ;

7. Credit card bills, the mortgage payment, and car repairs—no wonder my paycheck doesn't last till the end of the month.   —

8. Someone once defined a self-confident person as one who does crossword puzzles in pen instead of pencil.   -

( )

9. Three ways to save money on home repairs are (1) get several estimates, (2) avoid costly designer products, and (3) do it yourself.

;

10. I ordered several items online from Macy's: two suitcases, one maroon *Corrected* and one blue; an extra-large, machine-washable sweater and a canvas gym bag.

REVIEW TEST 2

CONNECT WRITING

Meet Tyler. He's trying to write instructions for the pet sitter who will be watching his two dogs, Goldie and Locks, while he is out of town. He's included a lot of information in the list, but his instructions aren't clear. He thinks it could be that he's used parentheses incorrectly. Help Tyler locate and correct all the parentheses mistakes in his instructions.

mhconnectwriting.com

On a separate piece of paper, write two sentences using each of the following punctuation marks: colon, semicolon, dash, hyphen, parentheses.

For additional materials on Chapter 29, visit www.mhhe.com/langan.

Commonly Confused Words

INTRODUCTORY ACTIVITY

Circle the five words that are misspelled in the following passage. Then write their correct spellings in the spaces provided.

If your a resident of a temperate climate, you may suffer from feelings of depression in the winter and early spring. Scientists are now studying people who's moods seem to worsen in winter, and there findings show that the amount of daylight a person receives is an important factor in "seasonal depression." When a person gets to little sunlight, his or her mood darkens. Its fairly easy to treat severe cases of seasonal depression; the cure involves spending a few hours a day in front of full-spectrum fluorescent lights that contain all the components of natural light.

1. You're
2. Whose
3. their
4. too
5. It's

Answers are on page 634.

Homonyms

The following commonly confused words are known as *homonyms*; they have the same sounds but different meanings and spellings. Complete the activities for each set of words, and check off and study any words that give you trouble.

COMMON HOMONYMS

all ready	knew	principal	to
already	new	principle	too
			two
brake	know	right	
break	no	write	wear
			where
coarse	pair	than	
course	pear	then	weather
			whether
hear	passed	their	
here	past	there	whose
		they're	who's
hole	peace		
whole	piece	threw	your
		through	you're
its	plain		
it's	plane		

ACTIVITY 1	**Homonyms**

all ready   completely prepared

already   previously, before

We were *all ready* to go, for we had eaten and packed *already* that morning.

Fill in the blanks: Phil was __all ready__ for his driver's test, since he had __already__ memorized the questions and regulations.

Write sentences using *all ready* and *already*.

__Tasha had all ready Taken her test__
__for Schod because, she had already study.__

brake   stop

break   come apart

Dot slams the *brake* pedal so hard that I'm afraid I'll *break* my neck in her car.

Fill in the blanks: While attempting to ~~brake~~ *breake* a speed record, the racecar driver had to __brake__ for a spectator who had wandered onto the track.

Write sentences using *brake* and *break*.

__I smash on the brake to not hit__
__the kido who chase the ball in the__
__street.__
__Shanita tryed breake the record for jump rope.__

coarse   rough

course   part of a meal; a school subject; direction; certainly (with *of*)

Micah muttered in a *coarse* tone, "Of *course* you know it all."

Fill in the blanks: The first _Course_, fresh oysters, included several _Coarse_ grains of sand.

Write sentences using *coarse* and *course*.

_____

_____

hear   perceive with the ear

here   in this place

If I *hear* another insulting ethnic joke *here*, I'll leave.

Fill in the blanks: Unless you sit right _here_ in one of the front rows, you won't be able to _hear_ a single thing the soft-spoken lecturer says.

Write sentences using *hear* and *here*.

I could not hear the movie because they were so loud in the Movie theater.

Danny came here to my house.

hole   empty spot

whole   entire

If there is a *hole* in the tailpipe, I'm afraid we will have to replace the *whole* exhaust assembly.

Fill in the blanks: If you eat the _Whole_ portion of chili, it will probably burn a _hole_ in your stomach.

Write sentences using *hole* and *whole*.

Jessie Dug a hole in the backyard.

the whole pie was gone.

its   belonging to it

it's   contraction of *it is* or *it has*

The kitchen floor has lost *its* shine because *it's* been used as a roller-skating rink by the children.

Fill in the blanks: Our living-room carpet has lost _its_ vivid color since _it's_ been exposed to so much sunlight.

Write sentences using *its* and *it's*.

_____

_____

knew	past tense of *know*
new	not old

   I *knew* that the *new* resident manager would work out fine.

Fill in the blanks: As soon as I put on my _____ white shoes, I _____ that my puppy would soil them.

Write sentences using *knew* and *new*.

_____

_____

know	to understand
no	a negative

   I never *know* who might drop in even though *no* one is expected.

Fill in the blanks: I _____ there are _____ openings in your company at present, but please keep my résumé in case anything turns up.

Write sentences using *know* and *no*.

_____

_____

pair	set of two
pear	fruit

   The dessert consisted of a *pair* of thin biscuits topped with vanilla ice cream and poached *pear* halves.

Fill in the blanks: We spotted a _____ of bluejays on our dwarf _____ tree.

Write sentences using *pair* and *pear*.

_____

_____

passed	went by; succeeded in; handed to
past	time before the present; by, as in "I drove past the house."

   After Edna *passed* the driver's test, she drove *past* all her friends' houses and honked the horn.

Fill in the blanks: Norman couldn't understand why he'd been _____ over for the promotion, because his _____ work had been very good.

Write sentences using *passed* and *past*.

_____

_____

peace   calm

piece   part

    The *peace* of the little town was shattered when a *piece* of a human body was found in the town dump.

Fill in the blanks: We ate in _____ until my two brothers started

fighting over who would get the last _____ of blueberry pie.

Write sentences using *peace* and *piece*.

_____

_____

plain   simple

plane   aircraft

    The *plain* truth is that I'm afraid to fly in a *plane*.

Fill in the blanks: The officials were surprised to find the stolen government

_____ parked in _____ view.

Write sentences using *plain* and *plane*.

_____

_____

principal   main; a person in charge of a school; amount of money
               borrowed

principle   law or standard

    My *principal* goal in child rearing is to give my daughter strong *principles* to live by.

Fill in the blanks: My _____ reason for turning down the part-

time job is that it's against my _____s to work on weekends.

Write sentences using *principal* and *principle*.

_____

_____

> **H I N T** It might help to remember that the *e* in *principle* is also in *rule*—the meaning of *principle*.

right   correct; opposite of *left;* something to which one is entitled

write   to put words on paper

It is my *right* to refuse to *write* my name on your petition.

Fill in the blanks: The instructor said if the students' outlines were not

_____, they would have to _____ them again.

Write sentences using *right* and *write.*

_____

_____

than   used in comparisons

then   at that time

I glared angrily at my boss, and *then* I told him our problems were more serious *than* he suspected.

Fill in the blanks: Felix hiked seven miles and _____ chopped firewood; he was soon more tired _____ he'd been in years.

Write sentences using *than* and *then.*

_____

_____

> **HINT**   It might help to remember that *then* (the word spelled with an *e*) is a time signal (*time* also has an *e*).

their   belonging to them

there   at that place; a neutral word used with verbs such as *is, are, was, were, have,* and *had*

they're   contraction of *they are*

The customers *there* are satisfied because *they're* being given a discount on *their* purchases.

Fill in the blanks: I told the owner of the video store that I'm going _____

right after work so that I can return _____ DVDs, and fortunately

_____ not going to charge me a late fee.

Write sentences using *their, there,* and *they're.*

_____

_____

threw   past tense of *throw*

through   from one side to the other; finished

When a character in a movie *threw* a cat *through* the window, I had to close my eyes.

Fill in the blanks: When Lee was finally _____ studying for her psychology final, she _____ her textbook and notes into her closet.

Write sentences using *threw* and *through.*

_____

_____

to	verb part, as in *to smile;* toward, as in "I'm going to school."
too	overly, as in "The pizza was too hot"; also, as in "The coffee was hot, too."
two	the number 2

Bryce went *to* college *to* earn a degree in computer science. (The first *to* means *toward;* the second *to* is a verb part that goes with *earn.*)

Movie tickets are *too expensive;* popcorn and drinks are expensive, *too.* (The first *too* means *overly;* the second *too* means *also.*)

The *two* couples went on a double date. (the number 2)

Fill in the blanks: My _____ coworkers are _____ polite _____ tell me the truth.

Write sentences using *to, too,* and *two.*

_____

_____

| wear | to have on |
| where | in what place |

I work at a nuclear reactor, *where* one must *wear* a radiation-detection badge at all times.

Fill in the blanks: At the college _____ Ann goes, almost all the students _____ very casual clothes to class.

Write sentences using *wear* and *where.*

_____

_____

| weather | atmospheric conditions |
| whether | if it happens that; in case; if |

Because of the threatening *weather,* it's not certain *whether* the game will be played.

Fill in the blanks: After I hear the _____ report, I'll decide _____ I'll drive or take the train to my sister's house.

CONNECT WRITING

Meet Roberto. He's working on his résumé to apply for a part-time construction job, but he thinks he may have used some words incorrectly. Help Roberto locate and correct all the commonly confused words in his résumé.

mhconnectwriting.com

Write sentences using *weather* and *whether*.

_____

_____

whose   belonging to whom

who's   contraction of *who is* and *who has*

The man *who's* the author of the latest diet book is a man *whose* ability to cash in on the latest craze is well known.

Fill in the blanks: The cousin _____ visiting us is the one _____ car was just demolished by a tractor trailer.

Write sentences using *whose* and *who's*.

_____

_____

your   belonging to you

you're   contraction of *you are*

Since *your* family has a history of heart disease, *you're* the kind of person who should take extra health precautions.

Fill in the blanks: If _____ not going to eat any more, could I have what's left on _____ plate?

Write sentences using *your* and *you're*.

_____

_____

Other Words Frequently Confused

Following is a list of other words that people frequently confuse. Complete the activities for each set of words, and check off and study the ones that give you trouble.

COMMONLY CONFUSED WORDS			
a	among	desert	learn
an	between	dessert	teach
accept	beside	does	loose
except	besides	dose	lose
advice	can	fewer	quiet
advise	may	less	quite
affect	clothes	former	though
effect	cloths	latter	thought

Commonly Confused Words

a, an   Both *a* and *an* are used before other words to mean, approximately, *one.*

Generally you should use *an* before words starting with a vowel (*a, e, i, o, u*):

an absence   an exhibit   an idol   an offer   an upgrade

Generally you should use *a* before words starting with a consonant (all other letters):

a pen   a ride   a digital clock   a movie   a neighbor

Fill in the blanks: When it comes to eating, I am lucky; I can eat like

_____ elephant and stay as thin as _____ snake.

Write sentences using *a* and *an.*

_____

_____

accept   receive; agree to

except   exclude; but

If I *accept* your advice, I'll lose all my friends *except* you.

Fill in the blanks: Everyone _____ my parents was delighted when

I decided to _____ the out-of-town job offer.

Write sentences using *accept* and *except.*

_____

_____

advice   noun meaning *an opinion*

advise   verb meaning *to counsel, to give advice*

Jake never listened to his parents' *advice,* and he ended up listening to a cop *advise* him of his rights.

Fill in the blanks: My father once gave me some good _____:

never _____ people on anything unless they ask you to.

Write sentences using *advice* and *advise.*

_____

_____

affect   verb meaning *to influence*

effect   verb meaning *to bring about something;* noun meaning *result*

My sister Sarah cries for *effect,* but her act no longer *affects* my parents.

Fill in the blanks: Some school officials think suspension will _____ students positively, but many students think its main _____ is time off from school.

Write sentences using *affect* and *effect.*

_____

_____

among   implies three or more

between   implies only two

At the end of the meal, my sister and I split the cost *between* the two of us rather than *among* all the people in our party.

Fill in the blanks: I told my assistant to look _____ my files for the report that I placed _____ two folders.

Write sentences using *among* and *between.*

_____

_____

beside   along the side of

besides   in addition to

Jared sat *beside* Jen. *Besides* them, there were ten other people at the Tupperware party.

Fill in the blanks: Elena refused to sit _____ Carlos in class because he always fidgeted, and, _____, he couldn't keep his mouth shut.

Write sentences using *beside* and *besides.*

_____

_____

can   refers to the ability to do something

may   refers to permission or possibility

If you *can* work overtime on Saturday, you *may* take Monday off.

Fill in the blanks: Joanne certainly _____ handle the project, but she _____ not have time to complete it by the deadline.

Write sentences using *can* and *may.*

_____

_____

clothes   articles of dress

cloths   pieces of fabric

I tore up some old *clothes* to use as polishing *cloths*.

Fill in the blanks: I keep a bag of dust _____ in the corner of

my _____ closet.

Write sentences using *clothes* and *cloths*.

_____

_____

desert   a stretch of dry land; to abandon one's post or duty

dessert   last part of a meal

Don't *desert* us now; order a sinful *dessert* along with us.

Fill in the blanks: I know my willpower will _____ me whenever

there are brownies for _____.

Write sentences using *desert* and *dessert*.

_____

_____

does   form of the verb *do*

dose   amount of medicine

Eve *does* not realize that a *dose* of brandy is not the best medicine for
the flu.

Fill in the blanks: A _____ of aspirin _____ wonders for Sue's

arthritis.

Write sentences using *does* and *dose*.

_____

_____

fewer   used with things that can be counted

less   refers to amount, value, or degree

I missed *fewer* writing classes than Rafael, but I wrote *less* effectively
than he did.

Fill in the blanks: Francesca is taking _____ courses this semester

because she has _____ free time than she did last year.

Write sentences using *fewer* and *less*.

_____

_____

former   refers to the first of two items named

latter   refers to the second of two items named

I applied for two jobs at the employment office; the *former* involves working with preschool children, and the *latter* involves working in sales.

Fill in the blanks: My toddler enjoys eating both fruits and vegetables; the _____ includes bananas and pears, and the _____ includes beans and squash.

Write sentences using *former* and *latter*.

_____

_____

> **HINT** Be sure to distinguish *latter* from *later* (meaning *after some time*).

learn   to gain knowledge

teach   to give knowledge

After Roz *learns* the new dance, she is going to *teach* it to me.

Fill in the blanks: My dog is very smart; she can _____ any new trick I _____ her in just minutes.

Write sentences using *learn* and *teach*.

_____

_____

loose   not fastened; not tight-fitting

lose   misplace; fail to win

I am afraid I'll *lose* my ring; it's too *loose* on my finger.

Fill in the blanks: Those slippers are so *loose* that every time I take a step, I *Lose* one.

Write sentences using *loose* and *lose*.

_____

_____

quiet   peaceful

quite   entirely; really; rather

After a busy day, the children were not *quiet*, and their parents were *quite* tired.

Fill in the blanks: After moving furniture all day, Vince was _____ exhausted, so he found a _____ place and lay down for a nap.

Write sentences using *quiet* and *quite.*

_____

_____

though   despite the fact that

thought   past tense of *think*

Though I enjoyed the band, I *thought* the cover charge of forty dollars was too high.

Fill in the blanks: Even _____ my paper was two weeks late, I _____ the instructor would accept it.

Write sentences using *though* and *thought.*

_____

_____

Incorrect Word Forms

Following is a list of incorrect word forms that people sometimes use in their writing. Complete the activities for each word, and check off and study any words that give you trouble.

INCORRECT WORD FORMS		
being that	could of	should of
can't hardly	irregardless	would of
couldn't hardly	must of	

Incorrect Word Forms   ACTIVITY 3

being that   Incorrect! Use *because* or *since.*

I'm going to bed now ~~being that~~ *because* I must get up early tomorrow.

Correct the following sentences.

1. Being that our stove doesn't work, we'll have tuna salad for dinner.

2. I never invite both of my aunts over together, being that they don't speak to each other.

3. I'm taking a day off tomorrow being that it's my birthday.

can't hardly   Incorrect! Use *can hardly* or *could hardly*.

couldn't hardly

    Small store owners ~~can't~~ `can` hardly afford to offer large discounts.

Correct the following sentences.

1. I couldn't hardly enjoy myself at the theater because my brother gave me a play-by-play account of the entire movie, which he had seen three times.

2. I can't hardly believe that I spent over fifty dollars on gasoline to fill up my SUV.

3. By one o'clock in the afternoon, everyone can't hardly keep from falling asleep in class.

could of   Incorrect! Use *could have*.

    I could ~~of~~ `have` done better on that test.

Correct the following sentences.

1. The sidewalk was so hot you could of toasted bread on it.

2. The moon was so bright you could of read by it.

3. The peach pie was so good that I could of eaten it all.

irregardless   Incorrect! Use *regardless*.

    ~~Irregardless~~ `Regardless` of what anyone says, he will not change his mind.

Correct the following sentences.

1. Irregardless of your feelings about customers, you must treat them with courtesy.

2. Jay jogs every day irregardless of the weather.

3. Anyone can learn to read irregardless of age.

must of   Incorrect! Use *must have, should have, would have*.

should of

would of

    I should ~~of~~ `have` applied for a loan when my credit was good.

Correct the following sentences.

1. I must of dozed off during the movie.

2. If Marty hadn't missed class yesterday, he would of known about today's test.

3. You should of told me to stop at the supermarket.

REVIEW TEST 1

These sentences check your understanding of *its, it's; there, their, they're; to, too, two;* and *your, you're.* Underline the correct word in the parentheses. Rather than guess, look back at the explanations of the words when necessary.

1. It seems whenever (your, you're) at the doctor's office, (your, you're) symptoms disappear.

2. The boss asked his assistant (to, too, two) rearrange the insurance files, placing each in (its, it's) proper sequence.

3. You'll get (your, you're) share of the pizza when (its, it's) cool enough (to, too, two) eat.

4. (Its, It's) a terrible feeling when (your, you're) (to, too, two) late (to, too, two) help someone.

5. (To, Too, Two) eat insects, most spiders use their (to, too, two) fangs to inject a special poison that turns (there, their, they're) victim's flesh into a soupy liquid they can drink.

6. (Its, It's) a fact that (there, their, they're) are (to, too, two) many violent shows on TV.

7. (There, Their, They're) is no valid reason for the (to, too, two) of you (to, too, two) have forgotten about turning in (your, you're) assignments.

8. If you (to, too, two) continue (to, too, two) drive so fast, (its, it's) likely you'll get ticketed by the police.

9. "My philosophy on guys is that (there, their, they're) just like buses," said Regina. "If you miss one, (there, their, they're) is always another one coming by in a little while."

10. "(Its, It's) about time you (to, too, two) showed up," the manager huffed. "(There, Their, They're) is already a line of customers waiting outside."

REVIEW TEST 2

The following sentences check your understanding of a variety of commonly confused words. Underline the correct word in the parentheses. Rather than guess, look back at the explanations of the words when necessary.

1. When (your, you're) (plain, plane) arrives, call us (weather, whether) (its, it's) late or not.

2. You (should have, should of) first found out (whose, who's) really (to, too, two) blame before coming in (hear, here) and making false accusations.

3. When Jack drove (threw, through) his old neighborhood, he (could hardly, couldn't hardly) recognize some of the places he (knew, new) as a child.

4. The (**affect**, effect) of having drunk (to, **too**, two) much alcohol last night was something like having (**a**, an) jackhammer drilling (among, **between**) my ears.

5. I was (quiet, **quite**) surprised to learn that in the (passed, **past**), (**our**, are) town was the site of (**a**, an) Revolutionary War battle.

6. Of (coarse, **course**) (its, **it's**) important to get good grades while (your, **you're**) in school, but it (**does**, dose) not hurt to (**know**, now, no) the (**right**, write) people when (your, **you're**) looking for a job.

7. If (your, **you're**) interested in listening to a great album, take my (**advice**, advise) and pick up a copy of *Sgt. Pepper's Lonely Hearts Club Band*; (its, **it's**) been voted the most popular rock album in history.

8. (Being that, **Since**) Barry has failed all five quizzes and one major exam and didn't hand in the midterm paper, he (though, **thought**) it would be a good idea (**to**, too, two) drop the (coarse, **course**).

9. (Their, **There**, They're) is (know, **no**) greater feeling (**than**, then) that of walking (threw, **through**) a forest in the spring.

10. I spent the (hole, **whole**) day looking (threw, **through**) my history notes, but when it came time to take the exam, I still (**could hardly**, couldn't hardly) understand the similarities (among, **between**) the Korean War, World War I, and World War II.

REVIEW TEST 3

On a separate piece of paper, write short sentences using the ten words shown below.

their	effect
your	passed
it's	here
then	brake
too (meaning *also*)	whose

For additional materials on Chapter 33, visit www.mhhe.com/langan.

Effective Word Choice

INTRODUCTORY ACTIVITY

CHAPTER PREVIEW

Slang
Clichés
Inflated Words
Wordiness

Put a check beside the sentence in each pair that makes more effective and appropriate use of words.

1. After shooting hoops with my bros, I downed a soda. _____S_____

   After playing basketball with my friends, I quickly drank a soda.

   _____

2. Even though my essay was short and sweet, I gave 110 percent.

   _____

   Even though my essay was concise, I tried my best. _____

3. I will endeavor to finalize the report subsequent to lunch. _____

   I will try to finish the report after lunch. _____

4. In the event that my daughter calls during the time that I am in a meeting, please tell her that I am unavailable at the present

   time. _____

   If my daughter calls while I am in a meeting, please tell her that I

   am unavailable. _____

Now see if you can circle the correct number in each case:

Pair (1, 2, 3, 4) contains a sentence with slang; pair (1, 2, 3, 4) contains a sentence with a cliché; pair (1, 2, 3, 4) contains a sentence with inflated words; and pair (1, 2, 3, 4) contains a wordy sentence.

Answers are on page 635.

Choose your words carefully when you write. Always take the time to think about your word choices, rather than simply using the first word that comes to mind. You want to develop the habit of selecting words that are appropriate and exact for your purposes. One way you can show sensitivity to language is by avoiding slang, clichés, inflated words, and wordiness.

Slang

We often use slang expressions when we talk because they are so vivid and colorful. However, slang is usually out of place in formal writing. Here are some examples of slang expressions:

I heard that Dominique's date was just *arm candy*.

House music is *sick.*

Josh is too *web shy*.

My boss hates it when I *reverse telecommute*.

The Red Bull I drank to *pull an all-nighter* was *fierce*.

Sadly, some of the designs on <u>Project Runway</u> don't have the *wow factor*.

I heard that Sam's *DJing* was *über cool*.

The photos you uploaded are *facebookable*.

Slang expressions have a number of drawbacks. They go out of date quickly, they become tiresome if used excessively in writing, and they may communicate clearly to some readers but not to others. Also, the use of slang can be an evasion of the specific details that are often needed to make one's meaning clear in writing. For example, in "Dominique's date was just arm candy," the writer has not provided specific details about Dominique's date necessary for us to understand the statement clearly. What was it about her date's appearance—physique, height, hair style, clothing, smile—that made this person so attractive? In general, then, you should avoid slang in your writing. If you are in doubt about whether an expression is slang, it may help to check a recently published hardbound dictionary.

| ACTIVITY 1 | **Avoiding Slang** |

Rewrite the following sentences, replacing the italicized slang words with more formal ones.

EXAMPLE

I was so *bummed* when my teacher *got on my case*.

<u>I was so discouraged when my teacher scolded me.</u>

> In item 1, consider: what do "two-timing" and "My bad" mean?

1. When I confronted my ex-boyfriend about *two-timing* me, he simply shrugged and said, *"My bad."*

   _____

   _____

2. My friend thinks that Chantel is *phat*, but I think she's too *emo*.

   _____

   _____

3. Rayna is on her cell phone *24-7*, but *it's all good.*

_____

_____

4. Joe wanted to *blow* the family dinner so that he could *hook up* with his friends.

_____

_____

5. Everyone at the gym thinks that Gavin is *juicing,* but he swears that he doesn't use *roids* to get his *six-pack.*

_____

_____

CONNECT WRITING

Meet Antonio. He works as a student intern at the career counseling center on his college campus. A former student has asked him to make sense of a meeting agenda from her new job. The agenda contains so many slang terms that she can't figure out what's going to be discussed at the upcoming meeting. Help Antonio locate and correct the slang used in the agenda.

mhconnectwriting.com

Clichés

Clichés are expressions that have been worn out through constant use. Some typical clichés are listed below.

COMMON CLICHÉS	
all work and no play	sad but true
at a loss for words	saw the light
better late than never	short and sweet
drop in the bucket	sigh of relief
easier said than done	singing the blues
had a hard time of it	taking a big chance
in the nick of time	time and time again
in this day and age	too close for comfort
it dawned on me	too little, too late
it goes without saying	took a turn for the worse
last but not least	under the weather
make ends meet	where he (*or* she) is coming from
needless to say	word to the wise
on top of the world	work like a dog

Clichés are common in speech but make your writing seem tired and stale. Also, they are often an evasion of the specific details that you must work to provide in your writing. You should, then, avoid clichés and try to express your meaning in fresh, original ways.

ACTIVITY 2 · Avoiding Clichés

Underline the cliché in each of the following sentences. Then substitute specific, fresh words for the trite expression.

EXAMPLE

My parents supported me through some <u>trying times.</u>

rough years

> **HINT**   In item 1, *to make a long story short* is a cliché.

1. To make a long story short, my sister decided to file for divorce.

   _____

2. As quick as a wink, the baby tipped over the open box of oatmeal.

   In a blink of eye knock

3. Any advice my friends give me goes in one ear and out the other.

   Any advice my friend give me

4. I felt like a million dollars when I got my first A on a college test.

   _____

5. These days, well-paying jobs for high school graduates are few and far between.

   _____

WRITING ASSIGNMENT

Write a short paragraph describing the kind of day you had yesterday. Try to put as many clichés as possible into your writing. For example, "I had a long hard day. I had a lot to get done, and I kept my nose to the grindstone." By making yourself aware of clichés in this way, you should lessen the chance that they will appear in your writing.

Inflated Words

Some people feel that they can improve their writing by using fancy, elevated words rather than simpler, more natural words. But artificial and stilted language more often obscures their meaning than communicates it clearly.

Here are some unnatural-sounding sentences:

The football combatants left the gridiron.

His instructional technique is a very positive one.

At the counter, we inquired about the arrival time of the aircraft.

I observed the perpetrator of the robbery depart from the retail establishment.

The same thoughts can be expressed more clearly and effectively by using plain, natural language:

The football players left the field.

His teaching style energizes students.

At the counter, we asked when the plane would arrive.

I saw the robber leave the store.

Following is a list of some other inflated words and the simple words that could replace them.

Inflated Words	Simpler Words
component	part
delineate	describe
facilitate	help
finalize	finish
initiate	begin
manifested	shown
subsequent to	after
to endeavor	to try
transmit	send

Avoiding Inflated Words

ACTIVITY 3

Cross out the two inflated words in each sentence. Then substitute clear, simple language for the inflated words.

EXAMPLE

Sally was ~~terminated~~ from her ~~employment~~.

Sally was fired from her job.

 In item 1, replace *query* and *associates* with simpler words.

1. Please query one of our sales associates.

    _____

    _____

2. The meteorological conditions are terrible today.

    _____

    _____

3. My parents desire me to obtain a college degree.

    _____

    _____

4. Do not protrude your arm out of the car, or an accident might ensue.

    _____

    _____

5. Many conflagrations are caused by the careless utilization of portable heaters.

    _____

    _____

Wordiness

Wordiness—using more words than necessary to express a meaning—is often a sign of lazy or careless writing. Your readers may resent the extra time and energy they must spend when you have not done the work needed to make your writing direct and concise.

Here is a list of some wordy expressions that could be reduced to single words.

Wordy Form	Short Form
a large number of	many
a period of a week	a week
arrive at an agreement	agree
at an earlier point in time	before
at the present time	now
big in size	big
due to the fact that	because
during the time that	while
five in number	five
for the reason that	because
good benefit	benefit
in every instance	always
in my opinion	I think
in the event that	if
in the near future	soon
in this day and age	today
is able to	can
large in size	large

plan ahead for the future	plan
postponed until later	postponed
red in color	red
return back	return

Here are examples of wordy sentences:

At this point in time in our country, the amount of violence seems to be increasing every day.

I called to the children repeatedly to get their attention, but my shouts did not get any response from them.

Omitting needless words improves these sentences:

Violence is increasing in our country.

I called to the children repeatedly, but they didn't respond.

Omitting Unnecessary Words

Rewrite the following sentences, cutting unnecessary words.

EXAMPLE

Starting as of the month of June, I will be working at the store on a full-time basis.

As of June, I will be working at the store full-time.

 In item 1, the first part of the sentence and *as of yet* are wordy.

1. It is a well-known and proven fact that there is no cure as of yet for the common cold.

   _____

2. The main point that I will try to make in this paper is that our state should legalize and permit gambling.

   _____

3. Due to the fact that Chen's car refused to start up, he had to take public transportation by bus to his place of work.

   _____

4. When I was just a little boy, I already knew in my mind that my goal was to be a stockbroker in the future of my life.

   _____

5. The exercises that Susan does every day of the week give her more energy with which to deal with the happenings of everyday life.

   _____

CONNECT WRITING

Meet Eva. She works as an intern at the career counseling center on her college campus. She's helping a student revise an email message to his new supervisor. The email is unclear because the student has written too many wordy phrases. Help Eva locate all the wordy phrases and revise the message using clear and concise wording.

mhconnectwriting.com

REVIEW TEST 1

Certain words are italicized in the following sentences. In the space provided, identify whether the words are slang (*S*), clichés (*C*), or inflated words (*IW*). Then replace them with more effective words.

___*S*___   1. Donna *came out of her shell* after she joined a singing group at school.

_____*became unshy,*_____

_____   2. The receptionist *penciled me in* for next Friday.

_____

_____   3. I'm *suffering from a temporary depletion of all cash reserves.*

_____

_____   4. That was *totally random* of me.

_____

_____   5. I got angry at the park visitors who did not put their *waste materials* in the *trash receptacle.*

_____

_____   6. Hearing I had passed the accounting final really *took a load off my mind.*

_____

_____   7. We all thought it was *too good to be true* when the instructor said that most of us would get A's in the course.

_____

_____   8. Fred *asserted to* the collection agency that he had sent the *remuneration.*

_____

_____   9. Even though Brad's married, he still enjoys *eye candy.*

_____

_____ 10. This book was written by a millionaire who *didn't have a dime to his name* as a boy.

_____

Rewrite the following sentences, omitting unnecessary words.

1. At 6:00 early this morning, I suddenly heard a loud and noisy banging by someone at the front door of my apartment.

_____

_____

2. The fact of the matter is that I did not remember until, of course, just now that I had an appointment to meet you.

_____

_____

3. We are very pleased to have the opportunity to inform you that your line of credit on your credit card with us has just been increased.

_____

_____

4. At this point in time, the company has no plan of adding to anyone's salary by giving a raise in pay in the near or distant future.

_____

_____

5. If you are out on the job market seeking a job, you just might benefit from professional help to assist you in your search for employment.

_____

_____

For additional materials on Chapter 34, visit www.mhhe.com/langan.

See if you can locate and correct the eight sentence-skills mistakes in the following passage written by Quang for a geography class. The mistakes are listed in the box below. As you locate each mistake, write the number of the sentence containing that mistake. Use the spaces provided. Then, on a separate sheet of paper, correct the mistakes.

Where in the World?

[1]Lines of latitude and longitude is the imaginary grid geographers use to locate places on the earth. [2]Latitude is the position of a point on the earths surface in relation to the equator. [3]The distance is measured in degrees beginning at the equator and going toward one of the earth's poles. [4]Any point on the equator has a latitude of zero degrees. [5]This is written 0°. [6]The north pole has a latitude of 90° north, and the South Pole has a latitude of 90° south. [7]As a result a point halfway between the North Pole and the equator would be located at 45° north. [8]Lines of longitude are imaginary lines running north and south, they divide the globe into 360 equal slices. [9]The main lines of longitude are called meridians. [10]All meridians pass through the North and South Poles. [11]The prime meridian or first meridian is the imaginary line that runs from the North Pole to the South Pole and passes through Greenwich, England, just outside London. [12]This line is 0° longitude. [13]So, now can you find your global address?

1	run-on _____	1	apostrophe mistake _____
1	mistake in subject-verb agreement _____	2	capitalization mistakes _____
1	missing comma after introductory words _____	2	missing commas around an interrupter _____

A WRITER'S CHECKLIST: Sentence Skills

Clear and Correct Sentences

✔ My paragraph/essay is free of fragments.

✔ My paragraph/essay contains no comma splices or fused sentences.

✔ Throughout, my sentence structure is varied.

Verbs, Pronouns, and Agreement

✔ In every sentence, my subjects agree with my verbs.

✔ I use verb tenses consistently.

✔ When I use pronouns, it is clear what (or which) noun they refer to.

Modifiers and Parallelism

✔ I use adjectives and adverbs correctly.

✔ My sentences contain no misplaced or dangling modifiers; it is clear what each modifier refers to.

✔ I have avoided faulty parallelism in my paragraph/essay.

Punctuation and Mechanics

✔ I use capitalization in appropriate places.

✔ I use end punctuation, apostrophes, quotation marks, commas, and other forms of punctuation correctly.

✔ I formatted my paper according to my instructor's guidelines or the instructions in Chapter 22.

Word Use

✔ I looked up any words whose meanings or spellings I was unsure of in a dictionary. I also used a spell-checker.

✔ I did not misuse any of the commonly confused words listed in Chapter 33.

✔ Throughout, I was careful to choose my words effectively, according to the guidelines in Chapter 34. I have avoided slang, clichés, inflated words, and wordiness.

CORRECTION SYMBOLS

Here is a list of symbols your instructor may use when marking papers. The numbers in parentheses refer to the pages that explain the skill involved.

agr	Correct the mistake in agreement of subject and verb (231–240) or pronoun and the word the pronoun refers to (252–262).
apos	Correct the apostrophe mistake (342–353).
bal	Balance the parts of the sentence so they have the same (parallel) form (295–303).
cap	Correct the mistake in capital letters (324–333).
coh	Revise to improve coherence (67–73; 76–77).
comma	Add a comma (365–378).
CS	Correct the comma splice (179–194).
DM	Correct the dangling modifier (289–294).
det	Support or develop the topic more fully by adding details (50–67; 75–76).
frag	Attach the fragment to a sentence or make it a sentence (162–178).
lc	Use a lowercase (small) letter rather than a capital (324–333).
MM	Correct the misplaced modifier (283–288).
¶	Indent for a new paragraph.
no ¶	Do not indent for a new paragraph.
pro	Correct the pronoun mistake (252–274).
quot	Correct the mistake in quotation marks (354–364).
R-O	Correct the run-on (179–194).
sp	Correct the spelling error (385–422).
trans	Supply or improve a transition (67–73).
und	Underline (359–360).
verb	Correct the verb or verb form (209–230; 241–251).
wordy	Omit needless words (428–431).

WC   Replace the word marked with a more accurate one (word choice).

?   Write the illegible word clearly.

/   Eliminate the word, letter, or punctuation mark so slashed.

^   Add the omitted word or words.

;/:/-/—   Add semicolon (380), colon (379); hyphen (382), or dash (381).

✓   You have something fine or good here: an expression, a detail, an idea.

Rowing the Bus

Paul Logan

PREVIEW	WORDS TO WATCH
There is a well-known saying that goes something like this: All that is necessary in order for evil to triumph is for good people to do nothing. Even young people are forced to face cruel behavior and to decide how they will respond to it. In this essay, Paul Logan looks back at a period of schoolyard cruelty in which he was both a victim and a participant. With unflinching honesty, he describes his behavior then and how it helped to shape the person he has become.	simulate (1) feigning (5) taunted (6) belittled (6) gait (7) rift (9) stoic (13)

When I was in elementary school, some older kids made me row the 1 bus. Rowing meant that on the way to school I had to sit in the dirty bus aisle littered with paper, gum wads, and spitballs. Then I had to simulate• the motion of rowing while the kids around me laughed and chanted, "Row, row, row the bus." I was forced to do this by a group of bullies who spent most of their time picking on me.

I was the perfect target for them. I was small. I had no father. And 2 my mother, though she worked hard to support me, was unable to afford clothes and sneakers that were "cool." Instead she dressed me in outfits that we got from "the bags"—hand-me-downs given as donations to a local church.

Each Wednesday, she'd bring several bags of clothes to the house and 3 pull out musty, wrinkled shirts and worn bell-bottom pants that other families no longer wanted. I knew that people were kind to give things to us, but I hated wearing clothes that might have been donated by my class-mates. Each time I wore something from the bags, I feared that the other kids might recognize something that was once theirs.

Besides my outdated clothes, I wore thick glasses, had crossed eyes, 4 and spoke with a persistent lisp. For whatever reason, I had never learned to say the "s" sound properly, and I pronounced words that began with "th" as if they began with a "d." In addition, because of my severely crossed eyes, I lacked the hand and eye coordination necessary to hit or catch flying objects.

As a result, footballs, baseballs, soccer balls and basketballs became my 5 enemies. I knew, before I stepped onto the field or court, that I would do something clumsy or foolish and that everyone would laugh at me. I feared humiliation so much that I became skillful at feigning• illnesses to get out of gym class. Eventually I learned how to give myself low-grade fevers so the nurse would write me an excuse. It worked for a while, until the gym teachers caught on. When I did have to play, I was always the last one cho-sen to be on any team. In fact, team captains did everything in their power to make their opponents get stuck with me. When the unlucky team captain was forced to call my name, I would trudge over to the team, knowing that no one there liked or wanted me. For four years, from second through fifth grade, I prayed nightly for God to give me school days in which I would not be insulted, embarrassed, or made to feel ashamed.

I thought my prayers were answered when my mother decided to **6** move during the summer before sixth grade. The move meant that I got to start sixth grade in a different school, a place where I had no reputation. Although the older kids laughed and snorted at me as soon as I got on my new bus—they couldn't miss my thick glasses and strange clothes—I soon discovered that there was another kid who received the brunt of their insults. His name was George, and everyone made fun of him. The kids taunted• him because he was skinny; they belittled• him because he had acne that pocked and blotched his face; and they teased him because his voice was squeaky. During my first gym class at my new school, I wasn't the last one chosen for kickball; George was.

George tried hard to be friends with me, coming up to me in the cafete- **7** ria on the first day of school. "Hi. My name's George. Can I sit with you?" he asked with a peculiar squeakiness that made each word high-pitched and raspy. As I nodded for him to sit down, I noticed an uncomfortable silence in the cafeteria as many of the students who had mocked George's clumsy gait• during gym class began watching the two of us and whispering among themselves. By letting him sit with me, I had violated an unspoken law of school, a sinister code of childhood that demands there must always be someone to pick on. I began to realize two things. If I befriended George, I would soon receive the same treatment that I had gotten at my old school. If I stayed away from him, I might actually have a chance to escape being at the bottom.

Within days, the kids started taunting us whenever we were together. **8** "Who's your new little buddy, Georgie?" In the hallways, groups of students began mumbling about me just loud enough for me to hear, "Look, it's George's ugly boyfriend." On the bus rides to and from school, wads of paper and wet chewing gum were tossed at me by the bigger, older kids in the back of the bus.

It became clear that my friendship with George was going to cause me **9** several more years of misery at my new school. I decided to stop being friends with George. In class and at lunch, I spent less and less time with him. Sometimes I told him I was too busy to talk; other times I acted distracted and gave one-word responses to whatever he said. Our classmates, sensing that they had created a rift• between George and me, intensified their attacks on him. Each day, George grew more desperate as he realized that the one person who could prevent him from being completely isolated was closing him off. I knew that I shouldn't avoid him, that he was feeling the same way I felt for so long, but I was so afraid that my life would become the hell it had been in my old school that I continued to ignore him.

Then, at recess one day, the meanest kid in the school, Chris, decided **10** he had had enough of George. He vowed that he was going to beat up George and anyone else who claimed to be his friend. A mob of kids formed and came after me. Chris led the way and cornered me near our school's swing sets. He grabbed me by my shirt and raised his fist over my head. A huge gathering of kids surrounded us, urging him to beat me up, chanting "Go, Chris, go!"

"You're Georgie's new little boyfriend, aren't you?" he yelled. The 11 hot blast of his breath carried droplets of his spit into my face. In a complete betrayal of the only kid who was nice to me, I denied George's friendship.

"No, I'm not George's friend. I don't like him. He's stupid," I blurted 12 out. Several kids snickered and mumbled under their breath. Chris stared at me for a few seconds and then threw me to the ground.

"Wimp. Where's George?" he demanded, standing over me. Someone 13 pointed to George sitting alone on top of the monkey bars about thirty yards from where we were. He was watching me. Chris and his followers sprinted over to George and yanked him off the bars to the ground. Although the mob quickly encircled them, I could still see the two of them at the center of the crowd, looking at each other. George seemed stoic,• staring straight through Chris. I heard the familiar chant of "Go, Chris, go!" and watched as his fists began slamming into George's head and body. His face bloodied and his nose broken, George crumpled to the ground and sobbed without even throwing a punch. The mob cheered with pleasure and darted off into the playground to avoid an approaching teacher.

Chris was suspended, and after a few days, George came back to 14 school. I wanted to talk to him, to ask him how he was, to apologize for leaving him alone and for not trying to stop him from getting hurt. But I couldn't go near him. Filled with shame for denying George and angered by my own cowardice, I never spoke to him again.

Several months later, without telling any students, George transferred 15 to another school. Once in a while, in those last weeks before he left, I caught him watching me as I sat with the rest of the kids in the cafeteria. He never yelled at me or expressed anger, disappointment, or even sadness. Instead he just looked at me.

In the years that followed, George's silent stare remained with me. It 16 was there in eighth grade when I saw a gang of popular kids beat up a sixth-grader because, they said, he was "ugly and stupid." It was there my first year in high school, when I saw a group of older kids steal another freshman's clothes and throw them into the showers. It was there a year later, when I watched several seniors press a wad of chewing gum into the hair of a new girl on the bus. Each time that I witnessed another awkward, uncomfortable, scared kid being tormented, I thought of George, and gradually his haunting stare began to speak to me. No longer silent, it told me that every child who is picked on and taunted deserves better, that no one—no matter how big, strong, attractive, or popular—has the right to abuse another person.

Finally, in my junior year when a loudmouthed, pink-skinned bully 17 named Donald began picking on two freshmen on the bus, I could no longer deny George. Donald was crumpling a large wad of paper and preparing to bounce it off the back of the head of one of the young students when I interrupted him.

"Leave them alone, Don," I said. By then I was six inches taller and, 18 after two years of high-school wrestling, thirty pounds heavier than I had been in my freshman year. Though Donald was still two years older than me, he wasn't much bigger. He stopped what he was doing, squinted, and stared at me.

"What's your problem, Paul?"   19

I felt the way I had many years earlier on the playground when I   20
watched the mob of kids begin to surround George.

"Just leave them alone. They aren't bothering you," I responded quietly.   21

"What's it to you?" he challenged. A glimpse of my own past, of row-   22
ing the bus, of being mocked for my clothes, my lisp, my glasses, and my
absent father flashed in my mind.

"Just don't mess with them. That's all I am saying, Don." My fingertips   23
were tingling. The bus was silent. He got up from his seat and leaned over
me, and I rose from my seat to face him. For a minute, both of us just stood
there, without a word, staring.

"I'm just playing with them, Paul," he said, chuckling. "You don't   24
have to go psycho on me or anything." Then he shook his head, slapped
me firmly on the chest with the back of his hand, and sat down. But he
never threw that wad of paper. For the rest of the year, whenever I was on
the bus, Don and the other troublemakers were noticeably quiet.

Although it has been years since my days on the playground and the   25
school bus, George's look still haunts me. Today, I see it on the faces of a few
scared kids at my sister's school—she is in fifth grade. Or once in a while
I'll catch a glimpse of someone like George on the evening news, in a story
about a child who brought a gun to school to stop the kids from picking on
him, or in a feature about a teenager who killed herself because everyone
teased her. In each school, in almost every classroom, there is a George with
a stricken face, hoping that someone nearby will be strong enough to be
kind—despite what the crowd says—and brave enough to stand up against
people who attack, tease, or hurt those who are vulnerable.

If asked about their behavior, I'm sure the bullies would say, "What's   26
it to you? It's just a joke. It's nothing." But to George and me, and everyone
else who has been humiliated or laughed at or spat on, it is everything. No
one should have to row the bus.

VOCABULARY IN CONTEXT

1. The word *simulate* in "Then I had to simulate the motion of rowing
   while the kids around me laughed and chanted, 'Row, row, row the
   bus'" (paragraph 1) means

   a. sing.

   b. ignore.

   c. imitate.

   d. release.

2. The word *rift* in "I decided to stop being friends with George. . . . Our
   classmates, sensing that they had created a rift between George and
   me, intensified their attacks on him" (paragraph 9) means

   a. friendship.

   b. agreement.

   c. break.

   d. joke.

READING COMPREHENSION QUESTIONS

1. Which of the following would be the best alternative title for this selection?

   a. A Sixth-Grade Adventure

   b. Children's Fears

   c. Dealing with Cruelty

   d. The Trouble with Busing

2. Which sentence best expresses the main idea of the selection?

   a. Although Paul Logan was the target of other students' abuse when he was a young boy, their attacks stopped as he grew taller and stronger.

   b. When Logan moved to a different school, he discovered that another student, George, was the target of more bullying than he was.

   c. Logan's experience of being bullied and his shame at how he treated George eventually made him speak up for someone else who was teased.

   d. Logan is ashamed that he did not stand up for George when George was being attacked by a bully on the playground.

3. When Chris attacked George, George reacted by

   a. fighting back hard.

   b. shouting for Logan to help him.

   c. running away.

   d. accepting the beating.

4. Logan finally found the courage to stand up for abused students when he saw

   a. Donald about to throw paper at a younger student.

   b. older kids throwing a freshman's clothes into the shower.

   c. seniors putting bubble gum in a new student's hair.

   d. a gang beating up a sixth-grader whom they disliked.

5. *True or false?* _____ After Logan confronted Donald on the bus, Donald began picking on Logan as well.

6. *True or false?* _____ The author suggests that his mother did not care very much about him.

7. The author implies that, when he started sixth grade at a new school,

   a. he became fairly popular.

   b. he decided to try out for athletic teams.

   c. he was relieved to find a kid who was more unpopular than he.

   d. he was frequently beaten up.

8. We can conclude that

   a. the kids who picked on George later regretted what they had done.

   b. George and the author eventually talked together about their experience in sixth grade.

c. the author thinks kids today are kinder than they were when he was in sixth grade.

d. the author is a more compassionate person now because of his experience with George.

DISCUSSION QUESTIONS

About Content

1. Logan describes a number of incidents involving students' cruelty to other students. Find at least three such incidents. What do they seem to have in common? Judging from such incidents, what purpose does cruel teasing seem to serve?

2. Throughout the essay, Paul Logan talks about cruel but ordinary school behavior. But in paragraph 25, he briefly mentions two extreme and tragic consequences of such cruelty. What are those consequences, and why do you think he introduces them? What is he implying?

About Structure

3. Overall, the author uses narration to develop his points. Below, write three time transitions he uses to advance his narration.

_____   _____   _____

4. Logan describes the gradual change within him that finally results in his standing up for two students who are being abused. Where in the narrative does Logan show how internal changes may be taking place within him? Where in the narrative does he show that his reaction to witnessing bullying has changed?

5. Paul Logan titled his selection "Rowing the Bus." Yet very little of the essay actually deals with the incident the title describes. Why do you think Logan chose that title?

About Style and Tone

6. Good descriptive writing involves the reader's senses. Give examples of how Logan appeals to our senses in paragraphs 1–4 of "Rowing the Bus."

Sight _____

Smell _____

Hearing _____

7. What is Logan's attitude toward himself regarding his treatment of George? Find three phrases that reveal his attitude and write them here.

WRITING ASSIGNMENTS

Assignment 1: Writing a Paragraph

Logan writes, "In each school, in almost every classroom, there is a George with a stricken face." Think of a person who filled the role of George in one of your classes. Then write a descriptive paragraph about that person, explaining why he or she was a target and what form the teasing took. Be sure to include a description of your own thoughts and actions regarding the student who was teased. Your topic sentence might be something like one of these:

> A girl in my fifth-grade class was a lot like George in "Rowing the Bus."
>
> Like Paul Logan, I suffered greatly in elementary school from being bullied.

Try to include details that appeal to two or three of the senses.

Assignment 2: Writing a Paragraph

Paul Logan feared that his life at his new school would be made miserable if he continued being friends with George. So he ended the friendship, even though he felt ashamed of doing so. Think of a time when you have wanted to do the right thing but felt that the price would be too high. Maybe you knew a friend was doing something dishonest and wanted him to stop but were afraid of losing his friendship. Or perhaps you pretended to forget a promise you had made because you decided it was too difficult to keep. Write a paragraph describing the choice you made and how you felt about yourself afterward.

Assignment 3: Writing an Essay

Logan provides many vivid descriptions of incidents in which bullies attack other students. Reread these descriptions, and consider what they teach you about the nature of bullies and bullying. Then write an essay that supports the following main idea:

> Bullies seem to share certain qualities.

Identify two or three qualities; then discuss each in a separate paragraph. You may use two or three of the following as the topic sentences for your supporting paragraphs, or come up with your own supporting points:

> Bullies are cowardly.
>
> ⌐ Bullies make themselves feel big by making other people feel small.
>
> Bullies cannot feel very good about themselves.
>
> Bullies are feared but not respected.
>
> Bullies act cruelly in order to get attention.

Develop each supporting point with one or more anecdotes or ideas from any of the following: your own experience, your understanding of human nature, and "Rowing the Bus."

Do It Better!

Ben Carson, M.D., with Cecil Murphey

PREVIEW	WORDS TO WATCH
If you suspect that you are now as "smart" as you'll ever be, then read the following selection. Taken from the book ***Think Big***, it is about Dr. Ben Carson, who was sure he was "the dumbest kid in the class" when he was in fifth grade. Carson tells how he turned his life totally around from what was a path of failure. Today he is a famous neurosurgeon at the Johns Hopkins University Children's Center in Baltimore, Maryland.	parochial (20) trauma (20) tenement (20) reluctantly (56) indifferent (58) acknowledged (67) obsidian (74)

"Benjamin, is this your report card?" my mother asked as she picked 1 up the folded white card from the table.

"Uh, yeah," I said, trying to sound casual. Too ashamed to hand it to 2 her, I had dropped it on the table, hoping that she wouldn't notice until after I went to bed.

It was the first report card I had received from Higgins Elementary 3 School since we had moved back from Boston to Detroit, only a few months earlier.

I had been in the fifth grade not even two weeks before everyone con- 4 sidered me the dumbest kid in the class and frequently made jokes about me. Before long I too began to feel as though I really was the most stupid kid in fifth grade. Despite Mother's frequently saying, "You're smart, Bennie. You can do anything you want to do," I did not believe her.

No one else in school thought I was smart, either. 5

Now, as Mother examined my report card, she asked, "What's this 6 grade in reading?" (Her tone of voice told me that I was in trouble.) Although I was embarrassed, I did not think too much about it. Mother knew that I wasn't doing well in math, but she did not know I was doing so poorly in every subject.

While she slowly read my report card, reading everything one word 7 at a time, I hurried into my room and started to get ready for bed. A few minutes later, Mother came into my bedroom.

"Benjamin," she said, "are these your grades?" She held the card in 8 front of me as if I hadn't seen it before.

"Oh, yeah, but you know, it doesn't mean much." 9

"No, that's not true, Bennie. It means a lot." 10

"Just a report card." 11

"But it's more than that." 12

Knowing I was in for it now, I prepared to listen, yet I was not all that 13 interested. I did not like school very much and there was no reason why I should. Inasmuch as I was the dumbest kid in the class, what did I have to look forward to? The others laughed at me and made jokes about me every day.

"Education is the only way you're ever going to escape poverty," she 14 said. "It's the only way you're ever going to get ahead in life and be successful. Do you understand that?"

"Yes, Mother," I mumbled.   15

"If you keep on getting these kinds of grades you're going to spend the 16 rest of your life on skid row, or at best sweeping floors in a factory. That's not the kind of life that I want for you. That's not the kind of life that God wants for you."

I hung my head, genuinely ashamed. My mother had been raising 17 me and my older brother, Curtis, by herself. Having only a third-grade education herself, she knew the value of what she did not have. Daily she drummed into Curtis and me that we had to do our best in school.

"You're just not living up to your potential," she said. "I've got two 18 mighty smart boys and I know they can do better."

I had done my best—at least I had when I first started at Higgins 19 Elementary School. How could I do much when I did not understand anything going on in our class?

In Boston we had attended a parochial• school, but I hadn't learned 20 much because of a teacher who seemed more interested in talking to another female teacher than in teaching us. Possibly, this teacher was not solely to blame—perhaps I wasn't emotionally able to learn much. My parents had separated just before we went to Boston, when I was eight years old. I loved both my mother and father and went through considerable trauma• over their separating. For months afterward, I kept thinking that my parents would get back together, that my daddy would come home again the way he used to, and that we could be the same old family again—but he never came back. Consequently, we moved to Boston and lived with Aunt Jean and Uncle William Avery in a tenement• building for two years until Mother had saved enough money to bring us back to Detroit.

Mother kept shaking the report card at me as she sat on the side of my 21 bed. "You have to work harder. You have to use that good brain that God gave you, Bennie. Do you understand that?"

"Yes, Mother." Each time she paused, I would dutifully say those 22 words.

"I work among rich people, people who are educated," she said. "I 23 watch how they act, and I know they can do anything they want to do. And so can you." She put her arm on my shoulder. "Bennie, you can do anything they can do—only you can do it better!"

Mother had said those words before. Often. At the time, they did 24 not mean much to me. Why should they? I really believed that I was the dumbest kid in fifth grade, but of course, I never told her that.

"I just don't know what to do about you boys," she said. "I'm going 25 to talk to God about you and Curtis." She paused, stared into space, then said (more to herself than to me), "I need the Lord's guidance on what to do. You just can't bring in any more report cards like this."

As far as I was concerned, the report card matter was over.   26

The next day was like the previous ones—just another bad day in **27** school, another day of being laughed at because I did not get a single problem right in arithmetic and couldn't get any words right on the spelling test. As soon as I came home from school, I changed into play clothes and ran outside. Most of the boys my age played softball, or the game I liked best, "Tip the Top."

We played Tip the Top by placing a bottle cap on one of the sidewalk **28** cracks. Then taking a ball—any kind that bounced—we'd stand on a line and take turns throwing the ball at the bottle top, trying to flip it over. Whoever succeeded got two points. If anyone actually moved the cap more than a few inches, he won five points. Ten points came if he flipped it into the air and it landed on the other side.

When it grew dark or we got tired, Curtis and I would finally go inside **29** and watch TV. The set stayed on until we went to bed. Because Mother worked long hours, she was never home until just before we went to bed. Sometimes I would awaken when I heard her unlocking the door.

Two evenings after the incident with the report card, Mother came **30** home about an hour before our bedtime. Curtis and I were sprawled out, watching TV. She walked across the room, snapped off the set, and faced both of us. "Boys," she said, "you're wasting too much of your time in front of that television. You don't get an education from staring at television all the time."

Before either of us could make a protest, she told us that she had been **31** praying for wisdom. "The Lord's told me what to do," she said. "So from now on, you will not watch television, except for two preselected programs each week."

"Just *two* programs?" I could hardly believe she would say such a ter- **32** rible thing. "That's not—"

"And *only* after you've done your homework. Furthermore, you don't **33** play outside after school, either, until you've done all your homework."

"Everybody else plays outside right after school," I said, unable to **34** think of anything except how bad it would be if I couldn't play with my friends. "I won't have any friends if I stay in the house all the time—"

"That may be," Mother said, "but everybody else is not going to be as **35** successful as you are—"

"But, Mother—"   **36**

"This is what we're going to do. I asked God for wisdom, and this is **37** the answer I got."

I tried to offer several other arguments, but Mother was firm. I glanced **38** at Curtis, expecting him to speak up, but he did not say anything. He lay on the floor, staring at his feet.

"Don't worry about everybody else. The whole world is full of 'every- **39** body else,' you know that? But only a few make a significant achievement."

The loss of TV and play time was bad enough. I got up off the floor, **40** feeling as if everything was against me. Mother wasn't going to let me play with my friends, and there would be no more television—almost none, anyway. She was stopping me from having any fun in life.

"And that isn't all," she said. "Come back, Bennie."   **41**

I turned around, wondering what else there could be.   **42**

"In addition," she said, "to doing your homework, you have to read 43 two books from the library each week. Every single week."

"Two books? Two?" Even though I was in fifth grade, I had never read 44 a whole book in my life.

"Yes, two. When you finish reading them, you must write me a book 45 report just like you do at school. You're not living up to your potential, so I'm going to see that you do."

Usually Curtis, who was two years older, was the more rebellious. But 46 this time he seemed to grasp the wisdom of what Mother said. He did not say one word.

She stared at Curtis. "You understand?"   47

He nodded.   48

"Bennie, is it clear?"   49

"Yes, Mother." I agreed to do what Mother told me—it wouldn't have 50 occurred to me not to obey—but I did not like it. Mother was being unfair and demanding more of us than other parents did.

The following day was Thursday. After school, Curtis and I walked 51 to the local branch of the library. I did not like it much, but then I had not spent that much time in any library.

We both wandered around a little in the children's section, not having any 52 idea about how to select books or which books we wanted to check out.

The librarian came over to us and asked if she could help. We explained 53 that both of us wanted to check out two books.

"What kind of books would you like to read?" the librarian asked.   54

"Animals," I said after thinking about it. "Something about animals."   55

"I'm sure we have several that you'd like." She led me over to a sec- 56 tion of books. She left me and guided Curtis to another section of the room. I flipped through the row of books until I found two that looked easy enough for me to read. One of them, *Chip, the Dam Builder*—about a beaver—was the first one I had ever checked out. As soon as I got home, I started to read it. It was the first book I ever read all the way through even though it took me two nights. Reluctantly• I admitted afterward to Mother that I really had liked reading about Chip.

Within a month I could find my way around the children's section like 57 someone who had gone there all his life. By then the library staff knew Curtis and me and the kind of books we chose. They often made sugges-tions. "Here's a delightful book about a squirrel," I remember one of them telling me.

As she told me part of the story, I tried to appear indifferent,• but as 58 soon as she handed it to me, I opened the book and started to read.

Best of all, we became favorites of the librarians. When new books 59 came in that they thought either of us would enjoy, they held them for us. Soon I became fascinated as I realized that the library had so many books—and about so many different subjects.

After the book about the beaver, I chose others about animals—all 60 types of animals. I read every animal story I could get my hands on. I read books about wolves, wild dogs, several about squirrels, and a vari-ety of animals that lived in other countries. Once I had gone through the animal books, I started reading about plants, then minerals, and finally rocks.

My reading books about rocks was the first time the information ever **61** became practical to me. We lived near the railroad tracks, and when Curtis and I took the route to school that crossed by the tracks, I began paying attention to the crushed rock that I noticed between the ties.

As I continued to read more about rocks, I would walk along the **62** tracks, searching for different kinds of stones, and then see if I could identify them.

Often I would take a book with me to make sure that I had labeled each **63** stone correctly.

"Agate," I said as I threw the stone. Curtis got tired of my picking up **64** stones and identifying them, but I did not care because I kept finding new stones all the time. Soon it became my favorite game to walk along the tracks and identify the varieties of stones. Although I did not realize it, within a very short period of time, I was actually becoming an expert on rocks.

Two things happened in the second half of fifth grade that convinced **65** me of the importance of reading books.

First, our teacher, Mrs. Williamson, had a spelling bee every Friday **66** afternoon. We'd go through all the words we'd had so far that year. Sometimes she also called out words that we were supposed to have learned in fourth grade. Without fail, I always went down on the first word.

One Friday, though, Bobby Farmer, whom everyone acknowledged • **67** as the smartest kid in our class, had to spell "agriculture" as his final word. As soon as the teacher pronounced his word, I thought, *I can spell that word.* Just the day before, I had learned it from reading one of my library books. I spelled it under my breath, and it was just the way Bobby spelled it.

If I can spell "agriculture," I'll bet I can learn to spell any other word in the **68** *world. I'll bet I can learn to spell better than Bobby Farmer.*

Just that single word, "agriculture," was enough to give me hope.   **69**

The following week, a second thing happened that forever changed **70** my life. When Mr. Jaeck, the science teacher, was teaching us about volcanoes, he held up an object that looked like a piece of black, glass-like rock. "Does anybody know what this is? What does it have to do with volcanoes?"

Immediately, because of my reading, I recognized the stone. I waited, **71** but none of my classmates raised their hands. I thought, *This is strange. Not even the smart kids are raising their hands.* I raised my hand.

"Yes, Benjamin," he said.   **72**

I heard snickers around me. The other kids probably thought it was a **73** joke, or that I was going to say something stupid.

"Obsidian, •" I said.   **74**

"That's right!" He tried not to look startled, but it was obvious he **75** hadn't expected me to give the correct answer.

"That's obsidian," I said, "and it's formed by the supercooling of lava **76** when it hits the water." Once I had their attention and realized I knew information no other student had learned, I began to tell them everything I knew about the subject of obsidian, lava, lava flow, supercooling, and compacting of the elements.

When I finally paused, a voice behind me whispered, "Is that Bennie 77 Carson?"

"You're absolutely correct," Mr. Jaeck said, and he smiled at me. If he 78 had announced that I'd won a million-dollar lottery, I couldn't have been more pleased and excited.

"Benjamin, that's absolutely, absolutely right," he repeated with 79 enthusiasm in his voice. He turned to the others and said, "That is wonderful! Class, this is a tremendous piece of information Benjamin has just given us. I'm very proud to hear him say this."

For a few moments, I tasted the thrill of achievement. I recall thinking, 80 *Wow, look at them. They're all looking at me with admiration. Me, the dummy! The one everybody thinks is stupid. They're looking at me to see if this is really me speaking.*

Maybe, though, it was I who was the most astonished one in the 81 class. Although I had been reading two books a week because Mother told me to, I had not realized how much knowledge I was accumulating. True, I had learned to enjoy reading, but until then I hadn't realized how it connected with my schoolwork. That day—for the first time—I realized that Mother had been right. Reading is the way out of ignorance, and the road to achievement. I did not have to be the class dummy anymore.

For the next few days, I felt like a hero at school. The jokes about me 82 stopped. The kids started to listen to me. *I'm starting to have fun with this stuff.*

As my grades improved in every subject, I asked myself, "Ben, is there 83 any reason you can't be the smartest kid in the class? If you can learn about obsidian, you can learn about social studies and geography and math and science and everything."

That single moment of triumph pushed me to want to read more. 84 From then on, it was as though I could not read enough books. Whenever anyone looked for me after school, they could usually find me in my bedroom—curled up, reading a library book—for a long time, the only thing I wanted to do. I had stopped caring about the TV programs I was missing; I no longer cared about playing Tip the Top or baseball anymore. I just wanted to read.

In a year and a half—by the middle of sixth grade—I had moved to the 85 top of the class.

VOCABULARY IN CONTEXT

1. The word *trauma* in "I loved both my mother and father and went through considerable trauma over their separating. For months afterward, I kept thinking that my parents would get back together . . . but he never came back" (paragraph 20) means

   a. love.

   b. knowledge.

   c. distance.

   d. suffering.

2. The word *acknowledged* in "One Friday, though, Bobby Farmer, whom everyone acknowledged as the smartest kid in our class, had to spell 'agriculture' as his final word" (paragraph 67) means

   a. denied.

   b. recognized.

   c. forgot.

   d. interrupted.

READING COMPREHENSION QUESTIONS

1. Which of the following would be the best alternative title for this selection?

   a. The Importance of Fifth Grade

   b. The Role of Parents in Education

   c. The Day I Surprised My Science Teacher

   d. Reading Changed My Life

2. Which sentence best expresses the main idea of this selection?

   a. Children who grow up in single-parent homes may spend large amounts of time home alone.

   b. Because of parental guidance that led to a love of reading, the author was able to go from academic failure to success.

   c. Most children do not take school very seriously, and they suffer as a result.

   d. Today's young people watch too much television.

3. Bennie's mother

   a. was not a religious person.

   b. spoke to Bennie's teacher about Bennie's poor report card.

   c. had only a third-grade education.

   d. had little contact with educated people.

4. To get her sons to do better in school, Mrs. Carson insisted that they

   a. stop watching TV.

   b. finish their homework before playing.

   c. read one library book every month.

   d. all of the above.

5. *True or false?* _____ Bennie's first experience with a library book was discouraging.

6. We can conclude that Bennie Carson believed he was dumb because

   a. in Boston he had not learned much.

   b. other students laughed at him.

   c. he had done his best when he first started at Higgins Elementary School, but he still got poor grades.

   d. all of the above.

7. We can conclude that the author's mother believed
   a. education leads to success.
   b. her sons needed to be forced to live up to their potential.
   c. socializing was less important for her sons than a good education.
   d. all of the above.

8. From paragraphs 70–80, we can infer that
   a. Bennie thought his classmates were stupid because they did not know about obsidian.
   b. Mr. Jaeck knew less about rocks than Bennie did.
   c. this was the first time Bennie had answered a difficult question correctly in class.
   d. Mr. Jaeck thought that Bennie had taken too much class time explaining about obsidian.

DISCUSSION QUESTIONS

About Content

1. How do you think considering himself the "dumbest kid in class" affected Bennie's schoolwork?

2. The author recalls his failure in the classroom as an eight-year-old child by writing, "Perhaps I wasn't emotionally able to learn much." Why does he make this statement? What do you think parents and schools can do to help children through difficult times?

3. How did Mrs. Carson encourage Bennie to make school—particularly reading—a priority in his life? What effect did her efforts have on Bennie's academic performance and self-esteem?

4. As a child, Carson began to feel confident about his own abilities when he followed his mother's guidelines. How might Mrs. Carson's methods help adult students build up their own self-confidence and motivation?

About Structure

5. What is the main order in which the details of this selection are organized—time order or listing order? Locate and write below three of the many transitions that are used as part of that time order or listing order.

   _____   _____   _____

6. In paragraph 65, Carson states, "Two things happened in the second half of fifth grade that convinced me of the importance of reading books." What two transitions does Carson use in later paragraphs to help readers recognize those two events? Write those two transitions here:

   _____   _____

About Style and Tone

7. Instead of describing his mother, Carson reveals her character through specific details of her actions and words. Find one paragraph in which

this technique is used, and write its number here: _____. What does this paragraph tell us about Mrs. Carson?

8.   Why do you suppose Carson italicizes sentences in paragraphs 67, 68, 71, 80, and 82? What purpose do the italicized sentences serve?

WRITING ASSIGNMENTS

Assignment 1: Writing a Paragraph

The reading tells about some of Carson's most important school experiences, both positive and negative. Write a paragraph about one of your most important experiences in school. To select an event to write about, try asking yourself the following questions:

Which teachers or events in school influenced how I felt about myself?

What specific incidents stand out in my mind as I think back to elementary school?

To get started, you might use freewriting to help you remember and record the details. Then begin your draft with a topic sentence similar to one of the following:

A seemingly small experience in elementary school encouraged me greatly.

If not for my sixth-grade teacher, I would not be where I am today.

My tenth-grade English class was a turning point in my life.

Use concrete details—actions, comments, reactions, and so on—to help your readers see what happened.

Assignment 2: Writing a Paragraph

Reading helped Bennie, and it can do a lot for adults, too. Most of us, however, don't have someone around to make us do a certain amount of personal reading every week. In addition, many of us don't have as much free time as Bennie and Curtis had. How can adults find time to read more? Write a paragraph listing several ways adults can add more reading to their lives.

To get started, simply write down as many ways as you can think of—in any order. Here is an example of a prewriting list for this paper:

Situations in which adults can find extra time to read:

Riding to and from work or school

In bed at night before turning off the light

While eating breakfast or lunch

Instead of watching some TV

In the library

Feel free to use items from the list above, but see if you can add at least one or two of your own ideas as well. Use descriptions and examples to emphasize and dramatize your supporting details.

Assignment 3: Writing an Essay

Mrs. Carson discovered an effective way to boost her children's achievement and self-confidence. There are other ways as well. Write an essay whose thesis statement is "There are several ways parents can help children live up to their potential." Then, in the following paragraphs, explain and illustrate two or three methods parents can use. In choosing material for your supporting paragraphs, you might consider some of these areas, or think of others on your own:

Assigning regular household "chores" and rewarding a good job

Encouraging kids to join an organization that fosters achievement: Scouts, Little League, religious group, or neighborhood service club

Going to parent-teacher conferences at school and then working more closely with children's teachers—knowing when assignments are due, and so on

Giving a child some responsibility for an enjoyable family activity, such as choosing decorations or food for a birthday party

Setting up a "Wall of Fame" in the home where children's artwork, successful schoolwork, and so on, can be displayed

Setting guidelines (as Mrs. Carson did) for use of leisure time, homework time, and the like

Draw on examples from your own experiences or from someone else's—including those of Bennie Carson, if you like.

A Change of Attitude

Grant Berry

PREVIEW	WORDS TO WATCH
Every college has them: students the same age as some of their professors, students rushing into class after a full day at work, students carrying photographs—not of their boyfriends or girlfriends, but of the children they too seldom see. In many cases, these students are as surprised as anyone to find themselves in college. In this essay, one such student describes his development from a bored high schooler to a committed college student.	decades (3) striven (3) suavely (4) immaculately (4) cliques (5) tedious (6) trudging (6) nil (6) smugly (8) deprivation (16) scowl (21) battering (22)

1   For me to be in college is highly improbable. That I am doing well in school teeters on the illogical. Considering my upbringing, past educational performance, and current responsibilities, one might say, "This guy hasn't got a chance." If I were a racehorse and college were the track, there would be few who would pick me to win, place, or show.

2   When I told my dad that I was going back to school, the only encouragement he offered was this: "Send me anywhere, but don't send me back to school." For my father, school was the worst kind of prison, so I was raised believing that school at its best was a drag. My dad thought that the purpose of graduating from high school was so you never had to go back to school again, and I adopted this working stiff's philosophy.

3   I followed my dad's example the way a man who double-crosses the mob follows a cement block to the bottom of the river. My dad has been a union factory worker for more than two decades,• and he has never striven• to be anything more than average. Nonetheless, he is a good man; I love him very much, and I respect him for being a responsible husband and father. He seldom, if ever, missed a day of work; he never left his paycheck at a bar, and none of our household appliances were ever carted off by a repo-man. He took his family to church each week, didn't light up or lift a glass, and has celebrated his silver anniversary with his first, and only, wife. However, if he ever had a dream of being more than just a shop rat, I never knew about it.

4   On the other hand, my dreams were big, but my thoughts were small. I was not raised to be a go-getter. I knew I wanted to go to work each day in a suit and tie; unfortunately, I could not define what it was I wanted to do. I told a few people that I wanted to have a job where I could dress suavely• and carry a briefcase, and they laughed in my face. They said, "You'll never be anything," and I believed them. Even now I am envious of an immaculately• dressed businessman. It is not the angry type of jealousy; it is the "wish it were me" variety.

Since I knew I was not going to further my education, and I didn't **5** know what I wanted to do except wear a suit, high school was a disaster. I do not know how my teachers can respect themselves after passing me. In every high school there are cliques• and classifications. I worked just hard enough to stay above the bottom, but I did not want to work hard enough to get into the clique with the honor roll students.

Also, I had always had a problem with reading. When I was a kid, **6** reading for me was slow and tedious.• My eyes walked over words like a snail trudging• through mud. I couldn't focus on what I was reading, and this allowed my young, active mind to wander far from my reading material. I would often finish a page and not remember a single word I had just read. Not only was reading a slow process, but my comprehension was nil.• I wasn't dumb; in fact, I was at a high English level. However, reading rated next to scraping dog poop from the tread of my sneakers. I didn't yet know that reading could be like playing the guitar: The more you do it, the better you get. As far as reading was concerned, I thought I was stuck in the same slow waltz forever.

In junior high and high school, I read only when it was absolutely **7** essential. For example, I had to find out who Spider-Man was going to web, or how many children Superman was going to save each month. I also had to find out which girls were popular on the bathroom walls. I'm ashamed to say that my mother even did a book report for me, first reading the book. In high school, when I would choose my own classes, I took art and electronics rather than English.

Even though I was raised in a good Christian home, the only things I **8** cared about were partying and girls. I spent all of my minimum-wage paycheck on beer, cigarettes, and young ladies. As a senior, I dated a girl who was twenty. She had no restrictions, and I tried to keep pace with her lifestyle. I would stay out drinking until 3:00 A.M. on school nights. The next morning I would sleep through class or just not show up. It became such a problem that the school sent letters to my parents telling them that I would not be joining my classmates for commencement if I didn't show up for class once in a while. This put the fear of the establishment in me because I knew the importance of graduating from high school. Nonetheless, I never once remember doing homework my senior year. Yet in June, they shook my hand and forked over a diploma as I smugly• marched across the stage in a blue gown and square hat.

Since I felt I didn't deserve the piece of paper with the principal's **9** and superintendent's signatures on it, I passed up not only a graduation party but also a class ring and a yearbook. If it were not for my diploma and senior pictures, there would not be enough evidence to convince a jury that I am guilty of attending high school at all. I did, however, celebrate with my friends on graduation night. I got loaded, misjudged a turn, flattened a stop sign, and got my car stuck. When I pushed my car with my girlfriend behind the steering wheel, mud from the spinning tire sprayed all over my nice clothes. It was quite a night, and looking back, it was quite a fitting closure for the end of high school.

After graduation I followed my father's example and went to work, **10** plunging into the lukewarm waters of mediocrity. All I was doing on my job bagging groceries was trading dollars for hours. I worked just hard enough to keep from getting fired, and I was paid just enough to keep from quitting.

Considering the way my father felt about school, college was a subject **11** that seldom came up at our dinner table. I was not discouraged, nor was I encouraged, to go to college; it was my choice. My first attempt at college came when I was nineteen. I had always dreamed of being a disk jockey, so I enrolled in a broadcasting class. However, my experience in college was as forgettable as high school. My habit of not doing homework carried over, and the class was such a yawner that I often forgot to attend. Miraculously, I managed to pull a C, but my dream was weak and quickly died. I did not enroll for the next term. My girlfriend, the one who kept me out late in high school, became pregnant with my child. We were married two days after my final class, and this gave me another excuse not to continue my education.

My first job, and every job since, has involved working with my hands **12** and not my head. I enjoyed my work, but after the money ran out, the month would keep going. One evening my wife's cousin called and said he had a way that we could increase our income. I asked, "How soon can you get here?" He walked us through a six-step plan of selling and recruiting, and when he was finished, my wife and I wanted in. Fumbling around inside his large briefcase, he told us we needed the proper attitude first. Emerging with a small stack of books, he said, "Read these!" Then he flipped the books into my lap. I groaned at the thought of reading all those volumes. If this guy wanted me to develop a good attitude, giving me books was having the opposite effect. However, I wanted to make some extra cash, so I assured him I would try.

I started reading the books each night. They were self-help, positive **13** mental-attitude manuals. Reading those books opened up my world; they put me in touch with a me I didn't know existed. The books told me I had potential, possibly even greatness. I took their message in like an old Chevrolet being pumped full of premium no-lead gasoline. It felt so good I started reading more. Not only did I read at night; I read in the morning before I went to work. I read during my breaks and lunch hour, when waiting for signal lights to turn green, in between bites of food at supper, and while sitting on the toilet. One of the books I read said that there is no limit to the amount of information our brains will hold, so I began filling mine up.

The process of reading was slow at first, just as it had been when I was **14** a kid, but it was just like playing the guitar. If I struck an unclear chord, I would try it again, and if I read something unclear, I would simply read it again. Something happened: The more I read, the better I got at it. It wasn't long before I could focus in and understand without reading things twice. I began feeling good about my reading skills, and because of the types of books I was reading, I started feeling good about myself at the same time.

The income from my day job blossomed while the selling and **15** recruiting business grew demanding, disappointing, and fruitless. We stopped working that soil and our business died, but I was hooked on reading. I now laid aside the self-help books and began reading whatever I wanted. I got my first library card, and I subscribed to *Sports Illustrated*. I found a book of short stories, and I dived into poetry, as well as countless newspaper articles, cereal boxes, and oatmeal packages. Reading, which had been a problem for me, became a pleasure and then a passion.

Reading moved me. As I continued to read in a crowded lunchroom, 16 sometimes I stumbled across an especially moving short story or magazine article. For example, a young Romanian girl was saved from starvation and deprivation● by an adoptive couple from the United States. I quickly jerked the reading material to my face to conceal tears when she entered her new home filled with toys and stuffed animals.

Not only did reading tug at my emotions; it inspired me to make a 17 move. All those positive-mental-attitude books kept jabbing me in the ribs, so last fall, at age twenty-seven, I decided to give college another try. Now I am back in school, but it's a different road I travel from when I was a teenager. Mom and Dad paid the amount in the right-hand column of my tuition bill then, but now I am determined to pay for college myself, even though I must miss the sound of the pizza delivery man's tires on my blacktop driveway. I hope to work my way out of my blue collar by paying for school with blue-collar cash.

As a meat-cutter, I usually spend between 45 and 50 hours a week with 18 a knife in my hand. Some weeks I have spent 72 hours beneath a butcher's cap. In one two-week period I spent 141 hours with a bloody apron on, but in that time I managed to show up for all of my classes and get all of my homework done (except being short a few bibliography cards for my research paper).

Working full-time and raising a family leave me little free time. If I am 19 not in class, I'm studying linking verbs or trying to figure out the difference between compound and complex sentences.

There are other obstacles and challenges staring me in the face. 20 The tallest hurdle is a lack of time for meeting all my obligations. For instance, my wife works two nights a week, leaving me to care for my two daughters. A twelve-hour day at work can lead to an evening coma at home, so when Mom's punching little square buttons on a cash register, I hardly have the energy to pour cornflakes for my kids, let alone outline a research paper.

Going to college means making choices, some of which bring criti- 21 cism. My neighbors, for example, hate my sickly, brown lawn sandwiched between their lush, green, spotless plots of earth, which would be the envy of any football field. Just walking to my mailbox can be an awful reminder of how pitiful my lawn looks when I receive an unforgiving scowl● from one of the groundskeepers who live on either side of me. It is embarrassing to have such a colorless lawn, but it will have to wait because I want more out of life than a half-acre of green turf. Right now my time and money are tied up in college courses instead of fertilizer and weed killer.

But the toughest obstacle is having to take away time from those 22 I love most. I am proud of the relationship I have with my wife and kids, so it tears my guts out when I have to look into my daughter's sad face and explain that I can't go to the Christmas program she's been practicing for weeks because I have a final exam. It's not easy to tell my three-year-old that I can't push her on the swings because I have a cause-and-effect paper to write, or tell my seven-year-old that I can't build a snowman because I have an argument essay to polish. As I tell my family that I can't go sledding with them, my wife lets out a big sigh, and my kids yell, "Puleeze, Daddy, can't you come with us?" At these times I wonder if my dream of a college education can withstand such an emotional battering,° or if it is even worth it. But I keep on keeping on because I must set a good example for the four little eyes that are keeping watch over their daddy's every move. I must succeed and pass on to them the right attitude toward school. This time when I graduate, because of the hurdles I've overcome, there will be a celebration—a proper one.

VOCABULARY IN CONTEXT

1. The word *cliques* in "In every high school there are cliques and classifications. I worked just hard enough to stay above the bottom, but I did not want to work hard enough to get into the clique with the honor roll students" (paragraph 5) means

   a. grades.

   b. schools.

   c. groups.

   d. sports.

2. The word *scowl* in "Just walking to my mailbox can be an awful reminder of how pitiful my lawn looks when I receive an unforgiving scowl from one of the groundskeepers who live on either side of me" (paragraph 21) means

   a. sincere smile.

   b. favor.

   c. angry look.

   d. surprise.

READING COMPREHENSION QUESTIONS

1. Which sentence best expresses the central idea of the selection?

   a. The author was never encouraged to attend college or to challenge himself mentally on the job.

   b. After years of not caring about education, Berry was led by some self-help books to love reading, gain self-esteem, and attend college.

   c. The author's wife and children often do not understand why he is unable to take part in many family activities.

   d. The author was given a high school diploma despite the fact that he did little work and rarely attended class.

2. Which sentence best expresses the main idea of paragraph 13?
    a. Influenced by self-help books, the author developed a hunger for reading.
    b. People who really care about improving themselves will find the time to do it, such as during the early morning, at breaks, and during the lunch hour.
    c. Self-help books send the message that everyone is full of potential and even greatness.
    d. There is no limit to the amount of information the brain can hold.

3. Which sentence best expresses the main idea of paragraph 22?
    a. The author's decision to attend college is hurting his long-term relationship with his wife and daughters.
    b. The author has two children, one age three and the other age seven.
    c. The author enjoys family activities such as attending his children's plays and building snowmen.
    d. Although he misses spending time with his family, the author feels that graduating from college will make him a better role model for his children.

4. The author's reading skills
    a. were strong even when he was a child.
    b. improved as he read more.
    c. were strengthened considerably in high school.
    d. were sharpened by jobs he held after high school graduation.

5. The author's father
    a. was rarely home while the author was growing up.
    b. often missed work and stayed out late at bars.
    c. was a college graduate.
    d. disliked school.

6. In stating that his graduation night "was quite a fitting closure for the end of high school," Berry implies that
    a. he was glad high school was finally over.
    b. car troubles were a common problem for him throughout high school.
    c. his behavior had ruined that night just as it had ruined his high school education.
    d. despite the problems, the evening gave him good memories, just as high school had given him good memories.

7. We can infer from paragraph 21 that the author
    a. does not tend his lawn because he enjoys annoying his neighbors.
    b. receives a lot of mail.
    c. is willing to make sacrifices for his college education.
    d. has neighbors who care little about the appearance of their property.

8. We can infer that the author believes children

   a. should be passed to the next grade when they reach a certain age, regardless of their test scores.

   b. should not require a great deal of time from their parents.

   c. fall into two categories: "born readers" and those who can never learn to read very well.

   d. benefit from having role models who care about education.

DISCUSSION QUESTIONS

About Content

1. The author looks back at this period of reading self-help books as one in which his attitude improved, eventually leading to his enrollment in college. Has a particular occurrence ever sharply changed your outlook on life? Was it something that you read, observed, or directly experienced? How did it happen? How did it change your point of view?

2. Berry writes that his father did not encourage him to go on to college. Nevertheless, he sees many positive things about his father. In what ways was his father a positive role model for him? In other words, is Berry's positive behavior as an adult partly a result of his father's influence? What do you see in your own adult behavior that you can attribute to your parents' influence?

3. Berry discusses some of the difficulties he faces as a result of being in college—struggling to find time to meet his obligations, giving up lawn care, spending less time with his family. What difficulties do you face as a result of fitting college into your life? What obligations must you struggle to fulfill? What activities remain undone?

About Structure

4. In most of his essay, Berry uses time order, but in some places he uses listing order. For example, what does Berry list in paragraphs 20–22?

_____

5. In closing his essay, Berry writes that at his college graduation, "there will be a celebration—a proper one." With what earlier event is he contrasting this graduation?

_____

About Style and Tone

6. In explaining that he followed his father's example, the author compares himself to "a man who double-crosses the mob [and] follows a cement block to the bottom of the river." In this comparison, Berry strikingly makes the point that his own actions led him to an undesirable situation. Find two other places where the author uses a

richly revealing comparison. Write those images below, and explain what Berry means by each one.

Image: _____

_____

Meaning: _____

Image: _____

_____

Meaning: _____

7. In the first sentence of Berry's essay, he tells us that it is "highly improbable" for him to be in college. What is his tone in this sentence and in the paragraph that follows?

RESPONDING TO IMAGES

Consider how this photograph of assembly-line workers is structured. Why do you think the photographer chose to take the picture from this particular angle?

WRITING ASSIGNMENTS

Assignment 1: Writing a Paragraph

Children are strongly influenced by the example of their parents (and other significant adults in their lives). For instance, the author of this essay followed his father's example of disliking school and getting a job that did not challenge him mentally.

Think about your growing-up years and about adults who influenced you, both positively and negatively. Then write a paragraph that describes one of these people and his or her influence on you. Supply plenty of vivid examples to help the reader understand how and why this person affected you.

The topic sentence of your paragraph should identify the person (either by name or by relationship to you) and briefly indicate the kind of influence he or she had on you. Here are some examples of topic sentences for this paper:

My aunt's courage in difficult situations helped me to become a stronger person.

My father's frequent trouble with the law made it necessary for me to grow up in a hurry.

The pastor of our church helped me realize that I was a worthwhile, talented person.

Assignment 2: Writing a Paragraph

Write a paragraph about one way that reading has been important in your life, either positively or negatively. To discover the approach you wish to take, think for a moment about the influence of reading throughout your life. When you were a child, was being read to at bedtime a highlight of your day? Did reading out loud in elementary school cause you embarrassment? Do you adore mysteries or true-crime books? Do you avoid reading whenever possible? Find an idea about the role of reading in your life that you can write about in the space of a paragraph. Your topic sentence will be a clear statement of that idea, such as:

I first learned to read from watching *Sesame Street.*

One key experience in second grade made me hate reading out loud in class.

My parents' attitude toward reading rubbed off on me.

Reading to my child at bedtime is an important time of day for both of us.

Books have taught me some things I never would have learned from friends and family.

There are several reasons why I am not a good reader.

A wonderful self-help book has helped me build my self-esteem.

Develop your main idea with detailed explanations and descriptions. For example, if you decide to write about reading to your child at bedtime, you might describe the positions you and your child take (Is the child in bed? On the floor? On your lap?), one or two of the stories the child and you have loved, some of the child's reactions, and so on.

Assignment 3: Writing an Essay

Berry's graduation-night celebration was a dramatic one and, he states, "a fitting closure for the end of high school." What was your senior prom or high school graduation celebration like? Did you participate in any of the planning and preparation for the events? Were finding a date and shopping for clothing for the prom fun or nerve-racking experiences? Was the event itself wonderful or disappointing? Write an essay telling the story of your graduation celebration from start to finish. Use many sharp descriptive details to help your readers envision events, decorations, clothing, cars, the weather, and so on. In addition, add meaning to your story by telling what you were thinking and feeling throughout the event.

You might try making a list as a way of collecting details for this paper. At first, don't worry about organizing your details. Just keep adding to your list, which might at one point look like this:

decorations committee

considered asking my cousin to go with me, if necessary

shopping for prom dress with Mom (and arguing)

afraid I'd be asked first by someone I didn't want to go with

talk of being up all night

pressed orchid corsage afterward

florist busy that week

working on centerpieces

feet hurt

Eventually, you will have enough information to begin thinking about the organization of your essay. Here's what the scratch outline for one such essay looks like:

Central idea: My high school prom was a mixture of fun and disappointment.

(1)   Before the dance

Work on the decorations com.

Anxiety over getting a date, finally relief

Worn out shopping for a dress

Last-minute preparations (getting flowers, having hair done, decorating ballroom)

(2)   Night of the dance

Picture-taking at home

Squeezing gown into car, hem gets stuck in car door and grease rubs on it

Beautiful ballroom

Rotten meal

Great band (even teachers yelling requests)

After two dances had to take off heels

Date kept dancing with others

Danced with my brother, who came with my girlfriend

Early breakfast served at hotel

(3)   After the dance

Total exhaustion for two days

Extensive phone analysis of dance with girlfriends

Never went out with that date again

Several years later, prom dress, wrapped in a garbage bag, went to Salvation Army

Perhaps you don't remember your prom or graduation night celebration very well, or don't wish to. Feel free to write about another important social event instead, such as a high school reunion, a family reunion, or your own or someone else's wedding.

Let's Get Specific

Beth Johnson

PREVIEW	WORDS TO WATCH
Some people are better writers than others. That's obvious to anyone who reads. There are writers whose material you just can't put down—and there are writers whose material you can't put down fast enough. One of the biggest differences between the skillful writer and the poor one is this: The successful writer uses specific, concrete language. Journalist and teacher Beth Johnson explains the power of specific language and demonstrates how any writer can become more skilled in its use.	instinctive (2) prospective (2) vividly (2) glaze (3) blandly (7) intuitively (8) swayed (8) parody (8) crave (9) anecdote (12) compelling (16) sustain (17)

Imagine that you've offered to fix up your sister with a blind date. "You'll 1 like him," you tell her. "He's really nice." Would that assurance be enough to satisfy her? Would she contentedly wait for Saturday night, happily anticipating meeting this "nice" young man? Not likely! She would probably bombard you with questions: "But what's he like? Is he tall or short? Funny? Serious? Smart? Kind? Shy? Does he work? How do you know him?"

Such questions reveal the instinctive● hunger we all feel for specific 2 detail. Being told that her prospective● date is "nice" does very little to help your sister picture him. She needs concrete details to help her vividly● imagine this stranger.

The same principle applies to writing. Whether you are preparing 3 a research paper, a letter to a friend, or an article for the local newspaper, your writing will be strengthened by the use of detailed, concrete language. Specific language energizes and informs readers. General language, by contrast, makes their eyes glaze● over.

The following examples should prove the point. 4

Dear Sir or Madam:

Please consider my application for a job with your company. I am a college graduate with experience in business. Part-time jobs that I have held during the school year and my work over summer vacations make me well-qualified for employment. My former employers have always considered me a good, reliable worker. Thank you for considering my application.

Sincerely,
Bob Cole

Dear Sir or Madam:

I would like to be considered for an entry-level position in your purchasing department. I graduated in June from Bayside College with a 3.5 GPA and a bachelor's degree in business administration. While at Bayside, I held a part-time job in the college's business office, where I eventually had responsibility for coordinating food purchasing for the school cafeteria. By encouraging competitive bidding among food suppliers, I was able to save the school approximately $2,500 in the school year 1998–1999. During the last three summers (1997–1999), I worked at Bayside Textiles, where I was promoted from a job in the mailroom to the position of assistant purchasing agent, a position that taught me a good deal about controlling costs. Given my background, I'm confident I could make a real contribution to your company. I will telephone you next Tuesday morning to ask if we might arrange an interview.

Sincerely,
Julia Moore

Which of the preceding letters do you think makes a more convincing 5
case for these job seekers? If you're like most people, you would choose
the second. Although both letters are polite and grammatically acceptable,
the first one suffers badly in comparison with the second for one important
reason. It is *general* and *abstract*, while the second is *specific* and *concrete*.

Let's look at the letters again. The differing styles of the two are evi- 6
dent in the first sentence. Bob is looking for "a job with your company."
He doesn't specify what kind of job—it's for the employer to figure out
if Bob wants to work as a groundskeeper, on an assembly line, or as a
salesperson. By contrast, Julia is immediately specific about the kind of
job she is seeking—"an entry-level position in your purchasing department." Bob tells only that he is "a college graduate." But Julia tells where
she went to college, what her grade point average was, and exactly what
she studied.

The contrast continues as the two writers talk about their work experi- 7
ence. Again, Bob talks in vague, general terms. He gives no concrete evidence to show how the general descriptions "well-qualified" and "good,
reliable worker" apply to him. But Julia backs up her claims. She tells
specifically what positions she's held (buyer for cafeteria, assistant purchasing clerk for textile company), gives solid evidence that she performed
her jobs well (saved the school $2,500, was promoted from mailroom), and
explains what skills she has acquired (knows about controlling costs). Julia
continues to be clear and concrete as she closes the letter. By saying, "I will
telephone you next Tuesday morning," she leaves the reader with a helpful, specific piece of information. Chances are, her prospective employer
will be glad to take her call. The chances are equally good that Bob will
never hear from the company. His letter was so blandly● general that the
employer will hardly remember receiving it.

Julia's letter demonstrates the power of specific detail—a power that **8** we all appreciate intuitively.• Indeed, although we may not always be aware of it, our opinions and decisions are frequently swayed• by concrete language. On a restaurant menu, are you more tempted by a "green salad" or "a colorful salad bowl filled with romaine and spinach leaves, red garden-fresh tomatoes, and crisp green pepper rings"? Would being told that a movie is "good" persuade you to see it as much as hearing that it is "a hilarious parody• of a rock documentary featuring a fictional heavy-metal band"? Does knowing that a classmate has "personal problems" help you understand her as well as hearing that "her parents are divorcing, her brother was just arrested for selling drugs, and she is scheduled for surgery to correct a back problem"?

When we read, all of us want—even crave•—this kind of specificity. **9** Concrete language grabs our attention and allows us to witness the writer's world almost firsthand. Abstract language, on the other hand, forces us to try to fill in the blanks left by the writer's lack of specific imagery. Usually we tire of the effort. Our attention wanders. We begin to wonder what's for lunch and whether it's going to rain, as our eyes scan the page, searching for some concrete detail to focus on.

Once you understand the power of concrete details, you will gain **10** considerable power as a writer. You will describe events so vividly that readers will feel they experienced them directly. You will sprinkle your essays with nuggets of detail that, like the salt on a pretzel, add interest and texture.

Consider the following examples and decide for yourself which came **11** from a writer who has mastered the art of the specific detail.

Living at Home

Unlike many college students, I have chosen to live at home with my parents. Naturally, the arrangement has both good and bad points. The most difficult part is that, even though I am an adult, my parents sometimes still think of me as a child. Our worst disagreements occur when they expect me to report to them as though I were still twelve years old. Another drawback to living with my parents is that I don't feel free to have friends over to "my place." It's not that my parents don't welcome my friends in their home, but I can't tell my friends to drop in anytime as I would if I lived alone.

But in other ways, living at home works out well. The most obvious plus is that I am saving a lot of money. I pay room and board, but that doesn't compare to what renting an apartment would cost. There are less measurable advantages as well. Although we do sometimes fall into our old parent-child roles, my parents and I are getting to know each other in new ways. Generally, we relate as adults, and I think we're all gaining a lot of respect for one another.

The Pros and Cons of Living at Home

Most college students live in a dormitory or apartment. They spend their hours surrounded by their own stereos, blaring hip-hop or rock music; their own furnishings, be they leaking beanbag chairs or Salvation Army sofas; and their own choice of foods, from tofu-bean sprout casseroles to a basic diet of Cheetos. My life is different. I occupy the same room that has been mine since babyhood. My school pictures, from gap-toothed first-grader to cocky senior, adorn the walls. The music drifting through my door from the living room ranges from Lawrence Welk to . . . Lawrence Welk. The food runs heavily to Mid-American Traditional: meatloaf, mashed potatoes, frozen peas.

Yes, I live with my parents. And the arrangement is not always ideal. Although I am twenty-four years old, my parents sometimes slip into a time warp and mentally cut my age in half. "Where are you going, Lisa? Who will you be with?" my mother will occasionally ask. I'll answer patiently, "I'm going to have pizza with some people from my psych class." "But where?" she continues. "I'm not sure," I'll say, my voice rising just a hair. If the questioning continues, it will often lead to a blowup. "You don't need to know where I'm going, OK?" I'll say shrilly. "You don't have to yell at me," she'll answer in a hurt voice.

Living at home also makes it harder to entertain. I find myself envying classmates who can tell their friends, "Drop in anytime." If a friend of mine "drops in" unexpectedly, it throws everyone into a tizzy. Mom runs for the dustcloth while Dad ducks into the bedroom, embarrassed to be seen in his comfortable, ratty bathrobe.

On the other hand, I don't regret my decision to live at home for a few years. Naturally, I am saving money. The room and board I pay my parents wouldn't rent the tiniest, most roach-infested apartment in the city. And despite our occasional lapses, my parents and I generally enjoy each other's company. They are getting to know me as an adult, and I am learning to see them as people, not just my parents. I realized how true this was when I saw them getting dressed up to go out recently. Dad was putting on a tie, and Mom one of her best dresses. I opened my mouth to ask where they were going when it occurred to me that maybe they didn't care to be checked up on any more than I did. Swallowing my curiosity, I simply waved good-bye and said, "Have a good time!"

Both passages could have been written by the same person. Both make 12 the same basic points. But the second passage is far more interesting because it backs up the writer's points with concrete details. While the first passage merely *tells* that the writer's parents sometimes treat her like a child, the second passage follows this point up with an anecdote* that *shows* exactly what she means. Likewise with the point about inviting friends over: The first passage only states that there is a problem, but the second one describes in concrete terms what happens if a friend does drop in unexpectedly. The first writer simply says that her room and board costs wouldn't pay for an apartment, but the second is specific about just how inadequate the money would be. And while the first passage uses abstract language to say that the writer and her parents are "getting to know each other in new ways," the second shows what that means by describing a specific incident.

Every kind of writing can be improved by the addition of concrete 13 detail. Let's look at one final example: the love letter.

Dear April,

I can't wait any longer to tell you how I feel. I am crazy about you. You are the most wonderful woman I've ever met. Every time I'm near you I'm overcome with feelings of love. I would do anything in the world for you and am hoping you feel the same way about me.

Love,
Paul

Paul has written a sincere note, but it lacks a certain something. That 14 something is specific detail. Although the letter expresses a lot of positive feelings, it could have been written by practically any love-struck man about any woman. For this letter to be really special to April, it should be unmistakably about her and Paul. And that requires concrete details.

Here is what Paul might write instead. 15

Dear April,

Do you remember last Saturday, as we ate lunch in the park, when I spilled my soda in the grass? You quickly picked up a twig and made a tiny dam to keep the liquid from flooding a busy anthill. You probably didn't think I noticed, but I did. It was at that moment that I realized how totally I am in love with you and your passion for life. Before that I only thought you were the most beautiful woman in the world, with your eyes like sparkling pools of emerald water and your chestnut hair glinting in the sun. But now I recognize what it means when I hear your husky laugh and I feel a tight aching in my chest. It means I could stand on top of the Empire State Building and shout to the world, "I love April Snyder." Should I do it? I'll be waiting for your reply.

Paul

There's no guarantee that April is going to return Paul's feelings, but 16 she certainly has a better idea now just what it is about her that Paul finds so lovable, as well as what kind of guy Paul is. Concrete details have made this letter far more compelling.

Vague, general language is the written equivalent of baby food. It is 17 adequate; it can sustain● life. But it isn't very interesting. For writing to have satisfying crunch, sizzle, and color, it must be generously supplied with specifics. Whether the piece is a job application, a student essay, or a love letter, it is concrete details that make it interesting, persuasive, and memorable.

VOCABULARY IN CONTEXT

1. The word *swayed* in "our opinions and decisions are frequently swayed by concrete language" (paragraph 8) means
   a. hidden.
   b. repeated.
   c. influenced.
   d. shown to be wrong.

2. The word *compelling* in "she certainly has a better idea now just what it is about her that Paul finds so lovable. . . . Concrete details have made this letter far more compelling" (paragraph 16) means
   a. forceful and interesting.
   b. long and boring.
   c. empty and vague.
   d. silly but amusing.

READING COMPREHENSION QUESTIONS

1. Which sentence best expresses the central idea of the selection?
   a. Communication skills of all types are useful throughout life.
   b. Always be specific when applying for a job.
   c. Specific language will strengthen your writing.
   d. Most people need help with their writing skills.

2. Main ideas may cover more than one paragraph. Which sentence best expresses the main idea of paragraphs 6 and 7?
   a. In letters of application for a job, Bob and Julia have included their background and job goals.
   b. Bob and Julia have written letters of application for a job.
   c. While Bob says only that he's a college graduate, Julia goes into detail about where and what she studied and her grades.
   d. While Bob's job-application letter is probably too vague to be successful, Julia's very specific one is likely to get a positive response.

3. Which sentence best expresses the main idea of paragraph 8?
   a. Julia's letter is a good example of the power of specific details.
   b. Our opinions and decisions are often influenced by specific language.

   c. We want to hear exactly what's in a salad or movie before spending money on it.

   d. When we know just what someone's "personal problems" are, we understand him or her better.

4. Johnson states that abstract language

   a. is rare.

   b. lets us clearly see what the writer's world is like.

   c. tends to lose our attention.

   d. makes us want to read more of the writer's piece.

5. Johnson feels that concrete language

   a. is hard to follow.

   b. makes readers' eyes glaze over.

   c. helps readers picture what the author is writing about.

   d. is not appropriate for a menu or a parody.

6. In paragraphs 6 and 7, the author suggests that Bob Cole

   a. is not qualified to enter the business world.

   b. is lying about his education and work experience.

   c. should have written a less wordy letter.

   d. should have written a more detailed letter.

7. Which of the following sentences can we assume Beth Johnson would most approve of?

   a. Shore City is an amusing but expensive place.

   b. Shore City is an interesting place to spend a bit of time.

   c. Shore City has an amusement park and racetrack, but all the hotel rooms cost over $100 a day.

   d. There is a city near the shore that has some interesting attractions, but its hotels are quite expensive.

8. We can infer from the reading that specific details would be very important in

   a. a novel.

   b. a history textbook.

   c. a biography.

   d. all of the above.

DISCUSSION QUESTIONS

About Content

1. At some earlier point in school, did you learn the importance of writing specifically? If so, do you remember when? If not, when do you think you should have been taught about the power of specific details in writing?

2. Johnson provides three pairs of examples: two job-application letters, two passages about living at home, and two love letters. Which pair most effectively makes her point for you about the value of writing specifically?

3. What kinds of writing will you be doing over the next few weeks, either in or out of school? Will it be papers for other classes, answers to essay questions, reports at work, letters of application for jobs, letters to friends, or other types of writing? Name one kind of writing you will be doing, and give an example of one way you could make that writing more specific.

About Structure

4. Essays often begin with an introduction that prepares readers for the author's central idea. How does Johnson begin her essay? Why do you think she chose this kind of introduction?

    _____

    _____

    _____

5. The authors of the papers on living at home are essentially using listing order. What are they listing?

    _____

6. Johnson takes her own advice and uses many concrete details in her essay. Locate two particularly strong examples of specific details in the reading that are not in the three pairs of samples, and write them below:

    _____

    _____

    _____

About Style and Tone

7. Johnson opens her essay in the second-person point of view. As a reader, how do you respond to being addressed directly? Why might Johnson have chosen this approach?

    _____

    _____

    _____

8. In paragraph 10, Johnson writes: "You will sprinkle your essays with nuggets of detail that, like the salt on a pretzel, add interest and texture." What kind of language is she using here?

    _____

    _____

    _____

RESPONDING TO IMAGES

The writer in this illustration plans to use three specific scenes to tell her story. How might the scenes be connected? What story do they tell? Be creative in your response, but make sure your ideas are based on specific visual details in the cartoon.

Copyright © Allen Swerling. Used with permission.

WRITING ASSIGNMENTS

Assignment 1: Writing a Paragraph

Using the same level of detail as Julia's application letter in the reading, write a one-paragraph letter of application for a part-time or a full-time job. Like Julia Moore, be sure to include the following in your paragraph:

> What kind of job you are applying for
> Where you have worked previously
> What positions you have held
> Evidence that you performed your job well
> Which skills you have acquired

Assignment 2: Writing a Paragraph

In this reading, "The Pros and Cons of Living at Home" is a strong example of a "pro and con" analysis—one that details the advantages and disadvantages of something. Think of a topic about which you have conflicting views. It could be a decision you are struggling with, such as changing jobs or moving to a larger (or smaller) house or apartment. Or it could be a situation in which you already find yourself, such as attending school while holding a job or having an elderly parent living with you. Write a paragraph in which you explain in detail what the pros and cons of the issue are.

Once you've chosen a topic, do some prewriting. A good strategy is to make two lists—one of the advantages and the other of the disadvantages. Here is a sample:

> Advantages of moving to a smaller apartment
>
> Save money on rent ($325 a month instead of $400 a month)
>
> Save money on utilities (smaller heating bill)
>
> Less space to clean (one bedroom instead of two)
>
> Disadvantages of moving to a smaller apartment
>
> Less space for all my furniture (big chest of drawers, sofa bed)
>
> No spare bedroom (can't have friends sleep over)
>
> Will get more cluttered (little space to display all my trophies, souvenirs, and sports equipment)

If you are not sure about which issue to write about, make lists for two or three topics. Then you'll have a better idea of which one will result in a better paper.

Use the lists of advantages and disadvantages as an outline for your paragraph, adding other ideas as they occur to you. Begin with a topic sentence such as "_____ has both advantages and disadvantages" or "I'm having a hard time deciding whether or not to _____." Next, write the supporting sentences, discussing first one side of the issue and then the other.

Be sure to include plenty of specific details. For inspiration, reread "The Pros and Cons of Living at Home" before writing your essay.

Assignment 3: Writing an Essay

Johnson uses sharp, concrete details to make a point she feels strongly about—that specific language gives writing real power. Write an essay persuading readers of the importance of something you believe in strongly. Be sure to include at least one or two concrete, convincing examples for every point that you make. You might write about the value of something, such as the following:

Regular exercise

Volunteer work

Reading for pleasure

Gardening

Spending time with young (or grown) children

Periodic intense housecleaning

Alternatively, you can write about the negative aspects of something, such as the following:

Excessive television watching

Compulsive shopping

Tabloid journalism

Procrastinating

Smoking

Following is an example of an informal outline for this assignment. As the writer developed this outline into paragraphs, she added, subtracted, and rearranged some of her examples.

Central idea: Cleaning out closets every now and then can be rewarding.

(1) I get rid of things I no longer need, or never needed:

   Pair of ten-year-old hiking boots, which I kept because they were expensive but that are thoroughly worn out

continued

Portable TV that no longer works

Yogurt maker given to me by my first husband on our anniversary

(2) I make room for things I do need:

All my shoes and pocketbooks, which can be arranged in neat rows on the shelves instead of crammed into cartons

Christmas presents I buy for my family in July and want to hide

(3) I find things that I thought were lost forever or that I forgot I ever had:

Box of photographs from our first family vacation

My bowling trophy

Presents I bought for last Christmas and forgot about

Tickets to Nowhere

Andy Rooney

PREVIEW	WORDS TO WATCH
Who doesn't love a "get rich quick" story? We eagerly read the accounts of lucky people who've become wealthy overnight just by buying the right lottery ticket. The hope that we might do the same keeps many of us "investing" in the lottery week after week. But syndicated columnist Andy Rooney thinks there's another lottery story that also deserves our attention.	gushed (6) digits (9) stowed (10) fidgeted (12) clutched (13)

1 Things never went very well for Jim Oakland. He dropped out of high school because he was impatient to get rich, but after dropping out he lived at home with his parents for two years and didn't earn a dime.

2 He finally got a summer job working for the highway department holding up a sign telling oncoming drivers to be careful of the workers ahead. Later that same year, he picked up some extra money putting fliers under the windshield wipers of parked cars.

3 Things just never went very well for Jim, and he was twenty-three before he left home and went to Florida hoping his ship would come in down there. He never lost his desire to get rich; but first he needed money for the rent, so he took a job near Fort Lauderdale for $4.50 an hour servicing the goldfish aquariums kept near the cashier's counter in a lot of restaurants.

4 Jim was paid in cash once a week by the owner of the goldfish business, and the first thing he did was go to the little convenience store near where he lived and buy $20 worth of lottery tickets. He was really determined to get rich.

5 A week ago, the lottery jackpot in Florida reached $54 million. Jim woke up nights thinking what he could do with $54 million. During the days, he daydreamed about it. One morning he was driving along the main street in the boss's old pickup truck with six tanks of goldfish in back. As he drove past a BMW dealer, he looked at the new models in the window.

6 He saw the car he wanted in the showroom window, but unfortunately he didn't see the light change. The car in front of him stopped short and Jim slammed on his brakes. The fish tanks slid forward. The tanks broke, the water gushed° out, and the goldfish slithered and flopped all over the back of the truck. Some fell off into the road.

7 It wasn't a good day for the goldfish or for Jim, of course. He knew he'd have to pay for the tanks and 75 cents each for the fish, and if it weren't for the $54 million lottery, he wouldn't have known which way to turn. He had that lucky feeling.

8 For the tanks and the dead goldfish, the boss deducted $114 of Jim's $180 weekly pay. Even though he didn't have enough left for the rent and food, Jim doubled the amount he was going to spend on lottery tickets. He never needed $54 million more.

9 Jim had this system. He took his age and added the last four digits° of the telephone number of the last girl he dated. He called it his lucky number . . . even though the last four digits changed quite often and he'd never won with his system. Everyone laughed at Jim and said he'd never win the lottery.

Jim put down $40 on the counter that week and the man punched out his tick- 10 ets. Jim stowed• them safely away in his wallet with last week's tickets. He never threw away his lottery tickets until at least a month after the drawing just in case there was some mistake. He'd heard of mistakes.

Jim listened to the radio all afternoon the day of the drawing. The people at 11 the radio station he was listening to waited for news of the winning numbers to come over the wires and, even then, the announcers didn't rush to get them on. The station manager thought the people running the lottery ought to pay to have the winning numbers broadcast, just like any other commercial announcement.

Jim fidgeted• while they gave the weather and the traffic and the news. Then 12 they played more music. All he wanted to hear were those numbers.

"Well," the radio announcer said finally, "we have the lottery numbers some 13 of you have been waiting for. You ready?" Jim was ready. He clutched• his ticket with the number 274802.

"The winning number," the announcer said, "is 860539. I'll repeat that. 860539." 14 Jim was still a loser.

I thought that, with all the human interest stories about lottery winners, we 15 ought to have a story about one of the several million losers.

VOCABULARY IN CONTEXT

1. The word *gushed* in "The tanks broke, the water gushed out, and the goldfish slithered and flopped all over the back of the truck" (paragraph 6) means
   a. dripped slowly.
   b. steamed.
   c. poured.
   d. held.

2. The word *digits* in "He took his age and added the last four digits of the telephone number of the last girl he dated" (paragraph 9) means
   a. letters.
   b. single numbers.
   c. rings.
   d. area codes.

READING COMPREHENSION QUESTIONS

1. Which of the following would be the best alternative title for this selection?
   a. A $54 Million Jackpot
   b. An Unnecessary Accident
   c. Foolish Dreams
   d. Moving to Florida

2. Which sentence best expresses the main idea of the selection?
   a. Everyone dreams of winning the lottery.
   b. The more money you invest in lottery tickets, the better your chances of winning.
   c. Jim Oakland's dreams of getting rich by winning the lottery were unrealistic.
   d. Jim Oakland is a very unlucky man.

3. *True or false?* _____ Jim dropped out of school because he was offered a good-paying job in Florida.

4. When Jim lost money as a result of his accident with the goldfish, he

    a. put himself on a strict budget.

    b. spent even more on lottery tickets.

    c. got a second job.

    d. moved back in with his parents to save money.

5. Jim never threw away his lottery tickets

    a. at all.

    b. until his next paycheck.

    c. until at least a month after the drawing.

    d. so that he could write off his losses on his tax return.

6. We can infer from paragraphs 6–7 that

    a. Jim's daydreams about getting rich made him careless.

    b. the driver in front of Jim should have gotten a ticket.

    c. the brakes on Jim's pickup truck were faulty.

    d. Jim slammed on his brakes because he'd suddenly realized that he'd never win the lottery.

7. In paragraph 9, the author suggests that Jim

    a. was good in math.

    b. did not date very often.

    c. never told anyone about his dreams of winning the lottery.

    d. never dated the same girl for very long.

8. Andy Rooney suggests that

    a. although few people win the lottery, it's still worth trying.

    b. most of what the public hears about lotteries shows how harmful they are.

    c. Jim Oakland gave up playing the lottery after losing the $54 million jackpot.

    d. playing the lottery harms far more people than it helps.

DISCUSSION QUESTIONS

About Content

1. Jim Oakland seemed to feel that lotteries were entirely good. Andy Rooney takes a more negative view. What is your opinion? On balance, are lotteries good or bad? On what are you basing your opinion?

2. Do you know anyone like Jim, someone who depends on luck more than on hard work or ability? If so, why do you think this person relies so much on luck? How lucky has he or she been?

3. What would be the good points of suddenly winning a large amount of money? What might be the downside? All in all, would you prefer to win or to earn the money you have? Why?

About Structure

4. As Rooney's piece went on, did you think that it was going to be about Jim Oakland winning the lottery—or losing it? What details contributed to your expectations?

About Style and Tone

5. At only one point in the essay does Rooney use a direct quotation. What is that point? Why do you think he chooses to dramatize that moment with the speaker's exact words?

6. One meaning of *irony* is a contradiction between what might be expected and what really happens. Rooney uses this type of irony in an understated way to contrast Oakland's goal with his actions. For instance, in paragraph 1, he states that Oakland was "impatient to get rich." In the same sentence he states, "he lived at home with his parents for two years and didn't earn a dime." Find one other spot in the selection where Rooney uses irony and write its paragraph number here:

   _____

7. Rooney refers to himself only one time in the essay, in the final paragraph. Why do you think he chooses to use "I" at that point? What is the effect?

8. How do you think Rooney feels about Jim? Does he admire his continued optimism about striking it rich? Does he think Jim is a bad person? Find passages in the essay that support your opinion about how Rooney regards Jim.

WRITING ASSIGNMENTS

Assignment 1: Writing a Paragraph

Write a paragraph about a time when you had good luck. Perhaps you found a twenty-dollar bill, or you happened to meet the person you are currently dating or are married to, or you were fortunate enough to find a job you like. Provide plenty of detail to let readers know why you consider your experience so fortunate. Your topic sentence may begin like this:

   A time I had incredibly good luck was the day that _____.

Assignment 2: Writing a Paragraph

As Andy Rooney describes him, Jim is a man who has relied on luck to make good things happen in his life, rather than on hard work or realistic planning. Do you know someone who drifts along in life, hoping for a lucky break but doing little to make it happen? Write a paragraph describing how this person goes about his or her life. Introduce that person in your topic sentence, as in these examples:

   My sister's former husband relies on luck, not work or planning, to get ahead in life.

   Instead of studying, my roommate hopes that luck will be enough to help her pass her courses.

Then give several specific examples of the person's behavior. Conclude by providing a suggestion about what this person might do in order to take the responsibility of creating his or her own "good luck."

Alternatively, write a paragraph about a person who plans logically and works hard to achieve his or her goals.

Assignment 3: Writing an Essay

Rooney uses just one example—Jim Oakland's story—to suggest the general point that people should not count on the lottery to make them rich. Write an essay in which you, like Rooney, defend an idea that many oppose or have given little thought to. Perhaps you will argue that high schools should distribute forms of birth-control to students or that alcohol should be banned on your college campus.

Develop your essay by describing in detail the experiences of one person. Your three supporting paragraphs may be organized by time order, describing the person's experience from an early to a later point; or they may be organized as a list—for example, showing how the person's experience affected him or her in three different ways. In your conclusion, make it clear, as Rooney does, that the one person you're writing about is intended to illustrate a general point.

Here is a sample outline for one such essay:

Thesis statement: Alcoholic beverages should be banned on this campus.

Topic sentence 1: Drinking affected Beverly's academic life.

Topic sentence 2: Drinking also affected Beverly's social life.

Topic sentence 3: Finally, drinking jeopardized Beverly's work life.

Conclusion: Many students, like Beverly, have their lives damaged and even ruined by alcohol.

Why Go to College?

Robert S. Feldman

PREVIEW	WORDS TO WATCH
Robert S. Feldman teaches psychology at the University of Massachusetts. This essay first appeared in *P.O.W.E.R Learning: Strategies for Success in College and Life*, a study-skills textbook. Feldman begins the selection by stating the reasons most students give for going to college. He goes on to explain seven other important reasons that many students never consider.	lofty (2) unreflective (2) diversity (9)

Congratulations. You're in college. 1

But *why?* Although it seems as if it should be easy to answer why 2 you're continuing your education, for most students it's not so simple. The reasons that people go to college vary from the practical ("I want to get a good job"), to the lofty • ("I want to learn about people and the world"), to the unreflective • ("Why not?—I don't have anything better to do").

Surveys of first-year college students show that almost three-quarters 3 say they want to learn about things that interest them, get training for a specific career, land a better job, and make more money (see **Figure 1.1**). And, in fact, it's not wrong to expect that a college education helps people find better jobs. On average, college graduates earn about 75 percent more than high school graduates over their working lifetime. That difference adds up: Over the course of their working lifetimes, college graduates earn close to a million dollars more than those with only a high school degree. Furthermore, as jobs become increasingly complex and technologically sophisticated, college will become more and more of a necessity.

But the value of college extends far beyond dollars and cents. Consider 4 these added reasons for pursuing a college education:

- **You'll learn to think critically and communicate better.** Here's 5 what one student said about his college experience after he graduated: "It's not about what you major in or which classes you take. . . . It's really about learning to think and to communicate. Wherever you end up, you'll need to be able to analyze and solve problems—to figure out what needs to be done and do it."

    Education improves your ability to understand the world—to 6 understand it as it now is, and to prepare to understand it as it will be.

- **You'll be able to better deal with advances in knowledge and** 7 **technology that are changing the world.** Genetic engineering . . . drugs to reduce forgetfulness . . . computers that respond to our voices. . . . No one knows what the future will hold, but you can prepare for it through a college education. Education can provide you with the intellectual tools that you can apply regardless of the specific situation in which you find yourself.

FIGURE 1.1
Choosing College
These are the most frequently cited reasons that first-year college students gave for why they enrolled in college when asked in a national survey.

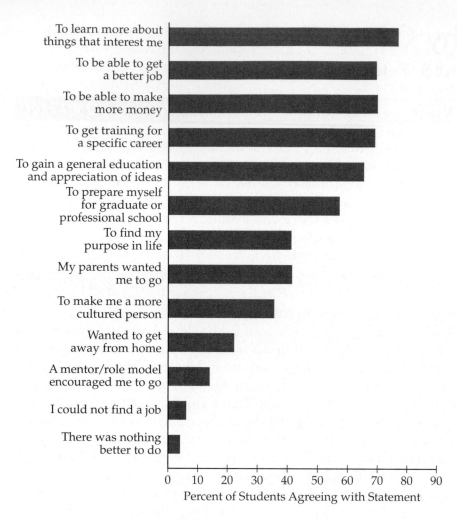

Percent of Students Agreeing with Statement

- **You'll learn to adapt to new situations.** College is a different world from high school. It presents new experiences and new challenges. Your adjustment to the college culture will prepare you for future encounters with new situations.   8

- **You'll be better prepared to live in a world of diversity.** The racial and ethnic composition of the United States is changing rapidly. Whatever your ethnicity, chances are you'll be working and living with people whose backgrounds, lifestyles, and ways of thinking may be entirely different from your own.   9

  You won't be prepared for the future unless you understand others and their cultural backgrounds—as well as how your own cultural background affects you.   10

- **You'll learn to lead a life of community service.** In its broadest sense, community service involves making contributions to the society and community in which you live. College provides you with the opportunity to become involved in community service activities, in some cases even getting course credit for it—a process called service learning. College also allows you to develop the skills involved in acting toward others with *civility* and respectful, courteous behavior.   11

- **You'll make learning a lifelong habit.** Higher education isn't   12
the end of your education. Education will build upon your
natural curiosity about the world, and it will make you aware
that learning is a rewarding and never-ending journey.

- **You'll understand the meaning of your own contributions to the**   13
world. No matter who you are, you are poised to make your own
contributions to society and the world. Higher education provides
you with a window to the past, present, and future, and it allows
you to understand the significance of your own contributions.
Your college education provides you with a compass to discover
who you are, where you've been, and where you're going.

VOCABULARY IN CONTEXT

1. The word *lofty* in "The reasons that people go to college vary from the
practical . . . to the lofty" (paragraph 2) means

   a. unclear.

   b. high-minded.

   c. selfish.

   d. appealing.

2. The word *diversity* in "You'll be better prepared to live in a world of
diversity" (paragraph 9) means

   a. variety.

   b. similarities.

   c. changes.

   d. difficulties.

READING COMPREHENSION QUESTIONS

1. What sentence best expresses the central point of this selection?

   a. Going to college can do more for you than increase your earning
power.

   b. A college education helps people understand world events better.

   c. Going to college exposes students to cultures other than their own.

   d. Most students go to college because they are undecided about their
future.

2. We can infer from what Feldman says that a few decades from now the
majority of Americans will be

   a. Whites.

   b. African Americans.

   c. Latinos.

   d. Latinos and African Americans.

3. A college education will enable you to deal with advances in technology because

   a. most college majors stress science and mathematics.

   b. a college education provides you with learning tools that you can apply to various situations.

   c. a college education can help you predict changes in the future.

   d. a college education will teach you to use current technological tools.

4. According to Feldman, American students need to understand cultures other than their own because

   a. Americans travel a great deal for business.

   b. other cultures will advance faster than American culture.

   c. America is becoming more diverse, and we are in greater contact with other cultures throughout the world.

   d. we need to make our economy more competitive with those of other countries.

5. *True or false?* _____ Feldman believes that after you have gotten a college education, you will have little need to continue learning.

6. *True or false?* _____ The author argues that it is important to understand how your talents and skills can contribute to society.

7. When surveyed, most students responded that they were attending college because they want to

   a. get a good job.

   b. learn more about things that interest them.

   c. learn about other cultures.

   d. make their parents happy.

DISCUSSION QUESTIONS

About Content

1. In paragraph 7, Feldman mentions three technological developments that are changing the world. Give three more examples of such things that have been developed in the past twenty years.

2. The author states that going to college with the idea of getting a better job is not unreasonable. What evidence does he use to back up this idea?

About Structure

3. The essay begins with a summary of reasons that explain why most students want to go to college. Should Feldman have discussed his own seven reasons for going to college before telling us what most students think? Why or why not?

4. Feldman includes a graph that presents "the most frequently cited reasons that first-year college students gave" for going to college. Why does he use a graph to convey this information? Why didn't he just summarize it in a separate paragraph?

About Style and Tone

5. Paragraph 13 includes an image—a mental picture—"Higher education provides you with a window to the past, present, and future, and it allows you to understand the significance of your own contributions." Using your own words, explain what Feldman means. Write your answer in the lines below.

   _____

   _____

   _____

6. Find another image Feldman uses, and explain what it means.

   _____

   _____

   _____

RESPONDING TO IMAGES

College is about more than academics. It can also teach us a great deal about how to work with and get along with others, many of whom come from different cultural backgrounds or have different values from people with whom we are used to associating. Using specific details, write an essay that uses your experiences in college thus far to prove this idea.

WRITING ASSIGNMENTS

Assignment 1: Writing a Paragraph

Feldman says that "Education will build upon your natural curiosity about the world . . ." (paragraph 12). Think about a subject that fascinates you—for example, the process by which mummies were made, the possibility that life exists in outer space, the intelligence of dolphins or other animals, wind power and other alternative methods for generating energy, or ways to stop air pollution. Write a paragraph that explains what it is about this subject that makes you curious about it.

   You might start by explaining how important, how exotic, or how strange you think your topic is. Then again, you can begin your paragraph with a question such as:

   What makes us want to learn more about global warming?

   Does it matter if there is intelligent life in outer space?

Here are a few more sample sentences you might use to start your paragraph.

After seeing the movie *The Mummy*, my interest in how Egyptians prepared their dead for burial became intense.

As a person who appreciates quiet, I have become obsessed with problems caused by inappropriate cell-phone use.

During the recent spike in gasoline prices, I have been learning all I can about alternative automobile fuels.

Assignment 2: Writing a Paragraph

The author claims that going to college will increase your chances of earning more money over your lifetime. However, for some people, college just isn't the right choice. Write a paragraph in which you discuss two or three career paths that you might have taken had you not chosen to go to college. Of course, you can discuss jobs that don't require a college education, but you might want to include those that require training through apprenticeships or the completion of trade school courses as well.

Assignment 3: Writing an Essay

Write an essay in which you explain at least three reasons for going to the college you are now attending.

If you just graduated from high school, you can begin the essay with an introduction that lists reasons—like those in Feldman's essay—that you chose to go to college and not enter the workforce immediately after high school. If you have been out of high school for some time and have just resumed your education, explain what caused you to return to school.

Then, in the body of the essay, develop at least three reasons that you chose to go to the college you are now attending. Here are four sample topic sentences for the body paragraphs for such an essay:

I applied to Wakefield College because it is close to home, making it possible for me to avoid room and board costs.

Firestone Community College has a top-rated hotel-restaurant management curriculum.

I was offered a half-tuition basketball scholarship to attend Townsend College.

I am attending Union Community College in order to improve my grades and eventually transfer to a prestigious university.

Round off your essay with a conclusion that tells the reader how the things you are learning in college will prepare you for a rewarding career and a satisfying life.

Consume Less, Conserve More

Al Gore

PREVIEW	WORDS TO WATCH
Al Gore was vice president of the United States under President Clinton from 1993 to 2001. Soon after losing the presidential election of 2000, Gore increased his efforts to make people become more environmentally conscious. This selection is taken from the conclusion to Gore's book *An Inconvenient Truth* (2006), which was made into a motion picture.	intrinsic (1) extraneous (4) aerate (8) decomposition (8) ferments (8) cooperatives (13) carbon offsets (14) sequestering (15)

In America, we have grown used to an environment of plenty, with   1
an enormous variety of consumer products always available and constant
enticement to buy "more," "new," and "improved." This consumer culture has become so intrinsic• to our worldview that we've lost sight of
the huge toll we are taking on the world around us. By cultivating a new
awareness of how our shopping and lifestyle choices impact the environment and directly cause carbon emissions, we can begin to make positive
changes to reduce our negative effects. Here are some specific ideas on
how we can achieve this.

Consume less

Energy is consumed in the manufacturing and transport of everything   2
you buy, which means there are fossil-fuel emissions at every stage of
production. A good way to reduce the amount of energy you use is
simply to buy less. Before making a purchase, ask yourself if you really
need it. Can you make do with what you already have? Can you borrow

or rent? Can you find the item secondhand? More and more Americans are beginning to simplify their lives and choose to reduce consumption.

▶ For ideas on how to pare down, visit www.newdream.org

Buy things that last

"Reduce, reuse, and recycle" has become the motto of a growing move- **3** ment dedicated to producing less waste and reducing emissions by buying less, choosing durable items over disposable ones, repairing rather than discarding, and passing on items that are no longer needed to someone who can make use of them.

▶ For more information about the three Rs, visit www.epa.gov/msw/reduce.htm

▶ To learn how to find a new home for something you no longer need, visit www.freecycle.org

Pre-cycle—reduce waste before you buy

Discarded packaging materials make up about one-third of the waste clog- **4** ging our landfills. Vast amounts of natural resources and fossil fuels are consumed each year to produce the paper, plastic, aluminum, glass, and Styrofoam that hold and wrap our purchases. Obviously, some degree of packaging is necessary to transport and protect the products we need, but all too often manufacturers add extraneous• wrappers over wrappers and layers of unnecessary plastic. You can let companies know your objection to such excess by boycotting their products. Give preference to those products that use recycled packaging or that don't use excess packaging. When possible, buy in bulk and seek out things that come in refillable glass bottles.

▶ For more ideas about how to pre-cycle, visit www.environmentaldefense.org/ article.cfm?contentid=2194

Recycle

Most communities provide facilities for the collection and recycling of **5** paper, glass, steel, aluminum, and plastic. While it does take energy to gather, haul, sort, clean, and reprocess these materials, recycling takes far less energy than does sending recyclables to landfills and creating new paper, bottles, and cans from raw materials. It has been suggested that if 100,000 people who currently don't recycle began to do so, they would collectively reduce carbon emissions by 42,000 tons per year. As an added benefit, recycling reduces pollution and saves natural resources, including precious trees that absorb carbon dioxide. And in addition to the usual materials, some facilities are equipped to recycle motor oil, tires, coolant, and asphalt shingles, among other products.

▶ To learn about where you can recycle just about anything in your area, visit www.earth911.org/master.asp?s=ls&a=recycle&cat=1 or www.epa.gov/epaoswer/ non-hw/muncpl/recycle.htm

Don't waste paper

Paper manufacturing is the fourth-most energy-intensive industry, not to **6** mention one of the most polluting and destructive to our forests. It takes an entire forest—more than 500,000 trees—to supply Americans with their Sunday newspapers each week. In addition to recycling your used paper, there are things you can do to reduce your overall paper consumption. Limit your use of paper towels and use cloth rags instead. Use cloth napkins instead of disposables. Use both sides of paper whenever possible. And stop unwanted junk mail.

▶ For information about how to remove your name from mailing lists, visit www.newdream.org/junkmail or www.dmaconsumers.org/offmailinglist.html

Bag your groceries and other purchases in a reusable tote

Americans go through 100 billion grocery bags every year. One estimate 7 suggests that Americans use more than 12 million barrels of oil each year just to produce plastic grocery bags that end up in landfills after only one use and then take centuries to decompose. Paper bags are a problem too: To ensure that they are strong enough to hold a full load, most are produced from virgin paper, which requires cutting down trees that absorb carbon dioxide. It is estimated that about 15 million trees are cut down annually to produce the 10 billion paper bags we go through each year in the United States. Make a point to carry a reusable bag with you when you shop, and then when you're asked, "Paper or plastic?" you can say, "Neither."

▶ To purchase reusable bags, learn more bag facts, and find out about actions you can take, visit www.reusablebags.com

Compost

When organic waste materials, such as kitchen scraps and raked leaves, 8 are disposed of in the general trash, they end up compacted deep in landfills. Without oxygen to aerate• and assist in their natural decomposition,• the organic matter ferments• and gives off methane, which is the most potent of the greenhouse gases—23 times more potent than carbon dioxide in global-warming terms. Organic materials rotting in landfills account for about one-third of man-made methane emissions in the United States. By contrast, when organic waste is properly composted in gardens, it produces rich nutrients that add energy and food to the soil—and of course also decreases the volume added to our landfills.

▶ For information about how to compost, visit www.epa.gov/compost/index.htm or www.mastercomposter.com

Carry your own refillable bottle for water or other beverages

Instead of buying single-use plastic bottles that require significant 9 energy and resources to produce, buy a reusable container and fill it up yourself. In addition to the emissions created by producing the bottles themselves, imported water is especially energy inefficient because it has to be transported over long distances. If you're concerned about the taste or quality of your tap water, consider using an inexpensive water purifier or filter. Also consider buying large bottles of juice or soda and filling your own portable bottle daily. Using your own mug or thermos could also help reduce the 25 billion disposable cups Americans throw away each year.

▶ For more information about the benefits of using refillable beverage containers, visit www.grrn.org/beverage/refillables/index.html

Modify your diet to include less meat

Americans consume almost a quarter of all the beef produced in the world. 10 Aside from health issues associated with eating lots of meat, a high-meat diet translates into a tremendous amount of carbon emissions. It takes far more fossil-fuel energy to produce and transport meat than to deliver equivalent amounts of protein from plant sources.

In addition, much of the world's deforestation is a result of clear- 11 ing and burning to create more grazing land for livestock. This creates further damage by destroying trees that would otherwise absorb carbon dioxide. Fruits, vegetables, and grains, on the other hand, require 95% less raw materials to produce and, when combined properly, can provide a complete and nutritious diet. If more Americans shifted to a less meat-intensive diet, we could greatly reduce CO_2 emissions and also save vast quantities of water and other precious natural resources.

▶ For more information about cows and global warming, visit www.earthsave.org/globalwarming.htm and www.epa.gov/methane/rlep/faq.html

Buy local

In addition to the environmental impact that comes from manufacturing 12 the product you are buying, the effects on CO_2 emissions from transporting those goods at each and every stage of production must also be calculated. It is estimated that the average meal travels well over 1,200 miles by truck, ship, and/or plane before it reaches your dining room table. Often it takes more calories of fossil-fuel energy to get the meal to the consumer than the meal itself provides in nutritional energy. It is much more carbon efficient to buy food that doesn't have to make such a long journey.

One way to address this is to eat foods that are grown or produced 13 close to where you live. As much as possible, buy from local farmers' markets or from community-supported agriculture cooperatives.• By the same token, it makes sense to design your diet as much as possible around foods currently in season in your area, rather than foods that need to be shipped from far-off places.

▶ To learn more about eating local and how to fight global warming with your knife and fork, visit www.climatebiz.com/sections/news_detail.cfm?NewsID=27338

Purchase offsets to neutralize your remaining emissions

So many things we do in our day-to-day lives—driving, cooking, heating 14 homes, working on our computers—result in greenhouse-gas emissions. It is virtually impossible to eliminate our personal contributions to the climate crisis through reducing emissions alone. You can, however, reduce your impact to the equivalent of zero emissions by purchasing carbon offsets.•

When you purchase carbon offsets, you are funding a project that 15 reduces greenhouse-gas emissions elsewhere by, for example, increasing energy efficiency, developing renewable energy, restoring forests, or sequestering• carbon in soil.

▶ For more information and links to specific carbon offsetting organizations, visit www.NativeEnergy.com/climatecrisis

VOCABULARY IN CONTEXT

1. The word *intrinsic* in "This consumer culture has become so intrinsic to our worldview that we've lost sight of the huge toll we are taking on the world around us" (paragraph 1) means
   a. harmful.
   b. beneficial.
   c. related to.
   d. fundamental.

2. The word *extraneous* in "all too often manufacturers add extraneous wrappers over wrappers and layers of unnecessary plastic" (paragraph 4) means
   a. additional.
   b. helpful.
   c. protective.
   d. essential.

READING COMPREHENSION QUESTIONS

1. Which of the following would make the best alternative title for this selection?
   a. The Climate Crisis: What One Person Can Do
   b. Why Everyone Should Recycle
   c. Our Carbon Footprint: It's Just Too Big
   d. A Planet in Jeopardy

2. Which of the following best captures the central point of the selection?
   a. Each person can help reduce civilization's harmful effects on the natural world and its climate.
   b. It is not hard to save energy.
   c. Recycling can reduce pollution and eliminate landfills.
   d. We need to encourage the use of alternative fuels.

3. Which of the following is not one of the questions Gore suggests you ask yourself before making a purchase?
   a. Can you find the item secondhand?
   b. Can you find the item for less online?
   c. Can you make do with what you already have?
   d. Can you borrow or rent the item?

4. Each week, it takes an entire forest to supply Americans with
   a. paper towels.
   b. unwanted junk mail.
   c. Sunday newspapers.
   d. napkins.

5. According to this selection, if organic waste is not properly composted it can

   a. increase the spread of disease.

   b. result in the emission of harmful methane.

   c. pollute groundwater with toxic chemicals.

   d. give off more emissions than cars and trucks.

6. *True or false?* _____ Americans consume almost a quarter of all the beef produced in the world.

7. Gore believes we should eat less meat because

   a. vegetable farmers are finding it hard to earn a living.

   b. cows, pigs, and other livestock have rights too.

   c. it takes more energy to provide protein from meat than from fruits and vegetables.

   d. eating too much meat is bad for our health.

DISCUSSION QUESTIONS

About Content

1. What does Gore mean by "greenhouse-gas emissions" (paragraph 14)? If necessary, look up this term on the Internet.

2. In your own words, summarize three ways Gore says we can reduce emissions:

   a. _____

   b. _____

   c. _____

3. Using what you have learned from this selection, take an energy inventory of the way you shop, the kinds of food you eat, or the way you recycle at home, in your dormitory, or anywhere else. How might you be able to save energy and reduce carbon emissions?

4. Is Gore optimistic about the future? How can you tell?

About Structure

5. One of the reasons this essay is easy to read is that Gore uses many subheadings to introduce various topics. Write a scratch outline using these major headings and subheadings as a way to create a visual of this essay's structure.

6. The author includes notes for further research after various subsections of the essay. How does doing this help him increase the persuasiveness and usefulness of the selection?

About Style and Tone

7. The author is aiming at a very wide audience. What is it about the kinds of words he uses that shows this? What do his frequent references to the Internet tell us about his intended readers?

8. At times, Gore uses technical terms such as "carbon offsets" without defining them. Should he have? Why or why not?

9. How would you describe the author's tone—his attitude toward his subject? Is it objective, passionate, skeptical?

10. The purpose of this essay is to get us to help solve the climate crisis and, therefore, save the planet. One of the ways Gore tries to persuade us is to appeal to our self-interest. Find places in which he does this.

WRITING ASSIGNMENTS

Assignment 1: Writing a Paragraph

Discuss ways in which you might conserve energy or reduce greenhouse gases by changing one thing in your daily routine. For example, you might buy in bulk and only use items that come in refillable glass bottles. You might use cloth rags instead of paper towels. You might carry a reusable bag with you when you shop. You might choose to only eat foods that are grown or produced where you live. Or you might follow another suggestion contained in the essay you just read.

In any event, be as detailed as you can in showing how what Gore advises might apply to your daily life.

Assignment 2: Writing a Paragraph

Thinking about the topics Gore addresses in his essay, take an audit of any area of your college campus: the student center, the gymnasium, a dormitory, or the college dining facility, for example. How effective is the college in producing less waste and reducing carbon emissions in this area of the campus? Write a paragraph in which you explain how the college might have a more positive effect on the environment in this area of the campus.

Assignment 3: Writing an Essay

Gore's essay is quite persuasive in that it shows us practical and relatively easy ways to address the crisis. Write an essay in which you persuade your reader that it is necessary we address the need to reduce the amount of nonbiodegradable garbage we produce.

However, instead of discussing what we might do to address the problem, as Gore does, paint a verbal picture of what might happen if we don't take action. For example, you might describe what our countryside, lakes, and oceans might look like if we continue to use plastic containers that do not degrade naturally. You might explain what our lifestyles will be like if we run out of fossil fuels and don't develop renewable sources of energy to replace them. Will we be able to generate electricity and heat for our homes? Will we be able to power our cars? Or will we go back to living as people did in the Middle Ages?

In other words, create a scene that a futurist or science fiction writer might dream up. If you need to gather information for this project, research some of the Internet sites Gore recommends in his essay. At any rate, remember that your purpose is to get your readers to see that there is real need to plan for the future—a future in which our lives and our relationship to the earth will be better, not worse, than they are now.

Anxiety: Challenge by Another Name

James Lincoln Collier

PREVIEW

What is your basis for making personal decisions? Do you aim to rock the boat as little as possible, choosing the easy, familiar path? There is comfort in sticking with what is safe and well known, just as there is comfort in eating bland mashed potatoes. But James Lincoln Collier, author of numerous articles and books, decided soon after leaving college not to live a mashed-potato sort of life. In this essay, first published in **Reader's Digest,** he tells how he learned to recognize the marks of a potentially exciting, growth-inducing experience, to set aside his anxiety, and to dive in.

WORDS TO WATCH

fabled (2)
pampas (2)
daunted (2)
wavered (7)
venture (10)
corollary (15)
insistent (15)

Between my sophomore and junior years at college, a chance came up for me 1 to spend the summer vacation working on a ranch in Argentina. My roommate's father was in the cattle business, and he wanted Ted to see something of it. Ted said he would go if he could take a friend, and he chose me.

The idea of spending two months on the fabled° Argentine pampas° was ex- 2 citing. Then I began having second thoughts. I had never been very far from New England, and I had been homesick my first weeks at college. What would it be like in a strange country? What about the language? And besides, I had promised to teach my younger brother to sail that summer. The more I thought about it, the more the prospect daunted° me. I began waking up nights in a sweat.

In the end I turned down the proposition. As soon as Ted asked somebody 3 else to go, I began kicking myself. A couple of weeks later I went home to my old summer job, unpacking cartons at the local supermarket, feeling very low. I had turned down something I wanted to do because I was scared, and I had ended up feeling depressed. I stayed that way for a long time. And it didn't help when I went back to college in the fall to discover that Ted and his friend had had a terrific time.

In the long run that unhappy summer taught me a valuable lesson out of which I developed a rule for myself: *do what makes you anxious; don't do what makes you depressed.* 4

I am not, of course, talking about severe states of anxiety or depression, which require medical attention. What I mean is that kind of anxiety we call stage fright, butterflies in the stomach, a case of nerves—the feelings we have at a job interview, when we're giving a big party, when we have to make an important presentation at the office. And the kind of depression I am referring to is that downhearted feeling of the blues, when we don't seem to be interested in anything, when we can't get going and seem to have no energy. 5

I was confronted by this sort of situation toward the end of my senior year. As graduation approached, I began to think about taking a crack at making my living as a writer. But one of my professors was urging me to apply to graduate school and aim at a teaching career. 6

I wavered.* The idea of trying to live by writing was scary—a lot more scary than spending a summer on the pampas, I thought. Back and forth I went, making my decision, unmaking it. Suddenly, I realized that every time I gave up the idea of writing, that sinking feeling went through me; it gave me the blues. 7

The thought of graduate school wasn't what depressed me. It was giving up on what deep in my gut I really wanted to do. Right then I learned another lesson. To avoid that kind of depression meant, inevitably, having to endure a certain amount of worry and concern. 8

The great Danish philosopher Søren Kierkegaard believed that anxiety always arises when we confront the possibility of our own development. It seems to be a rule of life that you can't advance without getting that old, familiar, jittery feeling. 9

Even as children we discover this when we try to expand ourselves by, say, learning to ride a bike or going out for the school play. Later in life we get butterflies when we think about having that first child, or uprooting the family from the old hometown to find a better opportunity halfway across the country. Any time, it seems, that we set out aggressively to get something we want, we meet up with anxiety. And it's going to be our traveling companion, at least part of the way, in any new venture.* 10

When I first began writing magazine articles, I was frequently required to interview big names—people like Richard Burton, Joan Rivers, sex authority William Masters, baseball great Dizzy Dean. Before each interview I would get butterflies and my hands would shake. 11

At the time, I was doing some writing about music. And one person I particularly admired was the great composer Duke Ellington. On stage and on television, he seemed the very model of the confident, sophisticated man of the world. Then I learned that Ellington still got stage fright. If the highly honored Duke Ellington, who had appeared on the bandstand some ten thousand times over thirty years, had anxiety attacks, who was I to think I could avoid them? 12

I went on doing those frightening interviews, and one day, as I was getting onto a plane for Washington to interview columnist Joseph Alsop, I suddenly realized to my astonishment that I was looking forward to the meeting. What had happened to those butterflies? 13

Well, in truth, they were still there, but there were fewer of them. I had benefited, I discovered, from a process psychologists call "extinction." If you put an in- 14 dividual in an anxiety-provoking situation often enough, he will eventually learn that there isn't anything to be worried about.

Which brings us to a corollary° to my basic rule: *you'll never eliminate anxiety by* 15 *avoiding the things that caused it.* I remember how my son Jeff was when I first began to teach him to swim at the lake cottage where we spent our summer vacations. He resisted, and when I got him into the water he sank and sputtered and wanted to quit. But I was insistent.° And by summer's end he was splashing around like a puppy. He had "extinguished" his anxiety the only way he could—by confronting it.

The problem, of course, is that it is one thing to urge somebody else to take on 16 those anxiety-producing challenges; it is quite another to get ourselves to do it.

Some years ago I was offered a writing assignment that would require three 17 months of travel through Europe. I had been abroad a couple of times on the usual "If it's Tuesday this must be Belgium"* trips, but I hardly could claim to know my way around the continent. Moreover, my knowledge of foreign languages was limited to a little college French.

I hesitated. How would I, unable to speak the language, totally unfamiliar with 18 local geography or transportation systems, set up interviews and do research? It seemed impossible, and with considerable regret I sat down to write a letter begging off. Halfway through, a thought—which I subsequently made into another corollary to my basic rule—ran through my mind: *you can't learn if you don't try.* So I accepted the assignment.

There were some bad moments. But by the time I had finished the trip I was 19 an experienced traveler. And ever since, I have never hesitated to head for even the most exotic of places, without guides or even advance bookings, confident that somehow I will manage.

The point is that the new, the different, is almost by definition scary. But each 20 time you try something, you learn, and as the learning piles up, the world opens to you.

I've made parachute jumps, learned to ski at forty, flown up the Rhine in a 21 balloon. And I know I'm going to go on doing such things. It's not because I'm braver or more daring than others. I'm not. But I don't let the butterflies stop me from doing what I want. Accept anxiety as another name for challenge, and you can accomplish wonders.

VOCABULARY IN CONTEXT

1. The word *daunted* in "The more I thought about [going to Argentina], the more the prospect daunted me. I began waking up nights in a sweat" (paragraph 2) means

    a. encouraged.

    b. interested.

    c. discouraged.

    d. amused.

2. The word *corollary* in "Which brings us to a corollary to my basic rule: *you'll never eliminate anxiety by avoiding the things that caused it*" (paragraph 15) means

    a. an idea that follows from another idea.

    b. an idea based on a falsehood.

    c. an idea that creates anxiety.

    d. an idea passed on from one generation to another.

*Reference to a film comedy about a group of American tourists who visited too many European countries in too little time.

READING COMPREHENSION QUESTIONS

1. Which of the following would be the best alternative title for this selection?

    a. A Poor Decision

    b. Don't Let Anxiety Stop You

    c. Becoming a Writer

    d. The Courage to Travel

2. Which sentence best expresses the main idea of the selection?

    a. The butterflies-in-the-stomach type of anxiety differs greatly from severe states of anxiety or depression.

    b. Taking on a job assignment that required traveling helped the author get over his anxiety.

    c. People learn and grow by confronting, not backing away from, situations that make them anxious.

    d. Anxiety is a predictable part of life that can be dealt with in positive ways.

3. When a college friend invited the writer to go with him to Argentina, the writer

    a. turned down the invitation.

    b. accepted eagerly.

    c. was very anxious about the idea but went anyway.

    d. did not believe his friend was serious.

4. *True or false?* _____ As graduation approached, Collier's professor urged him to try to make his living as a writer.

5. *True or false?* _____ The philosopher Søren Kierkegaard believed that anxiety occurs when we face the possibility of our own development.

6. *Extinction* is the term psychologists use for

    a. the inborn tendency to avoid situations that make one feel very anxious.

    b. a person's gradual loss of confidence.

    c. the natural development of a child's abilities.

    d. the process of losing one's fear by continuing to face the anxiety-inspiring situation.

7. The author implies that

    a. it was lucky he didn't take the summer job in Argentina.

    b. his son never got over his fear of the water.

    c. Duke Ellington's facing stage fright inspired him.

    d. one has to be more daring than most people to overcome anxiety.

8. The author implies that

    a. anxiety may be a signal that one has an opportunity to grow.

    b. he considers his three-month trip to Europe a failure.

    c. facing what makes him anxious has eliminated all depression from his life.

    d. he no longer has anxiety about new experiences.

DISCUSSION QUESTIONS

About Content

1. Collier developed the rule "Do what makes you anxious; don't do what makes you depressed." How does he distinguish between feeling anxious and feeling depressed?

2. In what way does Collier believe that anxiety is positive? How, according to him, can we eventually overcome our fears? Have you ever gone ahead and done something that made you anxious? How did it turn out?

About Structure

3. Collier provides a rule and two corollary rules that describe his attitude toward challenge and anxiety. Below, write the location of that rule and its corollaries.

   Collier's rule: paragraph _____

   First corollary: paragraph _____

   Second corollary: paragraph _____

   How does Collier emphasize the rule and its corollaries?

4. Collier uses several personal examples in his essay. Find three instances of these examples and explain how each helps Collier develop his main point.

About Style and Tone

5. In paragraph 3, Collier describes the aftermath of his decision not to go to Argentina. He could have just written, "I worked that summer." Instead he writes, "I went home to my old summer job, unpacking cartons at the local supermarket." Why do you think he provides that bit of detail about his job? What is the effect on the reader?

6. Authors often use testimony by authorities to support their points. Where in Collier's essay does he use such support? What do you think it adds to his piece?

7. In the last sentence of paragraph 10, Collier refers to anxiety as a "traveling companion." Why do you think he uses that image? What does it convey about his view of anxiety?

8. Is Collier just telling about a lesson he has learned for himself, or is he encouraging his readers to do something? How can you tell?

RESPONDING TO IMAGES

In his famous painting *The Scream*, expressionist painter Edward Munch creates an emotionally true (rather than logically realistic) landscape. Using specific details, write a paragraph that supports the main point in the previous sentence (which you can use as your topic sentence). *Hint:* Look up **expressionist** in a dictionary or online.

WRITING ASSIGNMENTS

Assignment 1: Writing a Paragraph

Collier explains how his life experiences made him view the term *anxiety* in a new way. Write a paragraph in which you explain how a personal experience of yours has given new meaning to a particular term. Following are some terms you might consider for this assignment:

Failure

Friendship

Goals

Homesickness

Maturity

Success

Here are two sample topic sentences for this assignment:

I used to think of failure as something terrible, but thanks to a helpful boss, I now think of it as an opportunity to learn.

The word *creativity* has taken on a new meaning for me ever since I became interested in dancing.

Assignment 2: Writing a Paragraph

The second corollary to Collier's rule is "you can't learn if you don't try." Write a paragraph using this idea as your main idea. Support it with your own experience, someone else's experience, or both. One way of developing this point is to compare two approaches to a challenge: One person may have backed away from a frightening opportunity while another person decided to take on the challenge. Or you could write about a time when you learned something useful by daring to give a new experience a try. In that case, you might discuss your reluctance to take on the new experience, the difficulties you encountered, and your eventual success. In your conclusion, include a final thought about the value of what was learned.

Listing a few skills you have learned will help you decide on the experience you wish to write about. To get you started, below is a list of things adults often need to go to some trouble to learn.

Driving with a stick shift

Taking useful lecture notes

Knowing how to do well on a job interview

Asking someone out on a date

Making a speech

Standing up for your rights

Assignment 3: Writing an Essay

Collier describes three rules he follows when facing anxiety. In an essay, write about one or more rules, or guidelines, that you have developed for yourself through experience. If you decide to discuss two or three such guidelines, mention or refer to them in your introductory paragraph. Then go on to discuss each in one or more paragraphs of its own. Include at least one experience that led you to develop a given guideline, and tell how it has helped you at other times in your life. You might end with a brief summary and an explanation of how the guidelines as a group have helped. If you decide to focus on one rule, include at least two or three experiences that help to illustrate your point.

To prepare for this assignment, spend some time freewriting about the rules or guidelines you have set up for yourself. Continue writing until you feel you have a central idea for which you have plenty of interesting support. Then organize that support into a scratch outline, such as this one:

Thesis: I have one rule that keeps me from staying in a rut—Don't let the size of a challenge deter you; instead, aim for it by making plans and taking steps.

Topic sentence 1: I began to think about my rule one summer in high school when a friend got the type of summer job that I had only been thinking about.

Topic sentence 2: After high school, I began to live up to my rule when I aimed for a business career and entered college.

Topic sentence 3: My rule is also responsible for my having the wonderful boyfriend (*or* girlfriend *or* spouse *or* job) I now have.

Five appendixes follow. Appendix A consists of parts of speech, and Appendix B is a series of ESL pointers. Appendixes C and D consist of a diagnostic test and an achievement test that measure many of the sentence skills in this book. The diagnostic test can be taken at the outset of your work; the achievement test can be used to measure your progress after you have studied these topics. Finally, Appendix E supplies answers to the introductory activities and practice exercises in Part 3. The answers, which you should refer to only after you have worked carefully through each exercise, give you responsibility for testing yourself. (To ensure that the answer key is used as a learning tool only, answers are not given for the review tests. These answers appear only in the Instructor's Manual; they can be copied and handed out at the discretion of your instructor.)

Parts of Speech

Words—the building blocks of sentences—can be divided into eight parts of speech. *Parts of speech* are classifications of words according to their meaning and use in a sentence.

This appendix explains the eight parts of speech:

nouns	prepositions	conjunctions
pronouns	adjectives	interjections
verbs	adverbs	

Nouns

A *noun* is a word that is used to name something: a person, a place, an object, or an idea. Here are some examples of nouns:

NOUNS			
woman	city	pancake	freedom
Alice Walker	street	diamond	possibility
George Clooney	Chicago	Hummer	mystery

Most nouns begin with a lowercase letter and are known as *common nouns*. These nouns name general things. Some nouns, however, begin with a capital letter. They are called *proper nouns*. While a common noun refers to a person or thing in general, a proper noun names someone or something specific. For example, *woman* is a common noun—it doesn't name a particular woman. On the other hand, *Alice Walker* is a proper noun because it names a specific woman.

ACTIVITY 1	**Using Nouns**

Insert any appropriate noun into each of the following blanks.

1. The shoplifter stole a(n) _____ from the department store.

2. _____ threw the football to me.

3. Tiny messages were scrawled on the _____ .

4. A _____ crashed through the window.

5. Give the _____ to Keiko.

Singular and Plural Nouns

A *singular noun* names one person, place, object, or idea. A *plural noun* refers to two or more persons, places, objects, or ideas. Most singular nouns can be made plural with the addition of an *s*.

Some nouns, like *box*, have irregular plurals. You can check the plural of nouns you think may be irregular by looking up the singular form in a dictionary.

SINGULAR AND PLURAL NOUNS	
Singular	**Plural**
goat	goats
alley	alleys
friend	friends
truth	truths
box	boxes

- For more information on nouns, see "Subjects and Verbs," pages 150–161.

Identifying Nouns

ACTIVITY 2

Underline the three nouns in each sentence. Some are singular, and some are plural.

1. Two bats swooped over the heads of the frightened children.

2. The artist has purple paint on her sleeve.

3. The lost dog has fleas and a broken leg.

4. Tiffany does her homework in green ink.

5. Some farmers plant seeds by moonlight.

Pronouns

A *pronoun* is a word that stands for a noun. Pronouns eliminate the need for constant repetition. Look at the following sentences:

The phone rang, and Malik answered the phone.

Lisa met Lisa's friends in the music store at the mall. Lisa meets Lisa's friends there every Saturday.

The waiter rushed over to the new customers. The new customers asked the waiter for menus and coffee.

Now look at how much clearer and smoother these sentences sound with pronouns.

The phone rang, and Malik answered it.

(The pronoun *it* is used to replace the word *phone*.)

Lisa met her friends in the music store at the mall. She meets them there every Saturday.

(The pronoun *her* is used to replace the word *Lisa's*. The pronoun *she* replaces *Lisa*. The pronoun *them* replaces the words *Lisa's friends*.)

The waiter rushed over to the new customers. They asked him for menus and coffee.

(The pronoun *they* is used to replace the words *the new customers*. The pronoun *him* replaces the words *the waiter*.)

Following is a list of commonly used pronouns known as *personal pronouns:*

PERSONAL PRONOUNS

I	you	he	she	it	we	they
me	your	him	her	its	us	them
my	yours	his	hers		our	their

ACTIVITY 3   **Using Personal Pronouns**

Fill in each blank with the appropriate personal pronoun.

1. André feeds his pet lizard every day before school. _____ also gives _____ flies in the afternoon.

2. The reporter interviewed the striking workers. _____ told _____ about their demand for higher wages and longer breaks.

3. Students should save all returned tests. _____ should also keep _____ review sheets.

4. The pilot announced that we would fly through some air pockets. _____ said that we should be past _____ soon.

5. Adolfo returned the calculator to Sheila last Friday. But Sheila insists that _____ never got _____ back.

There are several types of pronouns. For convenient reference, they are described briefly in the following box:

TYPES OF PRONOUNS

Personal pronouns can act in a sentence as subjects, objects, or possessives.

> *Singular:* I, me, my, mine, you, your, yours, he, him, his, she, her, hers, it, its
>
> *Plural:*   we, us, our, ours, you, your, yours, they, them, their, theirs

Relative pronouns refer to someone or something already mentioned in the sentence.

> who, whose, whom, which, that

Interrogative pronouns are used to ask questions.

> who, whose, whom, which, what

Demonstrative pronouns are used to point out particular persons or things.

> this, that, these, those
>
> **Note:** Do not use *them* (as in *them* shoes), *this here, that there, these here,* or *those there* to point out.

Reflexive pronouns are those that end in *-self* or *-selves*. A reflexive pronoun is used as the object of a verb (as in *Cary cut **herself***) or the object of a preposition (as in *Jack sent a birthday card to **himself***) when the subject of the verb is the same as the object.

> *Singular:* myself, yourself, himself, herself, itself
>
> *Plural:*   ourselves, yourselves, themselves

Intensive pronouns have exactly the same forms as reflexive pronouns. The difference is in how they are used. Intensive pronouns are used to add emphasis. (*I **myself** will need to read the contract before I sign it.*)

Indefinite pronouns do not refer to a particular person or thing.

> each, either, everyone, nothing, both, several, all, any, most, none

Reciprocal pronouns express shared actions or feelings.

> each other, one another

- For more information on pronouns, see pages 252–274.

Verbs

Every complete sentence must contain at least one verb. There are two types of verbs: action verbs and linking verbs.

Action Verbs

An *action verb* tells what is being done in a sentence. For example, look at the following sentences:

> Mr. Jensen *swatted* at the bee with his hand.
>
> Rainwater *poured* into the storm sewer.
>
> The children *chanted* the words to the song.

In these sentences, the verbs are *swatted*, *poured*, and *chanted*. These words are all action verbs; they tell what is happening in each sentence.

- For more about action verbs, see "Subjects and Verbs," pages 150–161.

ACTIVITY 4	Using Action Verbs

Insert an appropriate word in each blank. That word will be an action verb; it will tell what is happening in the sentence.

1. The surgeon _____ through the first layer of skin.
2. The animals in the cage _____ all day.
3. An elderly woman on the street _____ me for directions.
4. The boy next door _____ our lawn every other week.
5. Our instructor _____ our papers over the weekend.

Linking Verbs

Some verbs are *linking verbs*. These verbs link (or join) a noun to something that is said about it. For example, look at the following sentence:

The clouds *are* steel gray.

In this sentence, *are* is a linking verb. It joins the noun *clouds* to words that describe it: *steel gray*.

Other common linking verbs include *am, is, was, were, look, feel, sound, appear, seem,* and *become*.

- For more about linking verbs, see "Subjects and Verbs," pages 150–161.

ACTIVITY 5	Using Linking Verbs

In each blank, insert one of the following linking verbs: *am, feel, is, look, were*. Use each linking verb once.

1. The important papers _____ in a desk drawer.
2. I _____ anxious to get my test back.
3. The bananas _____ ripe.
4. The grocery store _____ open until 11:00 p.m.
5. Whenever I _____ angry, I go off by myself to calm down.

Helping Verbs

Sometimes the verb of a sentence consists of more than one word. In these cases, the main verb will be joined by one or more *helping verbs*. Look at the following sentence:

The basketball team *will be leaving* for their game at six o'clock.

In this sentence, the main verb is *leaving*. The helping verbs are *will* and *be*.

Other helping verbs include *do, has, have, may, would, can, must, could,* and *should*.

- For more information about helping verbs, see "Subjects and Verbs," pages 150–161, and "Irregular Verbs," pages 220–230.

Using Helping Verbs	ACTIVITY 6

In each blank, insert one of the following helping verbs: *does, must, should, could, has been.* Use each helping verb once.

1. You _____ start writing your paper this weekend.

2. The victim _____ describe her attacker in great detail.

3. You _____ rinse the dishes before putting them into the dishwasher.

4. My neighbor _____ arrested for drunk driving.

5. The bus driver _____ not make any extra stops.

Prepositions

A *preposition* is a word that connects a noun or a pronoun to another word in the sentence. For example, look at the following sentence:

A man *in* the bus was snoring loudly.

In is a preposition. It connects the noun *bus* to *man*. Here is a list of common prepositions:

PREPOSITIONS				
about	before	down	like	to
above	behind	during	of	toward
across	below	except	off	under
after	beneath	for	on	up
among	beside	from	over	with
around	between	in	since	without
at	by	into	through	

The noun or pronoun that a preposition connects to another word in the sentence is called the *object* of the preposition. A group of words beginning with a preposition and ending with its object is called a *prepositional phrase*. The words *in the bus,* for example, are a prepositional phrase.

Now read the following sentences and explanations:

An ant was crawling *up the teacher's leg.*

The noun *leg* is the object of the preposition *up. Up* connects *leg* with the word *crawling.* The prepositional phrase *up the teacher's leg* describes *crawling.* It tells just where the ant was crawling.

The man *with the black moustache* left the restaurant quickly.

The noun *moustache* is the object of the preposition *with.* The prepositional phrase *with the black moustache* describes the word *man.* It tells us exactly which man left the restaurant quickly.

The plant *on the windowsill* was a present *from my mother.*

The noun *windowsill* is the object of the preposition *on.* The prepositional phrase *on the windowsill* describes the word *plant.* It describes exactly which plant was a present.

There is a second prepositional phrase in this sentence. The preposition is *from,* and its object is *mother.* The prepositional phrase *from my mother* explains *present.* It tells who gave the present.

- For more about prepositions, see "Subjects and Verbs," pages 150–161, and "Sentence Variety II," pages 304–317.

| ACTIVITY 7 | **Using Prepositions** |

In each blank, insert one of the following prepositions: *of, by, with, in, without.* Use each preposition once.

1. The letter from his girlfriend had been sprayed _____ perfume.

2. The weedkiller quickly killed the dandelions _____ our lawn.

3. _____ giving any notice, the tenant moved out of the expensive apartment.

4. Donald hungrily ate three scoops _____ ice cream and an order of French fries.

5. The crates _____ the back door contain glass bottles and old newspapers.

Adjectives

An *adjective* is a word that describes a noun (the name of a person, place, or thing). Look at the following sentence:

The dog lay down on a mat in front of the fireplace.

Now look at this sentence when adjectives have been inserted:

The *shaggy* dog lay down on a *worn* mat in front of the fireplace.

The adjective *shaggy* describes the noun *dog;* the adjective *worn* describes the noun *mat.* Adjectives add spice to our writing. They also help us to identify particular people, places, or things.

Adjectives can be found in two places:

1. An adjective may come before the word it describes (a *damp* night, the *moldy* bread, a *striped* umbrella).

2. An adjective that describes the subject of a sentence may come after a linking verb. The linking verb may be a form of the verb *be* (he *is* **furious,** I *am* **exhausted,** they are **hungry**). Other linking verbs include *feel, look, sound, smell, taste, appear, seem,* and *become* (the soup *tastes* **salty,** your hands *feel* **dry,** the *dog seems* **lost**).

- For more information on adjectives, see "Adjectives and Adverbs," pages 275–282.

Using Adjectives	ACTIVITY 8

Write any appropriate adjective in each blank.

1. The _____ pizza was eaten greedily by the _____ teenagers.

2. Melissa gave away the sofa because it was _____ and _____.

3. Although the alley is _____ and _____, Jian often takes it as a shortcut home.

4. The restaurant throws away lettuce that is _____ and tomatoes that are _____.

5. When I woke up in the morning, I had a(n) _____ fever and a(n) _____ throat.

Adverbs

An *adverb* is a word that describes a verb, an adjective, or another adverb. Many adverbs end in the letters -*ly.* Look at the following sentence:

The canary sang in the pet store window as the shoppers greeted each other.

Now look at this sentence after adverbs have been inserted:

The canary sang *softly* in the pet store window as the shoppers *loudly* greeted each other.

The adverbs add details to the sentence. They also allow the reader to contrast the singing of the canary and the noise the shoppers are making.

Look at the following sentences and the explanations of how adverbs are used in each case:

The chef yelled **angrily** at the young waiter.

(The adverb *angrily* describes the verb *yelled.*)

My mother has an **extremely** busy schedule on Tuesdays.

(The adverb *extremely* describes the adjective *busy.*)

The sick man spoke **very** faintly to his loyal nurse.

(The adverb *very* describes the adverb *faintly*.)

Some adverbs do not end in *-ly*. Examples include *very, often, never, always,* and *well*.

- For more information on adverbs, see "Adjectives and Adverbs," pages 275–282.

ACTIVITY 9	**Using Adverbs**

Fill in each blank with any appropriate adverb.

1. The water in the pot boiled _____*slowly*_____.

2. Carla ____*always*____ drove the car through ____*fast*____ moving traffic.

3. The telephone operator spoke ____*calmly*____ to the young child.

4. The game show contestant waved ____*eagerly*____ to his family in the audience.

5. Wes ____*never*____ studies, so it's no surprise that he did ____*very*____ poorly on his finals.

Conjunctions

A *conjunction* is a word that connects. There are two types of conjunctions: coordinating and subordinating.

Coordinating Conjunctions

Coordinating conjunctions join two equal ideas. Look at the following sentence:

Kevin *and* Steve interviewed for the job, *but* their friend Anne got it.

In this sentence, the coordinating conjunction *and* connects the proper nouns *Kevin* and *Steve*. The coordinating conjunction *but* connects the first part of the sentence, *Kevin* and *Steve interviewed for the job,* to the second part, *their friend Anne got it.*

Following is a list of all the coordinating conjunctions. In this book, they are simply called *joining words.*

COORDINATING CONJUNCTIONS (JOINING WORDS)			
and	so	nor	yet
but	or	for	

- For more on coordinating conjunctions, see information on joining words in "Run-Ons," pages 179–194, and "Sentence Variety I," pages 195–208.

Using Coordinating Conjunctions   ACTIVITY 10

Write a coordinating conjunction in each blank. Choose from the following: *and, but, so, or, nor.* Use each conjunction once.

1. Either Jerome _____ Alex scored the winning touchdown.

2. I expected roses for my birthday, _____ I received a vase of plastic tulips from the discount store.

3. The cafeteria was serving liver and onions for lunch, _____ I bought a sandwich at the corner deli.

4. Marian brought a pack of playing cards _____ a pan of brownies to the company picnic.

5. Neither my sofa _____ my armchair matches the rug in my living room.

Subordinating Conjunctions

When a *subordinating conjunction* is added to a word group, the words can no longer stand alone as an independent sentence. They are no longer a complete thought. For example, look at the following sentence:

> Karen fainted in class.

The word group *Karen fainted in class* is a complete thought. It can stand alone as a sentence. See what happens when a subordinating conjunction is added to a complete thought:

> *When* Karen fainted in class

Now the words cannot stand alone as a sentence. They are dependent on other words to complete the thought:

> *When* Karen fainted in class, we propped her feet up on some books.

In this book, a word that begins a dependent word group is called a *dependent word*. Subordinating conjunctions are common dependent words. The following are some subordinating conjunctions:

SUBORDINATING CONJUNCTIONS			
after	even if	unless	where
although	even though	until	wherever
as	if	when	whether
because	since	whenever	while
before	though		

Following are some more sentences with subordinating conjunctions:

After she finished her last exam, Irina said, "Now I can relax."

(*After she finished her last exam* is not a complete thought. It is dependent on the rest of the words to make up a complete sentence.)

Lamont listens to audiobooks **while** he drives to work.

(*While he drives to work* cannot stand by itself as a sentence. It depends on the rest of the sentence to make up a complete thought.)

Since apples were on sale, we decided to make an apple pie for dessert.

(*Since apples were on sale* is not a complete sentence. It depends on *we decided to make an apple pie for dessert* to complete the thought.)

- For more information on subordinating conjunctions, see information on dependent words in "Fragments," pages 162–178; "Run-Ons," pages 179–194; "Sentence Variety I," pages 195–208; and "Sentence Variety II," pages 304–317.

| ACTIVITY 11 | Using Subordinating Conjunctions |

Write a logical subordinating conjunction in each blank. Choose from the following: *even though, because, until, when, before.* Use each conjunction once.

1. The bank was closed down by federal regulators _____ it lost more money than it earned.

2. _____ Paula wants to look mysterious, she wears dark sunglasses and a scarf.

3. _____ the restaurant was closing in fifteen minutes, customers sipped their coffee slowly and continued to talk.

4. _____ anyone else could answer it, Leon rushed to the phone and whispered, "Is that you?"

5. The waiter was instructed not to serve any food _____ the guest of honor arrived.

Interjections

An *interjection* is a word that can stand independently and is used to express emotion. Examples are *oh, wow, ouch,* and *oops.* These words are usually not found in formal writing.

"*Hey!*" yelled Maggie. "That's my bike."

Oh, we're late for class.

A Final Note

A word may function as more than one part of speech. For example, the word *dust* can be a verb or a noun, depending on its role in the sentence.

I *dust* my bedroom once a month, whether it needs it or not. (verb)

The top of my refrigerator is covered with an inch of *dust.* (noun)

Answers to Activities in Part 3

This answer key can help you teach yourself. Use it to find out why you got some answers wrong—to uncover any weak spot in your understanding of a given skill. By using the answer key in an honest and thoughtful way, you will master each skill and prepare yourself for many tests in this book that have no answer key.

CHAPTER 6: Subjects and Verbs

Introductory Activity (page 153)

Activity 1: Finding Subjects and Verbs (page 155)

1. Rachel poured
2. company offered
3. host introduced
4. Taryn adjusted
5. butt burned
6. bathroom is
7. Royden tripped
8. drink quenched
9. trimmer tossed
10. Volunteers collected

Activity 2: Subject and Linking Verbs (page 156)

1. parents are
2. I am
3. Tri Lee was
4. dog becomes
5. Liz seems
6. hot dog looks
7. people appear
8. students felt
9. cheeseburger has
10. phone seemed

Activity 3: Subjects and Verbs (page 156)

1. rabbits ate
2. father prefers
3. restaurant donated
4. Stanley looks
5. couple relaxed
6. Lightning brightened
7. council voted
8. throat kept
9. sister decided
10. I chose

Activity 4: Subjects and Prepositional Phrases (page 157)

1. ~~By accident,~~ my girlfriend dropped her set ~~of keys into the toilet at the public restroom.~~
2. ~~Before the trial,~~ the defense attorney quickly read ~~through her trial notes.~~
3. My two-year-old daughter Olivia sleeps ~~in my bed on stormy nights.~~
4. I applied ~~for a pre-approved credit card from my bank.~~
5. ~~On Friday nights,~~ my family watches movies ~~on our newly purchased LCD TV.~~
6. ~~Over the weekend,~~ Patrice wrote a five-page research paper ~~on indigenous rights for her political science class.~~
7. The wireless connection ~~from my neighbor's apartment~~ allows me access ~~to the Internet free.~~
8. ~~On Thursday,~~ several foreign-born soldiers received U.S. citizenship ~~during the naturalization ceremony at the Federal Building.~~
9. All my friends, ~~except Nino,~~ play the video game *Grand Theft Auto* ~~on their home computers.~~
10. The spicy horseradish ~~beneath the raw tuna in my nigiri sushi roll~~ burned the back ~~of my tongue.~~

Activity 5: Verbs of More than One Word (page 159)

1. Ellen has chosen
2. You should plan
3. Felix has been waiting
4. We should have invited
5. I would have preferred
6. Classes were interrupted
7. Sam can touch
8. I have been encouraging
9. Joe has agreed
10. students have been giving

Activity 6: Compound Subjects and Verbs (page 160)

1. Boards and bricks make
2. We bought and finished
3. fly and bee hung
4. twins look, think, act, and dress
5. salmon and tuna contain
6. I waited and slipped

7. girl waved and smiled
8. bird dived and reappeared
9. Singers, dancers, and actors performed
10. magician and assistant bowed and disappeared

CHAPTER 7: Fragments

Introductory Activity (page 162)

1. verb
2. subject
3. subject . . . verb
4. express a complete thought

Activity 1: Correcting Dependent-Word Fragments (page 165)

Activity 2: Combining Sentences to Correct Dependent-Word Fragments (page 166)

1. When the waitress coughed in his food, Frank lost his appetite. He didn't even take home a doggy bag.
2. Our power went out during a thunderstorm.
3. Tony doesn't like going to the ballpark. If he misses an exciting play, there's no instant replay.
4. After the mail carrier comes, I run to our mailbox. I love to get mail even if it is only junk mail.
5. Even though she can't read, my little daughter likes to go to the library. She chooses books with pretty covers while I look at the latest magazines.

Activity 3: Correcting -ing Fragments (page 168)

1. Desmond looked anxiously at his cell phone, waiting for his supervisor to return his call. He needed to call in sick to work.
2. Using one of the computers at the library, Hari could not access several Web sites, which he later learned were blocked.
3. A virus infected my computer. As a result, it destroyed data.

Activity 4: Correcting -ing or to Fragments (page 169)

1. Some workers dug up the street near our house, causing frequent vibrations inside.
2. I therefore walked slowly into the darkened living room, preparing to look shocked.
   or: I was preparing to look shocked.
3. Dribbling skillfully up the court, Luis looked for a teammate who was open.

4. Wanting to finish the dream, I pushed the Snooze button.
5. To get back my term paper, I went to see my English instructor from last semester.

Activity 5: Identifying and Correcting Fragments (page 171)

1. For example, she waits until the night before a test to begin studying.
2. My eleventh-grade English teacher picked on everybody except the athletes.
3. For example, he bought an air conditioner in December.

Activity 6: Identifying and Correcting Added-Detail Fragments (page 171)

1. My daughter faithfully watches the programs on the Disney Channel, including *Hannah Montana*, *Wizards of Waverly Place*, and *The Suite Life of Zack and Cody*.
2. There are certain snacks I love to eat when I watch TV, especially microwave popcorn.
3. For example, the ink-jet printer often needs a new printer cartridge.
4. By noon, the stadium parking lot was packed with tailgaters, with some of them grilling barbeque ribs and drinking ice-cold beer.
5. For example, free online game sites are filled with distracting marketing messages.

Activity 7: Correcting Missing-Subject Fragments (page 173)

1. Jack tripped on his shoelace and then looked around to see if anyone had noticed.
   or: Then he looked around to see if anyone had noticed.
2. I started the car and quickly turned down the blaring radio.
   or: And I quickly turned down the blaring radio.
3. Its orange-red flames shot high in the air and made strange shadows all around the dark room.
4. She also forgot to take my name.
5. She places herself in front of a seated young man and stands on his feet until he gets up.
   or: And she stands on his feet until he gets up.

Activity 8: Editing and Rewriting (page 174)

1. 2–3   If you think that these kids will simply outgrow their "baby fat," you're wrong.
2. 4–5   The number of overweight children in this country has doubled in the past twenty years, creating a health epidemic.

3. 6–7   Too many children spend hours watching television and <u>playing video games when they should be outside playing.</u>

4. 8–9   They consume sugary, high-calorie snacks <u>when they should be eating fresh fruits and low-fat yogurt.</u>

5. 15–16 <u>For example, everyone can be a positive role model.</u>

Activity 9: Creating Sentences (*page 174*)

CHAPTER 8: Run-Ons

Introductory Activity (*page 179*)

1. period
2. *but*
3. semicolon
4. *Although*

Activity 1: Correcting Fused Sentences (*page 181*)

1. month. Its
2. porch. They
3. make. It
4. do. He
5. shirt. A
6. B.C. The
7. cheaply. She
8. desk. She
9. fireplace. The
10. traffic. Its

Activity 2: Correcting Run-Ons: Fused Sentences and Comma Splices (*page 182*)

1. man. He
2. mailbox. Then
3. common. The
4. tiny. A
5. greyhound. It
6. Chinese. She
7. working. Its
8. lovely. It
9. drink. One
10. times. For

Activity 3: Writing the Next Sentence (*page 183*)

Activity 4: Connecting Two Thoughts (*page 184*)

1. , but
2. , and
3. , and
4. , so
5. , but
6. , so
7. , for
8. , but
9. , so
10. , for

Activity 5: Using Commas and Joining Words (*page 185*)

Activity 6: Using Semicolons (*page 186*)

1. Denny's; the
2. wedding; it
3. class; her
4. decreased; auto
5. ancient; it

Activity 7: Using Logical Transitions (*page 187*)

1. drive; however, the
2. art; otherwise, it
3. gasoline; as a result, spectators (*or* thus *or* consequently *or* therefore)
4. started; however, all
5. feelers; consequently, they (*or* as a result *or* thus *or* therefore)

Activity 8: Using Semicolons and Commas (*page 188*)

1. store; nevertheless, she
2. candy; as a result, he
3. strangers; however, he
4. schedule; otherwise, he
5. children; furthermore, she

Activity 9: Using Dependent Words (*page 189*)

1. since
2. Unless
3. because
4. After
5. although

Activity 10: Using Subordination (*page 189*)

1. Although I want to stop smoking, I don't want to gain weight.
2. Because it was too hot indoors to study, I decided to go down to the shopping center for ice cream.
3. Although he had hair implants, it looked very natural.
4. When Professor Williams scowled at the class, her facial expression told the story.
5. Although this world map was published only three years ago, the names of some countries are already out of date.

Activity 11: Editing and Rewriting (*page 190*)

1. When Mark began his first full-time job, he immediately got a credit card. <u>A used sports car was his first purchase.</u>
2. Then the began to buy expensive clothes that he could not afford. <u>He also bought impressive gifts for his parents and his girlfriend.</u>
4. To make matters worse, his car broke down, and <u>a stack of bills suddenly seemed to be due at once.</u>
5. Although Mark tried to cut back on his purchases, <u>he soon realized he had to cut up his credit card to prevent himself from using it.</u>
6. He also began keeping a careful record of his spending, <u>for he had no idea where his money had gone till then.</u>

Activity 12: Creating Sentences (*Page 191*)

CHAPTER 9: Sentence Variety I

Activity 1: The Simple Sentence (*page 195*)

Activity 2: The Compound Sentence (*page 196*)

1. I am majoring in digital media arts, for I hope to find a job doing video-game animation.
2. My children were spending too much time in front of the TV and computer, so I signed up my entire family for a one-year gym membership.
3. Nicole's skin was blemished and sun damaged, so she consulted with a plastic surgeon about a chemical face peel.
4. Riley insists on buying certified-organic fruits and vegetables, but I cannot distinguish organic from conventionally grown produce.
5. I was recently promoted to shift manager at work, so I need to drop down to part-time status at school next semester.

Activity 3: Writing Compound Sentences (*page 197*)

Activity 4: Creating Complex Sentences (*page 198*)

1. Lydia read the quarterly reports while her assistant drove them to the regional sales meeting.
2. When Keiko heard the punch line to the joke, she laughed hysterically.
3. Although I wanted to order the chef's seafood special, the kitchen ran out of fresh prawns.
4. Raymond refuses to drink from a public water fountain because he is afraid that he will catch an infectious disease.
5. Before I can register for a calculus class, I need to take the math placement exam.

Activity 5: Using Subordination (*page 199*)

1. As Carlo set the table, his wife finished cooking dinner.
2. Although Maggie could have gotten good grades, she did not study enough.
3. After I watered my drooping African violets, they perked right up.
4. Though the little boy kept pushing the "down" button, the elevator didn't come any more quickly.
5. I never really knew what pain was until I had four impacted wisdom teeth pulled at once.

Activity 6: Using *Who, Which,* or *That* (*page 200*)

1. Karen, who is an old friend of mine, just gave birth to twins.

2. The tea, which was hotter than I expected, burned the roof of my mouth.
3. I dropped the camera that my sister had just bought.
4. Ashaki, who is visiting from California, brought us some enormous oranges.
5. Liz used a steam cleaner to shampoo her rugs, which were dirtier than she had expected.

Activity 7: Writing Complex Sentences (*page* 201)

Activity 8: Using Joining Words and Dependent Words (*page* 201)

1. After . . . for
2. When . . . but
3. when . . . and
4. Because . . . so
5. but . . . because

Activity 9: Writing Compound-Complex Sentences (*page* 202)

Activity 10: Using Subordination or Coordination (*page* 202)

1. Though Jaylen likes loud music, his parents can't stand it, so he wears earphones.
2. After the volcano erupted, the sky turned black with smoke. Nearby villagers were frightened, so they clogged the roads leading to safety.
3. After Min-Yeng had a haircut today, she came home and looked in the mirror. Then she decided to wear a hat for a few days because she thought she looked like a bald eagle.
4. When I ran out of gas on the way to work, I discovered how helpful strangers can be. A passing driver saw I was stuck, so he drove me to the gas station and back to my car.
5. Our dog often rests on the floor in the sunshine while he waits for the children to get home from school. As the sunlight moves along the floor, he moves with it.
6. Because my father was going to be late from work, we planned to have a late dinner. But I was hungry before dinner, so I secretly ate a salami and cheese sandwich.
7. A baseball game was scheduled for early afternoon, but it looked like rain, so a crew rolled huge tarps to cover the field. Then the sun reappeared.
8. Cassy worries about the pesticides used on fruit, so she washes apples, pears, and plums in soap and water. Because she doesn't rinse them well, they have a soapy flavor.
9. Charlene needed to buy stamps, so she went to the post office during her lunch hour, when the line was long. After she waited there for half an hour, she had to go back to work without stamps.

10. After the weather suddenly became frigid, almost everyone at work caught a cold, so someone brought a big batch of chicken soup. She poured it into one of the office coffeepots, and the pot was empty by noon.

CHAPTER 10: Standard English Verbs

Introductory Activity (*page 210*)

played . . . plays
hoped . . . hopes
juggled . . . juggles

1. past time . . . -*ed* or -*d*
2. present time . . . -*s*

Activity 1: Using Standard Verb Forms (*page 211*)

1. drives
2. gets
3. practices
4. makes
5. brushes
6. falls
7. C
8. comes
9. watches
10. buzzes

Activity 2: Using Present Tense -*s* Verb Endings (*page 212*)

My little sister wants to be a singer when she grows up. She constantly hums and sings around the house. Sometimes she makes quite a racket. When she listens to music on the radio, for example, she sings very loudly in order to hear herself over the radio. And when she takes a shower, her voice rings through the whole house because she thinks nobody can hear her from there.

Activity 3: Using Standard Verb Forms: -*d* and -*ed* Endings (*page 213*)

1. spilled
2. jailed
3. burned
4. tied
5. measured
6. C
7. smashed
8. constructed
9. leveled
10. realized

Activity 4: Using Past Tense Verb Endings (*page 214*)

Brad hated working long hours, but he needed money to support his growing family and to pay for school. He started working at the auto body shop when he graduated from high school because he liked cars, but now the job bored him. He wished that he could spend more time at home with his wife and new baby girl. He also wanted to dedicate more time to his homework. Brad knew that he had made his own choices, so he decided to appreciate his job, his family, and his chance to move ahead in life.

Activity 5: Standard Forms of Irregular Verbs (*page 216*)

1. is
2. do
3. has
4. is
5. have
6. are
7. has
8. do
9. were
10. does

Activity 6: Identifying and Correcting Nonstandard Verbs (*page 216*)

1. ~~does~~ do
2. ~~be~~ is
3. ~~be~~ are
4. ~~has~~ have
5. ~~were~~ was
6. ~~have~~ had
7. ~~was~~ were
8. ~~done~~ did
9. ~~do~~ does
10. ~~have~~ has

Activity 7: Using Standard Forms of *be, have,* and *do* (*page 217*)

My cousin Rita has decided to lose thirty pounds, so she has put herself on a rigid diet that does not allow her to eat anything that she enjoys. Last weekend, while the family was at Aunt Jenny's house for dinner, all Rita had to eat was a can of Diet Delight peaches. We were convinced that Rita meant business when she joined an exercise club whose members have to work out on enormous machines and do twenty sit-ups just to get started. If Rita does reach her goal, we are all going to be very proud of her. But I would not be surprised if she does not succeed, because this is her fourth diet this year.

CHAPTER 11: Irregular Verbs

Introductory Activity (*page 220*)

1. *R* . . . talked . . . talked
2. *I* . . . read . . . read
3. *I* . . . sang . . . sung
4. *R* . . . tasted . . . tasted
5. *R* . . . picked . . . picked
6. *I* . . . made . . . made
7. *I* . . . felt . . . felt
8. *R* . . . typed . . . typed
9. *I* . . . became . . . become
10. *R* . . . mailed . . . mailed

Activity 1: Identifying Incorrect Verb Forms (*page 224*)

1. came
2. stood
3. built
4. swum
5. held
6. drove
7. written
8. blew
9. bought
10. knew

Activity 2: Using Present Tense, Past Tense, and Past Participle Verbs (*page* 224)

1. (a) sleeps
   (b) slept
   (c) slept
2. (a) rings
   (b) rang
   (c) rung
3. (a) write
   (b) wrote
   (c) written
4. (a) stands
   (b) stood
   (c) stood
5. (a) swims
   (b) swam
   (c) swum

6. (a) buys
   (b) bought
   (c) bought
7. (a) choose
   (b) chose
   (c) chosen
8. (a) eats
   (b) ate
   (c) eaten
9. (a) freezes
   (b) froze
   (c) frozen
10. (a) give
    (b) gave
    (c) given

Activity 3: Using *lie* and *lay* (*page* 227)

1. lies
2. Lying
3. laid
4. laid
5. lay

Activity 4: Using *set* and *sit* (*page* 228)

1. set
2. set
3. sit
4. set
5. setting

Activity 5: Using *rise* and *raise* (*page* 229)

1. rises
2. raised
3. rose
4. risen
5. raise

CHAPTER 12: Subject-Verb Agreement

Introductory Activity (*page* 231)

Correct: The postings on the college gossip site are very cruel.

Correct: There were many résumés for the supervisor to read.

Correct: Everybody wants wireless Internet access on campus.

1. postings . . . résumés   2. singular . . . singular

Activity 1: Words between Subjects and Verbs (*page* 232)

1. trail ~~of bloodstains~~ leads
2. clothes ~~in the hall closet~~ take
3. basket ~~of fancy fruit and nuts~~ was
4. instructions ~~for assembling the bicycle~~ were

5. Smoke ~~from the distant forest fires~~ is
6. Workers ~~at that automobile plant~~ begin
7. date ~~on any of the cemetery gravestones~~ appears
8. line ~~of cars in the traffic jam~~ seems
9. boxes ~~in the corner of the attic~~ contain
10. bags ~~with the new insulation material~~ protect

Activity 2: Verbs that Precede Subjects (*page* 233)

1. is noise
2. are berries
3. were cans
4. sits cabin
5. were students

6. stands cutout
7. was shape
8. were sneakers
9. are magazines
10. was row

Activity 3: Using Verbs with Indefinite Pronouns (*page* 234)

1. keeps
2. works
3. pays
4. have
5. slips

6. leans
7. expects
8. was
9. stops
10. has

Activity 4: Using Verbs with Compound Subjects (*page* 235)

1. seem
2. is
3. are
4. help
5. impresses

Activity 5: Using *who*, *which*, or *that* with Verbs (*page* 236)

1. has
2. goes
3. become
4. taste
5. are

Activity 6: Editing and Rewriting (*page* 236)

they do not think

there are enough creatures

guests . . . make

Everybody . . . thinks

somewhere that has

Activity 7: Creating Sentences (*page* 237)

CHAPTER 13: Consistent Verb Tense

Introductory Activity (*page* 241)

Mistakes in verb tense: Alex discovers . . . calls . . . present . . . past

Activity 1: Avoiding Unnecessary Tense Shifts (*page 242*)

1. answered	6. allowed
2. grabbed	7. showed
3. announced	8. stopped
4. worked	9. placed
5. called	10. crowded

CHAPTER 14: Additional Information about Verbs

Activity 1: Using the Correct Verb Tense (*page 247*)

1. have occurred	6. were raising
2. had finished	7. is organizing
3. have grown up	8. was presenting
4. am taking	9. have testified
5. had written	10. was playing

Activity 2: Using Infinitives, Participles, and Gerunds (*page 248*)

1. *P*	6. *P*
2. *G*	7. *P*
3. *I*	8. *P*
4. *G*	9. *G*
5. *I*	10. *I*

Activity 3: Making Sentences Active (*page 249*)

1. The paparazzi clamored to photograph the celebrities on the red carpet.
2. A large falling branch broke the stained-glass window.
3. The professor gave students a five-day extension on the research project.
4. A cigarette started the fire that destroyed the hotel.
5. Doctors must face the pressures of dealing with life and death.
6. The phlebotomist drew blood to randomly test employees for illegal drug use.
7. A thick layer of yellowish grease covered the kitchen shelves.
8. A group of volunteers removed trash in the neighborhood park.
9. Keith has gambled away thousands of dollars playing online video poker.
10. Women of all ages donated their "gently used" prom and bridal dresses to high school girls in need of gowns.

CHAPTER 15: Pronoun Reference, Agreement, and Point of View

Introductory Activity (*page 252*)

1. b	2. b	3. b

Activity 1: Pronoun Reference (*page 254*)

1. Sienna removed the blanket from the sofa bed and folded the blanket up.
2. The defendant told the judge, "I am mentally ill."
3. Before the demonstration, the leaders passed out signs for us to carry.
4. Kristy complained to Rachel, "My (or Your) boyfriend is being dishonest."
5. Because I didn't rinse last night's dishes, my kitchen smells like a garbage can.
6. A film on endangered species really depressed the students.

   or: Watching a film on endangered species really depressed the students.
7. The veterinarian said that if I find a tick on my dog, I should get rid of the tick immediately.
8. My sister removed the curtains from the windows so that she could wash the curtains.

   or: So that she could wash the curtains, my sister removed them from the windows.

   or: My sister removed the curtains from the windows so that she could wash the windows.

   or: So that she could wash the windows, my sister removed the curtains from them.
9. Richard said his acupuncture therapist could help my sprained shoulder, but I don't believe in acupuncture.
10. I discovered when I went to sell my old textbooks that publishers have put out new editions, and nobody wants to buy my textbooks.

    or: I discovered when I went to sell my old textbooks that nobody wants to buy them because publishers have put out new editions.

Activity 2: Pronoun Agreement (*page 255*)

1. them	4. them
2. their	5. it
3. they	

Activity 3: Using Pronouns Correctly (*page 257*)

1. his	6. his or her
2. his	7. her
3. its	8. he
4. her	9. her
5. them	10. his or her

Activity 4: Correcting Inconsistent Pronouns (*page 259*)

1. my blood
2. they know
3. they have
4. they should receive
5. I can avoid

6. their hands
7. she can worry . . . her own
8. we could
9. she can still have . . . her day
10. our rights

CHAPTER 16: Pronoun Types

Introductory Activity (*page 263*)

Correct sentences:

Andy and I enrolled in a Web design course.

The police officer pointed to my sister and me.

Meg prefers men who take pride in their bodies.

The players are confident that the league championship is theirs.

Those concert tickets are too expensive.

Our parents should spend some money on themselves for a change.

Activity 1: Identifying Subject and Object Pronouns (*page 266*)

1. her (*O*)
2. She (*S*)
3. me (*O*)
4. her and me (*O*)
5. he (*S*)
6. I (*am* is understood) (*S*)
7. they (*S*)
8. me (*O*)
9. We (*S*)
10. I (*S*)

Activity 2: Using Subject or Object Pronouns (*page 266*)

1. I
2. him *or* me
3. they
4. I *or* we
5. us
6. I *or* he *or* she *or* they *or* we
7. they *or* he *or* she
8. I *or* he *or* she *or* they *or* we
9. I *or* he *or* she *or* they *or* we
10. us *or* them

Activity 3: Identifying Correct Relative Pronouns (*page 269*)

1. that
2. that
3. who
4. which
5. whom

Activity 4: Using Relative Pronouns (*page 269*)

Activity 5: Correcting Possessive Pronouns (*page 270*)

1. hers
2. mine
3. ours
4. its
5. their

Activity 6: Correcting Demonstrative Pronouns (*page 271*)

1. This town
2. those seats
3. That dress
4. those chocolates
5. those potholes

Activity 7: Using Demonstrative Pronouns (*page 271*)

Activity 8: Using Reflexive Pronouns (*page 272*)

1. themselves
2. herself
3. himself
4. ourselves
5. themselves

CHAPTER 17: Adjectives and Adverbs

Introductory Activity (*page 276*)

adjective . . . adverb . . . *ly* . . . *er* . . . *est*

Activity 1: Using Comparatives and Superlatives (*page 278*)

tougher	toughest
more practical	most practical
quieter	quietest
more aggressive	most aggressive
clearer	clearest

Activity 2: Using the Correct Comparative and Superlative Forms (*page 278*)

1. best
2. dirtier
3. more considerate
4. worse
5. scariest
6. less
7. more stylish
8. sillier
9. slowest
10. most fattening

Activity 3: Using Adjectives or Adverbs (*page 279*)

1. badly
2. harshly
3. steep
4. frequently
5. truthfully
6. peacefully
7. bright
8. loudly
9. carefully
10. nicely

Activity 4: Using *well* or *good* (*page 280*)

1. well
2. good
3. good
4. well
5. well

CHAPTER 18: Misplaced Modifiers

Introductory Activity (*page 283*)

1. Intended: The grocery clerk was working at the supermarket.

   Unintended: The Mega Millions lottery was working at the supermarket.

2. Intended: The social worker works for the hospital.

   Unintended: The terminally ill patient's family works for the hospital.

Activity 1: Fixing Misplaced Modifiers (*page 284*)

1. At the back of his cage, the tiger growled at a passerby.
2. Lee hung colorful scarves made of green and blue silk over her windows.
3. Standing on our front porch, we watched the fireworks.
4. Jason has almost two hundred friends on Facebook.
5. With a smile, the salesclerk exchanged the blue sweater for a yellow one.
6. We all stared at the man with curly purple hair in the front row of the theater.
7. I love the cookies with the chocolate frosting from the bakery.
8. During their last meeting, the faculty decided to strike.
9. Larry looked on with disbelief as his car burned.
10. My cousin sent me instructions in a letter on how to get to her house.

Activity 2: Placing Modifiers Correctly (*page 285*)

1. Using caution, I rolled down my car window only a few inches for the police officer.
2. Tabloids all over the world publish unflattering photos of celebrities who are arrested for drunk driving or possession of illicit drugs.
3. The mongoose, which resembles the ferret, was brought to Hawaii to kill rats but has since destroyed much of the native plant life.
4. Led Zeppelin's fourth album has sold almost 22 million copies.
5. Elisa decided to undergo laser eye surgery at the university medical center to correct her astigmatism.

CHAPTER 19: Dangling Modifiers

Introductory Activity (*page 289*)

1. Intended: The grilled T-bone steak was sizzling.

   Unintended: The customer at the restaurant was sizzling.

2. Intended: Eric arrived home from college.

   Unintended: Eric's parents arrived home from college.

Activity 1: Correcting Dangling Modifiers (*page 291*)

1. A security guard pointed to the priceless painting that was hanging safely on a wall.
2. When I was five, my mother bought me a chemistry set.
3. C
4. Since the milk had turned sour, I would not drink it.
5. While I was updating my Facebook profile, my hot tea turned cold.
6. Pete hated to look at the kitchen sink, which was piled high with dirty dishes.
7. Because I locked my keys in the car, the police had to open it for me.
8. Because the plants were drooping and looking all dried out, the children watered them.
9. After I sat through a long lecture, my foot was asleep.
10. Since I was late, stopping for Starbucks was out of the question.

Activity 2: Placing Modifiers Correctly (*page 292*)

CHAPTER 20: Faulty Parallelism

Introductory Activity (*page 295*)

Correct sentences:

I use my TV remote control to change channels, to adjust the volume, and to turn the set on and off.

One option the employees had was to take a cut in pay; the other was to work longer hours.

The refrigerator has a cracked vegetable drawer, a missing shelf, and a strange freezer smell.

Activity 1: Using Parallelism (*page 296*)

1. (example: fast service)
2. howling dogs
3. rude
4. hiking
5. poor security
6. cleaned the apartment
7. having fun
8. inexpensive desserts
9. on the closet floor
10. sings in the church choir

Activity 2: Creating Nonparallel Sentences (*page 297*)

1. waited
2. cramming
3. illness
4. late buses
5. attracting
6. to suffocate
7. interrupted
8. financial security
9. birds chirping
10. breathed fire

Activity 3: Writing Parallel Sentences (*page 298*)

Activity 4: Editing and Rewriting (*page* 299)

1. Running is an exercise that can be good for you mentally, physically, and emotionallly.
2. A beginning runner should keep three things in mind: the warm-up session, the run, and the cool-down period.
4. Stretching reduces muscle stiffness, decreases the possibility of injury, and gradually increases the heart rate.
6. Your breathing should be steady and deep.
8. An adequate cool-down period allows time for the body to relax and the heart rate to normalize.

Activity 5: Creating Sentences (*page* 299)

CHAPTER 21: Sentence Variety II

Activity 1: Combining Sentences with *-ing* Words (*page* 304)

1. Gathering up their books and backpacks, the students began leaving the lecture hall.
2. Crossing the street with her daughter, Susan was involved in a hit-and-run accident.
3. Rushing to class, Arnold parked his motorcycle on the school lawn.
4. Acting quickly, the nurse brought the patient his pain medication.
5. Knowing that his team would lose the game, the football coach buried his face in his hands.

Activity 2: Using *-ing* Word Groups (*page* 305)

Activity 3: Combining Sentences with *-ed* Words (*page* 305)

1. Mary, startled by thunder, sat up suddenly in bed.
2. Married for fifty years, my parents decided to have a second wedding.
3. Frightened by the large dog near the curb, Erica wouldn't leave her car.
4. Dotted with mold, the old orange felt like a marshmallow.
5. Scott, determined to have plenty to eat during the movie, made a huge sandwich and popped popcorn.

Activity 4: Using *-ed* Word Groups (*page* 306)

Activity 5: Combining Sentences with *-ly* Words (*page* 307)

1. Hungrily, we ordered extra-large pepperoni pizzas and buffalo wings.

2. Suddenly, Nino left the party.
3. Lazily, I watched TV all afternoon.
4. Eagerly, David returned the customer's phone call.
5. Surprisingly, the visiting team won the game in double overtime.

Activity 6: Using *-ly* Words (*page* 308)

Activity 7: Combining Sentences with *to* Word Groups (*page* 308)

1. To make the tub less slippery, Lily put a thick towel on the bottom.
2. To keep raccoons away, we now keep our garbage in the garage.
3. To count his pulse, Bill pressed two fingers against the large vein in his neck.
4. To steam her face, my aunt opens her dishwasher when it begins drying.
5. To help out the homeless, we looked through our closets for unused clothing.

Activity 8: Using *to* (*page* 309)

Activity 9: Combining Sentences by Opening with Prepositional Phrases (*page* 309)

1. About once a week, we have dinner with my parents at a restaurant.
2. Before company came, I put the dirty cups away in the cupboard.
3. During my English exam, my eyes roamed around the room until they met the instructor's eye.
4. For twenty minutes, the little boy drew intently in a comic book without stopping once.
5. At the zoo, a playful young orangutan wriggled in a corner under a paper sack.

Activity 10: Using Prepositional Phrases (*page* 311)

Activity 11: Using Adjectives in a Series (*page* 311)

1. The old, peeling shingles blew off the roof during the blustery storm.
2. The lean, powerful dancer whirled across the stage with his graceful, elegant partner.
3. A large, furry rat scurried into the crowded kitchen of the restaurant.
4. The full, golden moon lit up the cloudy sky like a huge floating streetlamp.
5. The oval plastic doorbell of the large, ornate house played a loud rock tune.

Activity 12: Writing with Adjectives in a Series (*page 313*)

Activity 13: Combining Sentences with Verbs in a Series (*page 313*)

1. The robber scanned the liquor store for a surveillance camera, fidgeted with his dark sunglasses and baseball cap, and signaled to the clerk behind the counter that he had a handgun.
2. In the sports bar, Tanner placed a bet on his favorite basketball team, took a swig from his bottle of Budweiser, and sat back to watch the NBA playoff semi-finals.
3. The phlebotomist pressed down on Logan's forearm, slid the needle into his arm, and let out a heavy sigh as the needle missed his vein.
4. The comedy hypnotist invited a volunteer to the stage, quickly brought her into a trance, and offered her a clove of garlic, which she thought was a cashew nut.
5. The paparazzo stalked the Hollywood actor on vacation, adjusted his telephoto lens, and snapped hundreds of candid photos.

Activity 14: Using Verbs in a Series (*page 314*)

CHAPTER 22: Paper Format

Introductory Activity (*page 319*)

In "A," the title is capitalized and has no quotation marks around it; there is a blank line between the title and the body of the paper; there are left and right margins around the body of the paper; no words are incorrectly hyphenated.

Activity 1: Correcting Formatting Errors (*page 321*)

1. (example: Break words at correct syllable divisions (sis-ter))
2. Do not use quotation marks around the title.
3. Capitalize the major words in the title ("Being a Younger Sister").
4. Skip a line between the title and first line of the paper.
5. Indent the first line of the paper.
6. Keep margins on both sides of the paper.

Activity 2: Writing Titles (*page 321*)

1. Benefits of Pets
2. Learning How to Budget
3. The Value of a Study Group
4. A Special Relationship *or* Grandparents and Grandchildren
5. A Wise Decision

Activity 3: Rewriting Dependent Sentences (*page 322*)

1. Effective communication is often the key to a healthy relationship.
2. Reality TV shows are popular for several reasons.
3. Correct
4. The best vacation I ever had began when my friends from high school booked a one-week trip to Cancun, Mexico.
5. Most professional athletes say that they don't use steroids to enhance athletic performance.

CHAPTER 23: Capital Letters

Introductory Activity (*page 324*)

1–13: Answers will vary, but all should be capitalized.
14–16: On . . . "Let's . . . I

Activity 1: Capitalizing Names and Titles (*page 326*)

1. I . . . Boy Scouts
2. Friday . . . Thanksgiving . . . Target
3. Regal Cinema . . . If
4. New England . . . Republicans . . . Democrats
5. State Farm . . . Nationwide . . . Prudential Building
6. *Time* . . . *Newsweek* . . . California
7. Valentine's Day . . . Mother's Day
8. Pepsis . . . Fritos . . . Macintosh
9. Ford Taurus . . . Saturday
10. Broadway . . . *My Fair Lady*

Activity 2: Where Is Capitalization Needed? (*page 329*)

1. Uncle David
2. Motorola Razr . . . Bluetooth
3. United States President Jimmy Carter . . . Nobel Peace Prize
4. Pacific Islander . . . Samoa . . . East Coast
5. Principles . . . Marketing

Activity 3: Where Is Capitalization Unnecessary? (*page 330*)

1. husband . . . barbeque ribs
2. community college . . . technical writer
3. electronics store . . . televisions . . . players
4. community organizations . . . food drive
5. science teacher . . . tidal pools

Activity 4: Editing and Rewriting (*page 330*)

1. Lincoln, Memorial
2. Thursday, October

3. Uncle, Walt, Smithsonian, Institution
4. Now
5. Lincoln's
6. Potomac, River
7. Gettysburg, Address
9. Kodak

Activity 5: Creating Sentences (*page 331*)

CHAPTER 24: Numbers and Abbreviations

Introductory Activity (*page 334*)

Correct choices:

First sentence: 7:30 . . . 75 percent
Second sentence: Eighty-five . . . fifteen
Second sentence: 9 a.m.
Second sentence: hour . . . minutes

Activity 1: Using Numbers (*page 335*)

1. 2:30
2. five
3. eleven . . . seventy-seven
4. five . . . four
5. 15
6. 206
7. 15
8. two hundred
9. 7 . . . 2007
10. seven

Activity 2: Using Abbreviations (*page 336*)

1. newspaper . . . telephone
2. bushels . . . market . . . Route
3. Monday . . . September
4. psychology . . . England
5. chicken . . . macaroni
6. ounce . . . tablespoon
7. chemistry . . . Sunday . . . hours
8. January . . . company . . . year
9. license . . . medical
10. veteran . . . business . . . college

CHAPTER 25: End Marks

Introductory Activity (*page 339*)

1. depressed.   3. parked.
2. paper?   4. control!

Activity 1: Using End Punctuation (*page 340*)

1. door?   6. "Gotcha!"
2. message.   7. "Got milk?"
3. jerk?   8. storm.
4. shocked.   9. think?"
5. psychology.   10. officer.

CHAPTER 26: Apostrophes

Introductory Activity (*page 342*)

1. In each case, the 's indicates possession or ownership.
2. The apostrophes indicate omitted letters and shortened spellings.
3. In the first sentence, s indicates a plural noun; in the second sentence, 's indicates possession.

Activity 1: Combining Words (*page 343*)

you've   we're   couldn't
haven't   you'll   they'll
he's   we'd   doesn't

Activity 2: Forming Contractions (*page 343*)

1. didn't . . . wasn't   4. isn't . . . you've
2. doesn't . . . she's   5. We'd . . . don't
3. You're . . . can't

Activity 3: Using the Apostrophe (*page 344*)

Activity 4: Using Apostrophes Correctly (*page 345*)

1. Your . . . you're   4. There . . . they're
2. your . . . its   5. It's . . . they're
3. whose . . . Who's

Activity 5: Using 's to Show Possession (*page 346*)

1. singer's voice
2. Dawn's garage
3. Murphy's law
4. computer's memory
5. my wife's mother
6. yesterday's meat loaf
7. My sister's promotion
8. Alexis's bratty little brother
9. the referee's call
10. the tanker's hull

Activity 6: Identifying Possessive Nouns (*page 347*)

1. horse's   3. son's
2. brother's   4. comedian's

5. landlord's
6. Ted's
7. teller's
8. people's
9. studio's
10. girl's

Activity 7: Making Words Possessive (*page* 348)

1. (example: Aaron's)
2. bus's
3. computer's
4. Ross's
5. pizza's

Activity 8: Apostrophes vs. Simple Plurals (*page* 349)

1. parlors: parlor's, meaning "belonging to the parlor"
   aromas: simple plural meaning more than one aroma
   vents: simple plural meaning more than one vent
2. cars: car's, meaning "belonging to the car"
   streets: simple plural meaning more than one street
   buildings: simple plural meaning more than one building
3. Karens: Karen's, meaning "belonging to Karen"
   plants: simple plural meaning more than one plant
   stakes: simple plural meaning more than one stake
4. lakes: lake's, meaning "belonging to the lake"
   officials: simple plural meaning more than one official
5. positions: simple plural meaning more than one position
   exterminators: exterminator's, meaning "belonging to an exterminator"
6. candlelights: candlelight's, meaning "belonging to the candlelight"
   plates: simple plural meaning more than one plate
   goblets: simple plural meaning more than one goblet
7. Crackers: simple plural meaning more than one cracker
   slices: simple plural meaning more than one slice
   fathers: father's, meaning "belonging to my father"
8. insects: insect's, meaning "belonging to the insect"
   eggs: simple plural meaning more than one egg
   worms: simple plural meaning more than one worm
9. Seabirds: simple plural meaning more than one seabird
   oceans: ocean's, meaning "belonging to the ocean"
   surfers: simple plural meaning more than one surfer
10. daughters: daughter's, meaning "belonging to my daughter"
    prayers: simple plural meaning more than one prayer
    schools: simple plural meaning more than one school

Activity 9: Missing Apostrophes (*page* 350)

1. nurses' union
2. sisters' feet
3. lions' keeper
4. The Tylers' new flat screen TV
5. parents' wedding pictures

Activity 10: Editing and Rewriting (*page* 351)

1. My neighbor's dog
2. there's
3. the dog's constant barking . . . can't
5. my landlord's fence
7. I've
8. there's . . . the dog's behavior
9. that's . . . doesn't

Activity 11: Creating Sentences (*page* 351)

CHAPTER 27: Quotation Marks

Introductory Activity (*page* 354)

1. Quotation marks set off the exact words of a speaker.
2. Commas and periods following quotations go inside quotation marks.

Activity 1: Using Quotation Marks (*page* 356)

1. The chilling bumper sticker read, "You can't hug children with nuclear arms."
2. "One day we'll look back on this argument, and it will seem funny," Bruce assured Rosa.
3. "Hey, lady, this is an express line!" shouted the cashier to the woman with a full basket.
4. My grandfather was fond of saying, "Happiness is found along the way, not at the end of the road."
5. "When will I be old enough to pay the adult fare?" the child asked.
6. On his deathbed, Oscar Wilde is supposed to have said, "Either this wallpaper goes or I do."
7. The sign on my neighbor's front door reads, "Never mind the dog. Beware of owner."
8. "I'm not afraid to die," said Woody Allen. "I just don't want to be there when it happens."
9. My son once told me, "Sometimes I wish I were little again. Then I wouldn't have to make so many decisions."
10. "I don't feel like cooking tonight," Eve said to Adam. "Let's just have fruit."

Activity 2: Formatting Quotations (*page* 356)

1. The firefighter asked the neighbors, "Is there anyone else still in the building?"
2. "You'll have to remove your sunglasses," the security guard reminded the customers at the bank.
3. Upon eating a few drops of Horacio's homemade habanero sauce, Trudy yelped, "That's hot!"
4. "Good things come to those who wait," Zhao told himself as he waited in line for hours to buy an iPhone.
5. "If at first you don't succeed," my wife joked, "you should read the directions."

Activity 3: Writing with Quotation Marks (*page* 357)

Activity 4: Using Dialogue (*page* 358)

1. (example: Agnes said to me as we left work, "Henry got a raise.")
2. I said, "That's hard to believe, since Henry is a do-nothing."
3. Agnes replied, "Even so, he's gone up in the world."
4. I told her, "You must be kidding."
5. Agnes laughed and said, "Henry was moved from the first to the fourth floor today."

Activity 5: Converting Quotations into Indirect Statements (*page* 359)

1. Josh muttered that he is so tired of studying for finals.
2. The dental hygienist asked me if I brush and floss regularly.
3. Leona asked Matt if he would mind if she copied his lecture notes.
4. The security guard asked me if I had seen any suspicious activity in the building.
5. The delivery driver asked if I would mind signing for the package.

Activity 6: Using Quotations in Titles (*page* 360)

1. My sister just bought a TiVo so she won't have to miss any more episodes of General Hospital.
2. Rhianna grabbed the National Enquirer and eagerly began to read the article "I Had a Space Alien's Baby."
3. Our exam will cover two chapters, "The Study of Heredity" and "The Origin of Diversity," in our biology textbook, Life.
4. The last song on the bluegrass program was called "I Ain't Broke but I'm Badly Bent."
5. The classic 1980s movie Stand by Me was actually based on "The Body," a short story written by Stephen King.
6. At last night's performance of Annie Get Your Gun, the audience joined the cast in singing "There's No Business Like Show Business."
7. A typical article in Cosmopolitan will have a title like "How to Hook a Man without Letting Him Know You're Fishing."
8. One way Joanne deals with depression is to get out her Man of La Mancha album and play the song "The Impossible Dream."
9. I read the article "How Good Is Your Breakfast?" in Consumer Reports while munching a doughnut this morning.
10. According to a Psychology Today article titled "Home on the Street," there are 36,000 people living on New York City's sidewalks.

Activity 7: Editing and Rewriting (*page* 361)

3. . . . asked, "Has . . . before?"
4. "Once," she said.
5–6. "About . . . long."
8–9. "We're . . . ones."
10. asked, "Is . . . somebody?"
12. read, "Open . . . Emergency."
13. "I . . . there," she said, pointing to the sign.
15. "Can anyone hear me?" he asked.
16–17. "Yes, . . . minutes."
19. "I . . . quickly," he said softly, wringing his hands.
21–22. "Don't . . . time."

Activity 8: Creating Sentences (*page* 362)

CHAPTER 28: Commas

Introductory Activity (*page* 365)

1. a: card, . . . check, . . . ; ants, roaches,
2. b: car, . . . ; hiking,
3. c: leeches, . . . blood, . . . ; Derek, . . . arrested,
4. d: easy, . . . ; trees,
5. e: asked, . . . ; work, . . . said,
6. f: 1,500,000; Newark, New Jersey, . . . August 26, 2009,

Activity 1: Commas between Items in a Series (*page* 367)

1. sunglasses, a bottle of water, and a recent issue of *Every Day with Rachael Ray*
2. e-mail, play games, surf the Internet, download music, and send instant messages
3. igloo-shaped doghouse, several plastic toys, trampled flowers, and a cracked ceramic gnome

Activity 2: Necessary and Unnecessary Commas (*page* 367)

1. pennies, and a sock hidden under the seats
2. Squirrels, . . . and clouds of mosquitoes populate
3. spun to his left, . . . arms of the Panthers' center

Activity 3: Commas after Introductory Clauses (*page* 368)

1. airport,   2. library,   3. others,

Activity 4: More Necessary and Unnecessary Commas (*page* 368)

1. presents, . . . ribbon and tied
2. aisle, I saw a bead of sweat roll from her forehead
3. For example, I wrote a note to remind me that

Activity 5: Commas That Set Off Interruptions (*page 370*)

1. clerk, assisted by no one,
2. Craig, who were engaged for a year,
3. furniture, rusted beyond repair,

Activity 6: More Necessary and Unnecessary Commas (*page 370*)

1. gigantic, . . . the rest is deadwood
2. council, in a rare fit of wisdom
3. presidents of the United States,
4. aunt, a talkative woman,

Activity 7: Commas That Connect Complete Thoughts (*page 371*)

1. spacious, but
2. thunderstorm, so
3. C
4. space, for
5. C
6. supermarket, but
7. C
8. college, but
9. schoolwork, but
10. C

Activity 8: Setting Off Quotations with Commas (*page 372*)

1. speak,"
2. miseducated, " said John F. Kennedy,
3. building," muttered the patrol officer,

Activity 9: More Necessary and Unnecessary Commas (*page 372*)

1. poster in the subway station,
2. fine," . . . forgetting to kick."
3. think," the judge asked the defendant,

Activity 10: Adding Commas (*page 373*)

1. me, madam,
2. 6,000 . . . 15,000
3. 15, 1912.
4. Teresa, . . . Love,
5. Washington, D.C., . . . 50,000 . . . 6,500 . . . 114,000

Activity 11: Eliminating Unnecessary Commas (*page 374*)

1. We grew a pumpkin last year that weighed over one hundred pounds.
2. Anyone with a failing grade must meet with the instructor during office hours.
3. Last weekend a grizzly bear attacked a hiker who got too close to its cubs.
4. After watching my form on the high diving board, Mr. Riley, my instructor, asked me if I had insurance.

5. Rosa flew first to Los Angeles, and then she went to visit her parents in Mexico City.
6. The tall muscular man wearing the dark sunglasses is a professional wrestler.
7. Onions, radishes, and potatoes seem to grow better in cooler climates.
8. Whenever Vincent is in Las Vegas, you can find him at the blackjack table or the roulette wheel.
9. While I watched in disbelief, my car rolled down the hill and through the front window of a Chinese restaurant.
10. The question, sir, is not whether you committed the crime but when you committed the crime.

Activity 12: Editing and Rewriting (*page 375*)

On Tuesday, May 4, 2004, my husband~x~ and I were unable to sleep because of the loud music coming from your apartment. When I first heard the music, I didn't say anything to you because it was still early. But the music, along with loud~x~ laughter and talking, continued until around four o'clock in the morning. At midnight, my husband went into the hallway to see what was happening, and he ran into one of your guests. The man, who seemed very drunk, stared at him~x~ and said, "Go back to bed, old man." The next morning, we found beer cans, pizza boxes, and cigarette butts~x~ piled outside our door. This is unacceptable. We have written this letter to you as a warning. The next time something like this happens, we will call the police~x~ and the building manager. We don't want to cause trouble with you, but we will not tolerate another incident like what happened that night.

Activity 13: Creating Sentences (*page 376*)

CHAPTER 29: Other Punctuation Marks

Introductory Activity (*page 379*)

1. list:
2. chocolate-dipped
3. (1994–2008)
4. seriously;
5. abused—but happy

Activity 1: Using Colons (*page 380*)

1. diet:
2. summer:
3. columns:

Activity 2: Using Semicolons (*page 381*)

1. library; consequently,
2. crying; my
3. roommate; Rami . . . boyfriend; and

Activity 3: Using the Dash (*page 381*)

1. sea—shivering
2. —her third in three years—
3. time—eight

Activity 4: Using Hyphens (*page 382*)

1. rabbit-ear . . . high-definition
2. hole-in-the-wall . . . hoity-toity
3. hard-working . . . out-of-towners

Activity 5: Using Parentheses (*page 383*)

1. Americans (80 percent) had
2. hours (3:00 to 4:00 p.m.) are
3. often (1) make a list and then (2) check off items I have done.

CHAPTER 30: Dictionary Use

Introductory Activity (*page 386*)

1. fortutious (fortuitous)
2. hi/er/o/glyph/ics
3. be
4. oc/to/ge/naŕ/i/an (primary accent is on *nar*)
5. (1) identifying mark on the ear of a domestic animal (2) identifying feature or characteristic

Answers to the practice activities are in your dictionary. Check with your instructor if you have any problems.

Activity 1: Using a Dictionary (*page 387*)

arguing . . . friend . . . mortgage . . . reference . . . beautiful . . . marriage . . . achieve . . . tournament . . . ninety . . . appearance . . . representative . . . yesterday . . . unanimous . . . visitor . . . unusual . . . hammer . . . committed . . . vegetable

Activity 2: Marking Syllable Divisions (*page 387*)

2 . . . 3 . . . 4 . . . 5 . . .

Activity 3: Understanding Vowel Sounds (*page 388*)

pet . . . pie . . . pot . . . toe . . . cut . . . boot

Activity 4: Using the Schwa (*page 389*)

Activity 5: Using a Dictionary's Abbreviations Key (*page 390*)

plural . . . singular . . . adjective . . . adverb

Activity 6: Principal Parts (*page 391*)

choose - chose - chosen - choosing

know - knew - known - knowing

speak - spoke - spoken - speaking

Activity 7: Writing Plural Forms (*page 391*)

countries . . . volcanoes . . . curricula . . . women

Activity 8: Using Sentence Context (*page 391*)

Dictionary definitions:

1. Of foremost importance
2. requiring skillful or tactful handling
3. expressed objections or criticisms in bitter, harsh, or abusive language

Activity 9: Etymology (*page 392*)

magazine: from a French word meaning "storehouse"

anatomy: from the Greek anatome, meaning "dissection"

frankfurter: after Frankfurt, Germany

Activity 10: Usage (*page 393*)

informal . . . informal . . . informal . . . nonstandard . . . slang

Activity 11: Synonyms (*page 393*)

desire: covet, crave, want, wish

ask: question, inquire, query, interrogate, examine, quiz

cry: weep, wail, whimper, sob, blubber

CHAPTER 31: Spelling Improvement

Introductory Activity (*page 395*)

Misspellings:

akward . . . exercize . . . buisness . . . worryed . . . shamful . . . begining . . . partys . . . sandwichs . . . heros

Activity 1: Using Correct Endings (*page 397*)

1. hurried
2. admiring
3. denies
4. jabbing
5. magnified
6. committed
7. diving
8. hastily
9. propelling
10. nudges

Activity 2: Using Plural Endings or Forms (*page 398*)

1. buses
2. patches
3. therapies
4. batches
5. reefs
6. avocados
7. fifties
8. knives
9. daughters-in-law
10. theses

CHAPTER 32: Omitted Words and Letters

Introductory Activity (*page 402*)

bottles . . . in the supermarket . . . like a wind-up toy . . . his arms . . . an alert shopper . . . with the crying

Activity 1: Adding Missing Words (*page 403*)

1. I grabbed a metal bar on the roof of the subway car as the train lurched into the station.
2. For most of our country's history, gold was the basis of the monetary system.
3. Maggie made about a quart of French-toast batter— enough to soak a few dozen slices.
4. Several pairs of sneakers tumbled around in the dryer and banged against the glass door.
5. To err is human and to forgive is divine, but never to make a mistake in the first place takes a lot of luck.
6. Raccoons like to wash their food in a stream with their nimble, glove-like hands before eating.
7. When I got to the grocery store, I realized I had left my shopping list in the glove compartment of my car.
8. Reality shows are an inexpensive way for networks to make a high profit.
9. Soap operas, on the other hand, are very expensive to produce because of the high salaries of many cast members.
10. One memorable Friday the thirteenth, a friend of mine bought a black cat and a broken mirror and walked under a ladder. He had a wonderful day!

Activity 2: Using -s Endings (*page 404*)

1. sightseers . . . ghouls
2. sets . . . names
3. Dozens . . . beetles
4. dentists . . . restaurants . . . lines
5. workers . . . departments
6. lights . . . games . . . cars . . . persons
7. games . . . balls
8. shoes . . . jeans . . . months
9. stamps . . . pens
10. Workers . . . logs . . . chunks . . . chips

Activity 3: Writing with Plural Forms (*page 405*)

CHAPTER 33: Commonly Confused Words

Introductory Activity (*page 407*)

1. Incorrect: your   Correct: you're
2. Incorrect: who's   Correct: whose
3. Incorrect: there   Correct: their
4. Incorrect: to   Correct: too
5. Incorrect: Its   Correct: It's

Activity 1: Homonyms (*page 408*)

all ready . . . already
break . . . brake
course . . . coarse
here . . . hear
whole . . . hole
its . . . it's
new . . . knew
know . . . no
pair . . . pear
passed . . . past
peace . . . piece
plane . . . plain
principal . . . principle
right . . . write
then . . . than
there . . . their . . . they're
through . . . threw
two . . . too . . . to
where . . . wear
weather . . . whether
who's . . . whose
you're . . . your

Activity 2: Commonly Confused Words (*page 415*)

an . . . a
except . . . accept
advice . . . advise
affect . . . effect
among . . . between
beside . . . besides
can . . . may
cloths . . . clothes
desert . . . dessert
dose . . . does
fewer . . . less
former . . . latter
learn . . . teach
loose . . . lose
quite . . . quiet
though . . . thought

Activity 3: Incorrect Word Forms (*page* 419)

being that

1. Since (*or* Because) our stove doesn't work
2. since (*or* because) they don't speak to each other
3. since (*or* because) it's my birthday

can't hardly / couldn't hardly

1. I could hardly
2. I can hardly
3. everyone can hardly

could of

1. you could have
2. you could have
3. I could have

irregardless

1. Regardless of your feelings
2. regardless of the weather
3. regardless of age

must of / should of / would of

1. I must have
2. he would have
3. You should have

CHAPTER 34: Effective Word Choice

Introductory Activity (*page* 423)

Correct sentences:

1. After playing basketball with my friends, I quickly drank a soda.
2. Even though my essay was concise, I tried my best.
3. I will try to finish the report after lunch.
4. If my daughter calls while I am in a meeting, please tell her that I am unavailable.

   1 . . . 2 . . . 3 . . . 4

Activity 1: Avoiding Slang (*page* 424)

1. When I confronted my ex-boyfriend about cheating on me, he simply shrugged and said, "It was my fault."
2. My friend thinks that Chantel is attractive, but I think she's too emotional.

3. Rayna is on her cell phone all the time, but that's fine.
4. Joe wanted to quickly leave the family dinner so that he could meet his friends.
5. Everyone at the gym thinks that Gavin is taking steroids, but he swears that he doesn't use steroids to get his well-toned abdominal muscles.

Activity 2: Avoiding Clichés (*page* 426)

1. Substitute In brief for To make a long story short.
2. Substitute Very quickly for As quick as a wink.
3. Substitute is ignored for goes in one ear and out the other.
4. Substitute was delighted for felt like a million dollars.
5. Substitute rare for few and far between.

Activity 3: Avoiding Inflated Words (*page* 427)

1. Please ask one of our salespeople.
2. The weather is terrible today.
3. My parents want me to get a college degree.
4. Do not put your arm out of the car, or an accident might happen.
5. Many fires are caused by the careless use of portable heaters.

Activity 4: Omitting Unnecessary Words (*page* 429)

1. There is no cure for the common cold.
2. My main point is that our state should legalize gambling.
3. Because Chen's car wouldn't start, he took a bus to work.
4. Even when I was a boy, my goal was to be a stockbroker.
5. Susan's daily exercises energize her.

CREDITS

Photo Credits

Part 1

Page 3: © Corbis; p. 4: © Jamie Squire/Getty; p. 15: © Steven Weinberg/Stone/Getty; Chapter Opener 2: © Richard Lord Enterprises/The Image Works; p. 42: © Jeff Greenberg/Photo Edit.

Part 2

Page 45 top: © Photodisc/PunchStock; p. 45 bottom: © Digital Vision/Getty; CO 3: © Tim McGuire/Corbis; p. 51 top: © Darren Hopes/Getty; p. 51 bottom: © Frank May/dpa/Corbis; p. 52 top: © Nick White/Digital Vision/Getty; p. 52 middle: © Amanda Edwards/Getty; p. 52 bottom: © David Young Wolff/Photo Edit; p. 84: Library of Congress; CO 4 Superdome: top © Mario Tama/Getty; bottom © Mark Wilson/Getty; CO 4 Highway: © Mario Tama/Getty; p. 110 right: © David Buffington/Getty; p. 110 left: © McGraw-Hill Companies, Inc./Gary He, photographer; p. 125 both: © Angela Gaul; CO 5: © Reunion des Musees Nationaux/Art Resource, NY; p. 146 top right: © The Bridgeman Art Library/Getty; p. 146 top left: © Jim Zuckerman/Corbis; p. 146 bottom: © Vatican Museums and Galleries, Vatican City, Italy/Getty.

Part 3

Opener: © Owaki/Kulla/Corbis; p. 152 bottom: © Andrew Walsh; p. 152 top: Courtesy of Sheryl Stephen;

Section II Opener: © Natalie Hummel; p. 313: © Peter Adams/Getty; SO IV top: © Oren Levine; SO IV bottom: © Ryan Caiazzo; p. 351: © Nicole Hill/Getty; SO V: © Lisa Beebe.

Part 4

Opener: © Livia Corona/Taxi/Getty; p. 442: Courtesy of the Franciscan Sisters of Little Falls, Minnesota; p. 446: © Ryan McVay/Taxi/Getty; p. 455: © Bob Daemmrich/Photo Edit; p. 466: © BananaStock/PictureQuest; p. 468: Courtesy of Rose Del Castillo Guilbault; p. 473: © Royalty-Free/Corbis; p. 475: Courtesy of Firoozeh Dumas; p. 480: Library of Congress, Prints and Photographs Division; p. 483: © Joe Giza/Reuters/Corbis; p. 492: © Mark Peterson/Corbis; p. 499: © Left Lane Productions/Corbis; p. 501: © Larry Marcus of Minneapolis, MN; p. 508: © Louie Psihoyos/Corbis; p. 521: © Jason LaVeris/FilmMagic/Getty; p. 525: © Kevin S. Moul; p. 529: © BananaStock/PunchStock; p. 535: © Photodisc Red/Getty; p. 545: © ImageSource; p. 546: © Frank Capri/Hulton Archive/Getty; p. 551: © Kelly & Massa; p. 556: © Fabio Cardoso/zefa/Corbis; p. 565: © The McGraw-Hill Companies, Inc./Lars A. Niki, photographer; p. 566: © Eric Neitzel/WireImage/Getty.

Text/Line Art Credits

Chapter 35

p. 442 Sister Helen P. Mrosla, O.S.F., "All the Good Things." Originally, "Good Night, Sister, Thank You For Teaching Me" in *Proteus,* Spring, 1991. Reprinted with permission as edited and published by *Reader's Digest* in October, 1991.

p. 448 Paul Logan, "Rowing the Bus." Copyright © 1997. Reprinted by permission of the author.

p. 455 Rick Bragg, "All She Has—$150,000—Is Going to a University" from *The New York Times,* August 13, 1995. Copyright © 1995 The New York Times. All rights reserved. Used by permission.

p. 462 Mee Her, "Bowling to Find a Lost Father" from *Passages: An Anthology of the Southeast Asian Refugee Experience,* compiled by Katsuyo Howard. California State University, Fresno (1990). Reprinted with permission.

p. 468 Rose Del Castillo Guilbault, "Hispanic USA: The Conveyor-Belt Ladies" in *San Francisco Chronicle,* "This World," April 15, 1990. Reprinted by permission of the San Francisco Chronicle, via Copyright Clearance Center.

p. 475 The "F Word" from *Funny in Farsi: A Memoir of Growing Up Iranian in America* by Firoozeh Dumas.

Chapter 36

Chapter 37

INDEX

DESIGN AND MAKE
CURTAINS

HEATHER LUKE

NEW
HOLLAND

For Peter

First published in the UK in 1995 by
New Holland (Publishers) Ltd
London • Cape Town • Sydney • Singapore

Reprinted 1995 (twice)

24 Nutford Place
London W1H 6DQ
UK

P.O. Box 1144
Cape Town 8000
South Africa

3/2 Aquatic Drive
Frenchs Forest, NSW 2086
Australia

ISBN 1 85368 526 7 (hbk)
ISBN 1 85368 527 5 (pbk)

Managing Editor: Gillian Haslam
Editor: Coral Walker
Designers: Kit Johnson and Roger Daniels
Photographer: David Johnson
Illustrations: Lizzie Sanders

Typeset by Ace Filmsetting Ltd, Frome, Somerset
Reproduction by Hirt and Carter (Pty) Ltd
Printed in Hong Kong by South China Printing Company Ltd

ACKNOWLEDGEMENTS

My thanks to Sarah Westcott, Julie Troop and Jackie Pullman for their expert making up,
to Michael and Don for their on-site help. David Johnson for the brilliant photographs,
Carol Hicks for her hand modelling and the team whose inspiration and magic have
made the raw materials into a book – Yvonne, Gillian and Coral at New Holland. Special
thanks to Mary Stewart Wilson, Elizabeth Peck, Heather Phelps Brown and Jano Clarke
for allowing me to show you some 'vignettes' of their lovely homes.

We would like to thank the following suppliers for their help:
Osborne and Little for the fabrics on pages 27, 34, 37, 42, 57, 61 top left, 68;
Pierre Frey for the fabrics on pages 53, 62, 72 and the photograph on page 55;
Designers Guild for the photograph on page 18; Mulberry page 51 bottom right;
Byron and Byron for fittings on pages 43 top left, 46 right, 60 bottom right, 76; Wemyss
Houles for fittings on pages 27, 53, 66, 74; Artisan for the fittings on pages 39, 43 top left
and top right, 54, 58, 62 top, 63; Merchants for the fittings on pages 27, 54.

CONTENTS

INTRODUCTION

**Layers of vibrant silk organza are ruched
and draped to create a dramatic and
exciting window treatment with a
minimum of sewing skills.**

Whether motivated by pleasure or necessity, most of us at some time in our lives choose to make our own curtains. While first-time projects are propelled by adventure, novelty and enthusiasm, later homemade curtains can all too often be relegated to secondary rooms as we turn instead to a professional to handle the more important ones. However, it is these areas of the home which can give the curtain-maker the greatest satisfaction. Indeed, making curtains can be dull, but adding the element of 'design' to the task of making, elevates the project from the mundane to something exciting, absorbing and fulfilling.

In this book, I have brought together a mixture of designs; both rooms and windows which I have been commissioned to decorate, and window treatments which I have conceived and made specially for this book. Your own situation might be perfect for one of these designs, but my aim is to encourage you to create your own treatments, details and finishes.

Any window treatments you choose should reflect the period of your house and the style of your furnishings. If you feel unsure about mixing colours, textures and patterns, stay with the colours with which you feel most comfortable, but approach them in a new way. Collect scraps of fabrics and coloured papers, study books and magazines so that you can begin to understand just how colours work together and how you could use different combinations, patterns and textures. For example, red and yellow used with orange could be quite ghastly or very exciting, depending entirely on the tone of each colour. (The tone explains the amount of white added to the pigment; so a colour is described as light, medium or dark. The hue explains the intensity, for example, the amount of green and blue which create the colour aquamarine.)

Single colour or monochromatic schemes are created using tones and hues of the same colour. A good example is to think of a summer garden and to examine the number of different greens that sit comfortably together. Relate this theory to any colour: mix mauves, coral, raspberry and strawberry ice cream colours together under the banner 'pink'. Two-colour or related colour schemes are based on colours which are compatible. For example, use blue and green as separate colours in varying tones mixed with hues of blue-green and green-blue. Most schemes will also employ a complementary or accent colour, that is, a colour from the opposite side of the spectrum. Add a touch of red to blue and green, for instance.

Neutral mixes can be mouth-wateringly successful if you remember there is a whole range beyond the usual white, cream and black. Try the earth colours of sand, butter, stone, and brick with brass, steel, limed wood, dark oak or palest ash.

Texture, too, plays a vital part in your choice of fabric and in the way that a particular colour will look in situ.

Use ideas from contemporary and historical fashion, but always avoid 'trends' which might date your curtains. Classic fabrics and colours, perfectly made into curtains with detailed finishes which complement the overall room design, will stand the test of time. Of course, you may wish to change your curtains often and I have suggested simple and inexpensive ideas to accomplish this.

BASIC TECHNIQUES

STITCHES

Always ensure you start and finish all stitching with a double stitch, never use a knot.

Hemming stitch

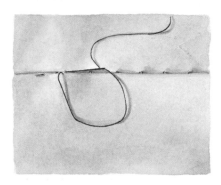

This stitch is used along the hems of lined curtains and the hems and sides of unlined curtains. Each stitch should be approximately 1.5 cm (⅝ in) in length. Slide the needle through the folded hem, pick up two threads of the main fabric, and push the needle directly back into the fold.

Herringbone stitch

Herringbone stitch is used over any raw edge which is then covered by another fabric. It is worked in the opposite direction to all other stitches. So right handers will work from left to right. Each whole stitch should be approximately 3 cm (1¼ in) for hems (a) and 8 cm (3¼ in) for side turnings (b). Stitch into the hem, from right to left, approximately 1.5 cm (⅝ in) to the right make a

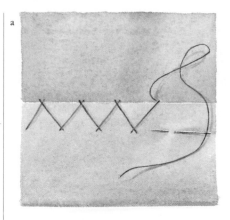

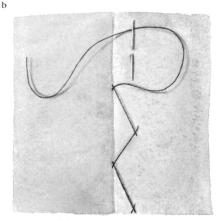

stitch into the curtain picking up two threads. Pull through and stitch 1.5 cm (⅝ in) to the right, making a stitch into the hem.

Ladder stitch

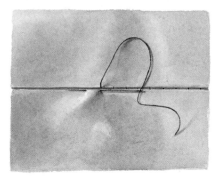

Ladder stitch is used to join two folded edges invisibly together. Slide the needle along the fold 5 mm (¼ in) and straight into the fold opposite. Slide along for 5 mm (¼ in) and back into the first fold, again directly opposite.

Long stitch

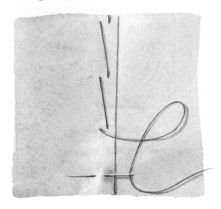

Long stitch is the most effective stitch to hold the side turnings of interlined curtains as it holds the interlining tight to the main fabric. Make a horizontal stitch approximately 1 cm (⅜ in) across. Bring the thread down diagonally by about 4 cm (1½ in) and repeat.

Slip stitch

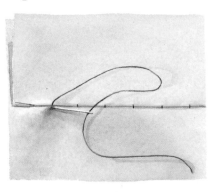

This stitch is used to sew linings on to curtains. Always use a colour thread which matches the main fabric. Make each stitch approximately 1.5 cm (⅝ in). Slide the needle through the main fabric and pick up two threads of the lining. Push the needle back into the main fabric exactly opposite and slide through a further 1.5 cm (⅝ in).

Lock stitch

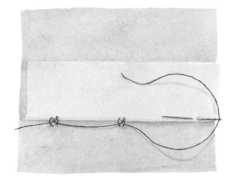

This stitch holds linings, interlinings and fabrics together, preventing them from separating, but still allowing some degree of necessary movement. Always use thread that blends with the background of the curtain fabric and the lining colour when stitching lining to interlining. Fold back the lining, secure the thread to the lining and make a small stitch in the main fabric just below. Make a large loop approximately 10 cm (4 in) long (slightly shorter for small items, like pelmets) and make a small stitch in the lining inside this loop. Stitch into the main fabric. Do not pull the stitch too tightly, but allow it to remain slightly loose.

Buttonhole stitch

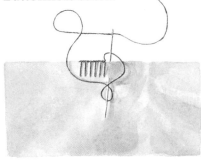

Used of course for buttonholes, but also wherever a raw edge needs to be strengthened or neatened. Work from left to right

with the raw edge uppermost. Push the needle from the back to the front, approximately 3 mm (⅛ in) below the edge. Twist the thread around the needle and pull the needle through, carefully tightening the thread so that it knots right on the edge of the fabric to form a ridge.

Blanket stitch

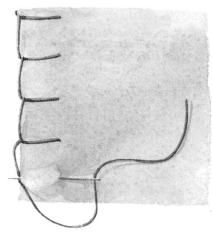

Originally used to neaten the raw edges of woollen blankets, its use is now mainly decorative. It is most comfortable worked from the side with the edge towards you. Push the needle from the front to the back, about 6 mm (¼ in) from the edge (this measurement will vary with large or small items). Hold the thread from the last stitch under the needle and pull up to make a loop on the edge.

PINNING

When pinning two layers of fabric together or piping on to fabric, always use horizontal and vertical pins to keep the fabric in place from both directions. The horizontal pins need to be removed just before the machine foot reaches them and the vertical ones – or cross pins – can remain

in place, so the fabrics are held together the whole time.

SEAMS

Flat seam

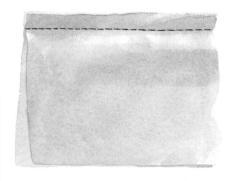

The most common and straightforward seam for normal use. With right sides together, pin 1.5–2 cm (⅝–¾ in) in from the edge at 10 cm (4 in) intervals. Pin cross pins halfway between each seam pin. These cross pins will remain in place while you are stitching to prevent the fabrics slipping. Once machine-stitched, open the seam flat and press from the back. Press from the front. Now press from the back, under each flap, to remove the pressed ridge line.

French seam

Use for sheers and unlined curtains or any occasion when the seam might be visible.

Pin the fabrics together with the wrong sides facing. Stitch 5 mm (¼ in) from the raw edges. Trim and flip the fabric over, bringing the right sides together. Pin again, 1 cm (⅜ in) from the stitched edge and stitch along this line to enclose the raw edges. Press from the right side, always pressing the seam in one direction only.

Flat fell seam

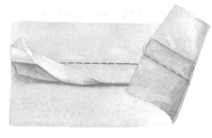

Use for neatening seams of heavier weight fabrics. Pin the fabrics together with the right sides facing and stitch 1.5–3 cm (⅝–1¼ in) from the raw edges. Trim one seam to just under half. Fold the other over to enclose the raw edge. Press down. Stitch close to the fold line.

MITRED CORNERS

When sides and hems are equal

1. Press the side seam over and the hem up. Position a pin through the point of the corner.

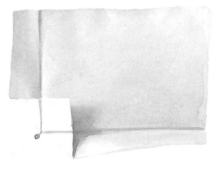

2. Open out the folds and turn in the corner at a 45° angle, with the pin at the centre of the foldline.

3. Fold the hem up and the sides in again along the original fold lines. Keep the pin on the point and make sure the fabric is firmly tucked into the folded lines.

When sides and hems are unequal

Follow step 1 as above, but when you reach step 2, the corner will not be folded to a 45° angle.

Instead, the corner of the fold will need to be angled away, towards the hem, leaving a longer fold on the side turnings so that the raw edges meet when the mitred corner is finished.

MAKING TIES

Ties are both useful and decorative and are used extensively throughout soft furnishings. For curtains, they are used primarily to tie a heading to a ring or pole. They are also used for tying cushion sides, seat pads and fastening loose covers.

Folded ties

Cut a strip of fabric four times the width of your finished tie and 3 cm (1¼ in) longer.

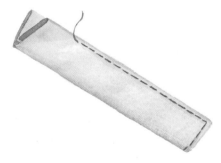

Press one short end under by 1 cm (⅜ in). Press in half lengthwise, fold each side to the middle, press, fold and stitch close to the folded edges.

Rouleau ties

Cut a strip of fabric four times the width of your finished tie and 3 cm (1¼ in) longer. Fold in half lengthwise, right sides together, enclosing a piece of cord which is longer than the strip of fabric. Stitch along the short side to secure the cord firmly. If the rouleau is quite wide, knot the cord as well. Stitch along the

length, 2 mm (⅛ in) towards the raw edge from the centre.

Trim the fabric across the corner, pull the cord through, at the same time turning the fabric right side out. Cut off the cord at the end. Press the raw edge under and slipstitch with small stitches.

PIPING

If piping is to be used in straight lines then it will be easier to cut it straight. If it is to be bent around corners, then it should be cut on the cross. For 4 mm (⅛ in) piping cord cut 4 cm (1½ in) wide strips. All joins should be made on the cross to minimise bulk when the fabric is folded.

To cut on the straight

Cut lengths as long as possible. Hold two strips, butting the ends together as if making a continuous length. Trim away both corners at a 45° angle. Hold together and flip the top one over. Stitch where the two pieces cross.

To cut on the cross

With the fabric flat on the table fold one bottom corner as if making a 30 cm (12 in) square. Cut along the fold line. Mark pencil lines from this cut edge at

4 cm (1½ in) intervals, and cut along these lines. Hold two pieces butting the ends together as if making a continuous strip. Flip the top one over and stitch together where the two fabrics cross.

Making up and pinning on

Press seams flat and cut away excess corners. Fold in half along the length and insert the piping cord. Machine stitch to encase, approximately 2 mm (⅛ in) from the cord. Keep the fabric folded exactly in half.

Always pin piping so that the raw edges of the piping line up with those of the main fabric.

To bend piping around curves, snip into the stitching line for the piping to lie flat. For a right angle, stop pinning 1.5 cm (⅝ in) from the corner, snip the piping right to the stitching line, fold the piping to 90° and start pinning 1.5 cm (⅝ in) on the adjacent side.

Joining

To join piping, overlap by approximately 6 cm (2¼ in). Unpick the casing on one side and cut away the cord so that the two ends butt up. Fold the piping fabric across at a 45° angle and cut along this fold. Fold under 1 cm (⅜ in) and pin securely before stitching.

BINDING

Binding one edge

1. Cut the binding strips to the width required (I use 1.5 cm (⅝ in) as an average.) Join the strips – always on the cross – to make the required length.
2. Pin the binding to the fabric, right sides together and stitch 1.4 cm (slightly less than ⅝ in) from the raw edges.

3. Neaten the raw edges to 1.4 cm (slightly less than ⅝ in). Press from the front, pressing the binding away from the main fabric. Fold the binding to the back, measuring the edge to 1.5 cm (⅝ in), keeping the fabric tucked firmly into the fold and pin at 8 cm (3¼ in) intervals. Turn to the back and herringbone the edge of the binding to the main fabric.

Binding a corner

Stop pinning short of the corner by the width of the finished binding. Fold binding back on itself to make a sharp angle and pin across this fold line. Pin on the adjacent side, the same distance from the edge. Stitch binding on, stopping at the pin and secure. Begin stitching again at the same point on the adjacent side. Press to mitre. Fold fabric to the back, mitring in the opposite direction.

UNUSUAL WINDOWS

Not all windows are neat-and-tidy rectangles or squares, set into a vertical wall. Irregular windows always tax the designer's imagination, how to dress them without spoiling the shape, where and how to hang the fittings. And how do you tackle windows set into sloping eaves? Try some of these ideas if you have a less than ordinary window shape.

Simple wooden buttons (right) do not take away from the window shape and could be painted to match the wall exactly. The voile can be hung to one side or right across with little effort.

I originally devised the method of 'curtaining' (far right) to cover hexagonal windows in an attic guest bedroom in Holland and have used this idea many times since. I think it is the perfect

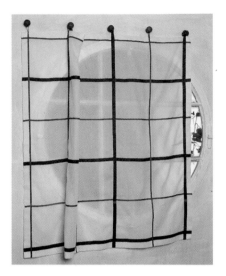

DESIGN AND MAKE CURTAINS

solution for almost any unusual window shape and for windows which need only little or occasional covering. The line of the frame is completely un-disturbed, the cover could be left either attached to the lower hooks or folded away when not in use.

Traditional curtains would have taken too much light from my bathroom (below left), so I had a swing metal frame made which sits back against the wall in the daytime and closes over each window at night.

Sloping windows are a recurrent problem with attic conversions. We chose primary colours to decorate this teenage girls' bedroom (right) and painted the poles to match the beds. Blue checked gingham tied back with unfinished strips of fabric cut on the cross provided just the right crisp, but informal, foil to the busy and colourful wallpaper.

A first-floor bedroom in a barn conversion left me with these problem windows (right). My brief was to create a romantic, feminine room from a vast space, so we first covered the walls in a fabric reminiscent of a cottage garden, specially printed for us in France, and then canopied the bed in silk and lace. I designed overlong silk curtains with bunched headings tied back to frame the wonderful woodland outlook. Sash ties with bows and lace under-curtains add the necessary feminine touches and reflect the bed canopy. A roller blind covered to match is discreetly hidden behind the heading during the day and is quick to pull down at night to keep out the dark and cold.

CURTAIN FITTINGS

CURTAIN TRACKS

For most uses, metal tracks with plastic runners and an enclosed pull-cording system are the best. These tracks are available in several different qualities to suit the weight and length of your curtains and are easily adaptable to 'top fit' on to a pelmet board or into the recess, or to 'face fit' to the wall, to a batten or directly on to the window frame. They are also available in telescopic lengths to suit a range of window sizes. You can also buy small tracks specifically for sheer curtains which often need to be fitted invisibly behind a pole or into a space behind the main curtains.

Cording is essential to protect interlined and long curtains. Attach cord weights which are heavy enough to keep the cords taut, and fit S clips to prevent them twisting. You might prefer to have a pulley system fitted which will keep the cords running in a continuous loop.

Side fittings, which hold the track to the wall, are available in several different sizes so that the track can be fitted either very close to the wall or some distance out. This facility allows the curtains to hang straight over a radiator or deep sill.

TRACK COVERS

Tracks are best unseen, so make a track cover to disguise the fittings. Cover it in the same fabric as the curtains or paint it to blend in with the wall. Make the top with wood and the front with plywood. The brackets will need to be housed into the wood to allow the fabric cover to fit neatly.

Cover the top, front and inside of the board with interlining and then the whole item with fabric. Starting at the back, work across the top, down the front and

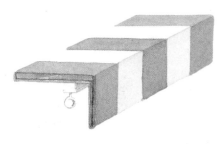

inside. Glue only in three places – at the back on the topside and the underside, and inside where the 6 mm (¼ in) front joins the board. Fit to the wall and camouflage the centre bracket and any side brackets with wallpaper or paint.

PELMET BOARDS

Pelmet boards need to suit the quality and weight of the curtaining and pelmets. Always add sides and fronts to the pelmet board to keep the pelmets from brushing against the curtains and to prevent the pelmet tipping backwards. Use wood for the top and 6 mm (¼ in) plywood for the front, with substantial brackets to hold the weight.

Paint the board to match the

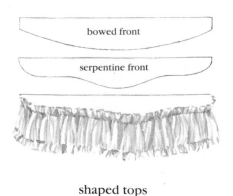

bowed front

serpentine front

shaped tops

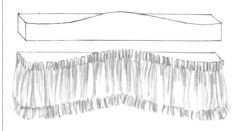

shaped fronts

window frame or cover the whole board with fabric to match the curtains. Ensure the front of the track is fitted approximately 50 mm (2 in) from the front of the board so that the heading can draw freely but without leaving a large gap. For a shaped board, choose a track which will bend to follow the front line.

CURTAIN POLES

There are so many different types of pole and finial style available in the shops that you will be spoilt for choice.

Choose poles which can be fitted as closely to the wall as possible with brackets which have fixings above and below the pole, otherwise heavy curtains could pull the fitting away from the wall. The end brackets should be positioned so that there is approximately 3 cm (1¼ in) from the fitting to the end of the pole, just enough space for one curtain ring. The curtain will then pull right to the end of the pole.

MEASURING AND PLANNING

The most successful window treatments have been carefully considered and designed before the fabric has even been purchased. Once you have taken accurate window measurements (see right) round them up or down to the nearest 5 mm (¼ in) and transfer them to graph paper. If you have neither scale rulers nor graph paper, work with a very simple scale, say, 1 cm = 10 cm or 1 in = 10 in, and a normal ruler.

Mark the room height, the position of the window and the space around the window. If there is a bay, beam or other obstacle, mark this also. Please don't be put off if you have no drawing experience. The examples here are deliberately simple to give you the confidence to try.

You will need tracing paper to place over your window plan and paper clips to hold them together. Experiment by drawing different curtains and fitting positions: long, short, with or without pelmets, formal or gathered headings, etc. You will soon begin to formulate suitable ideas.

Once you have a fairly definite concept, draw the window again, tidying up the measurements and draw the design as accurately as you can. Try to mark exactly where the fittings should be – how far to the side of the window and how far above. If you want to make a pelmet, mark the top,

sides and centre and shape the edge roughly.

Translate your ideas to the window by marking the walls around with a soft pencil and stand back to look. You will need to make an accurate template for a pelmet (see page 74). Most fittings can be cut to size, so ask someone to hold them in place for you to see what they will look like before they are finally fitted.

TAKING ACCURATE MEASUREMENTS

Measure the width and height at least three times so that you are aware if the window is not 'square' and if the floor or ceiling slopes.

Measurements to take

● From the top of the frame or reveal to the floor.
● From the ceiling (or under the cornice) to the top of the window.
● From the ceiling to the floor.
● The window width inside – noting any possible problems, eg, telephone sockets, etc.
● The window width outside.
● Measure the distance available all around the window for the curtain stack-back, avoiding pictures, bookcases, etc.

Stand back and check for any ugly fitments which might need to be covered. Measure and note unsightly double-glazing fittings, odd bits of wood, etc. Decide whether you need blinds and/or pelmets or fixed curtain headings. Plan how – and exactly where – they should be positioned. If a pelmet is to be used, make a template and tape it into position to check how it will look.

For curtains to hang outside reveal

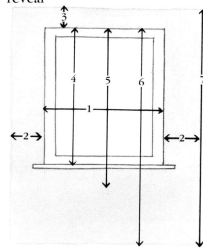

1 width of window
2 width of stack-back
3 top of architrave to ceiling
4 top of architrave to sill
5 top of architrave to below sill
6 top of architrave to floor
7 ceiling to floor

For curtains to hang inside reveal

1 width inside reveal
2 length from top of window to sill
3 depth of reveal

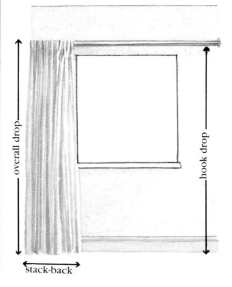

ESTIMATING FOR CURTAINS

HEADING REQUIREMENTS

Heading Type	Fullness Required
Gathered headings	
Tape	1.75 – 2.25
Ties	1.25 – 2.50
Handsewn	2.50 – 3.00
Bunched	2.25 – 2.50
Smocked	2.50 – 3.50
Pencil pleated	2.50 – 2.75
Hand Pleated	
Triple (French)	2.25 – 2.75
Goblets	2.25 – 2.50
Folded	
Pocket	2.00 – 3.00
Voiles	2.50 – 3.00

Most curtains look best with at least double fullness, but this may be reduced for short curtains which do not need the weight to hang well. If stack-back space is restricted, pleated headings will hold the curtain back into the smallest space. Allow only 1¼ to 1½ times fullness for a heavy fabric or one with a dominant design which needs to be seen.

HEADING ALLOWANCES

Bunched

Allow enough for a 10–12 cm (4–4¾ in) 'bunch' depending on the thickness of the fabric. Allow the hook drop plus 25–50 cm (10–20 in).

Frilled

Allow the frill above the hook drop and back to fit under the tape.

Allow the hook drop plus 12 cm (4½ in) for a 6 cm (2¼ in) frill, 16 cm (6½ in) for an 8 cm (3¼ in) frill, etc.

Pencil pleated

Allow the depth of the pleats. Allow the overall drop plus 6–8 cm (2¼–3¼ in).

Pocket headings

For voiles, allow 2 cm (¾ in) for the pocket and 2 cm (¾ in) above. Allow the overall drop plus 8 cm (3¼ in).

Bound headings

No allowance needed. Overall drop, no extra.

Smocked

Allow the depth of the smocking pattern. Allow the overall drop plus the depth of the smocking pattern.

Goblet/triple pleats

Allow double the depth of the pleat. Allow the overall drop plus 20 cm (8 in) for a 10 cm (4 in) pleat. Allow the overall drop plus 30 cm (12 in) for a 15 cm (6 in) pleat.

HEM ALLOWANCES

Unlined curtains	16 cm (6¼ in)
Lined curtains	16 cm (6¼ in)
Lined, bound hems, plain lining	8 cm (3¼ in)
Lined, bound hems, contrast lining	No extra fabric
Interlined curtains	12 cm (4¾ in)
Voile curtains	8–12 cm (3¼–4¾ in)

ESTIMATING FOR FABRIC

The quantity of fabric needed for each window is relative to the style of curtaining which you wish to make. The three factors are: the headings style, the fullness, and the curtain length. You will have already chosen your window treatment style following the guidelines on page 12 and from this you will know the fittings width and the overall drop of the curtains. The hook drop is the measurement from the top of the curtain hook and the bottom of the curtain fitting, to the hemline. The overall drop is from the top of the heading to the hemline. You will need to estimate these measurements from your plan, until the fittings are in position. The overall drop is from the top of the heading to the hemline.

Make allowances for any changes – for instance, if cupboards are to be fitted close to the window, or a possible change of flooring. Use the following as a guide.

EACH LENGTH

1. Find the overall drop

ceiling to floorboards	270 cm (106 in)
less allowance for carpet of 2 cm (¾ in)	268 cm (105¼ in)
less allowance for pelmet board of 2 cm (¾ in)	266 cm (104½ in)
plus overlong hem allowance of 5 cm (2 in)	271 cm (106½ in)

2. Add the hem and heading allowances

hem	12 cm (4¾ in)
heading	20 cm (8 in)
each cut length	303 cm (119 in)

3. Adjust for pattern repeat, if necessary

If the pattern repeat is 65 cm (25½ in)

303 cm ÷ 65 cm = 4.66
(119 in ÷ 25½ in = 4.66)
round up to 5.

Allow 5 repeats for each cut as each cut length must include complete pattern repeats.

5 × 65 cm = 325 cm
(5 × 25½ in = 127½ in)
Each cut length will need to be 325 cm (127½ in).

Note the fabric 'wastage': 325 cm (127½ in) is needed for each cut, yet only 303 cm (119 in) is actually needed for the curtain, so five pieces of 22 cm (8½ in) will be left.

At this point you can decide how best to use this spare fabric. You might decide to alter the headings, for example to have a frilled and bound heading rather than bound only, or to increase the heading fullness from frilled to bunched. Or this spare could be allocated for tiebacks, pelmets, etc, depending on the amount available.

Fabric pelmets can be very expensive, but can often be cut from the same piece of fabric, with each curtain cut. Another advantage is that the pattern is already matched.

Planning the fabric in this way means that you will never have wasted pieces, and will be aware when cutting of the importance of using the fabric wisely.

If the fabric you have chosen is expensive and the estimated cuts are just over a whole repeat (i.e. 4.1 repeats) you might decide to shorten the hem or heading allowance a little. Just enough to save costs without damaging the hanging quality.

Always allow an extra pattern repeat to the total amount of fabric estimated, to allow you to start your hemline in the position on the pattern which you choose.

HOW MANY WIDTHS

1. Select your fitting and divide the length in half for two curtains

180 cm ÷ 2 = 90 cm
(70 in ÷ 2 = 35 in)

2. Add the side return (10 cm/4 in) and the centre overlap (10 cm/4 in)

90 cm + 10 cm + 10 cm = 110 cm
(35 in + 4 in + 4 in = 43 in)

3. Multiply by the fullness needed for your heading

110 cm × 2.5 = 275 cm
(43 in × 2.5 = 107½ in, say 108 in)

4. Divide by the width of your fabric

275 cm ÷ 135 cm = 2.04
(108 in ÷ 54 in = 2)
Therefore, use two cuts per curtain

5. Multiply the number of widths by the cut lengths

Plain fabric
303 cm × 4 = 12.12 metres
(119 in × 4 = 13¼ yd)
You will need 12.12 m (13¼ yd)

Patterned fabric
325 cm × 4 = 13 metres
+ 65 cm for extra repeat = 13.65 metres
(127½ in × 4 = 14 yd
+ 25½ in = 14¾ yd)
You will need 13.65 m (14¾ yd)

MAKING TEMPLATES

Make accurate templates of anything which might prevent drapes hanging well. Cornices will usually be above the curtaining, but sometimes the side of the pelmet will need to return on to the cornice, there might be a plate rack or picture rail or pipes obstructing the fall of the curtains.

Use brown paper and a pencil to draw around the obstruction, if possible. If not, tear the paper roughly and cut in around it accurately with a sharp knife.

HAND-PLEATED HEADINGS

(Aim for pleats of 15 cm (6 in) and gaps between pleats of 12 cm (4½ in).

For a fitting size of 195 cm (76½ in) each curtain will be
97.5 cm + 10 cm + 10 cm = 117.5 cm
(38¼ in + 4 in + 4 in = 46¼ in)

1. Work out the number of pleats and gaps

97.5 cm ÷ 12 cm = 8.13
(38¼ in ÷ 4½ in = 8½),
say 8 gaps and therefore 9 pleats

2. Work out the fabric needed for the pleats

9 × 15 cm = 135 cm
(9 × 6 in = 54 in)

3. Add this plus side turnings to the curtain width

117.5 cm + 135 cm + 12 cm = 264.5 cm
(46¼ in + 54 in + 4½ in = 104¾ in)

4. Divide this by the fabric width

265 cm ÷ 135 cm = 1.96
(104¾ in ÷ 54 in = 1.92)

So, round up to allow two widths of fabric for each curtain.

If this calculation had worked out so that there was spare fabric in the widths, you could increase the size of the pleats to accommodate, or to cut away the excess. Conversely, if the fabric requirement calculated that you would only just need to cut into a full width, you could use slightly less fabric in each pleat.

If your room has two or more windows which vary in width, all curtains will need to have exactly the same size pleats and distance between pleats. In this case the widths will need to be cut down to exact measurements for each curtain.

PREPARATION

This is the key to successful sewing. Prepare well, and the work should go smoothly, with few errors. Look at various factors before you begin: where you are going to work, what you plan to work on, the fabric you plan to use, linings and interlinings. Here are some guidelines to bear in mind before you begin sewing.

THE WORKTABLE

If possible, you should stake your claim on one room which can be put aside for your own use, even if it is only while you are making your curtains.

A dining room or guest bedroom can be made into a temporary workroom with little effort. A worktable which is at least 2.5 × 1.2 m (8 × 4 ft) and preferably 3 × 1.5 m (10 × 5 ft) will make the whole job so much easier. You can buy a sheet of board in either of these sizes. Cover your dining table with thick felt so that the board can be rested safely on top.

Alternatively, make some sturdy legs which can be bracketed on to the underside of the board. This quickly made table can then be fitted temporarily over a guest bed. The space below can be used to store all your fabrics, linings and interlinings and the top will be wide enough for you to work on a whole width of fabric at a time. Pure luxury compared to hands and knees on the floor!

The height of the worktable should be whatever is comfortable for you; I use a table that is 95 cm (38 in) high.

Cover the top with heavy interlining and then a layer of lining. Staple these to the underside; pulling the fabrics very taut as you go. You will now have a soft surface which is ideal for pinning and pressing.

CUTTING OUT

Before you begin to cut the fabric, check it thoroughly for flaws. Try to cut around simple line flaws or incorporate them into headings and hems. If the fabric is badly flawed, return it.

Measure out each length and mark with pins to make sure that you have the correct amount of fabric. Always double check your measurements before cutting.

Fabric should ideally be cut along the grain and to pattern, but sometimes the printing method allows the pattern to move off grain. Make sure that the leading edges of all pairs of curtains match exactly. If necessary, allow the pattern to run out slightly to either side – but a 2 cm (¾ in) run-off is the most you should tolerate. Do not be tempted to follow the pattern and cut off the grain, as the curtain edges will not hang straight. As you cut each piece, mark the right sides and the direction of a plain fabric just in case there is a weave variation which is not noticeable until the curtains have been made up and hung.

Try not to fold your lengths at all, but if you do need to fold them, make sure it is always lengthwise. We have a series of poles fitted to the wall of the workroom over which each length is hung until it is ready for use. You might have a bannister rail which could serve the same purpose.

Join the widths and half widths as planned, using flat seams for all lined and interlined curtains (see page 7), French seams for lightweight unlined curtains (page 8), and flat fell seams for heavy unlined curtains (page 8).

PATTERN MATCHING

It is well worth spending a little time to make sure that all fabric patterns are matched correctly at the seam on each width. Curtains which are otherwise well made can easily be let down by cutting corners at this stage.

1. Place one of the lengths of fabric right side up on the worktable with the selvedge facing you. Place the next length over the first, right side down. Fold over the selvedge to reveal roughly 5 mm (¼ in) of pattern and press lightly.

2. Match the pattern to the piece underneath, and pin through the fold line along the whole length. You may need to ease one of the sides at times – using more pins will help. Go back and place cross pins between each pin. Machine or hand stitch along the fold line, removing the straight pins and stitching over the cross pins.

3. Press the seam from the wrong side and then again from the front. Use a hot iron and press quickly. Turn the fabric over again to the back and press under the seam to remove the pressed ridges. If the background fabric is dark or you are using a woven fabric, snip into the selvedges at

5 cm (2 in) intervals. If the background fabric is light, trim the selvedges back to 1.5 cm (⅝ in), removing any printed writing.

FABRIC WITH BORDERS

Some fabrics have printed or woven borders on one or both sides, so before cutting you need to determine where and how to use them. When the border is on both sides of the fabric, decide whether the border should appear on the leading and outside edges only, or whether one border should appear at each seam, in which case the extra border should be removed as the widths are joined.

I often prefer to remove the centre borders completely and use the extra lengths to allow the border to continue along the hem and 'frame' the curtain.

Where there is a border on one side of the fabric only, it should appear on the leading edge of each curtain. You will need to trim the border from the whole length and stitch it back on to each leading edge. Do check whether the border has a directional pattern and make sure that you pin it back on accordingly.

PREPARING LININGS

Cut out your lining fabric as closely to the grain as possible. Because this is often hard to see, allow about 5 cm (2 in) extra for each cut length.

Join lining widths with flat seams. If your curtains have half widths, it is easier to join all whole widths first and then cut the centre width through the middle. This avoids the possibility

of making up two left or right linings rather than a pair. Press all seams to lay open.

To make up the hems, place one lining on to the worktable, wrong side facing up, with one selvedge exactly along the edge of the table. It is unlikely that the cut line will be exactly straight, so turn up approximately 12 cm (4½ in) along the lower edge and press in place. Keep this folded line parallel to the bottom of the table. Trim the hem to 10 cm (4 in) from the fold and then fold it in half to make a 5 cm (2 in) double hem. Pin and machine stitch close to the fold line or slipstitch by hand.

INTERLININGS

It is important that interlining is cut out following the grain. If it is not stitched into the curtain exactly square, after a period of time it will fall down into the hemline. Use the grain line at headings and hems to help you.

Join all widths with flat seams and trim them back to 2 cm (¾ in), snipping into the selvedge at 5 cm (2 in) intervals.

WEIGHTS

To ensure that curtains hang and drape well, you should insert weights into curtain hems at each seam and at each corner. Make a lining cover for each weight to prevent it rubbing and possibly discolouring the fabric. Very heavy curtains or sheer curtains should have a length of fabric-covered chain weight threaded into the hem instead. Chain weight is available in different weights to suit all purposes.

DRESSING CURTAINS

Hand-headed curtains need to be dressed as soon as they are hung so that the pleats are trained to fall evenly. You will need to leave the curtains tied back for at least 48 hours and possibly up to 96 hours. The waiting will be well rewarded as your curtains will always hang well.

Begin by drawing the curtains to the stack-back position. Make sure that the heading is in order, the pleats are forwards and the gaps are folded evenly between each pleat. If the curtain hangs under a track or pole, the gaps will fold behind, if in front, the gaps will fold to the front.

Stand at eye level with the headings and take each pleat, smoothing it down through the curtain as far as you can reach to form a fold. Now, standing on the floor or lower down the step ladder and starting at the leading edge, follow these pleats through to waist height. From the leading edge fold each pleat back on to the last. Tie a strip of fabric loosely around the curtain to hold the pleats in place.

Kneel on the floor and follow the folds through into the hem. Finger press firmly. If the curtains are overlong, keep the pleats together and bend the curtain to one side. Tie another strip of fabric around the curtain hems to hold the pleats in place, loosely enough not to mark the fabric, but tight enough so that they do not slip down.

Springy fabrics may need to be readjusted several times, but this will become easier as the pleats are trained.

UNLINED CURTAINS

Unlined curtains are the simplest form of window covering to make and, with careful preparation and well chosen fabric, your curtains can look as good as any more complicated design. For those new to curtain-making, this is the place to start. If you need to make something quickly or perhaps find yourself on a very tight budget, unlined curtains using inexpensive fabrics but with plenty of fullness will make effective and very rewarding window treatments. I often use unlined curtains as draw curtains for the summer, allowing the sunlight to filter through while the heavier winter curtains are draped up to the sides.

Use silks, muslins, calicoes, and experiment with ribbons, braids, cords, ties, buttons and motifs to produce your own personalised finish. Turn to pages 40 – 47 to see how very good sheers and layered curtains can look.

Change heavy winter curtains to simple unlined cotton for the summer months. Crisp blue and white edging defines these white curtains and coordinating tablecloth.

MAKING UP

1. Place the cut and joined fabric for one curtain on to the worktable, with the right side facing down, lining up the hem and one side with two edges of the table. Smooth the fabric out, sweeping the edge of a metre rule or yardstick across the table and press to remove any creases. Turn in the side edge by 6 cm (2¼ in) using a small measuring gauge to make sure that the turning is even. Press lightly. Fold in half to give a 3 cm (1⅛ in) double turning. Pin and press again. Turn up the hem by 10 cm (4 in). Press lightly, then fold in half to make a 5 cm (2 in) double hem. Pin and press.

2. For medium to heavyweight fabrics, mitre the corner as shown here and described more fully on page 8.

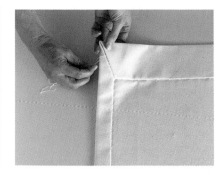

3. Stitch both the sides and the hem with neat slip stitches, 1.5–2 cm (⅝–¾ in) in length. Ladder stitch the corner, slipping in a fabric-covered weight.

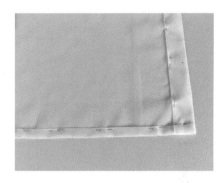

4. For sheer and lightweight fabrics, fold the sides and hems over so that the layers are exactly on top of each other, and slip stitch along the fold so that the stitches are almost invisible.

5. Measure from the hem to the top of the curtain to mark the hook drop of the finished curtain. If you do not yet have the exact measurements because the fittings are not in place, mark the estimated position. Measure at 30 cm (12 in) intervals and pin a line across the curtain. If you know the overall drop also mark this line with a row of pins.

6. Carefully move the curtain across the table and repeat with the other side.

7. Sheer, unlined curtains which will be used in doorways or open windows will need to be weighted along the hems to prevent them flapping about in any breeze. Insert a length of fabric-covered chain weight (see page 17) into the hem.

8. An attractive alternative to step 7 is to stitch several rows of decorative stitching to give the required weight and substance to the curtain hem.

LINED CURTAINS

The purpose of lining curtains is twofold – firstly, to protect the principal fabric from exposure to sunlight and/or the effects of condensation which will eventually cause fading and rotting, and secondly to add bulk.

Cotton sateen lining is available in three basic shades – ecru, cream and white, and in various qualities. A specialist furnishing fabric supplier will also be able to offer you coloured linings so that you can tone your lining with the main fabric. Lining fabric is relatively inexpensive and my advice is always to buy the best lining possible. If you look at several different qualities, you will immediately see the difference in the weight of yarn and quality of weave, and realise that saving costs on the lining fabric will be a false economy.

It is important that the lining you choose has been treated to withstand strong sunlight and dampness. However, while good curtain fabric will last for many years, linings should be replaced completely every 10–15 years. A window with a sunny aspect will need more linings and curtains than a north-facing window. Once a year, check the linings and replace the leading edge as soon as it starts to wear.

Lining curtains adds body as well as protecting the main fabric from the effects of strong sunlight or dampness. Over-sized gathered headings flop over informally.

DESIGN AND MAKE CURTAINS

MAKING UP

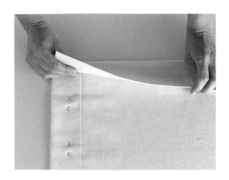

1. Place the fabric for one curtain on the worktable with the right side facing down, lining up the hem and one long side to two edges of the table. Smooth out the fabric and press to remove any creases. Turn in the side seams by 6 cm (2¼ in), using a small measuring gauge to make sure that the turning is even. Pin every 12–15 cm (4¾–6 in) and press. Turn up the hem by 16 cm (6½ in), checking that the pattern runs evenly across the width, and press lightly. Open out the fold and refold in half, to make an 8 cm (3¼ in) double hem. Pin and press.

2. Mitre the corners as shown here and described more fully on page 8. Make an angled mitre so that the hem and the side match along the diagonal.

3. Stitch the length of the side with herringbone stitches, approximately 5 cm (2 in) in length. Picking up only one thread at a time, slip stitch the hem, stitching a weight into each seam. Ladder stitch the mitre, slipping a weight into the corner.

4. Place the pre-prepared curtain lining (see page 17) on top of the curtain, wrong sides together, matching the seam lines and placing the top of the lining hem exactly on top of the curtain hem.

5. Turn back the lining and lock stitch to secure the lining twice across each width at equal distances and at all seams, using the same colour thread as the lining fabric. Reposition the lining and smooth out the creases.

6. Using scissors, score the lining along the folded edge of the curtain. Trim along this line. Turn the raw edge under leaving 3 cm (1¼ in) of curtain showing. Pin and stitch the edges of the curtain beginning 4 cm (1½ in) from the bottom corner and continuing until just below the heading.

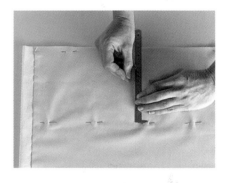

7. Measure from the hem to the top of the curtain and mark the hook drop of the finished curtain. If you cannot be exact because the fittings are not in place, mark the estimated position. Measure across the curtain at 30 cm (12 in) intervals and pin through both layers along the hook drop line. Mark the overall drop line with pins.

8. Fold the side to the middle and move the curtain across the table. Make up the other side in the same way.

INTERLINED CURTAINS

These curtains were made with unbleached artists' canvas, laundered first to take up the shrinkage and lined with a fine cotton pinstripe ticking. A mediumweight, cotton interlining was chosen to add enough body and weight to help hold back the leading edges and reveal the linings.

Apart from the practical advantages of offering additional insulation to your home – interlined curtains look and feel sumptuous and luxurious. These types of curtains always fall in generous folds and can be dressed to pleat back formally or to gather informally.

Light-flowing fabrics can be transformed into elegant drapes by first stitching the fabric to heavy interlining, allowing the body and weight of the interlining to hold the top fabric. Interlining linen or heavy cotton curtains for doorways and windows in country cottages and farmhouses will keep any draughts and cold from the room – much more effective and less expensive than double glazing or additional heating!

Interlining is available in several different weights, so you should choose the weight best suited to your needs. It is not necessary to put heavy interlining with heavy fabric and light with light – in fact, the opposite can transform a very lightweight fabric.

Always ask to test a length of interlining against your fabric. Hold fabric and interlining up together and see how the natural drape of the fabric is affected before you decide to buy.

Most interlinings are 90% cotton twill woven with approximately 10% of other fibres and brushed to encourage the fabric to hold heat. An interlining made wholly with manmade fibre is readily available, much less expensive and, although not as effective as the cotton interlining, is very light to work with, making stitching and handling easier.

MAKING UP

1. Place the fabric for one curtain on the worktable with the right side facing down, lining up the hem and one long side to two edges of the table. Smooth the fabric out, sweeping the edge of a metre rule or yardstick across the table. Clamp the fabric to the table at approximately 60 cm (24 in) intervals. Place the interlining on top, lining up the seams and hems and smooth out as before.

2. The interlining must now be locked to the main fabric at each seam and twice between each seam. Fold the interlining back on itself at the first seam and lock stitch all the way down using double thread. Stitch close to the hem but stop just short of the hook drop. Fold the interlining back flat, smooth out and then fold two thirds back again. Repeat the lock stitch for the whole length and again on the third of the width.

Your curtain is likely to be wider than your table; however, as interlined curtains should not be moved until they are stitched together, you must finish this part of the curtain before moving the other half on to the table.

3. Trim the interlining if necessary so that the sides of both the main fabric and the interlining are even. Remove the side clamps and turn back both fabric and interlining by 6 cm (2¼ in), using a small measuring gauge to make sure that the turning is even. With the tips of your fingers, check that the interlining is well tucked into the fold and a solid, firm edge is pinned in place. (A soft fabric might require the interlining to be locked to the main fabric along the folded edge. Use small stitches and make sure that they do not pull on the fabric at all.)

Trim the interlining along the hem if necessary and fold it up by 12 cm (4¾ in). Press lightly and pin securely.

4. Mitre the bottom corner following the instructions on page 8. Make a long mitre so that the 12 cm (4¾ in) hem and the 6 cm (2¼ in) side match along the diagonal. If you are using very heavy interlining with heavy fabric you might need to cut away the bulk of the interlining. Open out the mitre and trim along the folded diagonal line.

5. Stitch along the length of the side with long stitches approximately 5 cm (2 in) in length as shown on page 6 and along the hem with 2 cm (¾ in) herringbone stitches. Catch both layers of interlining but do not go through to the front fabric. Insert a weight into the mitre opening and ladder stitch to close with small, neat stitches.

6. Clamp the curtain back on to the table. Place the lining over the interlining, matching up the seam lines and allowing the lining to overhang the hem by approximately 10 cm (4 in). Smooth out with the ruler and lock the lining to the interlining along the same lines that hold the interlining to the main fabric. Start at the hemline and finish just before the hook drop.

7. With the point of the scissors, score the lining along the folded edge and trim to this line. Fold under the raw edge, leaving 3 cm (1¼ in) of the curtain fabric showing. Pin to secure. Trim the hem of the lining so that it is exactly 10 cm (4 in) longer than the curtain. Pin the lower, raw edge to the hem fold and take up the excess fabric by finger pressing a tuck into the lining along the stitched hemline. Press this fold downwards and pin to hold it in place. Fold the raw edge of the lining under so that the fold is 4 cm (1½ in) from the hem. Pin. Slip stitch the sides and hem from the hook drop to the edge of the table.

8. At this stage, measure from the hem to the top of the curtain to mark the hook drop of the finished curtain. If you do not yet have the exact measurement because fittings are not in place, mark the estimated position. Measure across the curtain at 30 cm (12 in) intervals and pin through all three layers at the hook drop measurement, to secure. Pin two or three more times between each of these to make a definite line.

9. Remove the clamps and carefully lift the curtain along the table. You should ask for some help to do this, so that the fabrics are disturbed as little as possible.

Re-clamp the other side of the curtain to the table. Continue smoothing the interlining against the main fabric, folding it back and locking in as before. Mark the hook drop all along to line up with the other side.

10. Check the exact overall drop measurements and mark with pins accordingly. Fold the lining back on itself along the pinned line. Remove the pins and carefully cut away the interlining along this line. Pin again to secure. Herringbone stitch the interlining to the curtain. Fold the main fabric over with the lining and continue with your chosen heading.

OVERLONG CURTAINS

The choice of curtain hem length is a purely personal one, however I usually advise and make curtains just 2–3 cm (¾–1¼ in) longer than floor length so that the fabric just bumps the floor. The reasons for this are several. Firstly, curtain fabric can drop or pull back in the time between making up and hanging, thus making it very difficult for an amateur to gauge an exact length. Secondly, very few window tops are parallel to the floor and overlong curtains make this variation less obvious. Old houses will almost always have draughts from around the window frame and below the skirting boards, which overlong curtains take up. And last, but by no means least, I *like* the look of curtains which just fall to the floor.

HEADINGS

A little spare fabric has been used to make alternately coloured tabs which, together with self-covered buttons, provide a striking and contemporary heading. Make your own tabbed or tied heading by following the step-by-step instructions on page 34.

Headings need to be both practical and decorative. Usually the functional qualities must override the decorative, but there are occasions when the window treatment will be for ornament only and then headings can be embellished with cords and tassels, rosettes and fringes with scant regard to function.

Hand-pleated headings are neat and tidy, suitable for formal window treatments and where the curtains need to pull back into a limited space. Gathered headings suit informal curtaining, as pleats may be pulled up at random and headings tied and buttoned to poles and rings. Hand gathered pleats are formal, especially if hand stitched or smocked. Rich and voluptuous headings can be created with excess fabric – turn into overlong frills flopping to the front of the curtain or scrunch randomly along the curtain top.

Tabbed headings are smart alternatives to any pleating or gathering and give a lovely decorative finish. Unfortunately, the use of these headings is restricted to windows where the curtain pole is easily reached as the headings have to be eased back by hand.

Headings can be finished with an almost infinite variety of detail. Buttons, ribbons, beads and sequins, braided edges, hand stitching and embroidery, contrast fabrics for double and triple frills, binding, backings and edgings, scallops and drapes – any or all to suit your window treatment.

The type of heading you use will depend on a number of factors: the size of the window, the style of the window treatment, whether the curtains need to be well stacked back or can be more decorative than practical.

HAND-PLEATED HEADINGS

Hand pleating encourages curtain headings to pull back evenly, providing a neat finish to the top of any curtains. Stiff heading buckram is used to support hand-pleated headings so that both the pleats and the gaps between keep their shape. Available in a variety of widths, the most useful are 10 cm and 15 cm (4 in and 6 in), both of which can be cut down if necessary. You should be able to buy heading buckram from a furnishing fabric specialist and some department stores. I prefer to stitch the buckram in place as the fusible type does not always stick evenly.

Goblet pleats make a less formal heading than French pleats, but take up more track space when curtains are pulled back.

MAKING UP

1. The hook drop and the overall drop will be the same for these headings. Measure double the depth of the buckram and trim the fabric evenly to this measurement. Fold the fabric over along the overall drop line and press lightly. Lay the fabric flat again, fold back the lining, and trim away the interlining along the pressed line. Herringbone stitch to hold the interlining in place.

2. Place the buckram on the fabric against the cut edge of the interlining and herringbone stitch.

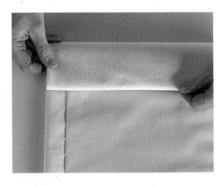

3. Fold the lining back. Fold the fabric over the bottom edge of the buckram and then fold again. Pin along and slip stitch the ends.

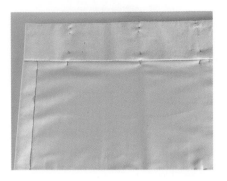

4. To position the heading pleats and gaps needed, refer to your plan (see pages 13–15). Measure the flat width of the curtain and deduct the finished width including the overlap and return. Divide the difference between the number of gaps. Keeping the pleat measurement as estimated, mark the overlap, the pleats, gaps, and return, across the width.

5. Fold and pin the pleats firmly in position at the top and bottom of the buckram. Machine down the length of each pleat and fasten securely. Remove all pins. Turn to the front and make pleats.

HAND HEADINGS

1. Triple pleats or French pleats are ideal for a formal finish, under pelmets and where curtains need to be pulled back into a limited space. Finish the pleat with a button covered in a contrast-coloured fabric or bind the top edge for smart detail.

Open out the pleat, place three fingers inside and flatten. Then lift the pleat and pinch in the centre fold. Push down to make three equal pleats. 1 cm (⅜ in) below the base of the pleat, stitch through the fabric to hold the pleat firmly in place. At the top of the pleat, stitch each piece in position so that it holds its shape.

Stitch across each of the three pleats and through the pleats just above the buckram.

2. Inverted pleats: Use for a contemporary finish and where the headings need to be clean-lined.

Stitch the pleats to fold to the inside of the curtain rather than the outside. Open up each one and press flat. Stitch across the top and down each side.

If stack-back space is limited, make double or triple pleats.

3. Goblet pleats: Taking up more space than triple pleats, goblets are often used for less formal curtains or when curtain headings are fixed. Decorate with knotted rope or gilded cord, or finish the goblet with large buttons, tassels or rosettes.

Open the pleat out fully and run a gathering thread around the base, 1 cm (⅜ in) below the buckram. Cut a rectangle of interlining, roll it up and stuff it into the goblet to give it a well-rounded shape. Cut the other pieces exactly the same size so that all pleats will be equal.

4. Cartridge pleats: Useful as an 'invisible' heading for fabric with a strong pattern or elegant simplicity which is better not disturbed by a more prominent heading. Use small pleats.

Open the pleats out fully and stuff with rolled up interlining to give a solid round shape. Make sure that the interlining for each pleat is cut and rolled equally.

1

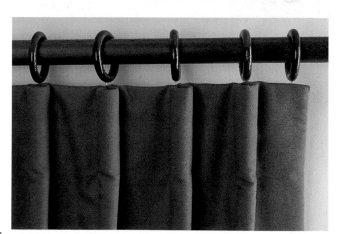

3

2

4

GATHERED HEADINGS

Gathered headings may be a simple frill at the top of the curtain, created by stitching on standard hook tape and pulling the cords, or they may be finished with a variety of details. A 6–8 cm (2¼–3¼ in) frill size is ideal with a pole fitting, as it will cover the bottom of the ring but only part of the pole. Adjust as necessary to suit the curtain fitting which you have chosen.

MAKING UP

For a 6 cm (2¼ in) frill you should have allowed 12 cm (4¾ in) plus 1.5 cm (⅝ in) to go under the tape. Cut away all excess fabric.

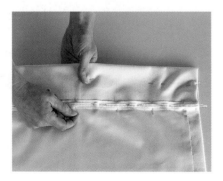

1. If your curtain is interlined, fold the lining back and trim away the interlining at the overall drop line. Fold fabric and lining over, pin on the tape and stitch close to the outer edges, always stitching with the heading towards the body of the machine. Pull the heading up to the required size and gather evenly across the width.

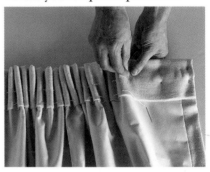

2. Make a hook band. Cut a piece of heading tape or heading buckram the width of the tape and of length equal to the finished heading size. Cut a strip of fabric three times this width and 4 cm (1½ in) longer. Fold the fabric over the band, trimming and herringboning the raw edge. Position hooks at the leading edge, at the return and at 11–13 cm (4¼–5 in) intervals across the width. Stitch securely to the back of the band to cover the tape.

3. Slipstitch the hook band neatly to cover the heading tape.

HAND GATHERED

1. Check your overall drop measurement and adjust pins accordingly. Fold the lining back and trim away the interlining, if used, along the overall drop line. Trim fabric and lining 7.5 cm (3 in) from this line and press to the back. Experiment with different stitch lengths to determine the stitch length you will need to obtain your required pleat size.

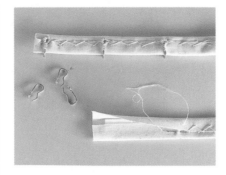

2. Divide the heading into 10 sections and mark each with a coloured tack. Make one row of stitches 3 cm (1¼ in) from the folded edge. Make a parallel row 3 cm (1¼ in) from the first. Pull up the two threads together evenly.

3. Make a hook band; divide into sections and match to the heading. Even out gathers, pin and slip stitch.

The binding for headings should be taken from a mid-tone in the fabric.

1. Tied and gathered: As an alternative to hooks, a pretty gathered or pleated heading might be tied to the pole or to curtain rings. Ties could be short and tied into a neat bow, or long and trailing. Plan the number of ties to be about 11–15 cm (4¼–6 in) apart and to suit the pole width. Divide the curtain by this number of gaps between ties and mark the tie positions. Make ties as on page 8 and pin under the tape. Secure each tie with double stitches as the tape is being stitched in place.

2. Scalloped frill: Check your overall drop and hook drop and adjust the pins accordingly. Make a scalloped template, pin this shaped edge along the overall drop line and cut around it through all layers. Using the same template, cut a facing from a strip of main fabric the length of the heading × the frill depth, plus 1.5 cm (⅝ in) to fit under the tape. Make up enough piping (see page 9) and stitch around the scallops. Pin the facing on with right sides together and stitch just

1

2

3

4

inside the previous stitching line. Trim, snipping into the corners. Press the scallops to shape. Pin and stitch the tape in place and cover with a hook band.

3. Adding ribbon: Check your overall drop and hook drop and adjust the pins accordingly. Add the frill depth plus 1.5 cm (⅝ in) to go under the tape and trim away all excess fabric. Trim away interlining along the overall drop line. Fold over the main fabric and lining and press. Turn the curtain to the front and position the ribbon so that it will finish just 1 cm (⅜ in) from the frill fold. Pin to the fabric only and stitch along both sides. Fold the frill over again and stitch tape to the hook drop measurement. Pull up, spreading gathers evenly and attach the hook band.

4. Pocket headings: Pocket or slot headings allow curtains to be threaded directly on to the pole or wire. They are often used for voiles and sheers and for curtains with a fixed heading which open on to ties or holdbacks rather than being pulled open and closed in the conventional manner. Allow 8–12 cm (3¼–4¾ in) for a curtain frill and 2 cm (¾ in) for voiles above the pocket.

Check your overall drop and trim away any interlining along this line. Add the frill return and twice the pocket depth, and trim away any excess fabric. (To find the pocket depth, add 10 per cent to the circumference of your pole for easement and divide in half.) Fold under, pin and then stitch along both the fold line and the stitching line which will become the top of the pocket.

BUNCHED HEADINGS

Bunched headings are very effective and extremely simple to make. And you can achieve very different looks using this same technique. For example, silk curtains finished with bunched headings look extremely sophisticated, yet heavy linen curtains with the same treatment will look very relaxed and have more of a country style.

Fine fabrics can be bunched successfully if at least three times the fullness of fabric has been used. Insert a length of scrunched organdie or fine net into the heading after the tape has been stitched on to give the curtain body and to help the folds fall correctly.

All interlined curtains make suitable candidates for bunched headings, but if medium or lightweight interlining has been used, insert a double layer into the heading before bunching.

Check the overall drop and hook drop, adjust the pins accordingly. Add the frill depth plus 1.5 cm (⅝ in) to go under the tape and cut away any excess fabric. Trim the interlining back another 2 cm (¾ in). Fold the heading down to the hook drop line, pin and stitch 3 cm (1¼ in) deep tape in place. Pull up and stitch on the hook band.

Turn the curtain to the front and bunch up the heading with your fingers. Using a long needle and double thread secure through the folds and into the back as often as needed to hold the shape without squashing the folds. Sew up the open ends by hand, gathering slightly.

Gathered headings are scrunched up and stitched in place. Hanging from a painted pole, they add an informal finish to these interlined curtains.

TABBED AND TIED HEADINGS

I used a little spare fabric to make alternately coloured tabs and buttons for a checkerboard effect; bought tapes or ribbons could be substituted if your time is limited. Most fabrics respond well to contrasting detail; striped and checked fabrics worked together, with perhaps a plain tone to add definition, are especially rewarding.

None of these headings is difficult to make if you have basic skills and like to experiment with cords, eyelets, ribbons, and even string, to create an individual finish. Some of the headings will not allow the curtains to be pulled back as far as you might wish, but they are ideal for decorative and fixed curtains. Most will allow the curtain to take up little space when pulled back, especially those threaded on to poles through large eyelets.

Always stiffen the headings with buckram, cotton heading tape or dressmakers' interfacing, to prevent the fabric flopping and looking untidy. Hand or machine stitch between the fabric and lining before binding, or insert into a folded heading. Unlined curtains will need a facing to cover the stiffening.

MAKING UP

1. Make fabric tabs in any size, but usually 2–4 cm (¾–1½ in) wide and long enough to fit easily over your pole. Allow enough for buttoning to the front and fixing to the back. Stitch securely to the curtain heading just beyond the overall drop before turning the heading over.

2. Stitch buttons to the front, securing them right through all layers of fabric. Use strong buttonhole thread to make sure that the tabs are secure, as this stitching will be holding the full weight of the curtain.

1. Add a 5 cm (2 in) border to the top of the curtain and stiffen it with heading buckram. Fit 20 mm (¾ in) eyelets to thread on to a 15 mm (⅝ in) pole.

2. Add 10 cm (4 in) to the overall drop, fold this in half and insert a 5 cm (2 in) band of stiffening; slip stitch along the fold. Punch 10 mm (⅜ in) eyelets and thread through double cords.

3. Add a 5 cm (2 in) border to the top of the curtain and stiffen with heading buckram. Fit 20 mm (¾ in) eyelets and 30 cm (12 in) ribbons to tie to the pole with little half bows.

4. Bind the curtain all round, stitching in 5 cm (2 in) of interfacing into the heading. Make ties measuring 1 × 45 cm (⅜ × 18 in). Stitch into the binding at regular intervals and tie to the curtain rings.

5. Bind the curtain all round, inserting 5 cm (2 in) soft interfacing into the heading. Cut tabs and bind these to match. Secure to the back of the heading and hold the front with a button.

6. Bind the curtain all round, inserting a soft interfacing into the heading. Stitch 100 cm (40 in) ties into the headings at intervals. Loop over the pole and tie in bows.

7. Add 10 cm (4 in) to the overall drop, fold in half, inserting a 5 cm (2 in) stiffening. Stitch 45 × 5 cm (18 × 2 in) piped tabs at regular intervals, loop over the pole and tie into half bows. Stitch in place.

8. Make a stiffened band with a shaped lower edge, the finished width of the curtain. Gather the curtain on to the band. Stitch ribbon loops, fold the band over and decorate with bought motifs.

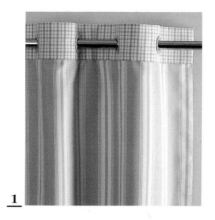

1

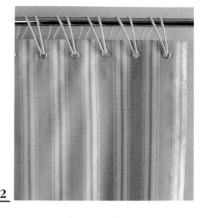

2

3

4

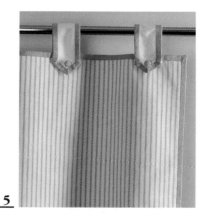

5

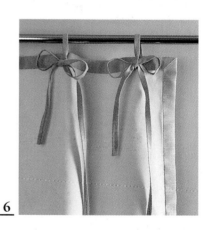

6

7

8

TIEBACKS AND HOLDBACKS

Decorate your fabric tiebacks with fresh flowers and greenery from the garden to match the table decorations for a summer party or a wedding meal.

Tiebacks need to be both practical and decorative, which makes them quite challenging to design and make.

First, choose a style which is in sympathy with your house and window treatment – a formal room will respond best to classic tiebacks, a muted colour scheme will need subtle tiebacks, while a pretty feminine room will be enhanced with bows and frills.

You will discover that tiebacks and holdbacks can also resolve many window dressing difficulties. Problems which I encounter time and again are curtains which, of necessity, hang too near a bathroom or kitchen sink, curtains in front of doors or where both curtains and maximum light are needed at different times of the day.

Many beautiful tiebacks can be bought 'off the peg' or made to order from a wide selection of trimmings (passementerie). Single or double tassels, cord loops or knotted ropes are just some suggestions. Brass and wooden arms or holdbacks are also available. Some will lie flat against the wall when not in use and twist around to hold the width of the curtain edge when needed.

Experiment with these and other ideas – use scarves or belts, add shells or wooden beads, and experiment with mixing fabrics – prints and checks, damasks with fine stripes. Imaginative use of paper, silk or dried flowers can look very attractive, while real flowers and greenery can also decorate curtains for a special occasion.

To measure for tiebacks, hold a tape or piece of rolled up fabric around your curtain. Lift the leading edge of the fabric and drape it to sit into the tieback in a gracious sweep. If the tieback is too loose it will keep slipping up and you will loose the drape, too tight and the fabric will crease and spoil the leading edge.

Fit tieback hooks in pairs, with the outer hook level with the outer edge of the curtain and the inner hook approximately 5 cm (2 in) inside. Tiebacks should have a brass ring sewn on to the inside, approximately 3 cm (1¼ in) in from the front edge, and a 5 cm (2 in) fabric loop to the back edge.

When the curtains are drawn, lift the tieback from the front hook only and let it fall flat behind the curtain. To tie your curtains back, pick the tieback up from behind the curtain and take it around to the front. Try to make this method a habit so the tiebacks remain the right way round and receive a minimum of handling.

Holdbacks will be fitted straight on to the wall or into the wooden frame. Hold the fitting at the edge of the curtain and pull back to the side to establish the best position for the holdback.

Formal and classical tieback fittings should be fitted approximately two thirds down whereas frilled and less formal ties can be fitted at almost any position complementary to the window treatment. Ask someone to hold your curtains back at several different points so that you can choose the hook position.

FABRIC TIEBACKS

MAKING A SASH

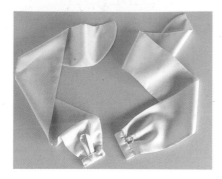

To establish the length of the sash, drape a length of scrap fabric around your curtain, trim to size, tie a bow or knot to the front or side of the curtain, pin in position and mark where the rings should be stitched to fit the tieback hook.

Cut fabric the length and twice the width of your template, fold in half with right sides together and stitch from each end to the centre, leaving a 12 cm (4¾ in) gap. Trim the seams back to 5 mm (¼ in), turn through, press and slip stitch the opening. Cut this length into two as shown, turn under the raw edges and pleat the sash ends to approximately 3 cm (1¼ in). Stitch to neaten and stitch a ring just inside one end and a fabric loop in the other. Fit on to the hook and tie into a bow or knot. Stitch so that the bow or knot cannot easily be undone.

Large bows and sashes for feminine window treatments can be made simply and quickly or in much more detail with contrast linings, pipings and ribbons.

MAKING A BOW

To make this bow, cut two pieces of fabric 45 × 12 cm (18 × 4¾ in) and piping to go all round. Stitch the piping to the right side of one piece, very close to the piping stitching line. Place the other piece of fabric over the top, pin carefully in place and stitch from the first side, keeping your stitching line just inside the last one. Leave a 12 cm (4¾ in) gap in the middle. Trim the seams to 5 mm (¼ in) and turn right side out. Pull the corners out with a pin and press along the seam line. Slip stitch the gap, pin the bow to the worktable and tie. Stitch the bow in position so that no one can come along and untie your beautiful creation.

MAKING A ROSE

Use different lengths and widths of fabric for different sized roses and buds. For this rose, cut one piece of fabric 1 m (1 yd) long, making it 14 cm (5½ in) at one end and 10 cm (4 in) at the other. Fold in half lengthwise and run a hand-stitched gathering thread 1.5 cm (⅝ in) in from the raw edges. Pull up to 50 cm (20 in) and, starting at the narrow end, roll up to make the rose, keeping the raw edges tight together. Stitch through all layers to hold the shape, cut a small square of fabric and stitch to the back to cover the frayed ends.

TIES

Simple ties also make very effective tiebacks, again for informal rooms. Tie a piece of tape or an offcut of fabric around your curtain to determine the length and width and follow the instructions on page 8. Checks and stripes can be bought inexpensively and are most effective used on the cross or in complementary colours and different weaves.

ROULEAUX

To make a rouleau measuring 45 × 6 cm (18 × 2¼ in) cut a strip of fabric 50 × 14 cm (20 × 5½ in) and a piece of polyester wadding 50 × 70 cm (20 × 28 in). Roll up the wadding and loosely herringbone. Press under 1.5 cm (⅝ in) along one length. Fold this strip over the wadding roll, pin the folded edge over the raw edge and slip stitch. Cut two small pieces to stitch over the ends, with a ring at one end and a fabric loop at the other.

A rouleau tieback (above) is decorative and is finished with rose in the same fabric. Below: the simplest treatments are so often the most effective.

LINENS AND SHEERS

Floaty drapes, in silk taffeta and muslin, allow maximum light into the room as well as framing the country-side view. Roller blinds keep out the darkness at night and pull up out of sight during the daytime behind a fabric-covered pelmet board.

Sheers encompass unlined and semi transparent curtaining which, although decorative in detail, is chosen and fitted for protection of some sort. Whether to give privacy, to block out excess sunlight, to cover exposed windows, to be 'dirt catchers' in a large city, or as under-curtains which can be used without the main curtains during the summer.

Fabrics used for sheets include muslins, very fine calicoes, organdie, silks, fine linens, linen scrim, lace and cotton voile. Any sheer fabrics used should be easy to clean and should not react to sudden changes in temperature.

Usually white, cream or off white, some linens and cottons can be bought unbleached and muslins, silks and voiles will all dye easily. Specialist furnishing and dressmaking fabric shops will be able to supply ready dyed sheers, but you could also dye your own. Last year, I needed a delicate shade of peachy-pink for a client which proved impossible to source. I solved the problem by steeping four handfuls of raspberry and blackcurrant tea in a bowlful of boiling water for 15 minutes, soaking the muslin for three hours before rinsing away any excess dye and leaving the curtains to dry naturally.

Sheer curtains need to be very full to show the fabric to its best and at least two and a half to three times the fullness for privacy.

1. Curtains are not necessary for privacy in many country situations, but a window dressing and some night time cover may be preferred. Jute scrim, more usually used for cleaning windows, and a fine tea towelling linen were selected for an inexpensive contemporary treatment.

The jute curtain was made with a pocket heading ruched on to a small pole which fitted on cup hooks behind the more decorative steel pole. Cotton ties were stitched into the flat heading of the white curtain and tied to curtain rings. The over-long jute and the floor length white linen add further to the informality of this unusual window treatment.

The gilded star holdbacks are just one example of the variety and fun element in contemporary interior design fittings.

Helpful reference
Pocket headings page 33, ties page 8, overlong curtains page 25

2. Often dark, heavy curtains are perfect for the winter months but feel too heavy if fully drawn throughout spring and summer. One solution is to make two pairs of curtains, the under-curtains only being used in warmer weather.

The sobriety of these main curtains is lightened with the addition of roses on the overlong drape of slubbed silk under-curtains with their fully gathered tape headings and self fabric ties. The outer curtains are completely flat, bound all around in charcoal grey, and lined with dark red. The border was cut from the width and stitched back on to the

leading edge and hem. Brass hooks – hand stitched to the curtain heading at regular intervals – encourage the curtain to pleat back into a very small space.

Helpful reference
Bound edges page 9, roses page 39, borders, pages 56–60, interlined curtains page 22, taped headings page 32, unlined curtains page 18, ties page 8.

3. My studio doors, although copied from a traditional French style, were double glazed, so do not need heavy curtaining, However, I do sometimes need to screen the intense sunlight in the summer when I am working. Steel bars were bent to shape for me by our local blacksmith and I made two flat muslin panels which

Fine linen is a heavier alternative to muslin for under-curtains. Linen is always prone to creasing, but it does filter the light beautifully and the even weave is ideal for hand stitching and to hold the scalloped edges.

double over the bars and slide easily on and off for washing.

The bars can swing back into the recess when the doors are open and to one side whenever the muslin panels are not needed.

4. Sometimes, when a blind is chosen as the preferred window treatment, you may find the window still needs softening. This fabric is most attractive as a flat blind, with the pictures depicting country events from a past way of life. The simple pelmet behind hides the fittings.

To make one the same, measure your window width and divide it into approximately 30 cm (12 in) sections. Add 6 cm (2¼ in) to each section to find the finished width and measure the depth required. Make a rectangle of fabric which is bound along the lower edge and lined. Make ties and buttons, divide the flat fabric into the number of sections needed and stitch the buttons in place, tying the ties around the buttons. Stitch a small brass ring behind each button and fit to small hooks which have been screwed into the window frame at the correct intervals. Finger pleat the hemline to look neat.

The organza curtain was cut 80 cm (32 in) over-long, seamed with French seams, 1 cm (³⁄₈ in) hems were slip stitched all around, and the heading pocketed to ruche on to a wire at the top and tied in a large knot.

Helpful reference
French seams page 8, pocket headings page 33, binding edges page 9, making ties page 8.

1

3

2

4

LAYERS

Two very different linens were chosen for the drapes: inexpensive jute scrim under fine linen, sewn with oversized pin tucks, and hand embroidered in feather stitch.

For the inexperienced, unlined curtains are by far the easiest window treatments to make and probably the most cost-effective, as they save the expense of linings and interlinings.

Easy to store, quick and inexpensive to make, layers of sheer curtains are ideal if you like to change your curtains each season. Unlined, sheer fabrics layer to create some fabulous, eye-catching treatments. Two strong colours such as green and blue or pink and red will vibrate with life and interest, rather like using a fabulous shot silk. Cream and white used together provide a restful, light combination with much more richness and variety than if either colour was used on its own.

There are also other interesting effects you can achieve with layers. A strong fabric, which might in itself be extremely attractive but at the same time a little overpowering, can be 'filtered' by hanging a lightweight voile in front.

The limitations of unlined curtains are that they do not stop draughts, keep out the early morning light or the darkness during the evening. One solution that I employ is to make a blind which hangs against the window frame, providing a 'picture' during the evening in the same manner as the outlook in the daytime. Roman blinds fold up during the daytime and can be interlined to provide some insulation at night. Roller blinds are also effective with layers of sheers as they can be made invisible during the daytime behind a small fitted pelmet board.

1. The printed linen blind against the window called the tune for the colours of these silk organza drapes. White has been used as a foil, with the mid blue ribbon detail picking up the background colour from the blind fabric. The vibrant blue chosen to frame the window reflects the flower centres and has the same ribbon detail, but this time in a toning shade. Thin brass rods were used to thread through the pocket headings of both layers. The outer layer was made with an extra flap of sheer fabric to form an attached pelmet.

Helpful reference

Unlined curtains page 18, pocket headings page 33, pelmets page 70, eyelet headings page 35.

2. Three layers of silk were chosen for their almost clashing tones and the quality of organza which allows each layer to be seen through the other. By shaping the hemlines, the three colours are always on show but the light is always filtered through all three, giving quite a different effect to each layer.

These hems were satin stitched by machine because I wanted the fabric to stretch and ruffle around the curves.

If you enjoy needlework, you might like to shell edge or feather stitch close to the edge.

The headings were all stitched together, ruched on to a narrow metal pole. Two lengths of fabric were wound very informally around a second pole and stitched at each end to tabs, which tie around the pole to hold the drape in place.

Helpful reference

Unlined curtains page 18, pocket headings page 33, pelmets page 70.

3. Yellow ochre, tan and red layers combine for an exotic effect. The headings of the top two layers were cut into deep scallops and edged with narrow ribbon in complementary colours. By tying each layer back individually, the colours can be seen in their own right and with added depths.

Helpful reference
Unlined curtains page 18, making ties page 8.

4. The whole scheme for this room was designed from the hand-printed olive leaf chosen for a half blind. Half blinds which pull up and down only a little way are very useful when the outlook from just the top half of a window needs to be obscured. The checked and buttoned edge was later picked up in the sofas and cushions.

The excellent quality of the cloth used for the blind, and the printing technique with its simple design, set a style which I was keen to keep in my interpretation. The walls were coloured and

stencil printed not to copy but to echo the olive leaf design. Two very different linens were chosen for the drapes to reflect the spirit of 'elegant naivete'. The sheers were made from very inexpensive jute scrim and the curtains were made of the best quality linen, sewn with oversized pin tucks and all hand embroidered in feather stitch using perlé thread with a slight sheen which contrasts beautifully and subtly with the matt linen weave.

DOOR CURTAINS

I like to leave my doors wide open on warm sunny days to filter strong breezes. The calico curtains tie to the same poles which hold my winter curtains. For fun, I embroidered them with the name of our house.

Door curtains are essential in most country homes for the winter months to rebuff the coldness from the window glass and to prevent the prevailing wind sneaking its way round door frames. Interline with heavy bump and use substantial fabrics for both front fabric and lining. Make curtains overlong so that they just sweep the floor. Give them double hems that can be let down and used to replace the first hem as it wears after a few years of constant rubbing on the floor.

Internal door curtains are also sometimes useful to temper draughts in winter or to dress a doorless opening.

At the back of my house there is a small area which always catches the early morning sun, making it an ideal spot for breakfast. The only drawback is that it opens on to the main garden, catching any westerly breeze. Instead of opening and closing the garden gate, I hang a patchwork curtain in the summer to keep the eating area draught-free. You could make a similar curtain with any patchwork pieces from your fabric box, arranging bits from old curtains, cushions and clothes creating a very personal melange.

Regular guests have been surprised to find the same curtain serving as a very acceptable single bedcover later in the year!

MAKING UP

My lovely patchwork 'door' curtain is made from pieces collected over the years. Just remember to check that any scraps you gather for this project are washable at the same temperature.

1. Cut squares of equal sizes and pin to a calico ground. Stitch each in place with a long tacking stitch.

2. Position cotton tape to cover all raw edges and stitch in place. Bind the outer edges with more tape and stitch cut lengths to the heading to tie the curtain on to hooks or a pole.

1. When I found this fabric for my new curtains I thought it would be fun to make a flat door curtain. You could adapt this idea to curtain the doors from a beach house or pool changing room, using towelling or deck-chair fabric. Or try a waterproof fabric in place of a shower door. It is also the perfect solution, in almost any fabric, for covering open shelves or alcoves.

Using three complementary fabrics or two fabrics and a binding tape, cut two pieces which fit the doorway exactly and two pieces for the flap, approximately 70 cm (28 in) deep. Pin the pieces together with right sides out. Bind both panels around the two sides and hem. Join together at the top. Stitch fabric ties to hold the two together. Fit a narrow metal bar into the door recess and slot the curtain over.

2. Often there is only space to one side of a doorway, so a curtain must be made and fitted to pull from one direction to completely cover the opening. A simple wooden holdback contains this curtain when the door is in use.

3. Door curtains in a restricted space need to be tied back to allow the door to open freely. I have one narrow curtain which pulls to the opening side of the door and a wider one pulling back to the hinged side.

4. A heavy Italian chenille bedcover at the end of a corridor leading to a guest room can be looped back or dropped down to close off the corridor without the barrier of a solid door.

_1_

_3_

_2_

_4_

CONTRAST LININGS

Simple ideas using fabric in a stylish way are often the most effective. I love the way that the simple gingham check opens to reveal fabric which would usually have been used for the front.

I almost always line curtains with a contrasting fabric, rather than the normal creams and ecrus. However, I rarely use a plain colour, which may be too strong viewed from outside, preferring instead simple stripes and two-coloured small prints which add to the overall design rather than making a statement. The element of surprise and delight when the curtains are pulled back to reveal another unexpected dimension is an additional pleasure.

Choosing two patterns to work so closely together can take much time and research, but when they work as well as this combination does, the time was more than well spent. The secret is to choose a complementary fabric which reflects something of the main fabric, while at the same time bringing in another dimension. When I designed the curtaining shown on page 71, I was thrilled to find such a perfect fabric for the lining, at once echoing the spirit of the toile and introducing the perfect cottage garden flowers threaded through the finest blue pinstripe.

The scallops, opposite, were cut using a template, but left uneven to look 'hand cut'. They were then edged with blanket stitch in embroidery thread, which is so simple but looks so very effective.

Where the linings are intended to be on show, the edges need to be finished neatly. One way to do this is to finish the edge with cord or piping. This piping (below) was chosen to pick up the main greeny blue colour, stitched to the lining before making up.

Checks and stripes always make pleasing combinations. Richly coloured curtains in browns and reds are bordered in a plain caramel and lined with a terracotta stripe (above right). The interlining is locked to the curtain fabric and the lining to the inter-lining before the binding is stitched on. The binding strips are pinned to the front and stitched on, through all layers, pressed,

folded to the back and hand stitched to cover the stitching line. The instructions on page 9 for binding edgings will help you. Before you take the curtain off the worktable, pin all around at about 5 cm (2 in) intervals with the pins at right angles to the edges. These pins will remain in place while the binding is stitched on, keeping the fabrics together and the lining straight.

Helpful reference

Interlined curtains page 22, bound edgings page 9, inverted pleat headings page 29.

Door curtains are often seen from both sides, in which case equal attention needs to be given to both fabrics. Fabrics that are very similar in weight and coordinate as perfectly as these do, look stunning, but you could use lighter and darker colourings and, with the right headings, make the curtain reversible for winter and summer.

MAKING UP

Neatening the edge

If curtains are equally valid from both sides, as in the case of room dividers, bed curtains and door curtains, each fabric should be stitched together right on the edge to create a neat finish. Stitching piping, cording, or fringing to either side neatens the edge and provides an anchor against which to stitch the other side.

Adding piping

A piped edge stitched to the lining before making up gives a firm line to stitch against and looks impressive.

Cut linings 3 cm (1¼ in) smaller all round than the flat curtain. Stitch piping to the sides and hem, place lining on to the curtain, lock in and stitch to the main fabric with small, neat running stitches through the back of the piping.

Patterned lining

Using a plain fabric on the front of a curtain and a patterned one on the inside can be very effective. To achieve this, the headings must remain in position while the curtains are held back. This lets the light shine through to show up the patterned lining.

Take the lining around to the front to make a narrow binding. Mitre the corner, as shown. Slip stitch the binding in place, just catching a thread from the lining side of the curtain.

BORDERS AND EDGINGS

Plain damask weave cotton is enhanced with an inset contrasting border and finished with fabric-covered buttons and ties. The under-curtains were first edged with a coordinating checked fabric before a linen cut fringe was stitched between the curtain and the lining.

It goes without saying that the edgings you choose will dramatically affect the style of your window treatment. Attention to the detailed finish of any curtaining will optimise the hard work which you have put in so far, and whether a simple binding or an elaborate fringe, the right edging will bring the fabric to life, enriching a wool damask, defining an all-over print or redefining a slubbed cotton.

There are so many different possibilities for edgings that you might find it difficult to make a choice – straight, frilled, double, single, on one side or four sides, buttoned, braided, scalloped, and so on. Curtains may appear harder or softer, more elegant or more informal, more contemporary or more traditional, depending on the style and colours of the edgings.

A formal room might suggest elegant passementerie while a contemporary setting demands a structured shape and defined lines. If you are as yet unsure how your other furnishings will take shape, it would be prudent to select an edging which subtly complements the main fabric as opposed to one which might prove to be too overpowering later on.

Consider the ways in which you might mix fringes and bindings, double or inset borders, braids with frills, a checked border against a traditional print, using large checks with small checks, large prints with small prints, but always choosing fabrics of a similar weight and content, so that both cloths will react to atmospheric changes in the same way.

BINDINGS AND BORDERS

Adding bindings and borders to curtains gives you the opportunity to experiment with different colours and textures. Borders may be wide, narrow, on the edge, or set in from the edge, and on as many sides of the curtain as you wish. Double and triple borders take time and need very accurate cutting and stitching but are always most effective. Try using one or two plain colours set into a pattern.

The really important factor to consider is that the fabrics must be of similar quality and content. It would be such a shame to have spent time choosing and making to find the fabrics reacting differently to room temperature

and pulling against each other. So a matt finish may be used with a sheen, pattern with plain, stripe with pattern, as long as the fibre content is the same and the weave similar.

The closely co-ordinated colours of the double curtains and edgings on page 57 are harmonious and quietly elegant.

MAKING BOUND EDGES

My standard edging size is 1.5 cm (⅝ in). I often adjust this a fraction either way, slightly more for a larger curtain or a deeper frill, and less for a dark colour or smaller frill. Order edging fabric to be at least as long as your curtains, so that the strips can be cut the length of the roll, entailing as few joins as possible, with none at all on the leading edge.

EDGING AN UNLINED CURTAIN

1. Cut and join enough strips of fabric 6 cm (2¼ in) wide to bind all edges.

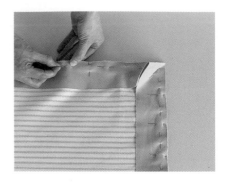

2. Place the curtain flat on to the worktable with the wrong side facing down. Pin the edging strip along the leading edge as shown. Stop pinning 1.5 cm (⅝ in) from the corner. Fold the edging over at a right angle and continue pinning along the hemline.

3. Stitch along the leading edge at exactly 1.4 cm (just under ⅝ in) from the raw edges. Stop stitching 1.5 cm (⅝ in) from the hem edge at the corner point. Fold the flap over and start stitching again at the other side of the flap, checking that the needle is inserted next to the last stitch.

These simple curtains made from ticking have been bound on all four edges with a deep yellow cotton to echo the colours of the ties and window seat.

4. From the right side, press the edging strip away from the curtain. Fold back under 1.5 cm (⅝ in), folding the edging tight against the seam, mitre the corner.

5. Turn the fabric over to the back. Mitre the corner by first folding the free side to the curtain edge and over again to enclose the raw edges. Snip the adjacent binding strip towards the corner, and fold the next length of binding over as before. Pin to hold in place. Slip stitch every 1 cm (⅜ in), picking up a machine stitch as you go so that no stitches are visible from the front.

BINDING A LINED CURTAIN

Follow the method above, but lock stitch the lining to the main fabric first and tack round all the edges to hold the pieces together.

BINDING AN INTERLINED CURTAIN

1. Cut and join enough strips of fabric 11 cm (4¼ in) wide, to bind all edges.

2. Place the curtain fabric on to the worktable and trim away the selvedge. If your curtains are small and you are using lightweight interlining, lock stitch the interlining to the curtain fabric and treat as one piece. Pin the binding to the curtain edge from the heading towards the hem. Stop pinning 9.5 cm (3½ in) from the hem. Fold the edging over at a right angle and continue pinning parallel with the hem.

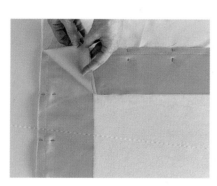

3. Stitch along the leading edge exactly 1.4 cm (just under ⅝ in) from the raw edge. It is important that the stitching line is very accurate to give an even edging. Stop at the corner 9.5 cm (3½ in) from the hem edge and secure the stitching. Fold the flap over and continue to stitch along the other side, starting 1.5 cm (⅝ in) from the leading edge. The stitches should meet at the corner.

4. Working from the front, press the binding away from the curtain. Fold the binding to the back of the curtain, measuring from the front 1.5 cm (⅝ in) all along as you pin. Carefully mitre the corner at the front.

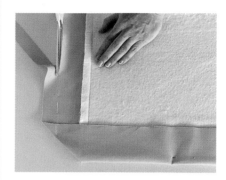

5. Fold over and mitre the back corner. Trim the binding on the leading edge only to 6 cm (2¼ in), leaving the hem.

Continue to make up the curtain following instructions on pages 24–25 stitching the lining to leave 1.5 cm (⅝ in) of the edging visible.

6. Herringbone stitch the hem and long stitch the sides to the interlining. Continue to make curtains following the instructions on pages 24–25, stitching the lining and leaving just 1.5 cm (⅝ in) visible.

MAKING AN INSET BORDER

The strips of fabric to make an inset border need to be cut 3 cm (1¼ in) wider than the finished border width. The outer border, or binding, should be cut to twice the finished width plus 3 cm (1¼ in). Cut and join enough strips to complete the edgings.

1. Place the curtain on the worktable, wrong side down, and pin the inset strips to the side, starting at the heading. Stop 1.5 cm (⅝ in) from the hem and fold the edging back on itself, allowing enough fabric so the border is mitred when finished. Continue pinning 1.5 cm (⅝ in) from the side edge. Repeat with other side. Stitch in place keeping 1.5 cm (⅝ in) from the raw edges.

2. Press from the front, away from the curtain. Press on the back, snipping along the short fold so that it lies flat.

3. With right sides together, pin the outside edging strip to the inset strip, mitring the corners as before. Stitch 1.5 cm (⅝ in) from the raw edges. Press from the front, away from the curtain and fold the edging under. Pin in place, turn over and mitre the corner.

4. Turn the fabric over and mitre the back corner, folding the border fabric in the opposite direction to keep the corner as flat as possible.

BOUGHT EDGINGS

Fringing, ribbons, cord and braids are readily available from furnishing fabric suppliers and department stores and they are an excellent way of edging your curtains quickly. Take a sample piece of fabric with you when shopping to ensure a good tonal match or contrast. Bear in mind the weight of fabric you are using and how the edging will be attached. Make sure you buy slightly more than slightly less, as the exact colour and style of edgings bought later may not match up.

1. I wanted the fringe to be less important on these under-curtains, so I stitched it behind a narrow border cut on the cross.

Adding a fringe to the leading edge of a curtain can make any fabric look elegant. Some fringes have decorative tops which ask to be shown, so these are best stitched to the front. Others have very plain tops and should be stitched between the top fabric and the lining.

Choose a linen or cotton fringe for linen or cotton fabrics and silk or a silky fibre for silk and damask fabrics.

2. I think ribbons will be taken much more seriously as a decorative detail in the next few years. I use ribbon for piping, for ties, or for binding edges. Plain or decorative ribbons are available in a vast selection of widths and colours, from matt ribbed hat ribbon to lustrous gold and silver creations

with wired edges which can be moulded into any shape, including the most marvellous bows. Embroidered cotton and linen ribbons are lovely for bedlinen and cushions as well as the leading edges of curtains.

3. Fan topped and fan edged braidings make particularly smart edgings for curtains, pelmets and cushions and are available in many colour combinations from interior decorators and furnishing fabric suppliers. I designed this jumbo fanned edging with my client especially for these hand-worked crewel curtains. A small passementerie company made up the edging together with matching cord which I used for cushions and tiebacks.

4. A coloured cord, hand-stitched to the edges and hems, adds a subtle finish to any curtain. Buy dainty 4–6 mm (⅛–¼ in) cord for lightweight curtains and up to 20 mm (½ in) cord for the heaviest wools and woven tapestries. Use contrasting colours for a smart finish, say red with navy, or related colours for a subtle finish such as apricot with soft pink. To make this padded edge, inset a roll of interlining all round before stitching the sides and hems in place. Stitch right through to the front to really secure the roll and stitch the cord to cover.

BORDERS ON THE CROSS

Instead of selecting a contrasting or complementary fabric for the borders, use the same fabric. Why not turn checks crosswise, cut stripes on the cross or in the opposite direction, or design a border cut in the same direction but with braiding between.

I designed the curtains opposite for a bedroom decorated only in red checks in varying scales. I wanted to add a border which was subtle enough not to become the focal point, but interesting enough to add another dimension. Cutting the fabric on the cross provided the diversion; brown ribbon details the change.

A simple unlined curtain in blue checked cotton would not be nearly as interesting without the cross cut borders (right). Jumbo piping covered with checked lining fabric cut on the cross provides a neat edge to these fun kitchen curtains (below).

MAKING UP

1. Cut the borders for the sides and hems across the grain of the fabric 12 cm (4¾ in) wide and for the heading 22 cm (8¾ in) wide. Place the ribbon along one edge of the right side of each border and stitch neatly in place, halfway across the ribbon width.

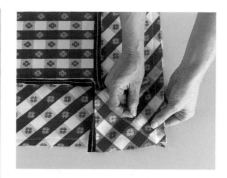

2. Pin the borders to the sides and hem with right sides facing and stitch with a 1.5 cm (⅝ in) seam. Pin across the corners to mitre and stitch.

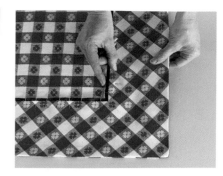

3. Press the seam flat and trim across the corner. Turn the border to the right side and press the seam lines. Press one half of the ribbon underneath the border and pin this edge flat on to the curtains to create a neat, even trim.

4. Stitch the border in place neatly along the edge of the ribbon trim.

5. To make the attached pelmet, line the heading border and pin to the curtains with right sides together. Make ties 1.5 × 60 cm (⅝ × 24 in) following the instructions on page 8. Insert in pairs and stitch the ties and border to the curtain securely, neaten the seam and fold the border to the front of the curtain.

FRILLED EDGES

One of my favourite commissions was a delightful Queen Anne house which was decorated with such attention to detail that it always reminds me of a grown-up dolls' house. Every item has been positioned perfectly and every edging designed to the last detail.

It interests me that in two dictionaries I find the word frill expounded as 'unnecessary ornament' and as a 'treat, bauble, delicacy'. This seems to sum up exactly how frilled edgings might fit into a design scheme. Frills are often completely unnecessary and could spoil the line; however, for some window treatments, frills are essential to make the design work. It is never right to frill everything, but often the effect of frills edging curtains or cushions does provide the 'treat' – the icing on the cake.

Frilled edgings are an extravagance, taking time and a considerable amount of extra fabric, but they do offer a softer look to curtains and drapes than more formal edgings and bindings. The opportunity for mixing fabrics and colours adds a fun element to the design process. Use magazines, books, shop windows, colour charts, small samples and scraps of fabrics for ideas. Balancing the scale of prints is essential – look carefully at the fabrics you plan to put together – you might need to alter the width of a stripe, the size of a check or the scale of a pattern for the perfect combination. Be careful that one colour or pattern does not overwhelm the others, and keep colourings within the same tonal range. Or you might prefer to make a strong statement, in which case, keep within the same tonal range, perhaps mixing forest green and deep terracotta red; or use one colour with a neutral – navy blue with white.

Overlong frills can be very effective – a 20 cm (8 in) frill stitched to the leading edge and hem and tied back tightly so that the frills fall with the drape, makes a different but equally strong statement.

BOUND AND BACKED FRILLS

1. Cut and join strips of fabric, allowing twice the overall drop of each curtain, 9 cm (3½ in) wide for the frill fabric and 12 cm (4¾ in) for the binding and backing. Pin each strip together, right sides facing and stitch along the length, 1.5 cm (⅝ in) from the edge. From the front, press the 12 cm (4¾ in) strip away from the narrower strip. Press under and pin, keeping an exact 1.5 cm (⅝ in) edging.

2. Fold under each end by 1.5 cm (⅝ in) stitch together with small ladder stitches. Run a gathering thread along the length 1.5 cm (⅝ in) from the raw edges. Measure the exact frill length, divide into 10 equal sections and mark with coloured marking tacks.

3. Pipe the leading edge of the curtain following the instructions on page 9. Divide the piped edge into 10 equal sections and mark with coloured marking tacks. Pull up the gathering thread and pin together, matching the section tacks. Spread the gathers evenly between as you go.

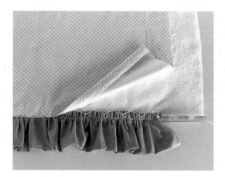

4. Stitch the frill to the piping line, keeping just inside the first stitching line. Trim the seam and layer to reduce the bulk if necessary. Herringbone stitch the piping and frilled edge to the main fabric or interlining. Slip stitch the lining close to the piping cord to enclose all raw edges.

SCALLOPED FRILLED HEMS

Create a template (see page 68) to make scallops along the curtain hemline, allowing 4–5 for each width of fabric. If the curtains are interlined, lock stitch the main fabric and interlining together and make up as one. Make piping (page 9) and stitch around the scallops, 1.5 cm (⅝ in) from the cut edge. Carefully snip into the points.

The attached skirt falls level with the floor so it needs to be shaped to fit the curtain scalloped edge before making up. I used scallops which measured 25 cm wide × 8 cm deep (10 × 3¼ in)

Lilac and yellow as a sophisticated colour combination translates equally well into this classical toile print, depicting scenes of traditional Chinese life. Glazed lilac linen has been used for the skirt and a small yellow ochre check to pipe the scallops. Sofas in lilac, piped with the same yellow check, with toile cushions echo the window treatment.

and allowed double fullness for gathering the skirt.

Divide the lined frill into 50 cm (20 in) sections and cut 8 cm (3¼ in) deep scallops, using the first template as a guide. Run a gathering thread 1.5 cm (⅝ in) from the raw edge, pull up and

pin to the piping line, spreading the gathers evenly into each section. Stitch close to the piping line and neaten the raw edges.

Do this with binding tape if the curtain is to be unlined, or slip stitch the lining to enclose the whole seam, if lined.

A pretty courtyard outlook needed curtains which would rarely be drawn, but would frame the window in a style compatible with the rest of the house. I decided to tie and drape these curtains high up away from the sink and other utensils., choosing another colourway of the same fabric to line and edge.

SCALLOPED EDGINGS

The window treatment opposite combines matt silk with a fine Italian cotton printed in a traditional paisley design. The paisley border has been joined to the leading edge with fine soft lemon cord, and a scalloped border in matt silk has been joined to the paisley border and hem, also with the cord. These curtains are shown over-long with the hems fanned out. Curtain headings are hand gathered in pencil pleats, with attached pelmets of paisley squares gathered up and stitched to hold. I have often used silk scarves for similar treatments.

Over-long curtains in crushed raspberry and caramel – with bold scallops – make an unusual but effective colour combination for an informal dining room, whether to accompany contemporary or traditional furnishings.

MAKING SCALLOPS

For the best effect, scallops should all be even in size and the best way to achieve this accurately, is to make a template using stiff paper and a round object like a saucer or the lid of a jar.

1. Cut a piece of card or a strip of heading buckram the length of the curtain and mark it into sections for each scallop. Also mark the depth of the scallop at the widest and narrowest points. Draw around a household object – like a saucer or bowl – to define the first shape. Trace this one and use it to repeat the shape. Cut out the template with scissors.

2. Pin this template on to the main fabric and draw round it.

3. Cut the scalloped edges, leaving 1 cm (⅜ in) seam allowance all round. Cut a strip of fabric for the facing which is the length of the curtain × the depth of the scallop. Pin the facing to the curtain, right sides together. Stitch around the scallops, keeping the stitching line an even 1 cm (⅜ in) from the raw edge. Trim seams and snip right into the points. Snip the curves as close to the stitching as possible so that they will lie flat when turned.

4. Turn out and press the scallops into even, rounded shapes. Continue to make up your curtains, lining or interlining as pages 18–25.

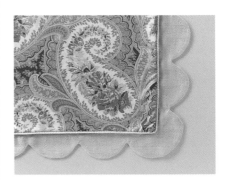

5. If the scalloped edge is to be a border to a curtain, in either a contrasting fabric or colour, you might like to pipe the curtain all round first. Always mitre the corners correctly.

PELMETS

If you want to use toile de jouy, use it everywhere. These two fabrics looked so good together that we almost had a problem choosing which was to be the curtain and which the lining. Doubled unlined pelmets trimmed in a hand-made picot edging are cut to perfection and seem to be as French as the fabric.

Pelmets provide the ultimate finishing touch to a window treatment; however, they can take as long to make as the curtains themselves and can cost much more if you indulge in elaborate trimmings and details.

Look at interiors magazines and books for ideas which might be compatible with your window style. Check out the latest fabrics and trimmings and the way in which fashion is influencing furnishings design. Nothing is ever absolutely *de rigueur* as it might be with say, a hemline, but there are certainly trends and details which can make all the difference between a successful and a mediocre window treatment.

Pelmets should, almost without exception, start from the ceiling and must always be deep enough to cover the window frame and any unsightly fittings. Double glazing, blind and security fittings are the worst offenders.

The rule of thumb for pelmet depth is an average of one-fifth on the curtain drop. This might be a good place to start, but use it as a guide rather than a rule; the ideas picked up from interiors magazines are probably just as reliable.

SWAGGED PELMETS

Swags and tails have become so much part of elegant period window treatments that I am often asked to explain how to make them. But to be able to cut and drape good swags takes an experienced curtain maker some time to learn and there are no short cuts to training and experience. I do teach experienced makers to design, drape and cut over a four day course, but as this time is not possible for most people I have adapted a very simple principle to show you how to make an elegant pelmet without draping.

It is still important that the numbers, depth and shape of the swags are well balanced. Have a pelmet board made which is 10 cm (4 in) deep (see page 12) and fit it in position. Drape and pin a length of chain or chain weight across the board to determine the swag sizes. Try out two or three swags on a pelmet board of up to 1.8 m (6 ft) wide and three or five after that.

When you are happy with the pelmet design, measure the drape and the distance along the board for the top of each swag, and the drape. Measure the depth of each swag. Add 4 cm (1½ in) to the width measurements and two and a half times the depth. Cut out one piece of fabric, mediumweight inter-lining and lining for each swag.

I use large thumb tacks to pin swags to pelmet boards. These are

easy to fit and simple to remove when the swags need shaking out or cleaning. Often there is only enough space between the board and ceiling to just fit two fingers and a thumb tack.

To make a very simple under swag, measure the depth from the pelmet board to the hemline of the

under swag and cut a semi-circle to this diameter. Leave unlined or line with the same lining used for the pelmets. Make three pleats across the top, with one central pleat, and stitch to a flat band. Finish the lower edge with fringe or braiding, or leave plain and fit to the pelmet.

MAKING UP

1. Make one swag at a time. Place one piece of fabric on to the worktable, right side down. Shape the lower edge to curve slightly from approximately 3 cm (1¼ in) on each side. Place the interlining on top and lock in approximately three times across the swag.

2. Trim away 2 cm (¾ in) of interlining from the sides and hem. Stitch the interlining to the fabric around the three sides with herringbone stitch.

3. Fold over the main fabric, press lightly, pin and herringbone to the interlining. Place the lining over and lock in along the previous lines.

4. With the point of your scissors, score the lining around the folded edges of the swag. Trim the lining 1 cm (⅜ in) outside this line. Fold under 2 cm (¾ in) and pin to the swag, leaving 1 cm (⅜ in) of the swag fabric showing.

5. Slip stitch all round. Now thread two large needles with double thread longer than the swag. Start from the hemline and secure the thread 1 cm (⅜ in) from one side and 3 cm (1¼ in) further in. Stitch the two threads parallel to each other, with exactly the same stitch size to the top. Experiment with the stitch size – longer stitches will give deeper pleats, small stitches will look like gathering. Here, I used stitches showing 1 cm (⅜ in) on the lining and 2.5 cm (1 in) in front.

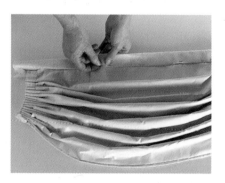

6. Repeat with the other side. Pull up both sides and secure the threads. If you are using a rosette or rose to finish the centre, pull up tightly. Cover a 5 cm (2 in) strip of heading tape with fabric and stitch to the top edge to enclose the raw edges. Pin the swags to the pelmet board with thumb tacks.

GATHERED PELMETS

Whether you have chosen to make a flat or a gathered pelmet you should always start from a basic template. Think of it in the same manner as a tailor's dummy over which you may drape, pleat and gather to your heart's content. A professional curtain maker might allow several hours to perfect a pelmet shape, so do not try or expect to rush this process. Time and care in preparation always show in the end result.

To make a template, stand back from your window and mark the wall or frame with a light pencil where you imagine the centre and sides will fall. Translate these measurements on to brown paper or newspaper, draw your design within them and cut out. Pin the template to the frame or wall along the top line. Stand back and pretend you are taller and shorter than you are so that you know what other people see. Adjust the template until you are happy with the shape.

Bowed pelmets emphasise the serpentine-shaped pelmet hem. Fancy lining and matching fan edging pick up the pink flowers from the chintz.

MAKING UP

1. Using a metal ruler, set square and a thick pencil, mark one half of the template into divisions. Use 4–5 cm (½–2in) spacing where there is little shaping and 2–3 cm (¾–1¼ in) divisions where there is more shaping. Number these divisions and cut into strips.

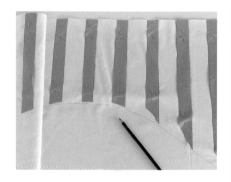

2. Make a toile in calico or spare fabric before cutting expensive fabric. Cut and join scrap fabric to the finished depth and three times the length of your template and clamp it to the worktable. Starting at the centre, place the paper strips parallel to the centre line, leaving gaps in between to create fullness. Two and a half times fullness is average, so leave 4.5 cm (1¾ in) for each 3 cm (1¼ in) paper strip. Add the pelmet board return and equivalent fullness.

3. When all the pieces are in place, cut around the lower edge, following the lowest point of each piece, and cut the return so that the hem line runs smoothly.

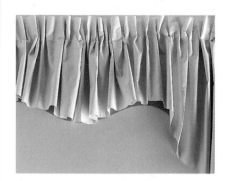

4. Fold the fabric in half and cut the other half to match. Run a large gathering thread through the pelmet approximately 6 cm (2¼ in) from the top and pull up to the template size. Fit to the window to check the shaping and make any adjustments. Pleat the gathers evenly and 'dress' the toile as if it were the real thing, remembering that the hem line will be weighted with trimmings or bindings and that the fabric will be of a superior quality to the toile.

5. From the template, plan the fabric cuts so that there is always a full width in the centre and part widths at either side. Cut out and join linings and interlinings to fit, but without the shaping.

6. Place the pelmet face down with the interlining over and lock stitch at 30 cm (12 in) intervals. Trim the interlining to shape around the lower edge.

7. If you are binding the lower edge, pin and stitch 1.5 cm (⅝ in) in from the raw edge. Press from the right side and fold neatly back to the wrong side. Herringbone stitch in place.

If binding is not being used, turn the sides and hem under 2 cm (¾ in) and press. Unfold and trim away the interlining. Fold the hem back and herringbone stitch.

8. Place the lining over and lock stitch to the interlining along the same lines. Score the lining along the edge of the pelmet fold and trim 1 cm (⅜ in) from this line. Fold hem under 1.5 cm (⅝ in) and slip stitch to the pelmet.

9. Tidy up the top edge if necessary. Measure from the top and turn over the heading allowance. Trim away any interlining and complete the headings.

UPHOLSTERED PELMETS

Upholstered pelmets are making something of a come-back after the excess of frills and chintzes in the last few years. Traditionally, flat pelmets would have been made with formal fabrics – damasks, brocades, velvets, and decorated with cords and braids. Unbleached linens and country stripes or plain cottons are contemporary alternatives.

Mix a strong, striped fabric on the pelmet with plain curtains, or use a floral chintz for the pelmet over plain curtains bordered in the same chintz. Woven or tapestry lambrequins, found in antiques shops or markets, can sometimes be adapted and reshaped to fit around a window. An elaborate pelmet with detailed fabric and trimmings could be used on its own with perhaps a blind or shutters beneath.

You will need to follow the instructions on page 15 to make up a flat template in a pleasing shape. Or you might prefer to draw the window on to graph paper, marking the centre and side depths, and designing your pelmet to accommodate these.

Scale up the design to full size on to brown paper. Cut out and fit on to the window frame. Check that the design is correct from all angles, and add or take away sections until you are satisfied with the result. Plan the fabric required.

MAKING UP

1. Cut, join and press the fabric and lining, remembering to use a full width of fabric at the centre. Cut out the interlining. Cut the pelmet from wood or pelmet buckram.

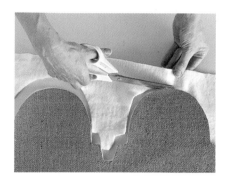

2. Spread a thin layer of glue over the front of the pelmet, place the interlining over the top, smoothing it out as you work. Carefully trim away any excess.

3. Place the main fabric on to the worktable, face downwards. Pin to the table and place the pelmet over the top, interlining side down. Line up seams and keep at right angles to the straight edge. Trim the fabric to 3.5 cm (1³⁄₈ in) all round the edge of the pelmet. Spread glue around the edges and fold the main fabric over.

4. Place the lining over the pelmet and pin around the edge to hold. Score along the pelmet edge with the point of your scissors and trim the lining 2 cm (³⁄₄ in) from this mark. Fold along the scored line and pin to the pelmet edge. Stitch the lining to the main fabric with a curved upholstery needle.

5. Slip stitch cord to the lower edge so that the lining is not visible from the front and stitch the fitting tape to the top edge.

At the bottom of each side, hand stitch small tabs which will be pinned into the window frame or wall to prevent the pelmet moving. Stitch heading tape or touch and close tape just below the top line. A deep pelmet should have two or three rows to hold it.

Fit to the pelmet board with large drawing pins through the heading tape or to the opposite side of the touch and close tape.

FLAT PELMETS

Cotton huckaback – used for commercial handtowels, mattress ticking and denim – proves that effective window treatments do not need to cost a great deal. The pelmet is simply a triangle of fabric, with the top fabric cut 10 cm (4 in) smaller and the lining 14 cm (5½ in) larger, piped and hand stitched over the smaller triangle. The long side of the triangle measures from the bottom of the 'dropped sides' and over the pelmet board.

The pelmet drape could have been hung over a pole and pulled up in the centre, caught in place with another piece of fabric.

CURTAIN CARE

Washing / cleaning

Unlined curtains are usually made when regular cleaning will be needed and should be washed or dry cleaned in accordance with the manufacturer's instructions. If frequent washing is essential, use a strong, hardwearing fabric, such as cotton, with enough substance to stand regular handling. To prevent shrinkage, either wash the fabric before making it up or over-cut the drops and make up the curtains with the shrinkage allowance so that this will be taken up at the first wash.

Make sure that every trace of detergent is removed. Sunlight can react with cleaning chemicals and cause fading. Always press while still damp, as pressing and steaming will keep fabric in shape. Try not to press over seams, only press up to them with the point of the iron. If you do need to press over a seam, slip a piece of cloth between the seam and the main fabric to prevent a ridge forming.

Airing

The best and most effective way to keep curtains clean and fresh is to choose a slightly breezy day, open the windows wide, close the curtains and allow them to blow in the breeze for a few hours. This will remove the slightly musty lining smell. If you can do this every few weeks your curtains will always stay fresh. This is more of a problem in the city, but is possible if you choose quiet, breezy spring and autumn Sundays.

Vacuuming

The regular removal of dust is vital to prevent particles of household dust settling into the fabric grain, as once dirt has penetrated it is very difficult and often impossible to remove with any satisfaction.

Vacuum all soft furnishings regularly with a soft brush, paying special attention to the inside of chair seats, pleats and frills. For delicate fabrics and pelmets make a muslin or fine calico 'mob cap', elasticated to fit over the end of the brush to soften the bristle/fabric abrasion.

Dry cleaning

Small furnishings, eg silk cushions, will need to be dry cleaned at regular intervals, so use a specialist furnishings dry cleaner and clean before dirt is ingrained.

Clean interlined curtains only when disaster strikes or before alterations. Regular care and attention will prevent curtains from becoming 'dirty'.

Alterations

If curtains need to be altered for any reason (like moving house) have them cleaned by a specialist dry cleaner before alterations are carried out. Remove stitching from the sides and hems to allow any ruckled fabric to be cleaned and to allow the fabrics to shrink at different rates.

Track maintenance

Periodically spray the inside of curtain track and the top of poles with an anti-static household cleaner or silicone spray to prevent dust building up and to ease the running.

Poles may be cleaned with a dilute household cleaner and a soft brush to remove dust from the crevices of decorative finials and the underside of curtain pole rings.

GLOSSARY

FIBRES

Acrylic Manmade from petrol, often mixed with more expensive fibres to keep the cost down. Not hardwearing, but useful for permanent pleating.

Cotton A natural fibre, cotton is very versatile, woven, knitted and mixed with other fibres. Used for any soft furnishings according to weight. It will lose strength in direct sunlight, so protect. Soft, strong, easy to launder, washable if pre-shrunk.

Linen Fibres found inside the stalks of the flax plant are woven to make linen cloth in almost any weight. Distinctive slub weave from very fine linen for under-curtains and sheers to heavy upholstery weight. A very strong fibre which is easy to work and will take high temperatures.

Silk From the cocoon of the silk worm, silk is soft and luxurious to touch. Fades in sunlight, so protect. Available in every weight, suitable for soft furnishings, from lampshades to heavy upholstery. Good mixed with cotton or wool.

Wool A natural fibre, liable to excessive shrinkage as the 'scales' on each fibre overlap, harden and 'felt'. Is warm to touch and initially resists damp. Ideal for upholstery and curtains.

Viscose Wood pulp woven into fibres which mixes well with other fibres helping them to take dyes and fireproofing. Washable and sheds dirt easily.

FABRICS

Brocade Traditionally woven fabric using silk, cotton, wool or mixed fibres, on a jacquard loom, in a multi or self coloured floral design. Brocades drape well and can be used for curtains, traditional bed drapes, covers and upholstery. Some are washable but most will need dry cleaning.

Calico Coarse, plain weave cotton in cream or white with 'natural' flecks in it. Available in many widths and weights for inexpensive curtains, bed drapes, garden awnings. Wash before use to shrink and press while damp.

Cambric Closely woven, plain weave fabric from linen or cotton with a sheen on one side. Use, wash and press as Calico. Widely used for cushion pad covers but also for curtains, covers and cushions.

Canvas Plain weave cotton in various weights suitable for upholstered chair covers, inexpensive curtains, slip covers, awnings and outdoor use. Available as unbleached, coarse cotton or more finely woven and dyed in strong colours.

Chintz Cotton fabric with Eastern design using flowers and birds, often with a resin finish which gives a characteristic sheen or glaze and which also repels dirt. The glaze will eventually wash out, so only dry clean curtains. Avoid using steam to press and never fold or the glaze will crack.

Corduroy A strong fabric woven to form vertical ribs by floating extra yarn across which is then cut to make the pile. Use for traditional upholstery. Press on a velvet pinboard while damp.

Crewel Plain or hopsack woven, natural cotton background embroidered in chain stitch in plain cream wool or multi-coloured wools. Soft but heavy, lovely for curtains, soft blinds, cushions and light-use loose covers. May be washed, but test a small piece first.

Damask A jacquard fabric first woven in Damascus with satin floats on a warp satin background in cotton, silk, wool and mixed fibres in various weights. Use for curtains, drapes and sometimes covers and upholstery, choosing different weights for different uses. Make up reversed if a matt finish is required. Suitable for curtaining which needs to be seen from both sides.

Gingham Plain weave fabric with equal width stripes of white plus one other colour in both warp and weft threads to produce blocks of checks or stripes in 100% cotton. Use for small windows in cottagey rooms, kitchens, children's bedrooms and slip covers. Mix with floral patterns and other checks and stripes.

Holland Firm, hardwearing fabric made from cotton or linen stiffened with oil or shellac. Used for blinds lightweight covers, curtaining and pelmets.

Lace Open work fabrics in designs ranging from simple spots to elaborate panels. Usually in cotton or a cotton and polyester mixture.

Moiré A finish usually on silk or acetate described as 'watermarked'. The characteristic moiré markings are produced by pressing plain woven fabric through hot engraved cylinders which crush the threads and push them into different directions to form the pattern. This finish will disappear on contact with water, so it is not suitable for upholstery.

Muslin White or off-white, inexpensive, open-weave cloth which can be dyed in pastel colours. Used for under-curtains and sheers in hot countries to filter light and insects.

Organdie The very finest cotton fabric with an acid finish giving it a unique crispness. Use for lightweight curtains, dressing tables and lampshades. Wash and press while damp.

Organza Similar to organdie and made of silk, polyester or viscose. Very springy and used for stiffening headings of fine fabrics, blinds to filter sunlight and to protect curtains. Use layers of varying tones or pastel colours over each other.

Provençal prints Small print designs printed by hand on to fine cotton for curtains, upholstery, cushions and covers. Washable, hard wearing, soft and easy to work with.

Silk noil Light to mediumweight silk, relatively inexpensive for interlining heavy curtains, slip covers, summer curtains and cushions.

Silk shantung Light to mediumweight silk woven with irregular yarns giving a dull, rough appearance. Use for curtains, cushions, light drapes and lampshades. Available in an extensive range of colours, gathers and frills.

Taffeta Woven from silk, acetate and blends. Used for elaborate drapes because it handles well and for its light-reflecting qualities.

Tartan Authentic tartans belong to individual Scottish clans and are woven or worsted fine twill weave with an elaborate checked design.

Traditional wool tartans are hardwearing for upholstering sofas and chairs, curtains and cushions.

Ticking Characteristic original herringbone weave in black and white, now woven in many colours and weights. Use for curtains and upholstery. Not usually pre-shrunk.

Toile de jouy Pastoral designs in one colour printed on to calico using copper plate printing techniques. Use for curtains, covers, upholstery, cushions and bedding.

Tweed Wool or worsted cloth in square or rectangular checked designs in few colours. Often used for shawls or more tightly woven for men's sporting clothes. However, use for upholstering stools, chairs, sofas or for curtains, pelmets and cushions.

Velvet Originally 100% silk, now made from cotton, viscose or other manmade fibres. Woven with a warp pile and additional yarn in loops which are up to 3 mm ($\frac{1}{8}$ in) depth to form a pile. Care needs to be taken when sewing or the fabrics will 'walk'. Press on a velvet pinboard. Dry clean carefully. Always buy good quality velvet with a dense pile which will not pull out easily.

Voile Fine, light plain weave cotton or polyester fabric dyed in many plain colours. Use for filmy curtains, bed drapes and under-curtains. Easily washable and little pressing necessary. Silk and wool voiles can be used for fine drapery.

INDEX